TERENCE CONRAN'S COMPLETE HOUSE & GARDEN DESIGN PROJECTS

CONSULTANT EDITORS
JOHN McGOWAN
& ROGER DuBERN

PROJECT PHOTOGRAPHY
HUGH JOHNSON
& NADIA MacKENZIE

SHELTON BOOKS

First published as two separate titles, *Terence Conran's DIY by
Design* and *Terence Conran's Garden DIY*, 1989 and 1991
by Shelton Books, an imprint of
Conran Octopus Limited
2-4 Heron Quays
London E14 4JP
a part of Octopus Publishing Group Ltd

This new formatted edition published 2000

British Library Cataloguing in Publication Data

A catalogue record for this book is available from the
British Library

ISBN 1 84091 133 6

Typeset by Servis Filmsetting Limited
Printed and bound in China

Consultant Editors JOHN MCGOWAN and ROGER DUBERN
Project Editor JOANNA BRADSHAW
Editors RICHARD DAWES and SIMON WILLIS
Editorial Assistant ROD MACKENZIE
Contributor ELIZABETH WILHIDE

Art Editors HELEN LEWIS and MERYL LLOYD
Design Assistant ALISON SHACKLETON
Illustrator PAUL BRYANT
Visualiser JEAN MORLEY

Photographers HUGH JOHNSON, SIMON LEE and
NADIA MACKENZIE
Photographic Stylist CLAIRE LLOYD
Photographic Assistants SIMON ANDERS and PETER WILLETT

Picture Research NADINE BAZAR
Production GRAHAM DARLOW, SHANE LASK and
SONYA SIBBONS

PLEASE NOTE
Before embarking on any major building work on your home, you
should also check the law concerning building regulations and
planning. It is also important to obtain specialist advice on
plumbing, gas and electricity, before attempting any alterations to
these services yourself.

While every effort has been made to ensure that all the
information contained in this book is correct, the publishers
cannot be held responsible for any loss, damage or injury caused
by reliance upon the accuracy of such information.

DIMENSIONS
Exact dimensions are given in metric followed by an approximate
conversion to imperial. Do not mix imperial and metric dimensions
when you are making a calculation.

Contents

CONTENTS

CONTENTS

INTRODUCTION
TO HOUSE PROJECTS

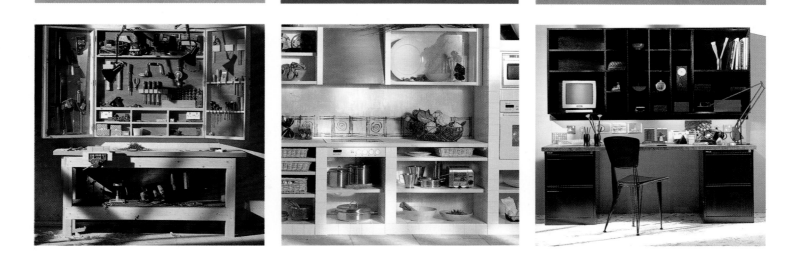

There is a growing passion for improving houses and apartments as people young and old, rich and poor, take satisfaction in making their homes comfortable and stylish. People everywhere restore, revamp, repair, and revitalize their homes, and in doing so many have discovered the pleasure of do-it-yourself projects.

This is a book that encourages the use of the talents of a designer as well as the traditional do-it-yourself skills of carpentry, decorating, plastering, and so forth. I have taken the simple, practical, everyday things around the house – the things for which we most often turn to home improvement, such as a set of shelves for books or a more congenial bathroom arrangement – and have shown how they can be designed and constructed to give you a stylish solution. For every room there are complete projects which will benefit any home. The way you finish them is entirely up to you and your choice of finish will personalize your work and make it *your* home.

Take, for example, the kitchen projects. These show how to create a completely new kitchen to fit any size room, or how to improve an existing one. As with all of the projects, the basic structures can be adapted and used in many different ways around the house. The appearance of the finished work will differ markedly by your choice of tiles, laminate, or wood surfaces, paint and stain colors, and by what goes into the kitchen when it is in use.

In addition to the projects, I have given ideas and inspiration to assist you with your work. The work of architects and designers, as well as amateurs and enthusiasts around the world, illustrates the opportunities that exist for dedicated home improvers to enhance the function and appearance of their homes, with style and by design.

I have started the book with a workbench and tool cupboard. Get them right and they will provide the example and temptation to encourage you to continue the good work.

Terence Conran.

TOOLS, MATERIALS, AND TECHNIQUES

Part 1 contains all the technical information you need to build the projects in this book. Essential tools, materials, and techniques are described in full, and are accompanied, where relevant, by explanatory diagrams. To help you locate the techiques, cross references are printed in bold throughout the project text, and at the top of every page.

Parts 2, 3, and 4 of the book are divided into the three main areas of the home: Kitchens and Dining Rooms, Living Rooms and Work Spaces, and Bathrooms and Bedrooms. Each section contains a lengthy introduction with detailed guidance and inspirational photographs for each room, followed by do-it-yourself projects. These consist of comprehensive tools and materials lists, a photograph of the finished project, and step-by-step diagrams.

Before starting work, plan each project carefully so that it can be tailored to your personal requirements. In particular, think about plumbing and electricity, so that pipe and cable runs can be modified if appropriate, so avoiding unnecessary upheaval once work has commenced.

TOOLS

TOOLS FOR PREPARATION

Adhesive spreader These are palm-size pieces of semi-flexible plastic with serrated or notched edges which are used to spread adhesives over wide surfaces, evenly, and at the correct rate. Because the size of the serrations or notches affects the spreading rate, adhesive manufacturers usually supply a spreader with their adhesives for brands where a spreader is required: mainly contact-types and tiling and flooring adhesives.

Bench stop and vise A woodwork vise is fitted to the underside of a bench, with the jaws level with the bench top. The jaws are lined and topped with hardwood to protect the work and any tools being used. Some vises also incorporate a small steel peg (a "dog") that can be raised above the main jaw level. This allows awkward or long pieces of wood to be clamped in position when used with a bench stop which is fixed at the opposite end of the bench stop.

Sliding bevel (1) Also called a bevel gauge, this is a type of square used to mark out lumber at any required angle. The sliding blade can be locked against the stock by means of a locking lever and the blade can form any angle with the stock.

Marking gauge (2) Essential for setting out woodworking joints, this is used to mark both widths and thicknesses with only a light scratch. The gauge comprises a handle, on which slides a stock bearing a steel marking pin. This movable stock can be locked in any position with a thumb screw so the steel pin is fixed at a precise point.

Mortise gauge (3) Similar to a marking gauge, it has two pins – one fixed, one adjustable – to mark out both sides of a mortise at the same time. Some types have an additional pin fixed below the beam so that the tool can be used as a marking gauge.

Contour gauge This is also called a shape tracer or a scribing gauge. It comprises a row of steel pins or plastic fingers held in a central bar. When pressed against an object, like a baseboard, the pins follow the shape of the object.

Utility knife A razor-sharp blade which is used to score a thin, accurate line for a saw or chisel to follow, ensuring a precise cut. The flat face of the knife can be run against the blade of a try square or straight-edge. A paring chisel is placed in the knife line for accurate paring of the last cut.

Miter box A simple open-topped wooden box which is used to guide saws into material at a fixed 45° or 90° angle, to ensure a square cut.

Plumb bob and chalk A plumb line is used to check verticals and mark accurate vertical lines, in chalk, on walls. A plumb bob is simply a pointed weight attached to a long length of string. Before use, the string can be rubbed with a stick of colored chalk. Hold the string in the required position at the top, wait for the plumb bob to stop swinging, then carefully press the string against the wall at the bottom and then pluck the string to leave a line on the wall. Most hardware stores stock chalk lines (plumb bobs with line winders and powdered chalk containers): these save time by automatically dusting the line with chalk as it is withdrawn.

Portable workbench A collapsible, portable workbench is vital for woodworking. A large, fixed workbench in a garage or shed is important, but the major advantage of the portable type is that it is lightweight and can be carried to the job, where it provides sturdy support when final adjustments have to be made.

A portable bench is like a giant vise – the worksurface comprises two sections which can be opened wide or closed tightly according to the dimensions of the work and the nature of the task. It can hold large and awkward objects.

Scribing block To fit an item neatly against a wall (which is very unlikely to be perfectly flat) the item has to be "scribed" flat to the wall using a small block of wood and a pencil (see **Techniques, page 91**). A scribing block is simply an offcut of wood measuring about 1in × 1in × 1in (25mm × 25mm × 25mm). The block is held against the wall, a sharp pencil is held against the opposite end of the block, and the block and the pencil are moved in a unit along the wall to mark a line on the item to be fitted. If you cut to this line, the item will then fit tightly against the wall.

Carpenter's level (9) Used for checking that surfaces are horizontal or vertical. A 24in (610mm) long level is the most useful all-round size. An aluminum or steel level will withstand knocks and it can be either I-girder or box-shaped in section. Ideally, a 9in (225mm) "torpedo" carpenter's level is also useful to have, for working in confined spaces such as alcoves and inside cupboards. It may be used in conjunction with a straight-edge over longer surfaces.

Steel measuring tape A 12ft (3.6m) or 18ft (5.5m) long, lockable tape (metal or plastic) is best, and one with a window in the casing that makes it easier to read measurements.

Steel bench rule Since the rule is made of steel, the graduations are very precise and indelible. A rule graduated on both sides in imperial and metric is the most useful. The rule can also serve as a precise straight-edge for marking cutting lines.

Straight-edge Can be made from a piece of 1 × 2in (25 × 50mm) scrap wood. It is used to tell whether a surface is flat and also for checking whether two points are aligned with each other.

Try square (4) An L-shaped precision tool comprising a steel blade and stock (or handle) set at a perfect right angle to each other on both the inside and outside edges. Used for marking cutting lines at right angles to an edge and for checking a square.

SUPPLEMENTARY TOOLS

Drill stand   Enables a power drill to be used with extreme accuracy when, for example, joining doweling (*see* **Techniques, page 30**). The hole will be perpendicular to the surface and its depth can be carefully controlled. The drill is lowered on to the work with a spring-loaded lever which gives good control and accuracy.

Metal detector   Pinpoints metal objects such as electric cables and water and gas pipes hidden in walls, ceilings, and floors. Electronically operated, it buzzes or flashes when metal is found.

TOOLS FOR SHARPENING AND CUTTING

Chisels   Used to cut slots in wood or to pare off thin slivers. Some chisels may be used with a mallet when cutting slots. When new, a chisel's cutting edge is ground and must be honed with an oilstone to sharpen it.
Mortise chisel (5) Used with a mallet for cutting deep slots.
Bench chisel (6) Used for undercutting in confined spaces, such as when making dovetail joints.
Firmer chisel (7) For general-purpose use around the home.
Paring chisel (8) Has a long blade for cutting deep joints or long grooves.

Doweling jig   A simple doweling jig clamps on to a piece of work, ensuring that the drill is aligned accurately over the center of the dowel hole to be drilled. It also guides the drill vertically.

DRILLS

Hand drill (10) For drilling holes for screws or for making large holes, particularly in wood. It will

make holes in metal and is useful where there is no power source. A handle attached to a toothed wheel is used to turn the drill in its chuck.
Power drill (11) These range from a simple, single-speed model (which will drill holes only in soft materials) to a multi-speed drill with electronic control. Most jobs call for something in between the two, such as a two-speed drill with hammer action. The two speeds enable most hard materials to be drilled and the hammer action means that you can also drill into the hardest walls.

DRILL BITS

You will need a selection of twist bits in various sizes and of different types for wood and metal, for use with a drill.

Brad-point bit (12) Used to make dowel holes in wood. The tip has two cutting spurs on the side and a center point to prevent the bit from wandering off center. Diameters range from $\frac{1}{8}$in (3mm) to $\frac{1}{2}$in (12mm).
Twist drill bit (13) Used with an electric drill for drilling small holes in wood and metal. Carbon-steel drills are for wood only: drilling into metal requires a high-speed steel drill.
Masonry bit (14) Has a specially hardened tungsten-carbide tip for drilling into masonry to the exact size required for an anchor. Special percussion drill bits are available for use with a hammer drill when boring into concrete.
Countersink bit (15) After a hole is drilled in wood, a countersink bit is used to cut a recess for the screwhead to sit in, so ensuring that it lies below the surface. Different types are available for use with a carpenter's brace and an electric drill. Head diameters are $\frac{3}{8}$in (9mm), $\frac{1}{2}$in (12mm), and $\frac{9}{16}$in (15mm). Carbon-steel bits can be used for wood, but high-speed steel bits can be used for wood, plastic, or metal.
Spade bit (16) Is used with an electric drill. It has a point at the end of the shank and its flat shank end allows it to slot into the drill chuck. Diameters are from $\frac{1}{4}$in (6mm) to $1\frac{1}{2}$in (38mm). For maxi-

mum efficiency the bit must be turned at high speed from about 1000 to 2000 rpm. It can be used to drill into cross grain, end grain, and manmade boards. Also known as a speedbore bit.
Auger bit (17) Has a tapered, square shank that fits into a carpenter's brace. It is used to make deep holes in wood, the usual lengths being up to 10in (250mm). Diameters range from $\frac{1}{4}$in (6mm) to $1\frac{1}{2}$in (38mm). The tip has a screw thread to draw the bit into the wood.
Forstner bit (18) A Forstner bit, or hinge-sinker bit, is primarily used for boring $1\frac{3}{8}$in (35mm) or 1in (25mm) diameter flat bottomed holes in cabinet and wardrobe doors to accept the hinge bosses on concealed hinges. Forstner bits are used in electric drills, ideally fitted in drill stands, and set to drill no deeper than $\frac{1}{2}$in (12mm).

Oilstone and honing guide   The first sharpens and the second maintains the correct angle for sharpening chisel and plane blades. An oilstone is a rectangular block of stone with grit on both sides. Oil is used as a lubricant while the blade is being sharpened on the stone, so you will need a can of fine oil nearby.
   The honing guide is an inexpensive tool which makes sharpening easier and more efficient. The blade of the tool to be sharpened is inserted at an angle and clamped in place, then the guide is repeatedly rolled back and forth on the surface of the oilstone.

Power router (19) This portable electric tool is used to cut grooves, recesses, and many types of joints in lumber, as well as to shape the edges of long lumber battens to form decorative moldings. A whole range of cutting bits in different shapes and sizes is available and when fitted into the router the bits revolve at very high speed (about 25,000 rpm) to cut the wood smoothly and cleanly (20). Although hand routers (which look like small planes) are available, whenever routers are referred to in this book, it is the power router to which the remarks are directed.

Tools

Saws

Circular saw (1) Invaluable for cutting large pieces of lumber or sheets of board. It will also cut grooves and angles. The most popular size has a diameter of 7¼in (184mm). Circular saws can be extremely dangerous and must be used carefully. The piece of work must be held securely and the blade depth set so that it will not cut into anything below the work. The tool should be fitted with an upper and lower blade guard. Support your work on scrap battens to avoid cutting into work-benches or floors.

Coping saw (2) Used to make curved or circular cuts. It has a narrow blade, which can be swiveled. When cutting, the blade can be angled as necessary so that the frame clears the edge of the work. Drill a hole close to the edge of the piece to be cut out, and thread the coping saw blade through the hole before reconnecting it to the handle and starting to cut.

Dovetail saw (3) Also called a gent's saw. This fine-tooth form of back saw with a stiffened back is ideal for making delicate and precise saw cuts. It is particularly useful for making dovetail joints.

Hand saws (4) Are used for rough cutting rather than fine carpentry. They have a flexible blade of 20–26in (510–670mm) in length, and a wooden or plastic handle. They are useful for general-purpose cutting of wood and fiberboards.

Saber saw (7) Will cut a variety of materials, and is much more versatile than a circular saw, although not as quick or powerful. It also cuts curves, shapes, angles, and holes in the middle of panels. The best models offer variable speeds – slow for hard materials and fast for soft. The latest models have either a reciprocating or a pendulum action. In these cases the blade goes backwards and forwards as well as up and down, which allows for much faster cutting on straight lines.

Compass saw (5) Also called a keyhole saw, it is designed to cut holes and shapes in wood. It has a narrow, tapered blade which will cut keyholes, for example. A hole is first drilled and the saw blade inserted to make the cut. Compass saws are useful for cutting holes for inset sinks where a power Saber saw is not available.

Back saw (6) For cutting the tenon part of a mortise and tenon joint (see **Techniques, page 28**), and also useful for other delicate and accurate work. It has a stiffened back and the blade is about 10–12in (250–300mm) long.

Surforms Available in a range of lengths from approximately 6–10in (150–250mm), these rasps are useful for the initial shaping of wood. However, further fine finishing by hand is needed to obtain a smooth surface. The steel blade has a pattern of alternating small teeth and holes through which waste wood passes, so that the teeth do not get clogged up. When blunt, the blade is simply replaced.

Supplementary Tools

Hacksaw For cutting metal. A traditional hack-saw has a wooden handle and a solid metal frame. The blade is tensioned by a wing-nut. Modern hacksaws have a tubular frame which is adjustable for different lengths of blade. A "junior" hacksaw is ideal for sawing small items or for working in confined spaces.

Hands Tools

Awl Used to make a small pilot hole in wood to take a screw. It is twisted into the wood with a continuous circular movement.

Clamps

For securing glued pieces of work while they are setting. There are many types of clamp, but the C-clamp is the most commonly used and is available in a wide range of jaw sizes.

Folding wedges are sometimes useful for securing an object while it is being glued. You can make two by cutting diagonally through a block of wood. For instructions on how to make and use folding wedges, see page 21.

Bar clamps These employ a long metal bar, and are indispensable for holding together large frameworks. Initially, rent rather than buy bar clamps, although you can improvise in some cases by making a rope tourniquet. This consists of a piece of rope which is tied around the object and a length of stick to twist the rope and so clamp the frame tightly.

Band clamp A nylon webbing clamp to apply even pressure around frames when they are being assembled. The webbing, like narrow seat-belt type material, is looped around the frame, pulled as tight as possible by hand, and then finally tightened by means of a screw mechanism or ratchet winder. Band clamps are cheaper alternatives to bar clamps.

C-clamp Also called a frame clamp or fast-action clamp, it is important for our projects that the jaws of the clamp open at least 8in (200mm). The lumber to be held in the clamp is placed between the jaws which are then tightened by turning a thumb-screw, tommy bar, or other type of handle. In the case of the fast-action clamp, one jaw is free to slide on a bar, and after sliding this jaw up to the workpiece, final tightening is achieved by turning the handle. In all cases, to prevent damage to the workpiece, scraps of wood are placed between it and the jaws of the clamp.

Hammers

Claw hammer (9) The claw side of the head of the hammer is used to extract nails from a piece of work quickly and cleanly.

Cross-peen hammer (10) The peen is the tapered section opposite the flat hammer head, and it is used for starting off small brads and tacks held in the fingers.

Tack hammer A smaller version of the cross-peen, this is useful for light work.

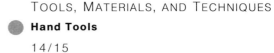
Mallet Most commonly used to strike mortise chisels, although if a chisel has an impact-resistant handle then a hammer may also be used. The tapered wooden head ensures square contact with the object being struck.

Nailset Used with a hammer to drive nails and brads below the surface so that they are hidden; the hole can then be filled. The pointed end is "cupped" to fit neatly over a nail or brad head.

Orbital sander Otherwise known as a finishing sander, this gives a fine, smooth surface finish to wood. A gritted sanding sheet is fitted to the sander's base plate. Sheets are graded from coarse to fine, and the grade used depends on the roughness of the surface to be sanded. Orbital sanders produce a great deal of dust, so always wear a mask when using one.

Pliers Used to remove nails and tacks from wood. The bevel-edged jaws grip the nail close to the surface of the wood, and the pliers are rocked back and forth to extract it.

PLANES

Smoothing plane (11) A general-purpose, hand-held plane for smoothing and straightening surfaces and edges. The plane is about 10in (250mm) long and its blade 2–2¼in (50–60mm) wide. The wider the blade the better the finish on wide lumber. There is a fine adjustment for depth of cut and a lever for lateral adjustment.

Block plane (12) Held in the palm of the hand, it is easy to use for small work and beveling edges. Also useful for planing end grain.

Jack plane (13) Longer than a smoothing plane, it is used for straightening long edges and is a good all-purpose plane.

Power plane (14) Finishes lumber to precise dimensions. A one-hand model is lightweight and can be used anywhere, whereas the heavier two-hander is intended for workbench use. A power plane will also cut bevels and rabbets.

Rasp A rasp is a type of coarse file for wood, available with flat or half-round surfaces. It is used to shape wood, often when scribing an edge to fit against a wall.

Sanding block and sanding paper A sanding block is used with sanding paper to finish and smooth flat surfaces. The block is made of cork, rubber, or softwood and the sanding paper is wrapped around it. Make sure in doing so that the paper is not wrinkled. Sanding paper used without a block tends to produce an uneven surface. Sheets of sanding paper are graded from coarse to fine and are selected according to the roughness of the surface to be sanded. Coarse paper is used for a very rough surface and fine paper for finishing.

Screwdrivers There is no single type of screwdriver that is better than the rest; personal preference is what matters. They come in many shapes and sizes, and the main differences are the type of tip (for slotted or Phillips screws), the length, and the shape of the handle, which varies from straight or fluted to bulb-shaped. Phillips screwdrivers can be used on most Phillips screws but certain speciality recess screws require their own special screwdrivers.

Ideally, you should have a range of screwdrivers for dealing with all sizes of screws. Ratchet models, which return the handle to its starting point, are easy to operate since your hand grip does not need to change. The spiral action screwdriver is very efficient (though very expensive) and it works like a bicycle pump rather than by turning the handle.

Cordless screwdriver A fairly new tool, it is expensive but can save much time and effort. Mainly used for Phillips screws.

SUPPLEMENTARY TOOLS

Metal file Gives a metal edge the required shape and finish. Most files are supplied with a removable handle which can be transferred to a

file of a different size. A flat or half-round file (one side flat, the other curved) are good general-purpose tools.

Hand staple gun A trigger-operated tool which fires a staple straight into a surface, usually fabric, fiberboard, or thin wood over a wooden batten. Its advantage over conventional nailing with a hammer is that, as it is used one-handed, the other hand is free to hold the work.

Power staple gun Easier to fire. Fires heavy-duty staples into thicker surfaces, such as ceilings. It is preferable to buy the same brand of gun and staples to prevent jamming.

Paintbrushes A set of paintbrushes for painting and varnishing should ideally comprise three sizes – 1in (25mm), 2in (50mm), and 3in (75mm). A better finish is always achieved by matching the size of brush to the surface – a small brush for narrow surfaces, a large brush for wide areas. Always clean thoroughly after use.

Electric paint sprayer Can produce a very smooth finish once its use is mastered. It may be preferable to hire rather than buy one – initially at least – since airless spray guns and compressors are expensive. Always work parallel to the surface you are spraying, applying two thin coats of paint rather than one thick coat.

Wrench A wrench is required for tightening carriage bolts, and any type that fits the head of the bolt is suitable. If the correct-size open-ended or ring wrench is not available, any type of adjustable wrench may be used.

Caulking gun Used to eject a bead of mastic-type waterproofing sealants (or caulking) into gaps where water might penetrate, such as around shower trays. A cartridge of caulking or sealant is held in the frame (or "gun"), and a plunger, pushes the caulking out of a nozzle at the end of the cartridge.

8 9 10 11 12 13 14

MATERIALS

LUMBER

Lumber is classified into two groups – softwoods and hardwoods. Softwoods come from evergreen trees and hardwoods from deciduous trees. Check lumber for defects before buying it. Avoid wood which is badly cracked or split, although you need not be concerned about fine, surface cracks since these can be planed, sanded, or filled. Do not buy warped wood, as it will be impossible to work with. Check for warping by looking along the length of a board to see if there is any bowing or twisting.

When you get your wood home, condition it for about ten days. As the wood will have been stored in the open air at the yard, it will be "wet." Once indoors, it dries, shrinks slightly and will warp unless stored flat on the ground. If you build with wood as soon as you get it home, your structure could run into problems later as the wood dries out. To avoid warping and aid drying, stack boards in a pile, with offcuts of wood placed between each board to allow air to circulate. This will lower the moisture content to about 10% and condition the wood, ready for use.

Softwood Softwood is much less expensive than hardwood and is used in general building work. Softwood is sold either by the *lineal* foot or the *board* foot. The former is based on the length of a piece of wood – for example, 8ft of 1 by 2 (1×2 in [25×50 mm]). The board foot is calculated by the thickness in inches × width in feet × length in feet – for example, 10ft of 1 by 6 would be 5 board feet: 1 in × $\frac{1}{2}$ ft (6in) × 10ft.

It is important to remember that standard softwood sizes refer to sawn sizes – that is, how it is sawn at a mill. When bought this way, softwood is suitable only for rough constructional work such as floor joists and basic frames. However, the smooth wood used for the projects in this book, for which appearance and accuracy are important, will need to have been planed. This is the state in which softwood is commonly sold in

MOLDINGS (see page 18)

local lumberyards; in the trade it is referred to as "S4S" (smooth 4 sides), and, since planing takes a little off each face, planed softwood is $\frac{1}{4}-\frac{3}{4}$ in (6–9mm) smaller in width and thickness than its stated size. Standard sizes should, therefore, be thought of as rough guides rather than exact measurements.

Hardwood Expensive and not as easy to obtain as softwoods, hardwoods often have to be ordered or bought from a specialist lumberyard. Many lumberyards will machine-plane lumber to your exact specifications. In home woodwork, hardwood is usually confined to moldings and beadings, which are used to give exposed sawn edges a neat finish.

SHEET MATERIAL BOARDS

Sheet material boards are mechanically made from wood and other fibers. They are versatile, relatively inexpensive, made to uniform quality, and are available in large sheets. Sheet materials are graded according to the quality of finished surfaces. It is worth buying the best you can afford, bearing in mind the purpose for which you will be using it. You need to know the advantages of each type of board before making your choice. All boards are made in sheets of 4×8ft (1220×2440mm), and most stockists will saw them to the size you require.

Hardboard Also called masonite, and the best known fiberboard. Common thicknesses are $\frac{1}{8}$in, $\frac{3}{16}$in, and $\frac{1}{4}$in (3mm, 4mm, and 6mm). As hardboard is weak and has to be supported on a framework, it is essentially a material for paneling. Denser types of tempered hardboard can be used for cladding partitions; softer types for bulletin boards.

Medium board Softer and weaker than hardboard, it is often, therefore, used in thicker sheets – usually $\frac{1}{2}$in (12mm).

Medium-density fiberboard (MDF) A good, highly compressed, general-purpose building board. You may find that it has to be ordered from a plywood wholesaler (your retail yard can do this for you), but it is worth it since it does not flake or splinter when cut, and leaves a clean, hard-sawn edge which does not need to be disguised as do other fiberboards. It also takes a very good paint finish, even on its edges. Thicknesses range from around $\frac{3}{16}$in to $1\frac{3}{8}$in (5mm to 35mm).

Particleboard Made by binding wood chips together under pressure, it is rigid, dense, and fairly heavy. Particleboard is strong when reasonably well supported, but sawing it can leave an unstable edge and can also quickly blunt a saw. Ordinary screws do not hold well in particleboard, and it is best to use twin-threaded screws (see **Screws, page 78**). Most grades of particleboard are not moisture-resistant and will swell up when wet. Thicknesses range from $\frac{1}{4}-1\frac{1}{2}$in (6–40mm), but $\frac{1}{2}$in, $\frac{3}{4}$in, and 1in (12mm, 19mm, and 25mm) are the most common.

Particleboard is widely available with the faces and edges veneered with natural wood, PVC, or plastic laminates. Colored finishes and imitation wood-grain effects are also available.

If used for shelving, particleboard must be well supported on closely-spaced brackets or bearers. The better-quality laminated boards are far stronger than plain particleboard.

Plywood Made by gluing thin wood veneers together in plies (layers) with the grain in each ply running at right angles to that of its neighbors. This gives the board strength and helps prevent warping. The most common boards have three, five, or seven plies. Plywood is graded for quality, taking into the account the amount of knots and surface markings present: N is perfect but often has to be ordered, followed by A, B, C, and D in decreasing order of quality; D is for rough work only. For example, A2 means that both faces are of very good quality; AC or ACX (the "X" stands

Square

Rectangular

Scoop

Quarter round

Corner

for exterior) denotes A grade on one side and C on the other, and is a good, economical option where only one side will be visible.

MR (moisture-resistant) plywood is for *internal* jobs where damp conditions prevail. Plywood is available with a range of surface veneers such as teak or mahogany, or with a plastic finish. Common thicknesses are $\frac{1}{8}$in, $\frac{1}{4}$in, $\frac{1}{2}$in, and $\frac{3}{4}$in (3mm, 6mm, 12mm, and 19mm).

Lumber core Made by sandwiching natural lumber strips between wood veneers, the latter usually of Far Eastern redwood or plain birch. Although plain birch is a little more expensive than redwood, it is of a much better quality. Lumber core is very strong, but can leave an ugly edge when sawn (gaps often appear between the core strips), making edge fixings difficult. It is graded in the same way as plywood and common thicknesses are $\frac{1}{2}$in, $\frac{3}{4}$in, and 1in (12mm, 19mm, and 25mm). It is a very rigid board and is therefore ideal for a long span of shelving.

Tongued-and-grooved boards Also called match boarding, or matching, this is widely used for cladding frameworks and walls. Each board has a tongue on one side and a slot on the other side. The tongue fits into the slot on the adjacent board to form an area of cladding; this expands and contracts according to temperature and humidity without cracks opening up between boards.

Ordinary tongued-and-grooved boards fit together like floorboards, but tongued and grooved boards for cladding have some form of decoration; this can be a beaded joint, or, more commonly, beveled edge which forms the attractive V-joint of tongued, grooved, and V-jointed (TGV) boards.

ADHESIVES AND FILLERS

Adhesives Modern types are strong and efficient. If they fail, it is because the wrong adhesive is being used or the manufacturer's instructions are not followed carefully. For all general indoor woodworking, use an aliphatic resin (yellow woodworker's glue) — all glue manufacturers produce their own brands. Use a two part resorcinol glue (guaranteed waterproof) in areas where there may be water splashing or condensation. If joints do not meet perfectly, use a gap-filling adhesive.

Ceramic tiles require their own special adhesive (of a thick, buttery consistency) which is supplied, ready mixed, in tubs. If tiles are likely to be regularly splashed — around sinks for example — you should use a waterproof tile adhesive. Some brands of adhesive can also double as grouting cement for filling the gaps between tiles.

Fillers If the wood is to be painted over, use a standard plastic wood filler — the type for repairing cracks in walls. This dries white and will be evident if used under any other kind of finish. When a clear finish is needed, fill cracks and holes with a proprietary wood filler or stopping. These are thick pastes and come in a range of wood colors. You can mix them together or add a wood stain if the color you want is not available. It is best to choose a color slightly paler than the surrounding wood, since fillers tend to darken when the finish is applied. Test the filler first on a waste piece of matching wood.

In fine work, a grain-filler is used to stop the final finish sinking into the wood. This is a paste, thinned with white spirit, and then rubbed into the surface. It is supplied in a range of wood shades.

FINISHES

The choice of finish is determined by whether the wood or board will be hidden, painted, or enhanced by a protective clear finish.

LACQUER

Quick-drying cellulose lacquer is the best finishing treatment to apply to wood furniture. It is resistant to heat, scratches, and solvents, and, when sprayed on, produces a superb finish.

POLISHES

French polish Refers to a particular polish, but it is also the collective term for all polishes made with shellac and alcohol. French polish is ideal where a light to medium brown tone is required. Although it gives a fine reflection, the finish itself is not highly protective.

Button polish Will give a more golden or orange tone.

White French polish or **transparent polish** Produces a clear finish, allowing the natural color of the wood to show through. French polishing demands great skill, and many people prefer to apply a clear polyurethane varnish with a conventional wax polish covering it.

PAINT

A liquid gloss (oil-based) paint is suitable for wood, and is applied after a suitable undercoat. Generally, two thin coats of gloss are better than one thick coat. Non-drip gloss paint is an alternative. It has a jelly-like consistency and does not require an undercoat, although a quality finish may need a second coat. Use a liquid gloss if you want to spray paint.

VARNISH

Normally applied by brush, varnish can also be sprayed on. It is available as a gloss, satin, or matt finish, all clear. However, varnish also comes in a range of colors, so that you can change the color of the wood and protect it simultaneously. The color does not sink into the wood, so that if the surface becomes scratched or marked then its original color will show through. For this reason, a wood stain or dye is sometimes used to change the color of wood. It sinks into the wood, but offers no protection, so a varnish or clear lacquer will also be needed.

| Half round | Twice rounded | Hockey stick | Reeded | Astragal |

MOLDINGS, BATTENS, AND DOWELS

Moldings Wood moldings are used as ornamentation and to cover gaps or fixtures in a wooden construction. The term "molding" encompasses everything from a simple, thin edge-banding to architraves and baseboards. A variety of shaped cutters produce many different shapes and sizes. In the unlikely event of your being unable to buy the shape of molding you want, you could make your own using a router.

Moldings are cut from hardwood – usually poplar or basswood. You can buy more exotic hardwood moldings, mahogany for example, from a specialist lumberyard. These are expensive and you may well prefer to buy a cheaper molding and then to stain or varnish it to obtain the color that you want.

Decorative moldings are available in standard lengths of 6ft, 8ft, 10ft, and 12ft. The following types are among those which are ideal for edging manmade boards and are available in a variety of sizes: half round (or bullnose); twice rounded; hockey stick; reeded; and astragal. Square or rectangular moldings range from $\frac{1}{4} \times \frac{1}{4}$in ($6 \times 6$mm) up to $\frac{1}{4} \times 1$in (6×25mm).

Other types of molding include scoop and quarter round, which cover gaps between the meeting parts of a structure. Corner moldings are a plain version of the scoop, and can be used inside or outside a joint.

When buying moldings, check each one to make sure that the length is straight and free from large or dead knots, which are likely to fall out and leave holes. Fungal staining is something else to watch for, especially if you intend to use a clear finish. If you need several lengths of moldings for the same job, check that you get a good match. Have a close look at the edges, color, and grain of each length, since mismatching can leave surface ripples or uneven edges.

Battens A general term used to describe a narrow strip of wood. The usual sizes are 1 × 1in (25 × 25mm) or 1 × 2in (25 × 50mm).

Battens serve one of two main functions. They can be screwed to a wall to serve as bearers for shelves. Alternatively, they can be fixed in a framework on a wall, with sheet material or boards mounted over them to form a new "wall."

Dowels Used to make framework joints or to join boards edge-to-edge or edge-to-face.

Hardwood dowels are sold in diameters of $\frac{1}{4}$in, $\frac{3}{8}$in, and $\frac{1}{2}$in (6mm, 9mm, and 12mm). You can buy packs of dowels cut to length (either 1in or $1\frac{1}{2}$in [25mm or 38mm]), or you can buy long lengths and cut them to size. Generally speaking, dowel lengths should be about one-and-a-half times the thickness of the boards being joined.

Dowels are used in conjunction with adhesive and, when the joint is complete, it is important to let excess adhesive escape from the joint. Dowels with fluted (finely grooved) sides and beveled ends will help this process. If you have plain rather than shaped dowels, make fine sawcuts along the length and bevel the ends yourself.

NAILS

Nails are generally sold by their penny (or "d") size. The most common are 2d (1in), 4d ($1\frac{1}{2}$in), 6d (2in), 8d ($2\frac{1}{2}$in), and 10d (3in).

Common nails With large, flat, circular heads, these are used for strong joints where frames will be covered, and the nails will be hidden.

Annular threaded nails Used where really strong attachments are required.

Round finishing nails Used when the finished appearance is important. The heads of these nails are driven flush with the wood's surface or countersunk so they are unobtrusive. They are also used when nailing a thin piece of wood to a thicker piece and there is a risk of splitting the wood. This is likely when nailing close to the end of the wood, or if the nail is too large.

Brads For attaching thin panels, these fine, round wire nails will be required. These have tiny, unobtrusive heads that can be driven in flush with the wood's surface or punched below it.

Hardboard pins Copper-plated and with a square cross-section. They have deep-drive diamond-shaped heads that sink into the surface – ideal for securing hardboard and other boards to lumber in areas subject to condensation, where steel pins could cause black staining.

Masonry nails For securing lumber battens to walls as an alternative to screwing and anchoring. Where a quick and permanent attachment is required, use the hardened-steel type.

SCREWS

All types of screws are available with either conventional slotted heads or with Phillips heads. The latter look neater and are the better type to use, especially if you are inserting screws with an electric screwdriver.

For most purposes, screws with flat heads are ideal as, when countersunk, the head lies flush with the surface after insertion. Round-head screws are used for attaching metal fixtures such as shelf brackets and door bolts, which have punched-out rather than countersunk screw holes. Ovalhead screws are often used alone or with metal screw cups where a neat appearance is important.

Wood screws These have a length of smooth shank just below the head. When joining two pieces of wood, this produces a strong clamping effect as the screw is tightened, but there is also a possibility of the unthreaded shank splitting the wood, so extra care is required.

Twin-threaded screws Quicker to insert than ordinary wood screws and less likely to split wood. Except for larger sizes, they are threaded along

NAILS AND SCREWS

1 Screw cup; 2 Wall anchor bolt; 3 and 4 Frame fixing (nylon plug and plated screw); 5 Veneer pin; 6 Hardboard pin; 7 Brad; 8 Round finishing nail; 9 Common nail; 10 Annular threaded nail; 11 Masonry nail; 12 Countersunk screw with slotted head; 13 Countersunk screw with Phillips head; 14 Round-head screw; 15 Ovalhead screw; 16 Dome-head screw; 17 Twin-threaded screw

their entire length, giving an excellent grip in wood, and also in fiberboard, particleboard, lumber core, and plywood. The best types are zinc-plated (rust-resistant) and hardened (stronger and less prone to head damage by an ill-fitting screwdriver).

WALL FIXTURES AND BOLTS

The choice of wall fixture depends on the type of wall and the size and weight of the object being attached to it.

Anchors Use a masonry drill bit to drill a hole which matches the size of screw being used (a No 10 bit with a No 10 screw, for example). Insert the anchor in the hole, then insert the screw through the object being fitted and into the anchor. Tighten the screw for a secure attachment.

Solid wall fixtures The method of attaching to a solid brick or block wall is to use an anchor. Traditional fiber anchors have been superseded by plastic versions which will accept a range of screw sizes, typically from No 8 to No 12.

Stud wall fixtures To guarantee a secure fixture, you should locate the lumber uprights (studs) which form the framework of the wall and drive screws into them. If you want to attach something heavy and the lumber uprights are not in the required position, then you must attach horizontal battens to the lumber uprights, since otherwise the fitting will be unsafe.

Cavity-wall fixtures Used on hollow walls, which are constructed from wallboard partition or lath and plaster, which are found in modern and old houses respectively. There are many types of these fixtures including spring toggle, gravity toggle, and nylon toggle, and nearly all of them work on the same principle: expanding wings open up to grip the back of the wallboard or lath and plaster, securing the attachment.

Wall anchor bolt For heavier objects, such as a kitchen unit which will be heavily loaded, a more robust attachment using a wall anchor bolt is advisable. It is similar to an anchor in principle, but has its own heavy-duty machine screw. You need to make a much larger hole in the wall, typically $\frac{3}{8}$in (10mm) in diameter. The sleeve of the anchor expands in the hole as the bolt is tightened and grips the wall firmly.

LATCHES

Magnetic catches Most useful on smaller doors which are unlikely to distort. There must be perfect contact between the magnet fitted to the cabinet frame and the strike plate which is fitted to the door. The other important factor is the pulling power of the magnet – on small cabinet doors a "pull" of $4\frac{1}{2}$–$6\frac{1}{2}$lb (2–3kg) is sufficient. On wardrobe doors an 11–13lb (5–6kg) "pull" is needed.

Magnetic push latches are also useful, especially for small, lightweight doors. Push on the door inwards and it springs open just enough to be grasped and fully opened by the fingers.

Mechanical latches Common types are the spring-loaded ball catch and the roller catch. Again, alignment is vital to success, which is why adjustable types are favored. A mechanical push latch is activated by pressure on the door itself, so a door handle is not necessary.

Peglock catches Particularly suitable for kitchen and bathroom cabinets, where atmospheric conditions can cause doors to warp.

HINGES

The easiest types of hinge to fit are those which do not have to be recessed into the door or door frame – flush, decorative flush (for lightweight doors), or cranked (for cupboard doors). For fitting flaps, piano hinges are used. They are sold in 6ft (1.8m) lengths, and are cut to the required size with a hacksaw. For fitting heavy doors or for

a very neat finish, butt hinges, which are recessed, are a good alternative.

Concealed (or European) hinges are used for particleboard and MDF doors. A special drill bit is required to cut cylindrical holes in the door, but the hinges are adjustable once fitted.

SLIDING DOOR TRACKS

Doors can either be suspended from above or supported from below. The track for glass or panel doors is made from PVC and comes in a variety of colors. The door simply slides along the channel in the track.

Top-hung track Small tongued sliders or adjustable wheel hangers attached to the top edge of the door sit in the track. Small guides keep the bottom edges of the door aligned.

Bottom-roller track The door slides on small rollers located in the track. Guides attached at the top of the door keep it aligned in the track.

TILES

Ceramic tiles Especially popular for kitchens and bathrooms, where durable and waterproof surfaces are essential. There is an enormous range available, and prices vary according to size, shape, and the purpose for which they are required: floor tiles need to be much stronger than wall tiles. Common sizes are $4\frac{1}{4} \times 4\frac{1}{4}$in (108 × 108mm) and 6 × 6in (150 × 150mm), but rectangular shapes are also widely available.

"Universal" tiles have angled edges which ensure that uniform joint spacing is left when the tiles are butted up against each other.

Tiles are sold by the square foot or in boxes of 25 or 50, which will cover one half or one square yard (meter). After calculating the number of tiles required, allow a few extra to cover breakages. Unless you are using only one box, do not use the tiles straight from the box – mix them up with other boxes to disguise any slight color variations.

5   6   7   8   9   10   11   12   13   14   15   16   17

TECHNIQUES: SAWING AND CUTTING

WOOD

Wood is available either sawn or planed. Sawn wood is rough in appearance, but is close in width and thickness to the dimensions you specify when ordering. Planed wood is smoothed on all sides, but planing removes $\frac{1}{4}$–$\frac{3}{4}$in (6–19mm) from both the nominal width and the thickness. Sawn wood is ideal for building frameworks, but choose planed wood where a smooth finish is important. Wood should be straight and relatively knot-free. The surface should also be undamaged.

When building a framework of critical thickness (such as the basic kitchen unit modules on page 86) you may find it difficult to obtain wood of exactly the required thickness. If so, buy wood that is slightly oversized and plane it down.

After building, a fine surface can be obtained by sanding, either by hand with sanding paper wrapped around a sanding block, or by using an electric orbital sander. In both cases, start with medium-grade sanding paper and finish with fine, and only sand in line with the grain, rather than across it, as this can scratch the wood.

Wood finishes If a varnish, wax polish, or paint finish is required, it can be applied easily with a brush (or rag). An alternative, often used by professional furniture makers, is to finish woodwork with a quick-drying cellulose lacquer (see **Materials, page 17**), which can be applied with a paint sprayer. Before spraying, make sure that any holes are filled with stainable wood filler, and stain the surface, if required, before sanding it smooth. The first coat of lacquer is applied as a sealer. Leave it to dry for 30–60 minutes, then rub down the surface with fine sanding paper. Next, apply a second, finishing, coat of lacquer.

MEASURING AND MARKING SQUARE

Mark cutting lines lightly with a hard pencil, then use a utility knife to score against a straight-edge or try square along the rule to create a sharp, splinter-free line.

To mark lumber square, use a try square with the stock (handle) pressed against a flat side of the lumber, called the face side or face edge. Mark a line along the square, using a knife in preference to a pencil, then use the square to mark lines down the edges from the face mark. Finally square the other face side, checking that the lines join up right around the lumber.

Check a try square for accuracy by pressing it against a straight-edge. Mark along the blade, then turn the handle over to see if it aligns with the line from the other side.

If you are measuring and marking a number of pieces of the same length, then clamp them together and mark across several of them at the same time.

SPACING BATTEN

This is simply an offcut of wood, about $\frac{3}{4}$in or 1in square (19mm or 25mm square), which is used to ensure that any slats to be fixed across a frame are spaced an equal distance apart. To ascertain the length to cut the spacing batten, simply bunch all the slats at one end of the frame. Measure to the other end of the frame and divide by the number of spaces (which you can count while you have the slats laid side by side). The resulting measure is the length to cut the spacing batten, which is used to set each slat into its exact position.

BRACING

When making a door or any similar frame, it is vital that it should be square, with corners at perfect right angles. You can ensure this by using one of two bracing methods.

3-4-5 method Measure three units along one rail, four units down the adjacent rail, then nail a bracing batten accurately to one of the unit marks. Pull into square so that the bracing batten measures five units at the other unit mark, forming the long side of a triangle. Saw off the batten ends flush with the frame but do not remove the batten until frame is fitted in place. For large doors such as those on wardrobes, fix two battens on opposing corners.

1 Marking Lumber to Length and Square All Around
Mark across the face of the lumber with a utility knife held against a try square blade. Move knife around corners and mark sides, and finally mark other side to join up the lines.

2 Using Spacing Battens to Space Out Slats Evenly
Bunch the slats together evenly at one end of the frame, then measure to the other end of the frame. Divide this number by the number of spaces required; cut spacing batten(s) to this length.

Try square method Nail a batten into one rail, pull into square by using a try square, and then nail the batten into the adjacent rail.

MAKING FOLDING WEDGES

Folding wedges are very useful for clamping large frames on a bench top during assembly. Folding wedges are always used in pairs, but more than one pair may be used to hold a large framework.

Make each pair of wedges from a piece of lumber (hardwood is ideal for this) measuring $1\frac{1}{2}$in × $1\frac{1}{2}$in × 13in (38mm × 38mm × 330mm). Make the wedges by sawing the lumber diagonally into two pieces.

To use the wedges, a wooden batten is first nailed to the bench and the item to be clamped is placed against the batten. Another batten is nailed to the bench, parallel with the first, and about $1\frac{3}{4}$in (45mm) away from the item. The wedges are now placed between the item and the second batten. The ends of the wedges are then knocked inwards with two hammers, thereby clamping the frame.

❸ **Bracing a Frame Square**
Nail a batten across a corner of the frame so that the 3-4-5 shape triangle is formed.

SAWING AND CUTTING

Cross-cutting to length by hand Hold the lumber firmly with the cutting line *(see* **Measuring and Marking Square, page 20** *)* overhanging the right-hand side of the workbench (if you are right-handed). With the saw blade vertical and the teeth on the waste side of the line, draw the handle back to start the cut. To prevent the saw from jumping out of place, hold the thumb joint of your other hand against the side of the saw blade.

Rip-cutting by hand With the lumber or board supported at about knee height, start the cut as described above, then saw down the waste side of the line, exerting pressure on the down cut only. If the saw blade wanders from the line, clamp the edge of a lumber batten exactly above the cutting line on the side to be retained, and saw along it.

Using a portable power saw If the cutting line is only a short distance from a straight edge, adjust

❹ **Making Folding Wedges**
Saw wood diagonally. Nail batten to bench; wedges fit between batten and item being clamped.

the saw's fence so that when it is run along the edge of the lumber, the blade will cut on the waste side of the cutting line. If the lumber is wide, or the edge is not straight, clamp a batten to the surface so that the saw blade will cut on the waste side of the line when it is run along the batten.

Ensuring a straight cut When cutting panels or boards using a power circular saw or a Saber saw, the best way to ensure a straight cut is to clamp a guide batten to the surface of the work, parallel with the cutting line, so that the edge of the base plate can be run along the batten. Obviously, the batten position is carefully adjusted so that the blade cuts on the waste side of the cutting line. Depending on which side of the cutting line the batten is clamped, when using a circular saw, it is possible the motor housing will damage the batten or the C-clamps holding it in place. In this case; replace the batten with a wide strip of straight-edged plywood clamped to the work far enough back for the motor to clear the clamps.

❺ **Cross-cutting to Length**
Hold the lumber firmly. Steady the saw blade with your thumb joint as you start to cut.

❻ **Straight Power-saw Cutting**
Top **Use the rip fence of the saw if cutting near the edge.** *Above* **Cutting alongside the batten as a guide for obtaining a straight cut.**

❼ **Cutting with a Back Saw**
Start the cut as for a hand saw. As the cut progresses keep the blade horizontal.

TECHNIQUES: CUTTING AND PLANING

CUTTING A CIRCLE

With a Saber saw Mark the circle on the face of the panel. If you do not have a compass, a good makeshift alternative can be made with a loop of string pivoting on a thumb tack at the circle's center. Hold a pencil vertically in the loop at the perimeter to draw the circle.

For a neat, splinter-free edge, carefully score around the cutting line with a sharp utility knife.

To start the cut, drill a hole about $\frac{3}{8}$in (10mm) in diameter just on the waste side of the line. Insert the Saber saw blade through this hole and start the cut from this point, sawing carefully just on the waste side of the cutting line. By scoring the cutting line it will be easier to follow the line and get a smooth edge.

With a coping saw Mark out the circle, score the cutting line, and drill a hole just on the waste side as above. Disconnect the blade from one end of the frame, pass the blade through the hole, and re-connect it to the frame. It will be best to clamp

the piece of work vertically when cutting the circle. The blade can be turned in the frame as necessary to help the frame clear the piece of work, but even so, with a coping saw you will be restricted in exactly how far you are able to reach away from the piece of work. If the circle is some way from the edge, use either a power Saber saw or a hand compass saw to cut it.

With a compass saw A compass saw, similar to a keyhole saw, has a stiff, triangular pointed saw blade attached to a simple handle. A very useful compass saw blade is available for fitting in a knife handle.

Because this saw has no frame, it is very useful for cutting circles and other apertures, like keyholes, anywhere in a panel.

Preparation of the circle for cutting, such as marking out, scoring, and drilling for the blade, is the same as for the other methods. When cutting with a compass saw, keep the blade vertical and make a series of rapid, short strokes without exerting too much pressure.

CUTTING CURVES

The technique is basically the same as for cutting a circle, except that there will be no need to drill a hole in order to start the cut. You can use a Saber saw, coping saw, or compass saw to make the cut. A coping saw is ideal for making this cut because most of the waste can be removed with an ordinary hand saw, since you will be cutting close to the edge of the wood, and the saw frame, therefore, will not get in the way.

CUTTING GROOVES AND SLOTS

The easiest way to cut grooves (or dados) is to use a router with a bit set to the depth required for the groove. Use a straight-sided router bit. Ideally, the router bit should be the exact width of the groove or slot, so that it can be cut from one setting. If this is not possible, then use a smaller router bit and cut the groove or slot in two or more goes. Make the first cut along the waste side of the line with a batten clamped in line with the

groove to guide the base of the router. If a deep groove is required, it may be necessary to make a shallow cut first, then a deeper one.

To cut dados by hand, start by marking out the groove with a utility knife which will ensure a neat finish. Hold the piece of work on a bench, and with a back saw, make vertical cuts just inside the marked lines to the depth of the dado. If the dado is wide, make a series of other vertical cuts in the waste wood. Now chisel out the waste, working from each side to the middle. Finally, with the flat side of the chisel downwards, pare the bottom of the dado so that it is perfectly flat.

CUTTING RABBETS

A rabbet is an L-shaped step in the edge of a piece of lumber.

To cut a rabbet by hand, use a marking gauge to mark the rabbet width across the top face of the piece of work and down both sides. Mark the depth of the rabbet across the end and sides.

Hold the lumber flat and saw down on the waste side of the marked line

① Straight Rip-cutting
Clamp a straight batten alongside the cutting line and saw beside the batten. A wedge holds the cut open.

② Using a Power Saber Saw
For a straight cut, clamp a batten alongside line. Cut a circle by following line.

③ Cutting Circles by Hand
***1* Drill a small hole and cut circle using a compass saw. *2* Making the cut with a coping saw.**

④ Chiseling a Groove
After making saw cuts at side, chisel out waste from each side. Finally pare base flat.

to the depth of the rabbet. Then use a chisel to cut out the waste one bit at a time along the end grain.

It is very easy to cut a rabbet using a router, and in this case it is not necessary to mark out the rabbet unless you want a guide to work to. However, do practice on scrap wood to be sure of setting the router to cut to the correct depth and width.

If using a straight cutter, adjust the guide fence on the router so that the cutter cuts to the correct width, then adjust the cutting depth so that the router will cut to the correct depth. When the router is correctly set up, simply hold it flat on the piece of work and move it against the direction of the cutter's rotation.

If you are using a cutter with a guide pin, simply adjust the depth of cut and then run the cutter along the edge of the wood to form the rabbet. The cutter will follow irregularities in the wood, so make sure the wood is perfectly straight.

MAKING A V-BLOCK

A V-block is useful for holding circular items steady while they are being worked on. Make the block from a length of 2 × 3in (50 × 75mm) S4S lumber – the actual length should be a little longer than the item to be held. The V is made to a depth of about 1in (25mm) in the 3in (75mm) side of the lumber. Cut the V using a circular saw with the blade tilted to 45°. Clamp the block firmly and fit the saw with a guide fence to keep the cut straight. Cut up one side and down the other. Practice on scrap wood while adjusting the depth and width of cut to give the correct size V-shape. Alternatively, you can use a V-cutter bit in a router. It may take two or three passes with the router to make the V to the full depth and width of the cutter.

PLANING

By hand Make sure that the plane blade is sharp and properly adjusted. Stand to one side of the work with your feet slightly apart so you are facing the work and feeling comfortable. Plane from one end of the piece of work to the other, starting the cut with firm pressure on the leading hand, transferring it to both hands, and finally to the rear hand as the cut is almost complete. Holding the plane at a slight angle to the direction of the grain can sometimes improve the cutting action.

With a power plane Remove ties and loose clothing; overalls are ideal. Wear goggles and a painter's mask. Turn the adjuster knob to set the depth to cut and start the plane. Begin with a shallow cut and increase the cutting depth if necessary. Make sure the work is clamped in place.

Stand comfortably to one side of the work and, holding the plane with two hands, set it into the work at one end and pass it over the surface to the other end. Push the plane forwards steadily; not too fast or you will get a wavy surface finish. When you have completed the work, switch off and make sure that the blades stop spinning before resting the plane down with the cutting depth set at zero.

DRILLING

To ensure that screwheads lie flush with the surface of plywood, particleboard or other material use a countersink drill bit.

To minimize the risk of splitting lumber, drill pilot and clearance holes for screws. For small screws, pilot holes can be made with an awl.

The **clearance hole** in the lumber should be fractionally smaller in diameter than the screw shank.

The **pilot hole** in the lumber to receive the screw should be about half the diameter of the clearance hole. The depth of the pilot hole should be slightly less than the length of the screw.

Drilling vertical holes To ensure vertical holes, mount the drill in a drill stand. If this is not possible, stand a try square on edge so that its stock (handle) is resting on the work alongside the drilling position, and the blade is pointing up in the air. Use this as a sighting guide and line up the drill as close as possible with the square to ensure the drill is vertical. It is also helpful if an assistant can stand back and sight along the drill and square from two sides to ensure the drill is held straight.

---

⑤ Making a V-block
Cut out a V in a block of 2 × 3in (50 × 75mm) lumber using a circular power saw tilted to cut at 45°.

⑥ Drilling Vertical Holes
With a drill stand, not only will the drill bit be held vertical, but depth is also controlled.

⑦ Freehand Drilling Guide
When drilling it can be helpful to stand a try square alongside the drill to ensure accuracy.

⑧ Drilling Depth Guide
There are various guides to control drilling depths, such as rings for drills, and masking tape.

Techniques: Wall Fixtures

Screwing

When screwing one piece of wood to another, make sure that half of the screw penetrates into the bottom piece of wood. The screw's thickness should not exceed one-tenth of the width of the wood into which it has to be inserted. Keep screws at a distance of five times their shank diameter from the side edge of the wood, and ten times the shank diameter from its end.

Nailing

The correct length of nail to use is two-and-a-half to three times the thickness of the lumber being nailed. However, check that the nail will not pierce right through the two pieces being nailed. Wherever possible nail through the thinner piece of wood into the thicker piece.

Nails grip best if driven in at an angle ("**skew nailing**"). A row of nails should be driven in at opposing angles to each other. Framework joints are usually held by skew nailing. Clamp or nail a block of wood temporarily against one side of the vertical piece to stop it sliding as the first nail is started.

To prevent wood from splitting, particularly if nailing near an edge, blunt the points of the nails by hitting them with a hammer before driving them home. Blunt nails will cut through lumber fibers neatly, while pointed nails are more likely to push the fibers apart like a wedge, leading to splitting.

Wall Fixtures

Solid wall The normal attachment for a solid wall is a wood screw and plastic anchor. Before drilling the fixing hole, check with a metal detector that there are no pipes or cables hidden below the surface. Drill the holes for the anchor with a masonry drill bit in an electric drill. The anchor packing will indicate the drill size to use. Switch to hammer action if the wall is hard. The screw should be long enough to go through the fixture and into the wall by about 1in (25mm) if the masonry is exposed, and by about $1\frac{3}{8}$in (35mm) into a plastered wall.

If the wall crumbles when you drill into it, mix up a cement-based plugging compound (available from home improvement stores). Turn back the screw half a turn before the compound sets (in about five minutes). When it is hard (in about one hour) the screw can be removed and a heavy attachment made.

If your drill sinks easily into the wall once it has penetrated the plaster layer, and a light gray dust is produced from the hole, you are fixing into lightweight concrete blocks. In this case, special winged anchors for soft blocks should be used.

To make a quick, light-to-medium weight attachment in a solid wall, a masonry nail can be used. Choose a length that will penetrate the material to be attached, and pierce an exposed masonry wall by $\frac{5}{8}$in (16mm) and a plastered wall by about 1in (25mm). Wear goggles in case the hardened nail snaps when you strike it, and hammer it gently through the material to be attached and into the wall.

Lath and plaster For a strong attachment, screw directly into the main vertical studs to which the laths are nailed. You can find these studs with a metal detector (*see* **Stud wall**, below).

For a lightweight attachment you can screw into the wood laths. These can be located by probing with a pointed implement such as an awl. Then insert a twin-thread wood screw. For medium-to-heavyweight attachments into lath and plaster, drill between the laths and use a cavity-wall fitting suitable for lath and plaster, such as a spring toggle, gravity toggle, or nylon toggle.

Stud wall For a strong attachment into a gypsum wallboard-covered stud wall, make a screw fixing directly into the vertical studs. You can find these by tapping the wall to check where it sounds most dense, and then probing these areas with a pointed implement until a firm background is found. Alternatively, you can make a small hole in the wall, and push a stiff wire into it horizontally until an obstruction is felt, which will be the stud. Withdraw the wire and hold it on the surface of

① Drilling Holes for Screws in Lumber
Drill a clearance hole in the thinner piece. Countersink this hole, then drill a hole to slightly less than screw length. *Inset* To counterbore, drill to the diameter of the screwhead to required depth, then as above.

② Techniques for Joining Wood by Nailing
Nail should be two-and-a-half to three times the thickness of the lumber being joined. Assemble frames on bench by nailing against batten. *Inset* Blunt nail points to avoid splitting lumber.

the wall so that the edge of the stud can be marked. By drilling about 1in (25mm) to the farther side of this mark, the center of the stud will be found and a screw can be inserted.

To avoid making holes in the surface of a wall, a metal detector can be used. Move it over the wall to locate a pattern of nails and mark this on the surface. Vertical rows of nails indicate a stud. Alternatively, use one of the newer electronic stud and joist detectors. This is moved over the surface to detect a change in density between the different construction materials. A change indicates the position of a stud.

If a fixture cannot be made into a stud, a lighter fixture can be made into gypsum wallboard by using a fixture designed for that material. Follow the manufacturer's instructions for the size of hole required, which can be made in gypboard with an ordinary twist drill bit.

Cavity wall Cavity walls comprise a solid inner leaf of bricks or concrete blocks surfaced with plaster and separated from the outer leaf of

bricks or stone blocks by a cavity about 2in (50mm) wide.

When tapped, a cavity wall sounds solid. For fixtures, treat it is a solid wall (see page 24).

BEVELED BATTENS

These provide a very secure method of holding heavy objects on to a wall. The battens are formed by sawing a strip of wood lengthways with the saw blade set at 45°. This results in two interlocking pieces of wood. One piece, with the sloping face pointing upwards and the narrower face facing the wall, is screwed to the wall. The other piece, with the sloping face pointing downwards and the narrower side facing the item to be hung, is screwed to the item to be attached. When the item is lifted into place, the battens interlock and produce a very secure attachment.

For security, the battens should be formed by sawing a 1 × 4in (25 × 100mm) strip of lumber lengthways. Screws should be applied to the wall and into the item to be hung at about 8in (200mm) intervals. Use No 10 wood screws –

1½in (38mm) long into the item to be hung, and 2½in (65mm) long into the wall. Anchors will also be required.

ATTACHING RIGHT-ANGLED BRACKETS

These are right-angled steel strips pre-drilled for screw fixing and are useful for attaching lumber frames to walls and ceilings, as long as the brackets are positioned out of sight.

Decide where you want the bracket, hold it in place on the frame and use a pencil to mark the center of one screw fixing position. Drill a pilot hole and attach the bracket with one screw. Repeat for the other brackets. Position the frame and check that it is vertical. Mark center points of the bracket fixing holes on the wall or ceiling. Remove the frame and use a masonry drill to make anchor holes at the required positions. Press anchors into holes. Before replacing the frame and screwing brackets in place, check that brackets are still accurately positioned on the frame. Drill pilot holes for the remaining screw fixings, and insert the screws.

TYPES OF WALL FIXTURES

Anchor for solid walls

Anchor for soft building blocks

Spring-toggle anchor for cavity walls and ceilings

Gravity toggle anchor for cavity walls

Nylon toggle (above)

Anchor for gypsum wallboard (below)

③ Skew Nailing for Strength
Assemble frames by skew nailing (driving nails at an angle). The joint will not then pull apart.

④ Using a Nailset
For a neat finish, use a nailset to drive nail heads below the surface, then fill indentation.

⑤ Using Beveled Battens
For a secure fixing on a wall use beveled battens made by sawing a batten lengthwise at 45°.

TECHNIQUES: WOOD JOINTS

WOOD JOINTS

Butt joint This is the simplest frame joint of all. The ends of the lumber to be jointed must be cut square so that they butt together neatly. Corner and "T" joints can be formed, which are glued and nailed for strength. Corrugated fasteners can also be used to hold these joints, especially where the sides of the frames will be covered to hide the fasteners. When "T" joints are being formed from inside a frame, they can be skew nailed (see page 24).

Corner joint This is a simple "knock down" fixture attached with screws; it is used to attach boards at right angles. They are described as "knock down" joints because some are in two parts for easy disassembly, and even the simple attachments can be unscrewed. They do not look very attractive, but are useful where they will be hidden – by a fascia, for example.

Miter joint Popular for making picture frames, but suitable for other

② Corner Fitting Joints
Ideal for joining wood and boards at right angles. *Top* A one-piece fitting. *Bottom* A two-part type. Both are easily fitted using screws.

① Simple Butt Joints
Top Corner and *below* "T" joints can be formed by skew nailing or by using corrugated fasteners.

right-angled corner joints. Cut the joint at 45° using a miter box as a guide. A simple miter joint is glued and nailed, but a stronger joint can be made using dowels, or by making oblique saw cuts into which wood veneers are glued.

Half-lap joint Also known as halving joints, these join wood of similar thickness at corners or to form "T" or "X" joints (mid-lap and cross-lap joints). Cut each piece to half its thickness. Use a try square to mark the width of the cut-outs and a marking gauge set to half the thickness of the wood to mark their depth. Be sure to cross-hatch the waste wood with a pencil so that the correct side is removed. To form an end-lap joint, saw down as for making a tenon joint (see page 28). To form a mid- or cross-lap, saw down on each side of the "T" cut-out to the depth of the central gauge line, then chisel out the waste.

Dado joint Used mainly for shelving, this is basically a slot into which a shelf fits. The "through" dado joint

③ Types of Half-lap Joints
Top A corner-lap joint. *Bottom left* A mid-lap joint. *Bottom right* A cross-lap joint.

④ Forming a Half-lap Joint in Lumber Battens
Mark width of the cut-out. Mark half the thickness of the wood with a marking gauge. Cross hatch area to be removed. Saw down sides with a back saw, then chisel out the waste.

⑤ Cutting Miter Joints
Miters make right-angled corner joints. Using a miter box as a guide for ensuring a 45° angle, cut out the joint with a back saw.

6 **Forming Miter Joints**
Top Glue and nail together a simple miter joint. *Bottom* Reinforce the joint with a corner block, dowels, or wood veneer.

8 **Types of Dado Joint**
Top A through dado joint. *Middle* A through dado joint on the side of a central support. *Bottom* A corner dado joint.

7 **Stages in Forming a Through Dado Joint**
Mark width of the dado according to the thickness of the wood being joined. Use a utility knife. Mark depth with a marking gauge. Cut down the sides with a back saw. Chisel out the waste, working from both sides to the middle.

goes to the full width of the shelf, while a "stopped" dado joint is taken only part of the way across the board. Chisel the waste away from each side. In the case of a stopped dado, chisel the waste from the stopped end first. If you have a router, it is easier to cut a dado joint by running the router across the board against a batten clamped at right angles to the board to guide the router accurately.

A rabbet joint is similar to a dado joint at the top of a board, and can be cut in a similar way *(see* **Cutting rabbets, page 22** *).*

Bare-faced rabbet-and-dado joint This type of dado joint, used at the corners of a frame, is a much stronger joint than the common butt joint or lap joint because the rabbet of one piece is held in a dado cut in the other piece. The joint will be held just with good aliphatic resin wood-working glue, and by nailing or screwing down through the top into the upright. However, because of the short grain of the outside of the dado, this piece is left overlong while the joint is made, and then the "horn" (the excess timber) is cut off neatly, flush with the side of the joint. The rabbet should be no thicker than half the width of the lumber being jointed.

Carefully mark out the joint with a utility knife, a try square, and a marking gauge. The depth of the dado (groove) should be about one-third to a half the thickness of the upright. Cut the sides of the dado to the required depth using a back saw held vertical, or a carefully set circular saw. Clamping a batten alongside the dado will help to keep the cut straight. Remove the waste with a chisel, working from both sides to the middle, and holding the chisel with the flat side downwards. Alternatively, cut the dado with a router *(see* **Cutting grooves and slots, page 22** *).*

Mark out the vertical piece so that the rabbet will exactly fit in the dado. Use a marking gauge to mark out the rabbet. The rabbet is cut with a router or with a hand saw and chisel to form the tongue *(see* **Cutting rabbets, page 22** *).*

9 **Stages in Making a Bare-faced Rabbet-and-dado Joint**
Leave a "horn" of surplus lumber to support the short grain which will be on the outside of the groove. Mark width of piece being joined. Mark and cut dado as before. Saw off horn.

TECHNIQUES: WOOD JOINTS

Mortise and tenon joint A mortise and tenon joint can be marked out with a mortise gauge. Mark out the tenon (the tongue) so that it is one-third of the thickness of the piece of wood. The mortise (the slot) is marked at the same width in the other piece. The length of the mortise should match the width of the tenon being fitted. Drill out most of the waste with a series of holes using a drill bit slightly smaller than the mortise width. Working from the center, chop out the mortise with a chisel to the depth required. If making a through joint (in which the end of the tenon is visible), turn the wood over and complete the mortise from the other side.

Hold the tenon piece upright, but sloping away from yourself, secure in a vise, and use a back saw carefully to cut down to the shoulder. Then swivel the wood around to point the other way, and saw down to the other side of the shoulder. Next, position the wood vertically and cut down to the shoulder. Finally, place the wood flat and saw across the shoulder to remove the

2 Marking and Cutting a Mortise and Tenon Joint
Mark the length of the mortise slot to match the size of the rail being joined. Set the mortise gauge to the width of the chisel being used to cut out the mortise slot. (Chisel should be about one-third the width of wood being joined.) Use the mortise gauge to mark the mortise, and also the tenon, on the rail. Drill out the mortise and complete the cut with a chisel. Use a back saw to cut out the tenon.

1 Mortise and Tenon Joints
Top A common or stopped mortise and tenon joint. *Below* Through mortise and tenon joint.

3 Making a Haunched Mortise and Tenon Joint
Leave rail over-long. Mark out as before but allow for shoulder at top. Cut mortise slot, then saw down sides of a shoulder. Finish mortise using a chisel. Cut tenon as shown.

waste. Repeat for the waste on the other side of the tongue. Check that the two pieces fit well before gluing and assembling the joint. For added strength and a better appearance, cut small additional shoulders at each end of the tenon. These joints are the type used in the Wardrobe with Hinged Doors project (see page 212 for instructions).

Haunched mortise and tenon joints For joints at the corner of a large frame, such as the doors in the Japanese Wardrobe project (page 238), a square "haunch" or shoulder can be left in the tenon to increase its effective width and considerably strengthen the joint.

The joint is marked out with a try square, utility knife, and marking gauge as for an ordinary mortise and tenon, but allowance is made for a square shoulder at the top as shown in the diagram.

To prevent the small amount of cross-grain lumber above the mortise from being pushed out when the mortise slot is cut, the rail is left overlong at this stage to create a "horn"

⑤ Shouldered Tenon Joint
For enhanced strength and appearance, cut small additional shoulders at each end tenon. Do this by sawing down.

④ Making a Bare-faced Mortise and Tenon Joint
Tenon is offset to one side. Mark and cut as shown here.

which is cut off after the joint has been made and assembled.

Bare-faced mortise and tenon joint If the tongue of a tenon joint is offset to one side, this produces a bare-faced tenon as shown in the diagram. This produces a strong joint where narrow rails, such as the trellis rails in the Japanese Wardrobe doors (page 238), meet the thicker frame rails. The mortise slots in the frame rails can be cut farther back from the front edge for extra strength, and the bare-faced tenons of the trellis rails allow the front faces of these rails to lie flush with the front face of the door.

A bare-faced tenon is cut in the same way as a half-lap joint (or halving joint).

Dovetail joint A dovetail joint is made so that the "pins," which are the protruding fingers, interlock in both parts of the joint, giving a joint of great pull-out strength. The joint can only come apart in the same way as it was assembled.

A sliding bevel is used to mark out

a central dovetail pin on one rail, and the dovetail shape is cut out using a dovetail saw or fine-toothed back saw to leave a central pin.

The thickness and shape of the pin is marked on the other piece, called the "post," and the marks are extended on to the ends using a try square. The post is held upright and the waste inside the two outer pins is cut out using a dovetail saw, while a coping saw is used to cut across the bottom of the waste. The sides are pared down to size with a chisel.

⑥ Marking Out and Cutting a Dovetail Joint
Mark a line the thickness of the matching piece. Using a mortise gauge, mark top of the pin. Mark sides of pin with sliding bevel set at slope of 1 in 6. Cut pin with back saw. Hold pin on other piece. Mark dovetail and cut out waste with back and coping saws. Pare base accurately with chisel to achieve good fit.

Dowel joint Dowels are a strong, simple, and hidden means of joining wood together.

Use pre-cut grooved dowels with beveled ends (*see* **Materials, page 18**). These range from $\frac{1}{4}$in (6mm) diameter by 1in (25mm) long to $\frac{3}{8}$in (10mm) by 1$\frac{1}{2}$in (38mm). The dowel length should be about one-and-a-half times the thickness of the wood being jointed. If you need to use doweling of a larger diameter (as used in the cupboard door frames in the Tiled Kitchen or for the Alcove Shelves and Cupboards), cut your own lengths of dowel. Cut grooves down the length of dowel to allow glue and air to escape, and bevel the ends. The dowel lengths should be twice the thickness of the wood being joined.

On both pieces of wood, use a marking gauge to find the center line, and mark with a pencil. Drill the dowel holes to half the dowel length with the drill held in a drill stand, or aligned with a try square stood on end. Drill the dowel holes in one of the pieces to be jointed, insert center points in the holes, then bring the two pieces of the joint together so they are carefully aligned. The center points will make marks in the second piece of wood where the dowel holes should be drilled. Drill the holes to half the length of the dowels, plus a little extra for glue. Where dowels are used for location rather than strength, such as for joining worktops, set the dowels three-quarters into one edge and a quarter into the other.

Put glue in the holes and tap the dowels into the holes in the first piece with a mallet. Apply glue to both parts of the joint; bring them together and clamp them in position until the glue has set.

GLUING

All joints are stronger if glued. Make sure that surfaces to be joined are clean and well-fitting. Clamp surfaces together while the glue is setting, but not so tightly that all the glue is squeezed from the joint. Use waterproof glue for joints that may be subject to dampness. If the parts do not fit tightly, use a two-part resorcinol glue.

❶ Types of Dowel Joint
Dowels can join panels edge to edge and join frames at corners. They can be hidden or have ends exposed.

❷ Dowels to Join Panels
Right **Mark dowel positions. Drill holes, insert center points. Mark second piece.**

❸ Making a Doweled Frame
If edge of frame will not be seen, drill holes for dowels after making frame. Hammer dowels home; cut ends flush after glue dries.

❹ Using a Doweling Jig
If dowels are to be hidden, a doweling jig makes it easy to drill holes that align in both pieces.

SCRIBING AND LEVELING

Scribing long lengths When you are fitting a worktop, horizontal panel, shelf, or vertical panel to a wall, you are likely to find that it will not touch the wall at every point since it is extremely unlikely that the wall will be flat and square. To avoid such gaps, it is necessary to scribe the item to the wall.

Hold the item in place and as close to its final position as possible. If it is a worktop, make sure that it is level and at right angles to whatever is next to it. If it is an upright, make sure that the front edge is held plumb. Where the gap is at its widest, pull the panel forward so that the gap is 1in (25mm). Take a block of wood 1in (25mm) long and place it on the panel, against the wall, at one end. Hold a pencil against the other end of the block, and draw the pencil and block along the wall so that the pencil makes a line, which reproduces the contours of the wall.

With a Saber saw or a compass saw, cut along the line. Where the line is too close to the edge to saw,

shape the panel to the line using a tool such as a Surform or a wood rasp. Press the panel against the wall and check that it fits neatly all the way along.

Scribing in alcoves It is more difficult to scribe in an alcove because a horizontal panel will usually fit neatly only *after* it has been scribed to the walls.

Using a large wooden square (you can make one from lumber battens following the 3-4-5 principle of producing a right-angled triangle [*see* page 20]), find out if one, or both, of the side walls are square and flat. If they are, you can carefully measure between them at the required height of the worktop. Then saw off the ends of the worktop to this length and position it, before finally scribing it to the rear wall as described above.

If the side walls of the alcove are not square, you can mark out the worktop using a cardboard template (*see* **Using templates**) of each side wall and part of the rear wall which you then scribe to fit.

Using a contour gauge This device (*see* **Tools, page 12**) is used for reproducing a complicated shape and is useful if you have to fit, for example, a worktop around something such as a decorative wood molding. It comprises a row of movable pins or narrow plastic strips held in place by a central bar. When pressed against a shape, the pins follow the outline of the shape. The contour gauge is then held on the item to be fitted and the shape transferred to it by drawing around the contour gauge with a pencil. After use, realign the pins.

Using templates When cutting around an awkward-shaped object, such as a pipe, it is a good idea to make a template of the obstruction. Make the template from cardboard or thick paper. Cut and fold the template to make it as accurate as you can. When you are satisfied that you have a good fit, place the template on the item to be fitted, and mark around it to produce a cutting line. Alternatively, glue the template in position and cut around it.

Leveling battens When attaching battens to a wall with masonry nails, first lay the battens on the floor and drive the nails almost all the way through them. On the wall, use a carpenter's level to position the batten horizontally and draw a pencil line along the top edge of the batten. Hold the batten in position and drive a masonry nail at one of the ends part of the way into the wall. Check that the top of the batten aligns with the guide line, then rest the carpenter's level on the batten and, with the bubble central, drive a nail into the wall at the other end of the batten. Make sure that the batten is level, then drive in all the nails.

If attaching the batten with screws, drill clearance holes in the batten as above and, with a pointed tool, mark the wall through a screw hole at one end of the batten. Drill and anchor the wall at this point (*see* **Wall fixtures, page 24**) then screw the batten to the wall. Level the batten as above, mark the other screw positions, then remove the batten and drill and anchor the wall. Finally, screw the batten in place.

5 Scribing Long Lengths to Fit Against a Wall
Where gap is widest pull panel forwards so gap is 1in (25mm). Hold pencil against 1in (25mm) wide block; move block and pencil along wall to draw cutting line. Cut along this line.

6 Attaching Leveling Battens to a Wall
If attaching with masonry nails drive these into battens first. Hold batten in place and mark wall. Holding batten on marked line, insert nail at end. Recheck level; drive in other nails.

TECHNIQUES: FITTING DOORS AND HINGES

Leveling kitchen units Floors are rarely level, so that when installing kitchen units you must work from the highest spot in the room. Assemble the units and temporarily place them in position. Take a long, straight wooden batten and place this on the top of the units. Place a carpenter's level on the horizontal batten, to find the highest unit. Work from this unit and bring all the other units up to this level by shimming pieces of plywood or hardboard underneath them. After this is done, the top can be installed, and the doors and shelves fitted.

Alternatively, if you have yet to construct the support units, you can build each one to the exact height required to compensate for differences in floor level. This leveling technique is very useful for old properties where floors are invariably uneven. First, lay straight battens around the floor where the units will be positioned – one batten at the front edge and one at the back. Work from the high point and shim the battens so that they are level. Mark on them the positions of the

units and at each point measure the gap to the floor. Increase the height of each unit by this amount.

Finding verticals Use a plumb line to mark a vertical line on a wall. Tap a nail into the wall where you want the vertical to be, and tie the plumb line to it. When the line is steady, hold a scrap of wood on the wall so it just touches the string and mark the wall at this point. Repeat the procedure at a couple of other places. Alternatively, rub the plumb line with chalk. When it stops swinging, press it against the wall, then pluck the string to leave a vertical chalk line on the wall.

HANGING DOORS

Hinged cupboard or wardrobe doors There are two ways to fit hinged doors; they can be **inset** to fit between side frames, or they can be **flush overlay** where the doors cover the side frames.

Inset doors look attractive, but they are harder to fit than flush overlay doors because they must be very accurately made to achieve a

uniform gap all round the opening. Flush overlay doors cover the frame and hide any uneven gaps. Also, the concealed hinges that are normally used to hang a flush overlay door are adjustable, making it easy to alter the door so that it opens and closes correctly.

Sliding cupboard and wardrobe doors Small doors slide in double U-channel tracks made from lumber or plastic. Shallow U-channel track is fitted along the bottom front edge of the opening and a deeper track is fitted at the top, to the underside of the front edge. The grooves in the track should match the door thickness and it is important to fit the top track exactly vertically above the bottom track. Make sliding doors so that they overlap each other by about $1\frac{3}{4}$–2in (45–50mm). Their height should be the distance from the bottom to the groove in the top track, plus $\frac{1}{4}$in (6mm). After assembly of the frame unit, the door can be fitted by lifting it up and into the top track, and then slotting it into the bottom track.

Heavier doors must be hung using an overhead- or bottom-track roller system. Fitting is usually straightforward if you follow the manufacturer's instructions. Even if the track has not been fixed exactly horizontal, there is usually a means of adjusting the doors so that they move and close smoothly.

FITTING HINGES

Inset doors **Flush hinges** are the easiest to fit. They are simply screwed to the edge of the door and the frame, and require no recessing. However, they cannot be adjusted after fitting. The inner flap of the hinge is screwed to the edge of the door, while the outer flap is screwed to the inner face of the frame.

Attach the hinges at equal distances from the top and bottom of the door. With a tall or very heavy door, fit a third hinge centrally between the other two. Mark the hinge positions on the edge of the door with the hinge knuckle (joint) in line with the door front. Drill pilot holes and screw on the inner flap. Hold the door in place or rest it on something

① Using a Contour Gauge
To reproduce complicated shapes, press the gauge against objects; use it as a pattern.

② A Method of Leveling Kitchen Units
Temporarily position the units or the partition frame. Place carpenter's level on a straight batten to find the highest unit. Pack plywood or hardwood pieces under other units to bring them to this height.

③ Fitting Sliding Door Track
Heavy doors are best hung on bottom track. Track screws to floor and rollers are inset in door bottoms.

to raise it to the correct height, making sure that it is accurately aligned at the top and bottom, and mark the positions of the hinges on the frame. Remove the door and extend these lines using a try square. Hold the door against the frame so it is in an open position, and screw the outer hinge flaps in place, so that they match up with the guide lines.

Butt hinges are conventional flapped hinges and are available in steel (commonly) or in brass, which is better for high quality work. They are attached in the same way as flush hinges, except that the hinge flaps have to be recessed into the lumber using a chisel or router.

Mark out the hinge positions as for flush hinges, making sure that the hinges are not positioned so that the fixing screws will go into the end grain of cross members and be likely to pull out.

The length of the hinges are marked out first, using a utility knife, then the width of the hinge and the thickness of the flap are marked using a marking gauge. With a chisel held vertical, and a mallet, cut

down around the waste side of the recess, then make a series of vertical cuts across the full width of the recess. Remove the waste by careful chiseling, then finally pare the bottom of the recess flat using the chisel held flat-side downwards.

If you are careful, you can remove the bulk of the waste from a hinge recess using a straight bit in a router. The bit is set to cut to the depth of the recess, and afterwards the corners can be finished off using a chisel.

Flush overlay doors Modern, adjustable **concealed hinges** are the most commonly used. There are many types available, and they come with full installation instructions. Some types are face-fitted and simply screw in place on the inside face of the door, but usually a special Forstner bit is used to drill a wide, flat-bottomed hole for the hinge body in the rear surface of the door. Next the base plate is screwed to the side frame. Finally, the hinge is attached to the base plate and the adjusting screws are turned until the door fits perfectly.

6 **The Stages in Fitting a Butt Hinge**
Using a try square and a utility knife, mark out the length of the hinge. With a marking gauge mark width and thickness of hinge flap. With chisel vertical, cut around outline of hinge. Make series of cuts across width of recess. Pare out the waste, then check that the flap lies flush. Once this is done, screw the butt hinge in place.

4 **Fitting a Flush Hinge**
Flush hinges are very easy to fit. Screw the outer flap to the frame and the inner flap to the door.

5 **Fitting a Butt Hinge**
Butt hinges must be recessed into the door frame so that hinge flaps are flush with the surface.

7 **Fitting Face-fixed Concealed Hinges**
This hinge is simply screwed to the inside face of the door and frame.

8 **Fitting Recessed Concealed Hinges**
Blind hole is drilled for hinge body. The base plate arm is adjustable.

TECHNIQUES: FITTING CATCHES AND LOCKS

FITTING CATCHES

Many types of concealed hinges have built-in closers, so catches are not required. With conventional hinges, **magnetic catches** are popular. The magnet is fitted to the side of the cabinet and the catch plate is then positioned on the magnet. The door is closed on to the catch and pressed hard so that the catch plate marks the door. The door is opened and the catch plate is then simply screwed to the door.

Ball catches are very neat devices. On the central edge of the door a hole is drilled to accept the body of the ball catch, which is pressed into place. The door is closed and the ball marks the edge of the cupboard. The door is opened and the striker plate carefully positioned to coincide with the center of the ball. If you are recessing the striker plate, its outline should be drawn around, using a utility knife. The strike plate is then recessed into the cabinet so that it lies flush with the surface enabling the catch to operate smoothly.

① Magnetic Cupboard Catch
A magnetic catch is screwed to the inside face of a cabinet and the catch plate is screwed to the frame.

FITTING DOOR LIFT MECHANISMS

Actual fitting instructions vary with the type of mechanism, but basically all screw inside the cupboard on the side of the frame, close to the top. Two lift mechanisms are required per door, and they are designed to throw the door upwards and outwards, and clear of the ceiling.

With the more sophisticated type (fig 4, left-hand illustration), the mechanism is screwed to the side face of the frame just below the top of the cupboard, and just inside the front edge. It is held with three screws. The lift-up flap is screwed to the opening part of the mechanism with two screws, the top screw being fixed down from the top edge of the flap by the thickness of the cupboard top plus $1\frac{1}{8}$in (28mm). This ensures that the flap opens without damaging the cupboard front or the ceiling.

FITTING LOCKS

The neatest lock is a **cabinet mortise lock**. To fit, mark the center line

② Fitting a Ball Catch
Drill door edge centrally for ball catch body which is pressed in place. Striker plate fixes to frame.

③
Fitting a Cabinet Mortise Lock to a Cupboard Door
1 Mark the center line on the door edge and measure and mark the width and thickness of lock on the door edge. *2* Use a brad-point bit to clear out mortise and clear out the slot with a chisel. *3* Push lock into mortise slot and mark around cover plate. *4* Cut recess for plate; form keyhole using compass saw.

④
Fitting Top-hinged Door Lift Mechanism
Two types of door lift mechanism are shown below. On the left is a combined hinge and stay, and on the right is a conventional stay. Both are designed to throw the door upwards and then to keep it held open.

in the edge of the door and measure and mark the width and thickness of the lock body. Using a brad-point drill bit of the same thickness as the lock body, drill out a series of overlapping holes to remove the bulk of the waste, and clear out the slot with a chisel. Push the lock into the mortise slot, mark around the cover plate and cut a recess. Measure the lock for the keyhole position, mark this on the front face of the door, drill the hole and saw a slot for the key. Close the door, turn out the lock bolt to mark the cabinet side, and fit the lock strike plate there.

A straight **cupboard lock**, as used on the Tool Cupboard project (page 45), is very easy to install. It simply screws to the back of the door after the keyhole has been cut out with a compass saw.

Start by making a thick paper template of the outline of the lock with a cut-out for the keyhole accurately positioned. Hold the template on the face of the door and mark the keyhole. Drill a hole at the top to the correct size, and below this drill a line of smaller holes which can be en-

larged into a slot for the keyhole. You can use a compass saw (which is also known as a keyhole saw) for this purpose.

Hold the lock in place behind the door, and fit the key to position the lock accurately. Mark and drill the fixing lock positions. Screw the lock in place. A brass keyhole escutcheon fitting may be supplied, and this is simply tapped into place in the keyhole flush with the face of the cabinet front.

In the case of the Tool Cupboard project, it will be necessary to cut away part of the door side rail to allow the lock to fit flush with the edge of the door. To do this, hold the lock against the edge of the door and mark the outline of the lock. Drill through the side rail, within this outline, and carefully chisel away the waste so that the lock fits snugly when slipped into place behind the door front.

Once the lock has been installed, the door should be closed and the key operated so that the lock bolt marks the edge of the other door. With a chisel, cut a rabbet in this

position for the lock bolt, and then cover the recess with a strike plate (also supplied with the lock). This is held in position, and its outline is marked with a knife. A shallow recess is then cut with a chisel so that the plate can be screwed in place, flush with the surface.

A **cut cupboard lock**, or **drawer lock**, is harder to fit because a recess has to be cut behind the cupboard or drawer front. A double recess is required – one for the lock mechanism, and the other for the back plate which is also recessed into the edge of the door or drawer for a neat fit and a smooth finish.

Hold the lock in position and mark the outline of the back plate on the back and the edge of the door. Also mark where the mechanism rabbet is required. First cut out the mechanism rabbet using a chisel, then make the shallower rabbet for the back plate. When the lock fits accurately, cut out the keyhole, then screw the lock in position. Attach the keyhole escutcheon and the strike plate as described above, and check that the lock works smoothly.

● **Fitting Cut Cupboard Lock**
1 **First chisel out the recess for the mechanism, then make a shallower rabbet for the lock back plate. 2 When lock fits neatly, cut out keyhole.**

● **Fitting a Surface-mounted Cupboard Door Lock**
Make a template of lock outline. *1* Hold template on the door at lock position. *2* Drill hole and saw a slot. *3* Position the lock with the key in place. *4* Screw the lock to the door.

● **Fitting a Cupboard Lock on a Framed Door**
1 **Hold the lock in position behind the frame and mark its outline. *2* Drill within the outline and chisel out waste. *3* Slide the lock through the aperture and fit as on left.**

TECHNIQUES: TILING

Plan tiling with equal gaps at each side

First row supported on batten

Fit tiles neatly around a window

Overlap tiles at external corners

Use cut tiles in internal corners

① Tools for Tiling
Top to bottom **Adhesive spreaders – metal and plastic; scoring tool; cutting pliers; tile nippers; heavy-duty cutter; spacers; file; saw; grout spreader.**

② Making a Gauging Rod
Lay out a correctly spaced row of tiles and on a batten accurately mark tile widths including spacers.

Planning When tiling, accurate laying out is essential. The tiles must be applied absolutely level, and, after tiling, no cut edges should show. Only factory-glazed edges, or half-round edge (bullnose) tiles which are made to be seen, should be visible. With the frames of the basic kitchen units (page 86) note that the frame width is designed so that the front face tiles exactly cover the ends of the frames and the edges of the tiles glued to each side. Tiles on the side panels are arranged so that cut tiles are right at the back of the units. Similarly, if any tiles have to be reduced in height, these cut tiles should be at floor-level where they will be less noticeable.

When tiling a plain wall, centralize the tiles on it, using cut tiles of equal width at each end. If the wall has a prominent window, arrange the tiles to give it a neat border. In both cases, adjust the height of the tiles by having cut tiles at floor or base-board level. Plan your tiling scheme so that part-tiled walls and low vertical surfaces, such as the side of a plinth, have whole tiles on the

top row. You may have to compromise on the best overall arrangement for the room. To deal with window reveals (recesses), have glazed edges visible around the front of the reveal, and have cut tiles butting up to the window frame.

Laying out Start by making a gauging rod. This is simply a length of straight lumber about $\frac{1}{2} \times 1\frac{1}{2}$in ($12 \times 38$mm), on which pencil lines are drawn to indicate tile widths, including spacers. To mark the lines, lay out a row of tiles along the gauging rod, with spacers between them — unless tiles incorporating spacers are being used. Draw a line across the gauging rod to coincide with the center of each joint. If rectangular tiles are used, a second rod will be required for tile heights.

Use the gauging rod(s) to lay out accurately the tile positions. When you are satisfied with the arrangement, nail a straight lumber batten (about $\frac{1}{2} \times 1\frac{1}{2}$in [$12 \times 38$mm]) horizontally across the full width of the area to be tiled to support the first row of complete tiles. Next, nail vertical battens at each side to support

③ Setting out the Wall
Centralize tiles on a dominant feature like a window, and fix batten one tile height above floor.

④ Starting to Attach tiles
Also fix vertical battens at each side. Spread adhesive in corner and press tiles firmly into place.

Plumb bob   Carpenter's level

the last row of complete tiles at the sides and to keep the tiling square. Use the gauging rods to mark off on the wall battens the exact tile widths and heights, as this will help you to keep the tiling square. If you are tiling a plastered wall, nail the tiling battens with lightly driven-in masonry nails. If tiling on wood or plywood use common nails.

TILING TOOLS

Adhesive spreader A simple notched plastic tool which evenly spreads a bed of tile adhesive.

Tile cutter There are various types of tile cutters available. Some resemble a pencil and have a tungsten-carbide tip which is drawn across the tile to score the surface where the break is required. A better type is a cutter resembling a pair of pincers. This has a cutting wheel to score a cut line, as well as jaws between which the tile is placed before the cutter handles are squeezed, pincer-like, to make the cut. A heavy-duty cutter for thick, large tiles consists of a jig with a cutting-lever arm.

Tile saw Consists of a tungsten-carbide rod-saw blade fitted into a frame. It will cut tiles to any shape: L-shaped, curved, etc. The tile to be sawn is clamped in a vise.

Tile spacers Nowadays it is common for tiles to be supplied with plain edges, rather than with built-in spacer lugs molded on the edges of the tiles. Spacer tiles are simply butted together and are automatically evenly spaced as they are positioned. However, with plain edge tiles it is important to place spacers between the tiles as they are positioned. This creates even gaps for grouting between the tiles.

Tile nippers A plier-like device for removing narrow strips which are too small to be handled by a conventional cutter. It will also cut shaped tiles.

Tile-file Useful for cleaning up sharp and uneven edges of a cut tile.

Grout spreader Flexible rubber blade for spreading grout cement into joints.

Sponge For cleaning away adhesive and grout from the surface of a fixed tile.

Tiling process Establish tile positions by laying out, then begin tiling in a bottom corner and spread adhesive over about 1 square yard. Rake it out evenly using the notched spreader supplied with the adhesive. Working from a corner, press the tiles into the adhesive with a slight twisting motion. If tiles without spacers are used, hold them evenly apart with plastic wall-tile spacers. These can either be pressed well into the joints and left in place, or they can protrude from the surface, in which case they can be pulled out after an hour or so and re-used elsewhere. Fit whole tiles only: tiles cut to fit around obstacles can be fitted later.

Cutting edge tiles Wait for 12 hours after the main area of tiling has been completed, before removing the setting-out battens. Tiles can then be cut to fill the gaps around the perimeter. Measure the space into which the tile is to fit, remembering to allow for the spacers between tiles. Use a tile cutter to cut a straight line across the surface of the tile, then smooth rough edges using a tile file. Use a notched spreader to

apply adhesive direct to the back of the tile, and press it into place.

Cutting around difficult shapes To cut around a pipe, snap the tile along the center line of the pipe, then score the pipe's outline on the surface. For a neat finish, saw around the pipe outline using a tungsten-carbide rod-saw held in a conventional hacksaw frame. Alternatively, nip away the pipe cutout by snapping off small pieces of the tile, using tile nippers or a pair of pliers. Tiles to be laid around basins and window openings can also be scored along the cutting line and then nipped. Alternatively, the cutout can be sawn out, which is likely to avoid breakages if the part to be cut out is close to the edge of the tile.

Finishing off Once the tiles are firm they should be grouted with a waterproof grout applied with a rubber spreader. When the grout is just beginning to set, use a small rounded stick to press the grout into the joint lines, then wipe off the excess grout with a damp sponge. When the grouting has dried, polish the tiles' surface with a dry duster.

⑤ Cutting Tiles to Size
Score along glazed side, then break tile along line using a cutting tool. Saw awkward shapes.

⑥ Cutting Around Pipes
Mark position of hole on face of tile. Snap tile along center line. Score outline, then nip out waste.

⑦ Grouting Tiles to Finish
Use rubber blade squeegee to press grout into joints. As grout sets, press rounded stick along joints.

⑧ Drilling a Hole in Tiles
Stick masking tape on drill point. Use masonry drill bit. Switch to hammer action when tile drilled through.

WORKBENCH AND TOOL CUPBOARD

This is the starting point for all serious do-it-yourself enthusiasts. If you make this well it will lead you to undertake many other projects. You will also have a solid bench to work on and practical, safe storage for your tools – two ingredients that will make your work more enjoyable, comfortable, and efficient.

The workbench should be made first. For simplicity, I have used a ply-covered fire-door with a solid lumber core; this is just as tough as the conventional solid beech top used for most professional benches, but is much cheaper. The frame is made from pine, and houses a plywood shelf for large pieces of equipment. A woodworker's vise and retractable stop for planing have been fitted to the bench.

The tool cupboard is secured to the wall with beveled battens, and its two wings (which double as doors) are fitted with locks, and fold back against the wall when the cupboard is in use. It is essential to incorporate lockable doors on a tool cupboard, especially in a household such as mine, where tools vanish with unfailing regularity. All your tools, attachments, nails, and screws have their own storage area and are easily visible, so there is no excuse not to return them to their rightful place when your work is finished; searching around for missing tools never fails to upset the enjoyment of woodwork.

Work lamps are clamped to the top of the cupboard to provide sufficient light where it is most needed, and the gap behind the cupboard allows wiring to be installed for electrical outlets.

Several coats of clear, shiny varnish were applied to the cupboard to give it a thoroughly professional look. Enjoy it and use it well.

Adjustable work lamps

Lockable doors open out to wall

Fire-retardant door blank used for workbench top

Vise & Stop

light tools

Heavy tools

light tools

tool Cupboard hung on wall with 2 sets of beveled battens

Wiring runs behind tool cupboard for electrical outlets

Shelf for large or very heavy tools

WORKBENCH

A sturdy woodworking bench helps you to achieve good results, and constructing your own will provide valuable woodworking experience.

For a neat and solid construction, the top and bottom rails are rabbeted into the bench legs. To speed up and simplify the job, omit the rabbets and simply glue and screw the rails to the sides of the legs, using a woodworking adhesive.

The top of the workbench is a solid-core, fire-retardant flush door blank measuring 6ft 8in × 24in (2050 × 610mm). The top should overhang the frame – by 4in (100mm) at each end, by $\frac{1}{2}$in (12mm) at the back and by at least 1in (25mm) at the front. The overhang allows enough space for C-clamps to hold items to the bench top. The overall height of the bench is 37in (940mm), a comfortable working height for a person about 6ft (1.8m) tall. Decide what is a comfortable working height for you, and adjust the leg lengths accordingly.

The rail lengths are dependent on the size of the door blank used, to give the overhangs mentioned

MATERIALS

Part	Quantity	Material	Length
LEGS	4	6 × 6in (150 × 150mm) S4S softwood	35$\frac{1}{2}$in (902mm)
TOP RAILS	2 long 2 short	2 × 6in (50 × 150mm) S4S softwood	To suit door size
BOTTOM RAILS	2 long 2 short	1 × 6in (25 × 150mm) S4S softwood	To suit door size
BENCH TOP	1	Solid core, fire-retardant flush door blank	6ft 8in × 24in (2050 × 610mm)
BENCH TOP BATTENS	2	2 × 2in (50 × 50mm) S4S softwood	Length of the sides between the legs
SHELF	1	$\frac{1}{2}$in (12mm) AC grade plywood	As above
BENCH VISE	1		
HANGING BARS	2	1in (25mm) dowel	To suit bench width

TOOLS

FOLDING PORTABLE WORKBENCH/VISE

UTILITY KNIFE

STEEL BENCH RULE

TRY SQUARE

HAND SAW

BACK SAW

CHISEL about $\frac{3}{4}$in (19mm) wide bench type

CHISEL about 1in (25mm) wide firmer type

DRILL (hand or power)

TWIST DRILL BITS

COUNTERSINK BIT

MARKING GAUGE

ROUTER (an alternative to a chisel for cutting rail rabbets)

above. Whether or not you rabbet the rails into the legs will also affect the length of the rails. The long rails fit inside the shorter end ones. If you rabbet the rails, note that the top rails are thicker than the bottom ones. So the top rails will be shorter than the bottom rail lengths by the difference in thickness between the two rails.

SPADE BIT to make cut-out for bench stop, and holes for hanging bars

TWIST DRILL BIT to make holes for bench-stop bolt

SABER SAW (or compass saw or coping saw) to make vise cut-out

MALLET

BAND CLAMP (or rope and scrap of wood to make tourniquet)

SCREWDRIVER (Phillips or slotted, depending on screw type)

SMOOTHING PLANE

SANDING BLOCK and SANDING PAPER

WRENCH to fit coach screws to install vise

MARKING THE LEGS

Mark the legs to length, squaring the cutting line on all faces, and then cut the legs. Check they are of identical length by standing them together and comparing their heights.

If the rails are to be rabbeted into the legs, mark out the rabbets (see **Techniques, page 22**).

MARKING FOR TOP RAIL

Line up one of the short rails flush with the top of the leg to mark off the depth of the rabbet. Line up a try square underneath to mark off the line squarely. Score a line on to the leg with a utility knife. Mark all four faces of the leg (see **Techniques, page 20**).

1 **Marking and Making the Leg Rabbets for Rails**
Left Mark rabbets for the top and bottom rails. *Center* Top rabbets are cut with a back saw; bottom rabbets with a back saw and chisel. *Right* The leg rail after rabbeting has been done.

BENCH STOP

BOLT SLOT

BENCH TOP
SUPPORTING BATTEN

TOP END RAIL

COACH BOLT
(for bench stop)

BOTTOM END RAIL

LEG

HANGING BAR

TOP SIDE RAIL

BOTTOM SIDE RAIL

WOOD STRIP

WOODEN JAWS

VISE

SHELF

BASIC ASSEMBLY OF
WORKBENCH AND PARTS

WORKBENCH

Set the marking gauge to the thickness of the top rail and mark this off on to the top, inner and outer faces of the leg, as shown (fig 1, page 40). Repeat the whole procedure for the other three legs.

MARKING LEG FOR BOTTOM RAIL

For the top of this rail to finish 14in (350mm) from the ground, measure this distance up the leg and mark with a pencil. Put the rail in place underneath and line up your try square underneath. Remove the rail and score a line with a utility knife for the position of the bottom of the rail. Replace the rail against the try square, then move the square to the top of the rail. Remove the rail again and score a line with a utility knife for the position of the top of the rail. Lining up in this way ensures greater accuracy. Continue lines round to the other three faces.

Re-set the marking gauge to the thickness of the lower rail and mark this thickness off on to the inner and outer faces of the legs as shown (fig 1, page 40).

CUTTING FOR TOP RAIL

Hold the leg in a portable workbench or clamp it to a solid table or saw horse and, cutting on the waste side of the line, make the horizontal cuts first, using a back saw to the marked depths. Then make the vertical cuts, using a back or hand saw, on both the outer faces. Remove any waste with a chisel. Alternatively, use a router, with the depth set to the thickness of the rails.

Repeat this procedure for the other three legs.

CUTTING OUT FOR BOTTOM RAIL

Make horizontal cuts with a back saw on the outer faces of one leg at the top and bottom of the rail position, to your marked depths. To cut out the rabbet, make a series of cuts with a back saw down to the marked depths, about ½in (12mm) apart; then pare out the waste with a bench chisel and a mallet *(see* **Techniques, page 22** *).*

Repeat for the other three legs until the surface is flat.

END FRAME ASSEMBLY

The rails must fit tightly. If necessary, make the rabbet so that they are fractionally undersized and plane down the rails slightly until they fit tightly in the rabbets.

Apply glue to the leg rabbets and position the bottom rail, so that it is flush with the sides. Drill and countersink through the rail into the legs and screw them together with 2in (50mm) No 10 screws – three on each leg. Repeat at the top for the top rail, gluing and screwing as before, using 2½in (65mm) No 10 screws.

Repeat the whole procedure for the second end frame. If you want to simplify construction by not using rabbets, simply glue and screw the rails to the face of the legs. However, make sure that the frames are assembled square, and that the rails overhang the legs by the thickness of the rail.

Clean up, plane, and bevel all the outer edges, then remove any excess glue and sand down all the surfaces for a smooth finish.

ADDING THE LONG RAILS

Stand the two end frames upright and fit the bottom long rails in place, gluing the leg rabbets as before. Remember that the tighter the legs fit, the stronger the frame will be. For a sturdy frame, the shoulders must be pulled up tightly before screwing them together. To do this, use either a band clamp or a rope tourniquet around the frame at the height of the rail joints. If using rope, loop a thin piece of wood in the rope on each side and twist it around to make the frame secure.

Glue and fit the top rails and then tighten them together with a clamp or a rope tourniquet.

Pilot-drill and screw through the rails into the legs in three places, as with the end frames. Once the rails have been screwed, the clamp can be removed.

Clean up, and bevel the top and bottom edges of the bottom rails and the bottom edges of the top rails. Sand down the framework and plane the top of the framework and the top rail flush.

1 **Assembling the Workbench End Frame**
Lay the legs on a flat surface and check that bottom rail fits tightly into the rabbet. Glue and screw in place. Attach top rail in a similar way, then repeat for the legs at the other end.

2 **Adding the Side Rails and Supporting Battens**
Glue and nail the bottom side rails into the leg rabbets first, then repeat for the top rails. In each case hold the frame tightly together with a rope tourniquet to keep it square. *Inset* Corner detail.

SECURING THE BENCH TOP

Take two battens of 2 × 2in (50 × 50mm) S4S, cut to the length of the sides between the legs. Drill and countersink the battens on two adjacent faces for screws to secure the side and top (ours had five along the side, six along the top). Choose the best side of the frame as the front. At the back, clamp one of the battens in place to the inside of the frame, flush with the top of the top rail, and screw through the side into the rail. The front batten is attached after installing the vise.

Put the top in place, equalizing the overhang each end and allowing $\frac{1}{2}$in (12mm) overhang at the back, and the remainder at the front (enough to take a cramp). Do not screw the top down yet.

INSTALLING A VISE

You will need a vise that fits into the top rail. There is a wide range of woodworking vises to choose from. All have wide-opening jaws and are designed to fit to the underside of the bench top, on the front edge close to a leg, so that the top edge of the jaws (after the lining has been fitted – see below) is level with the bench top. Some smaller vises simply clamp on to the underside of the workbench, but it is best to use one that is designed to be bolted in place. A square body seating will ensure easy fitting to the bench top.

Choose the largest vise you can afford – a jaw opening of about 13in (330mm) is ideal but maximum openings range from $4\frac{1}{2}$in (115mm) up to about 15in (380mm). The larger vises often have a useful quick-release mechanism which allows you to pull the jaw out and in without having to wind the handle as with a normal vise. Make sure that the body of the vise and the sliding jaw have holes to take the plywood liners which protect the work, the vise, and your tools.

The method of fitting varies slightly according to the make of vise chosen, but this is how we installed ours. Remember that the top of the steel jaws must finish a little way down from the worktop, say $\frac{1}{2}$in (12mm), to allow for a wooden strip, which is part of the jaw liners, to be fitted easily.

Measure the depth of the vise. Subtract from this the thickness of the worktop, minus $\frac{1}{2}$in (12mm) (see fig 3). You will need a shim (cut from a scrap of wood) of the same thickness to go under the bench top and to fit between it and the vise.

MAKING THE CUT-OUT FOR THE VISE IN THE SIDE RAIL

You will first need to make a template of the vise. Put the vise on end with its shim and draw around it on to a piece of thick paper or card. Simplify the lines of the template to make cutting the side rail easier. Cut out the template and hold it to the underside of the bench top, about 12in (300mm) in from the front left hand for a right-handed person (or from the right for a left-handed

person), and draw around the template on the top rail.

To make the cut-out, remove the bench top, and cut around the line with a power Saber saw or by hand with a compass saw or coping saw.

Clamp the second bench top supporting batten in place to the front top rail as before (see **Securing the Bench Top, left**) and screw it in place, cutting out the section where the gap has been left for the vise with a compass saw or coping saw. Screw the top back in place through the battens.

Slide the vise into position, with the shim in place. Drill pilot holes up through the fixing holes in the bottom of the vise, through the shim, and into the worktop. Secure the vise tightly in place using lag screws and washers.

MAKING THE WOODEN JAW LINERS

The liners are wooden pieces attached inside the jaws of the vise so as to finish flush with the top of the bench. They serve to protect work while it is being held in the vise.

From $\frac{1}{2}$in (12mm) plywood, cut two pieces slightly longer than the steel jaws of the vise. The width of the plywood should equal the distance between the top of the bench and the runner of the vise.

Cut a piece of scrap hardwood to the same thickness as the distance between the top of the steel jaws and the top of the worktop, and to the same length as that of the wooden jaw liners. Glue in place to the front edge of the bench, flush with the worktop, so that it rests on the vise.

ATTACHING THE REAR WOODEN JAW LINER

Mark through the holes in the front of the vise on to one of the wooden jaw liners. Transfer the marks to the other line. Drill and countersink the liners at these marks and screw into the worktop through these holes and the holes in the vise back.

ATTACHING THE FRONT WOODEN JAW LINER

Close the vise with the front wooden jaw clamped in place, and screw through the front holes into the jaw.

③ Fitting the Bench Vise
Thickness of shim is depth of vise, less thickness of worktop minus the wooden strip.

④ Fitting the Wooden Jaw Liner to the Vise
Jaw liners (made from $\frac{1}{2}$in [12mm] plywood) finish flush with the bench top. The rear jaw liner is fixed by screwing it into the worktop. Screw through the front of the vise to attach the front liner.

WORKBENCH

THE BENCH STOP

A bench stop which can be raised above the bench top is useful for pushing against while large pieces of work are planed or chiseled.

The bench stop fits just outside and tangent to the front leg at the vise end. To mark the position of the bench stop on the bench top, square around from the outer edge of the leg using a pencil and try square. The line should be continued from underneath, up the front edge, and on to the top of the workbench. Measure back from the front edge to coincide with the leg. Square off the line from the side with a try square.

Take a piece of hardwood batten about 1 × 1½in (25 × 38mm) and cut to about 10–12in (250–300mm) long. Mark around the end of the batten in position behind the pencil marks on the worktop as shown: that is, to the *outside* of them. Check that the lines will allow the bench stop to fit alongside the leg. Go over the pencil marks with a utility knife.

Using a spade bit as near as possible in size to (but smaller than) the bench top cut-out, drill right through the worktop. Clamp a piece of packing underneath the hole, so that you can then pare out the edges down on to the packing, to avoid breaking the wood underneath. Take care to pare out fractionally *within* the line. Check occasionally with a try square that you are cutting down square. Keep cleaning out until the batten slots into the hole, but stop when the fit is still fairly tight.

INSTALLING BENCH STOP

We used a 6in (150mm) long, ⅜in (9.5mm) diameter carriage bolt with a washer and a wing nut. Mark where the bolt is to be on the leg. (This must be far enough down to clear the top rail.) Fit the stop in place flush with the top. Transfer the bolt mark on to the bench stop – this will be the top of the slot. Move the stop up to the highest position required, that is, about 3–4in (75–100mm), and mark off the bolt position for the bottom of the slot.

Take the bench stop out. Mark off the center line and drill a line of holes ⅜in (9.5mm) in diameter along the length of the slot, with a shim held underneath. Clean out the slot with a chisel until the bolt slides freely inside. Alternatively, use a router to make the slot.

At the marked line on the leg, mark a vertical line in the exact center of the bench stop position, to make sure that the bolt fits in the middle of it. Use a ⅜in (9.5mm) drill bit to drill right through the leg at this point. Slide the stop into place and push the bolt through from the inside of the leg and through the slot. Secure the screw in place with a washer and a wing nut.

ATTACHING THE SHELF

Measure the outside dimensions of the frame and cut a piece of ½in (12mm) thick plywood to this size. Make notches for the legs by measuring and cutting with a power Saber saw or small hand saw. Clean up and bevel the top edges of the shelf and then slot it in place on the bottom rails.

ATTACHING HANGING BARS

These hanging bars are fitted beween the long rails at the opposite end to the vise, and are very useful for hooking things on, such as C-clamps, a dustpan and brush, a paint tin, and other essential items that you may need close by.

Cut two lengths of 1in (25mm) dowel to the width of the underframe, plus a little extra for planing off afterwards. Mark dowel positions about 12in (300mm) and 24in (600mm) in from each of the rail ends, in the center of both the back and front top rails of the bench.

Using a spade bit of the same diameter as the dowel, drill holes at the marks, through the rails, back and front. Put dowels through the holes, hammering them in after smearing the ends with aliphatic resin glue. Plane off the ends flush with the rails.

THE VISE AND BENCH STOP
Often the vise can be used in conjunction with the stop to hold large items.

1 Installing the Bench Stop
Enlarge the line of holes in the stop to form a slot. Slot in bench is formed in the same way.

TOOL CUPBOARD

It is important to store tools in a safe and secure place where they are also readily accessible when required. Properly stored tools stay sharp and rust-free, and with each tool in its correct place you will not waste time looking for tools.

This cupboard provides an ideal place to store tools. It is secured to the wall of the workshop or garage where you would normally do home improvements. When the cupboard is in use, the doors open out flat to the wall on each side for easy access to the tools. You can plan it to suit your needs, leaving space for new tools as you buy them.

The rack incorporates outlets for power tools, and adjustable lamps to give excellent illumination of the worksurface below. When not in use, the lamps can be pushed out of the way, and the doors closed. For safety, the cupboard is permanently screwed to the wall through beveled battens, and the doors have a lock for security and to keep the tools out of the way of children.

MAIN CUPBOARD SECTION

Cut the back panel by sawing the full sheet of ½in (12mm) plywood in half to form two 48 × 48in (1220 × 1220mm) sheets. Use a circular saw (or hand saw), running the sole plate against a straight batten clamped to the surface of the plywood sheet to ensure a straight cut (see **Techniques, page 21**).

Measure the exact height of the back panel and cut two pieces of 1 × 4in (25 × 100mm) lumber to this length to form the side rails. Glue and screw these rails on-edge to the back panel with screws about every 9in (230mm), through from the back. Use 1in (25mm) No 8 screws.

Cut two pieces of 1 × 4in (25 × 100mm) lumber about 48in (1220mm) long for the top and bottom rails. Position the pieces and mark off the internal lengths. Cut them squarely to fit between the side rails. Glue and screw these pieces in place on to the back panel as with the side rails. Using 2in (50mm) No 8 screws, attach the sides to the top and bottom rails by inserting two screws into each corner joint.

Finish by removing excess glue and planing any protruding edges. Sand smooth.

DOOR SECTIONS

The door front panels are formed by cutting the remaining 48 × 48in (1220 × 1220mm) panel in half to form two 24 × 48in (610 × 1220mm) panels. The waste incurred by cutting provides the curf (the gap between the two doors).

Cut two pieces of 1 × 3in (25 × 75mm) lumber to length for the side rails. Glue and screw these in place as with the main section.

Again using 1 × 3in (25 × 75mm) lumber, measure for the top and bottom rails as above, and glue in place between the side rails, screwing through the door front. Insert two screws in each corner to secure the sides to the top and bottom.

ORGANIZING THE INSIDE

The inside of the tool cupboard can be organized to suit your own needs, but, for safety, heavy equipment *must* be in the main cupboard.

MATERIALS

Part	Quantity	Material	Length*
SIDE RAILS	2	1 × 4in (25 × 100mm) S4S lumber	48in (1220mm)
TOP & BOTTOM RAILS	2	As above	As above
CUPBOARD SHELVES	3	As above	As above
MOUNTING BATTENS	2	As above	As above
SHELF DIVIDERS	4	As above	4in (100mm)
DOOR SIDE RAILS	4	1 × 3in (25 × 75mm) S4S lumber	48in (1220mm)
DOOR TOP & BOTTOM RAILS	4	As above	24in (610mm)
BOLT MOUNTING BATTEN	1	As above	48in (1220mm)
SLOTTED SHELVES	2	As above	24in (610mm)
SHELF EDGING STRIPS	3	1 × 1in (25 × 25mm) S4S lumber	48in (1220mm)
CHISEL MOUNTING SLOTS	1	2 × 2in (50 × 50mm) S4S lumber	As above

From 1 sheet of N or A grade ½in (12mm) plywood 8 × 4ft (2.44 × 1.22m)

BACK PANEL	1		48 × 48in (1200 × 1200mm)
DOOR PANELS	2		24 × 48in (610 × 1220mm)

Also required: Offcuts of planed lumber and plywood to make tool-mounting blocks

*Approximate lengths only – refer to text for actual size

TOOLS

STEEL BENCH RULE

UTILITY KNIFE

TRY SQUARE

CIRCULAR SAW (or hand saw or Saber saw)

DRILL (hand or power)

TWIST DRILL BIT

MASONRY DRILL BIT

SPADE BIT

COUNTERSINK BIT

COPING SAW or POWER SABER SAW to cut blocks to fit tool handles

BACK SAW

TWO C-CLAMPS

SCREWDRIVER (Phillips or slotted, depending on type of screws being used)

SMOOTHING PLANE

SANDING BLOCK and SANDING PAPER

TOOL CUPBOARD

The other safety note concerns electrical outlets. If you put these in as we have, they will be at a convenient working height and the cables serving them can be run neatly in conduit in the gap created behind the cupboard by the beveled battens on which it is mounted. It is most important to ensure that the cupboard is screwed firmly to the wall, and to keep a note of the position of the cable runs if you drill the back panel to mount tools in the future. The same caution must be applied to the wiring of lamps if these are attached to the top of the cupboard.

SHELVES FOR THE MAIN CUPBOARD

Cut the shelves from 1 × 4in (25 × 100mm) lumber to the same length as the top and bottom rails. Work out the position of the shelves by laying the cupboard down and trying equipment in place.

When the shelves are correctly positioned, mark the center line on to the sides, and continue the line on to the back to give a line for the screw positions. Glue the shelves in place and screw through from the back and through the sides.

Decide, according to your requirements, how you want to partition the shelves. For the dividing pieces, measure and cut them to size from the same size of lumber as the shelves. Put the dividers in place and mark around them on the inside of the cupboard. Take the dividers away, and drill through the back panel from the front so that you can see where to screw from the back. Replace the dividers, countersink the fixing holes in the back panel, and then screw through from the back into the dividers.

Nail 1 × 1in (25 × 25mm) battens in place at the front of the shelves to prevent things falling off. Place small strips across the shelves where planes will be positioned so that the plane blades do not rest on them and get damaged.

MOUNTING TOOLS

Some tools, such as power drills and mallets, can be mounted on solid blocks of wood.

Roughly draw around the shape of the handle on to a piece of thick paper, and cut wood to this shape with a Saber saw or coping saw.

To fit the handles in place, screw through from the back using the method for fitting shelf dividers.

For the chisel slots use a piece of 2 × 2in (50 × 50mm) lumber with a row of holes drilled to a diameter smaller than the chisel handles.

Using a spade bit, drill a row of holes through the middle of the block. With a back saw, cut slots in the front as shown to allow the chisel blade to turn in through the slot.

Various springs, clips, and hooks can be used to hold other tools.

SHELVES FOR THE DOORS

These shelves have slots cut in them to a variety of sizes, providing a useful way to store screwdrivers, marking gauges, and other tools that are longer than they are wide.

Drill holes in the middle of the shelves and cut through them from the front to form slots in the same way as with the chisels. Install the shelves as with the main cupboard.

Try squares are held in place by pieces of 1 × 3in (25 × 75mm) lumber rabbeted using a back saw.

ATTACHING THE TOOL MOUNTS

An advantage of this tool cupboard is its versatilty. You can organize it to suit your precise requirements, but leave enough space for more tools to be added later.

① Forming the Chisel Slots
Holes are drilled in 2 × 2in (50 × 50mm) lumber with beveled edge, and slots are cut out.

② Making a Saw Holder
A block of wood shaped to fit inside a saw handle is screwed to a turn-buckle made from plywood or MDF.

③ Attaching the Door Hinges
Doors carry a lot of weight so hinges must be substantial and secured with long screws.

DOOR TOP RAIL

DOOR FRONT

BACK

BACK TOP RAIL

SHELF DIVIDER

SLOTTED SHELF

EDGING BATTEN

SIDE RAIL

DOOR BOTTOM RAIL

TOOL CUPBOARD ASSEMBLY

MOUNTING SAWS

Tools with open handles, such as saws, can be mounted on shaped blocks of wood fitted with turn-buckles that fit inside the handles.

Use a piece of wood slightly thicker than the handle and draw around the inner shape of the handle on the wood. Cut out the wood to this shape with a Saber saw or coping saw. Cut a piece of $\frac{1}{4}$in (6mm) plywood or MDF to the same shape.

Screw the block to the door using two screws. Screw the turn-buckle to the block with one central screw which is secure but will allow the turn-buckle to turn.

Screw hooks can be placed as necessary in the front doors.

HANGING THE DOORS

Hang the doors on the main cupboard using three butt hinges for each (see **Techniques, page 33**).

The left-hand door is secured with two swan-neck (flush) bolts which fit into catch plates attached to the bottom rail and to the underside of the top shelf (the top rail is not easy to reach). To make it possible to install the bolts, screw a strip of 1 × 3in (25 × 75mm) lumber to the inside edge of the door's side rail. Attach a lock (see **Techniques, page 35**) and door handles.

SECURING TO THE WALL

For safety, the cupboard is hung on beveled battens (see **Techniques, page 25**). Cut two lengths of 1 × 4in (25 × 100mm) lumber to the width of the cupboard. To bevel the battens, cut each piece lengthwise through half of its thickness with the saw blade angled at 45°. The top section is screwed to the cupboard back, and the lower part to the wall.

Screw the top-section battens to the back of the cupboard about 7in (180mm) down from the top, and about 10in (250mm) up from the bottom, using seven 1$\frac{1}{2}$in (38mm) No 10 screws in each.

Put the lower-section battens in place under the top-section battens and measure down from the top to the bottom edge of the lower batten. Decide where the cupboard is to sit on the wall, then measure this distance down and fix the lower batten to the wall at this height with 2$\frac{1}{2}$in (65mm) No 10 screws and anchors.

Measure down and secure the upper batten in the same way, or sit the cupboard on the first batten and mark the wall for the other batten.

Secure the cupboard firmly to the wall by screwing through the back into the lower-section battens. This is most important if electrical outlets are to be installed in the cupboard.

PART 2

KITCHENS AND DINING ROOMS

By designing and building your own kitchen which is very often the most important room in the house, you will get more satisfaction from it than any off-the-shelf kitchen can ever give. The final result will be a kitchen that is tailored exactly to your own requirements in terms of style and practicality.

As you plan your kitchen, you should consider many alternatives until you know precisely what you want to achieve. On the following pages are many inspirational ideas and suggestions for kitchens and utility rooms which can be adapted to your own design. In addition, there is a complete kitchen, and utility room units, to build yourself as well as many original and classic designs for kitchen fittings from plate racks to display shelves. Begin with a minor project if you lack confidence and skill, and gradually build up your hand-made kitchen.

Whether you are creating a whole kitchen from scratch, improving an existing one, or merely adding a wooden knife rack, building it yourself gives your kitchen a truly personal element. It also provides an opportunity to have kitchen fixtures you know are well designed and well built.

ASSESSING THE WORKLOAD

The level of change you wish to make to a kitchen will depend upon a number of factors. If you want your kitchen completely replaced and redesigned you must consider just how much you are capable of doing. Building and installing new units, worksurfaces, and shelves is not beyond the skills of most do-it-yourself enthusiasts. However, if you are intending to redesign the layout and move services – water and waste piping, electrical outlets, light fixtures, and gas fixtures – then the undertaking is considerable. In addition, you must consider the legal restrictions imposed upon work involving gas, water, and electricity. It is often illegal and possibly dangerous for you to undertake it yourself.

The moving of units will disrupt existing flooring, tiling, and plasterwork. And while your own capabilities may stretch to woodworking and decorating, they might not enable you to lay floors and replaster walls. Budget for professional help as necessary and get estimates before you start work so that you do not begin with a grand plan and run out of money half way through.

If you are relatively happy with the position and capacity of existing units but are unable to live with the style, then consider revamping them with new doors and worksurfaces.

Small changes can often be made to transform an existing kitchen completely: a new set of shelves for displaying kitchen

ASSESSING AND PLANNING

Building a complete, coordinated, and fully fitted kitchen such as this one in natural wood (above) requires careful planning. Moving fixtures can involve new plumbing and rewiring, both of which will require professional assistance and costly upheaval. The time, effort, cost, and skills required to create such a kitchen must be honestly assessed before work begins to avoid problems later.

There are plenty of smaller projects to undertake in the kitchen. Perhaps the most simple, functional, visually effective, and easily assembled is a stainless steel hanging bar (previous page). Pots, pans, and other cooking utensils hang from butchers' hooks. The bar can be attached between two kitchen units or two walls, or can be suspended from the ceiling.

objects, or a plate rack in natural wood, for example. Another simple device is a steel hanging bar for storing everything from pie slicers to saucepans, making the kitchen a more practical place to cook in.

Once you have decided exactly what you want to undertake, map out a schedule and a budget. You may find that you cannot afford the time or the money to do all the work immediately, in which case decide on priorities. Include in your budget an amount in excess of the cost of materials and professional help as a contingency against possible problems – say ten percent on top of your basic estimate.

Consider well in advance the amount of disruption that will be caused to what is a major room in your home. Will you be able to continue to use the kitchen while it is being redesigned? Other arrangements may have to be made for cooking. Prepare your family for the mess that will result from the work. Above all consider safety, particularly if children are likely to use the area while work is in progress.

You will enjoy the work and be pleased with the results if you have not undertaken more than you can handle. Make sure that you have purchased all the materials necessary for each stage of the process before you start, and that you have the right tools for the job. Finishing, detailing, and decorating can take more time, effort, and expense than actual construction, but are important and must never be underestimated.

FORM AND FUNCTION

As you plan your new kitchen, or make alterations to an existing one, always consider how you want the room to function and to look when finished. The beauty of this kitchen is the quality of the materials used – natural wood, mosaic tiles, and marble – combined with a simple yet elegant design. It is effective because it has been made with faultless precision and a great deal of attention to detail. There are no brackets to break the graphic line of the shelves, no decorative detail to detract from its minimal style, and nothing is placed on show unless it is as attractive as the kitchen itself.

MATERIAL EFFECTS

More than anything else, it is the materials which you choose for your kitchen fixtures that will influence the overall feel and appearance of the room. Let us consider two basic styles of kitchen and the materials which fashion them.

In recent years, kitchens used on an industrial scale – in restaurants, hotels, and other places where cooking is quite literally an industry – have become a powerful influence on domestic kitchens.

An industrial-looking kitchen tends to have a formal, high-tech atmosphere, streamlined and sleek in appearance, with an emphasis on efficiency and hygiene. The two qualities valued most by professional chefs are durability and ease of cleaning. It is not easy to turn the industrial kitchen into part of the living room nor to make it cozy. This is a style for a separate kitchen – a serious cooking cen-

ter, where rustic ideas are inappropriate. This does not mean, however, that an industrial influence will make your kitchen look like the inside of a laboratory or chemical plant. It does mean using high quality materials with a minimum of decorative detailing. Walls are faced with white ceramic tiles, and can extend to the ceiling, have a painted wall area above them, or be broken up for variety's sake with bands of colored tiles.

Stainless steel is indisputably the most popular choice for professional-looking worktops. Very easy to clean and thus hygienic, stainless steel wears gracefully and looks attractive even when it has been scratched and lost its gleam. Stainless steel is quite expensive, however, and can be substituted by laminates or a worktop made from white ceramic tiles, terrazzo (marble chips), or granite.

PROFESSIONAL POLISH

Borrow ideas from professional kitchens when planning which materials to use in a kitchen. In this large and luxurious arrangement, created for some very serious cooking indeed (above right), the style is strictly professional and incorporates an enormous extractor hood, double swing doors, and an open charcoal grill. The materials are functional, durable, and attractive, not homely and decorative.

In a smaller kitchen and on a small domestic scale, similarly strong materials can be equally effective (above left). Stainless steel has been used for professional-looking fixtures, and marble slip tiles provide a hardwearing floor.

Many domestic kitchens these days double as eating rooms and living rooms, and it is common for members of a household to spend a great deal of time there. If you plan to use your kitchen for this purpose, it needs to look and feel livable with a more cozy atmosphere.

Natural materials are marvelous for this type of kitchen: they look and feel welcoming as well as elegant, and the great popularity of the country-style kitchen bears this out. Wood, stone, terrazzo, granite, and slate are generally more tolerant of all the knocks, scratches, and dirt stains which occur naturally in a kitchen than are manmade materials, which scar and deteriorate rather than age gracefully. Even though marble stains if oil or alcohol touches its surface, it retains a pleasing patina of age; but if a white laminate suffers a deep stain, it sits upon the surface as an unsightly scar. Wood that is chipped, scratched, or stained will appear comfortably lived in, while old laminates will start to break up and disintegrate after a lot of wear. Wooden worksurfaces will last longer if a tough hardwood such as beech is used. Obviously, synthetics have their advantages and can be used effectively, and a lot less expensively, in a kitchen or dining room than natural materials. Tiled and vitreous-enameled surfaces are other options which age well and are durable. Most people will use some laminate surfaces in their kitchen and it is worthwhile considering juxtaposing them with, for instance, an old wooden kitchen table, or a weathered butcher's block. Such a contrast of old with new, natural with synthetic, is highly effective and invariably interesting.

SURFACE COORDINATION

The gleaming appeal of polished stainless steel has been enhanced in this kitchen (above left) by choosing only steel utensils and then storing them on a stainless steel hanging bar. The colors in the kitchen are muted and the design is plain so that the room has a studied coordination about it.

Another kitchen (above right) shares this overall approach of coordination but has been achieved using different materials. Simple bricks, painted white, form the basis of the kitchen. The storage units are finished in white laminate, and the floor is warm terracotta quarry tiles. These elements blend well with the wooden high shelf and the large basket above the stove.

MATERIAL EFFECTS

UNDERSTATED ELEGANCE

Gleaming terrazzo (stone and marble chips set in concrete) on the worktop, the palest wood for units, doors, and floor, and muted shades on other surfaces and objects, give this kitchen its understated elegance (right). A small open-plan kitchen shows a truly original design, which could be achieved by doing-it-yourself (below left). Warm, natural, polished wood has been used for the plate rack, worktop, and floor. The doors and units are painted in a pale finish. In a separate, small galley kitchen (below right), the paint on the walls and doors is again pale. It offsets the rich finish of the terrazzo worktop which incorporates a section of wood to act as a built-in chopping board – easily achieved and highly practical.

HAND FINISHED

Doing-it-yourself means implementing original ideas using unusual materials and finishes. One-room living in an open-plan loft (opposite above) dictates that only a corner is available for use as a kitchen. This design could be equally effective in an office, workshop, or studio. Concrete blocks form the base of the island unit which is topped with a laminated worktop. The blocks echo the rough-cast concrete of the walls. All the materials used here are strong and basic like the building they are placed in.

In a small space, such as this attic kitchen (opposite below left), contrasting surfaces could be unattractive, so the wood paneling on the sloping walls has been bleached to match and blend with the wooden worktop.

A useful pass-through from kitchen to dining room (opposite below center) incorporates an attractive closet. The kitchen is beautifully finished in wood paneling which has been painted a clear, bright eau de nil, a color which continues beyond the pass-through to the dining room. The whole door panels stand out in strong geometric relief.

When the kitchen is on show (opposite below right), the appearance is very important. Anyone would be happy to eat and relax next to this line of white units with their marble worktop and a wall of marble slips (tiles).

KITCHEN LAYOUT

Finalizing the exact location of every unit and appliance in your kitchen involves careful planning at an early stage to avoid problems later on. A kitchen is, first of all, a work area, so you should make sure that it will be easy and efficient to use. You should check the location of your doors and lights, then calculate how best to arrange the areas intended for food preparation, cooking, and eating. Bear in mind that you will want to have your cooking utensils within easy reach, saucepans near to the stove, and so on.

If there are children about, make certain that any electrical outlets and open shelves will be safely out of reach. Storage should also be considered before you set to work; think about how much space you will need for cleaning and laundry equipment, cutlery, dishes, laundry products, and food.

As you begin to plan your layout, give thought also to what outside doors can let in – muddy boots and drafts for example – and weigh these disadvantages with the positive reasons for having an outside door in the kitchen: easy access to a garden or a trash can, and to fresh air. How these elements affect your kitchen design depends on how you want to use your kitchen. Some people prefer to be left on their own while working in the kitchen; others love having people wandering in and out, making the kitchen the social center of their home.

If you own a lot of attractive kitchen equipment, think about building a special shelving system to display it to advantage. As with a row of cups hanging on hooks, great esthetic pleasure can be derived from allowing a kitchen's function to determine its form or shape. Do also consider, though, that anything displayed in a kitchen accumulates grease and dust, so think about cleaning chores too as you finalize the plans for your kitchen.

While kitchens should be designed to encourage easy cooking and mobility, the particular plan you choose will depend on your own preferences.

There are five basic floor plans. One is the linear or single-line kitchen, with everything lined up against one wall — excellent if the wall is long enough or if the kitchen is basically a passage. The galley or corridor kitchen, arranged along two facing walls, should have the sink and the stove on the same side of the kitchen and give enough room for bending down – at least 48in (1200mm) between the facing units. Such a kitchen is not recommended unless built against a dead end or a window. The L-shape kitchen is very popular – deservedly, for it combines well with a living or dining area in the kitchen and makes good use of limited wall space. A U-shaped kitchen is ideal for a small area, like an alcove, and offers one of the most convenient and adaptable arrangements of space for preparation and cooking; usually the worktops here run in an unbroken sequence, and one leg of the U can be used to divide the room, with an eating area beyond it. Lastly, there is an island kitchen, a favorite with professional or very confident cooks who appreciate its adaptability and the way it can display their culinary prowess; an island unit can also act as a room divider.

The sink should be positioned at the center of a kitchen, beneath a window if possible (for natural light), not in a corner where it is difficult to get at. It should have food preparation areas on either side. Since moving a sink requires plumbing alterations, you may wish to leave your sink where it is, regardless of placement.

The strong, geometric lines of a modern building have been reflected in this architect's design for the kitchen. Gleaming white units and shelves, in big, chunky shapes house only white, black, chrome, and yellow objects.

KITCHEN LAYOUT

We have mentioned the five commonly used kitchen layouts, but there is no need to stick rigidly to any of these plans. In nearly all kitchens there is a vast potential for flexible space management, using the differing heights of base units, shelving, and built-in or free-standing stoves.

Central islands in particular provide opportunities both to divide a kitchen and to focus attention on the cooking going on there – if so desired. Breakfast bars can serve this function just as effectively as island cooking centers but in a different way – by clearly marking out the cooking from the eating areas. If there is room in your kitchen, it is always best to make some clear distinction between the two.

The sink, stove, and preparation areas, along with the refrigerator, should form a "work triangle" whose sides when combined should not exceed 20–23ft (6–7m) in length. This results in having no two work centers more than a double arm-span apart, to avoid needless exhaustion. Nor should they be uncomfortably close, which would cause cramping. A cramped kitchen can lead to accidents, so plan the layout to allow more than one person at a time to move around the room safely.

Cooktops should *not* be placed under windows – someone could get burned trying to open the window. Neither should a cooktop or a stove come at the end of a run of cabinets – it is best to have a worktop on either side of it, although it could be placed in a corner.

You should also consider the washing machine, if this is going to be in the kitchen. Washing machines do have a tendency to leak or flood at least once in their lifetime, so bear this in mind when planning drainage and choosing a floor covering. For plumbing reasons, if both a washing machine and a dishwasher are planned for your kitchen it is best to keep them close together and near the sink.

AROUND THE KITCHEN TABLE

A niche has been carved in a storage unit for slotting a round table into neat and secure alignment with the open display storage of this small kitchen (opposite above).

Purposefully combining old and new can be very attractive as in this standard, modern, white kitchen (opposite below). The polished wood floor complements a rustic wooden table. It has been placed at an interesting angle for practical reasons as well as for visual interest.

If the table is to be used for more formal occasions, it is best separated from the working kitchen. A screen (above) has been built in as part of the kitchen. The table is a neat extension of that screen, so is linked to, but effectively separated from, the kitchen itself.

CORNER KITCHEN

In a tight narrow corner, precise planning and a design with an eye to detail are required to make the best use of what small space there is (left). Here, there are neatly arranged fixtures and a maximum amount of storage space.

KITCHEN LIGHTING

In kitchens even more than in other rooms, imaginative lighting is essential, so plan it from the start. Natural light sources should be considered first. Think carefully about what will be placed near a window or glazed door and whether it will benefit from sunshine and a view. The sink may or may not require this privilege. A table could be more deserving if you intend to sit there regularly. General electric lighting for kitchens should aim to give the maximum adaptability – and lights should be able to be directed differently for different activities. Avoid a single central ceiling light, because of the shadows it will throw on worksurfaces as well as its marked lack of esthetic appeal.

Worksurfaces must be highlighted for safe and efficient food preparation – fluorescent tubes built into wall-mounted cabinets avoid the problem of the cook working in his or her own shadow. Check

that the light bulbs will be hidden from both sitting and standing eye-levels.

Systems of track holding a number of lights with separate switches are useful in kitchens, as are pivoting hinged fixtures mounted under kitchen wall cabinets to provide downward illumination on to worksurfaces. If you also eat often in the kitchen in the evenings, put in a dimmer control to fade out all the kitchen clutter by the sink and worksurfaces when you are eating.

There are many different types of lighting fixtures and bulbs. Fluorescent bulbs use less electricity and last far longer than incandescent bulbs. However, they not only give an unattractive light but have the disadvantage of flickering slightly which many find unpleasant. They also emit an irritating hum.

Incandescent bulbs, also available as track lights, are preferable except where it is vital to avoid the heat they give off or

where long life is essential. They range usually from 40 to 150 watts in lighting power. Incandescent lamps can shatter from thermal shock if splashed with cold water and so need completely enclosed fixtures near wet or steamy places, above a sink or cooktop, for example.

Low-voltage tungsten halogen is excellent in kitchens, particularly in the form of small spots. It gives a clear, white light and makes glass, china, ceramics, chrome, and metal truly gleam.

Tungsten strips installed below shelves prevent a large handsome hood casting a shadow over the cooktop (above left).

Knocking out the walls of a kitchen has allowed natural light into an otherwise dark corner (above right), and downlighters have been installed at strategic points.

A small kitchen in a corridor has the benefit of French doors that lead to the garden and provide natural light (opposite). Underneath closets, strip lights illuminate the worksurface and downlighters add extra light elsewhere.

ESSENTIAL SERVICES

Getting essential services correctly installed, moved, or altered is not an optional extra when remodeling your
kitchen, and should be budgeted for from
the start, particularly as there are no real
money-saving short cuts to good plumbing, gas, and electrical installations.

When planning a kitchen, work out the
maximum number of machines you are
likely to need in it. It is more convenient
to install all the supply and waste pipes at
one time than merely to deal with your
present demands. Supply pipes and outlets for equipment not yet purchased can
be capped off until needed.

All gas appliances and heating should
be installed by experts – a gas company or
one of their approved contractors. Most
modern appliances have built-in safety
devices against gas leaks.

Although not in itself poisonous when
burnt, gas, whether natural, propane, or
butane, can give off noxious fumes and
water vapor. Rooms with gas appliances
therefore need good ventilation. Take
care both to avoid gas flames being
affected by drafts and to keep gas storage
safely outside.

Fatal accidents in the home are seldom
caused by electrocution, but rather by
fires arising from overloading electrical
outlets, faulty wiring, inadequate insulation, or overheating. These are very real
dangers. Only qualified electricians can be
relied upon to install electrical systems
that satisfy legal requirements, which
vary from state to state.

*These three kitchens were custom-designed for
particular spaces using distinctive ideas to suit
the specific style, cooking, storage, and display
requirements of the owners. All the essential
services – wiring, plumbing, lighting – were
planned in minute detail before work began and
no rearrangement could now be achieved
without major and costly disruption to the layout
and finish of each kitchen.*

SCREENING AND SEPARATING

Today, modern kitchens are at the heart of family life, and modern cooks do not want to be locked away surrounded by pots while the rest of the family and/or guests are talking elsewhere. Yet some division between cooking and eating areas is desirable. To mark this division without isolating the cook, several approaches have been evolved.

Island units, sometimes containing a stove, are an obvious way of dividing the cooking and eating/living areas, as are units jutting out in peninsular forms. Such plans guard the work triangle from interruption while allowing the cook to take part in any conversation. Often, a peninsular unit can double as a breakfast bar, which makes it easier for food to be served hot from the stove. Most breakfast bars are at worktop height (36in [915mm]), so bar stools are required. Clearly these are not very safe for young children, nor comfortable for the elderly.

The simplest screen is a purpose-built partition made with wood stud and finished to match your kitchen decoration. It can be of any height to suit your kitchen design. You can incorporate storage and display into the structure with a high shelf for display, shelves on one or both sides, or attach hooks or a wire mesh for hanging utensils and pans.

Other forms of screening can be devised, utilizing whatever appeals to you and what you happen to have, such as pots, pans, or bottles of preserved fruits. If, however, you plan on having, and often using, a separate dining room, think about installing a pass-through between the kitchen and dining room. When shut, this will leave the dining room as a quiet room and keep especially pungent smells inside the kitchen. When open, the cook can talk fairly easily to the rest of the household and pass through dishes with the minimum delay.

COUNTER DIVIDERS

In two spacious open-plan areas (above), the kitchen is separated from the main room with a breakfast bar. This has been simply achieved by installing a worktop which overlaps a basic unit on the side facing into the main room, so creating a space beneath it for sitting and for storing stools. By adding a sink to this worktop, plates can be cleared easily from the main room to this counter, which has a dishwashing machine below it on the kitchen side.

COOK'S PASS-THROUGH

In this unusual arrangement (opposite), a pass-through between kitchen and dining room runs directly behind the cooktop. Designed for a virtuoso cook rather than a busy family, it allows direct delivery of sizzling hot dishes to the table. Behind the cooktop, a simple island unit, consisting of a stack of drawers, has an extended wooden worktop which effectively divides the kitchen and provides chopping and preparation space close to the stove.

STYLING DETAILS

As these three kitchens show, what you choose to display in a kitchen, and how you display it, is as important to its style as the basic design. By planning, building, finishing, and then equipping your kitchen yourself, you can ensure a harmonious result. The detail is a crucial element in the overall visual impact of the room.

COUNTRY KITCHEN

Display lots of your favorite decorative china intermingled with fresh food in baskets and dried food in glass storage jars if you want to evoke an informal, colorful, country atmosphere, abundant and pretty in appearance (above left). This approach will work only if you are prepared to clean the china regularly, since it will attract grease and dirt if on display. Also, ensure that your basic kitchen provides a sympathetic background to this gentle jumble. A traditional dresser is an ideal background for your display, but here a very simple and inexpensive kitchen of plastic laminated fiberboard has been given a dresser effect by hanging mugs from the top shelf on butcher's hooks and using the worktop under the shelves as part of the display. Nothing overtly modern or hard in appearance has been allowed to intrude and spoil the effect.

METALLIC EFFECTS

By contrast, another cook prefers to display stainless steel utensils with chrome and glass kitchenware (below left). The result is equally effective and harmonious because here all that is soft and pretty has been expelled. The hanging bar and the shelf are also metallic and the speckled background enhances the gleaming, utilitarian display.

In another tiny kitchen this approach has been taken to its stylistic conclusion (opposite). The whole kitchen is sharp and metallic: everything is either gray, stainless steel, or chrome, with one white wall providing definition for a professional hanging bar and its polished pans. A single pretty plant in a terracotta pot provides a strong point of contrast in an otherwise hard environment.

A PLACE FOR EVERYTHING

If you like a generally informal, cozy approach to your kitchen style, remember that the general clutter this may well entail requires a large space. If you have only a small kitchen, perhaps of the galley type, you will have to impose a certain discipline to make controlled use of a space in which only one person can cook. In such a case, a more high-tech and practical design may be appropriate.

If you do have a spacious kitchen, you can afford to spread out expansively, but take care that your kitchen does not become chaotic and unattractive. An informal arrangement can create in effect a still-life of fruits, vegetables, pots, dishes, and attractive kitchen utensils.

A Welsh dresser, although the most well-known, is by no means the only way of displaying objects of interest, charm, or beauty. Think about building pigeon-holes to store and display spice or herb jars, interesting old bottles – or interesting new ones for that matter. Despite the potential that space gives you for disorder, try to arrange objects neatly and in a manner that is appealing to the eye. If uncertain about what to display, work on the principle – if you've got it, show it!

Shelf edge-banding (a strip of hardwood fastened to the front edge of the shelf) adds support which can be useful for long shelves. Both shelf edge-banding and back battens are essential if you are intending to store heavy objects, such as casserole dishes. Place on the highest shelves those things you use infrequently. Always incorporate an extra-wide edge-banding that projects slightly above the shelf to prevent objects falling down.

Although it seems obvious, it is difficult to overemphasize the importance of really strong and secure attachments for all wall cabinets and shelves, especially when heavy crockery or pots and pans are going to be stored on them.

AN ORDERLY DISPLAY

Where space for storage is limited, a kitchen has been allowed to extend into a hallway (opposite above). Here an entire wall has been given over to open shelves. Cleverly but very simply designed and constructed, this unit echoes the open shelves in the kitchen beyond, and fills the wall, framing an existing window. The arrangement works well because of the order the shelves impose. They are narrow and placed at varying depths to accommodate certain items precisely, so that clutter cannot accumulate and everything is clearly accessible and easily found. The supports form partitions which ensure that the storage is grouped so that a wide range of objects can be placed together without looking haphazard, cluttered, or randomly arranged.

IN A STRAIGHT LINE

Shelves placed so that they follow the contours of a room, and are regularly spaced, provide a strong geometric grid for neat open displays. A pigeon-hole effect allows for a formal display (opposite below left) of china and glass. Each square is self contained and highlights the objects it houses.

Another simple but highly effective design (opposite below right), with fiberboard and laminated shelves on battens across an alcove, contains a more relaxed display of everyday dishes and glass.

SMART JARS

Dried foods, when stored in large glass storage jars in neat rows, look extremely attractive, and give a kitchen a traditional atmosphere. Storage jars remind us of old-fashioned shops and wholesome home cooking. Here (left) they are displayed to great effect on a custom-made unit which blends perfectly with its surroundings. It is made from simple wood or fiberboard and covered in white tiles so that it appears to be part of the wall it stands on. The depths of the three shelves match precisely the height of the jars. Antique salt containers and old olive oil bottles standing on polished wood add to the traditional effect.

FLOORING

Bear in mind when choosing the particular type of floor covering for your kitchen that it should reflect and enhance the style of the rest of the kitchen – starkly modern white tiles could be out of place in a farmhouse style kitchen, for example. A floor is a crucial influence on a kitchen. The type of flooring you decide on will be partly dictated to you by the sort of subfloor you have underneath. Although there are ways around the problem, you may not be able to put terracotta or ceramic tiles on top of wooden joists, as lumber bends and moves, potentially causing cracking of the tile joints or even of the actual tiles. Equally, if you choose sheet vinyl or vinyl tiles – both common floor coverings – cold, potentially damp concrete or stone underneath will require particleboard or hardboard as sub-flooring beneath it. You may be restricted by not being on solid foundations or by needing to insulate sound from the level below.

Be careful that the floor of a kitchen in an older building is not too uneven and that it relates properly to the levels of adjoining rooms. Any abrupt change of level could be dangerous as well as unsightly so calculate beforehand exact levels, rehanging doors if necessary.

Sheet vinyl is probably the most common and least expensive form of kitchen floor covering and comes in a variety of different colors and patterns. Many of these can give very pleasing imitations of ceramic or even polished wooden floors. Vinyl lasts well, can be cleaned easily, is waterproof, and resistant to oils, fat, and most chemicals – though not to heat. It can be laid on hardboard, over floorboards, and can be cushioned underneath for greater warmth and comfort. Even cheaper than sheet vinyl, vinyl composition comes in the form of brittle tiles. A textured finish on vinyl shows fewer stains and is more slip-resistant.

Although vinyl flooring is extremely popular and practical, cork tiling is also

TERRACOTTA TILES

In the rustic kitchen of an old country house, the furniture is freestanding and old fashioned (below left) and the materials are natural. A floor of terracotta quarry tiles is the natural and traditional choice for such a room. Quarry tiles age beautifully, are durable, and highly attractive. However, traditional tiles of this kind are best used at ground-floor level and the subfloor must be carefully considered before you start work.

CHECKERBOARD CERAMIC

Elegant checkerboard squares, traditionally in ceramic tiles or stone, look good in most kitchens. Here (below right), the checkerboard design on the floor echoes the square tiles below the worksurface and on the walls. If a floor is not suitable for ceramic tiles, a similar effect can be easily achieved by using patterned vinyl flooring instead. This is relatively cheap and easy to maintain.

worth considering. It is an excellent insulator, for both sound and heat, and is pleasantly warm to walk on. Cork tiles are easy to clean, but may chip and dent.

Ceramic tiles look splendid, are long-lasting, and easy to clean. They can feel cold underfoot, however (this will depend in part on your heating arrangements), are expensive and, as mentioned, are not suitable for all types of floor. Terracotta tiles add visual as well as literal warmth underfoot.

Heavy-duty quarry tiles are extremely hard-wearing: they are non-slip and extremely tough, but the weight of them makes them impractical for a floor above

ground level, and upper floor kitchens are better off with good quality vinyl flooring. Terracotta, granite, and marble are also tough and durable, as are wooden floors, as long as they are heavily sealed in areas of constant use.

Linoleum, for many years regarded as old-fashioned and unattractive, is enjoying a revival, with some extremely good designs available. Sheet lineoleum is hardwearing, manufactured to industrial standards, and not difficult to lay, but it usually requires a hardboard sub-floor.

Wood is also worth considering for the kitchen, although it does absorb grease stains and requires regular scrubbing in

order to keep it clean. Painted floors are impractical, as are carpet and coir.

Whichever floor covering you choose, do not attempt to lay it yourself without advice either from the retailer or the manufacturer. Always check that the surface or sub-floor on which it is to be laid is correctly prepared and treated.

Make absolutely sure that you are using the right adhesive and the correct edging; that there is no dampness below the floor; and that you are equipped with precisely the right tools for the laying and trimming. If you are not confident, call in experts to lay the floor for you – this will be less expensive than re-doing it yourself.

DURABLE RUBBER

Synthetic rubber stud flooring is available in sheets or large tiles. Its appeal lies partly in its smart, contemporary appearance and partly in its excellent durability and ease of maintenance. The range of colors available makes it suitable for a wide variety of modern kitchen styles. Here (below left), bright red has been used to provide a splash of color in an otherwise completely white kitchen.

NATURAL CORK

Cork is a warm surface for a kitchen floor; it has the advantages of being a natural material which is easy on the eye, and is a relatively inexpensive alternative to wood. It is not as durable as vinyl or rubber, but ages pleasantly and, if properly sealed and polished, it is not difficult to maintain. In this neat and functional kitchen (below right), wall-to-wall cork tiling provides a perfect complement to the wooden table and chairs.

UTILITY ROOMS

A utility room should be functional, practical, and labor-saving, but it does not need to be a large room. It should have enough space for a washing machine and clothes dryer, a sink and drainer, storage cupboards, and a drying rack.

In a self-contained utility room, clothes can be washed, dried, and ironed, household cleaning equipment stored, and essential chores such as shoe cleaning and clothes mending performed. Dangerous materials such as bleach and cleaning fluids should always be kept out of reach of children, preferably in childproof wall-mounted closets.

Utility rooms need to be carefully planned and fitted, so consider first your sink, washer, and dryer; these should be positioned to allow easy access for repairs, servicing, and ventilation. A double sink with a generous draining board is particularly useful in a utility room, where clothes can be soaked, bleached, and washed by hand. Decide whether your existing plumbing system is adequate for your equipment. If not, call in professional help to make any necessary alterations. Remember that laundry equipment can leak occasionally, so the floor should be easy to clean.

If space in the utility room is limited, a drying rack can be suspended from the ceiling and an ironing board can even fold down from the wall.

An open utility area is hidden when not in use by a large Venetian blind (above). The ironing board folds out from a cupboard when needed.

A changing area for a baby, below a port-hole window on to the garden, has been incorporated into this attractive utility room, created in a lean-to extension (below left).

Utility rooms can often be installed in narrow spaces (opposite and below right) where a line of units houses the machines and a sink. Use the space above for useful cabinets or shelves where dangerous cleaning materials can be safely stored out of children's reach.

DINING ROOMS

Today, eating rooms are frequently incorporated into the living room or kitchen. The short leg of an L-shaped living room or one corner or a wall of a kitchen often act as the eating room. The kitchen table itself is frequently where a family gathers to eat, and a separate dining room – with all the suggestions of formality that dining conveys – has become something of a rarity or luxury. A totally separate dining room is therefore something worth cherishing.

Traditionally, the formal dining room was a place of ostentatious and magnificent display. Carefully segregated from the kitchen, which was frequently a food-chilling distance off, it boasted suites of matching furniture in mahogany or walnut, on which gleamed the family silver. Above these, the walls were crowded with family portraits. Meals were served with a matching formality.

Recently the reaction to such formality, plus the fact that many homes do not have the space for a dining room proper, has obscured the real potential of dining rooms. An elegant but welcoming and attractive eating room is the perfect setting for relaxed, leisurely, sociable meals. Comfortable chairs and soft lighting encourage guests to linger, talking, over their food and wine; eating together is a supremely social act.

But a dining room can serve other functions besides just eating and entertaining, important though these two are. A desk in one corner can make it an extra room for quiet study, a comfortable armchair another place for reading.

The dining room is also a place for display, particularly if it is not in as frequent use as the other living areas. It can offer a place to exhibit treasured or "best" objects such as dishes, glasses, candlesticks, and racks of wine.

If you like, and can afford, antique or reproduction formal furniture such as mahogany sideboards, then your dining room style is set and you can enhance it best with beautifully finished shelves and a flattering lighting system. However, as an alternative, consider building a display unit or a fitted sideboard. Display crystal glasses on glass shelves, a china collection on open plate racks, or open a pass-through between the kitchen and dining room and make it a decorative feature.

Far from being outdated, an imaginatively planned dining room greatly enhances a home and your lifestyle.

DECORATIVE DISPLAYS

In a cool, sleek room the modern dining table and chairs are placed beside a wall of display shelving (opposite above). Here, books and music equipment are on show, but such a structure could be equally effective for storing china or glass.

A collection of ceramic pots is magnificently displayed in a dining room (below right) on shelves built into a false alcove. The pots are perfectly lit from a spotlight (not shown) placed above them.

An attractive unit (opposite below left) has been designed like a traditional dresser top. A larger unit (opposite below right) creates a fitted dresser, with a backing of wood paneling and drawers incorporated below a wide central shelf. With its gently mottled paint finish, it is the perfect background for a display of 1930s china.

DINING AREAS

An antique table and chairs are placed in a section of an open-plan layout (below left) to provide a formal dining room atmosphere. Note the attractive display shelves which are part of the adjoining kitchen and act as a screen.

In an old house, a creative modern design (opposite below center) incorporates a fitted metal table with window shelves.

THE KITCHEN SYSTEM

The problem faced by many people when trying to install a fitted kitchen is that most walls are out of true and uneven, and are often not at right angles to the floor. The whole process of installing your immaculate factory-made cabinets can easily become a nightmare, which is made worse when walls are covered with pipes and electrical wiring.

This system is designed to make the installation and scribing of kitchen fixtures as simple as possible; it allows existing pipework to run behind the fixtures and, most importantly, allows you to decide for yourself what sort of finish is most suited to your personal style.

This is a kitchen system that enables you to plan your space in the best possible way, allowing you to put all your cooking equipment on display or, if you prefer, shut away behind closed doors. You can incorporate gleaming new modern equipment, or use existing oven ranges and refrigerators. The dimensions are flexible and the permutations are innumerable.

Hardwood top with sink let in

washing Machine

Hardwood drainer

Towel rod

Doors on frame (details opposite)

Marble or stone worktop

space for trays

open shelves

tiled (or painted) uprights

FRONT ELEVATION

High level oven range or microwave with refrigerator below, built into floor-to-ceiling partition

open shelves

open shelves

drawer

Cook top recessed into work top

doors (details below)

through-section of Kitchen partition: Softwood frame clad with plywood,

and tiled

Module of tile

door frame fits tightly between floor & underside of worktop, and between partitions

use Kitchen door hinges & magnetic catches.

Door handles made from grooved hardwood dowels

Kitchen doors & frame

PAINTED KITCHEN

THE KITCHEN SYSTEM: PAINTED KITCHEN

In this rustic kitchen, the basic partition units have been painted rather than tiled. Open shelves have been incorporated in between the partitions and a rod for hanging towels has been built-in underneath the sink. A tiled worktop lies over the partition units and provides a workspace that is both practical and easy to clean.

To complete the country atmosphere, traditional slatted shelves, a hanging bar for kitchen utensils, and a knife rack have been mounted on the wall. These provide extra storage, are easy to construct, and make stylish additions to the basic kitchen system.

LAUNDRY ROOM

Using much the same basic system as the kitchen, the sturdy uprights of the laundry unit support a traditional deep-glazed ceramic Belfast sink which is set beneath a solid maple "butcher block" worktop. A washing machine and clothes dryer can be placed on floor plinths and are here housed on either side of the sink, underneath the worktop, to give a neat, symmetrical appearance.

A slatted shelf is built-in under the sink and between the two partition units to provide storage for laundry detergent and other essential cleaning materials. Below the shelf there is room for a large laundry basket for dirty clothes.

A drying rack on a pulley can be built and positioned over the unit for drying clothes, sheets, and large items such as duvets. With an area like this, doing the laundry could almost become a pleasure.

Constructed from dowels in a triangular frame

traditional drying rack suspended from ceiling

Worktop made from laminated particle board with hardwood edge

Hardwood draining board

Recessed Belfast Sink

Washing machine & clothes dryer installed under worktop

tiled frame & tiled plinth

towel rod & towel hide storage area from view.

Shelf for laundry detergents
Basket for dirty clothes

THE KITCHEN SYSTEM

The basic element of this kitchen is the upright partition, which is tiled. Alternatively, it could be painted, clad in tongued, grooved, and V-jointed lumber, or covered with melamine or plastic laminate.

The width of the partition panels is adjusted to match the width of the tiles being used so that they exactly cover the edges of the tiles that are fixed to the sides of the panels. The spacing between the partitions is adjusted to suit the width of the appliances, shelves, and cupboards to be fitted. A worktop covers the tops of the panels, and overhangs them by $\frac{3}{4}$in (20mm). As the overall width of the worktop affects the front-to-back depth of the partition panels, it is important to decide on the worktop depth right at the beginning (see **Worktops, page 92**).

The upright partition panels are assembled, clad (skinned), tiled, grouted, and battened ready for fixing the shelves, before the partitions are fitted in place.

BASE UNITS

When building base units of a critical thickness, you may find it difficult to obtain wood of exactly the required thickness. In this case, buy wood that is slightly oversized and plane it to the correct thickness.

Height You may have to modify slightly the height of the panels to suit the tiles you are using and the equipment to be fitted into the kitchen. The working height used in this project is $36\frac{1}{2}$in (930mm), which allows for a worktop thickness of $1\frac{1}{2}$in (40mm), while the overall height of the basic element – the upright partition panel – is 35in (890mm). This height is based on using whole tiles to cover the partition panel (eight tiles high).

Depth The front-to-back depth of the partition panel is $24\frac{3}{4}$in (630mm), which allows a $25\frac{1}{2}$in (650mm) deep

worktop to overlap the panel by $\frac{3}{4}$in (20mm). If you buy a standard $23\frac{1}{2}$in (600mm) deep worktop you should reduce the partition panel depth to $22\frac{3}{4}$in (580mm).

At the back of the panel, the rear stud is inset by 2in (50mm) to allow for scribing, if required, for pipe and conduit runs. This space can also be used to provide ventilation for oven ranges and refrigerators. Gas appliances must have a separate flue. Allowance has been made in the design for a back panel and/or a door to be fitted, if required.

Spacing You can adjust the spacing between partition panels to suit appliances, your preferences for cupboard widths, and so on. Our panels are $23\frac{1}{2}$in (600mm) apart.

Shelves The design allows the top shelf to rest one tile's height down from the top of the partition panel and to line up with the tiled fascias. When hardwood edge-banding is added, the shelf finishes flush with the front edge of the partition.

Intermediate shelves are also in line with the fascia tiles, but are set half-a-tile back from the front edge. This looks neat and allows doors to be installed on the front if desired. (The top shelf is not included in this case.) All shelves rest on wooden battens, which are hidden by the front edge-banding on the shelves.

Floor plinths These are optional, but they give a neat finishing touch, and are useful if the floor is uneven. The underside of the plinths can be shimmed as necessary if the floor is uneven, and the front edge scribed to the floor before tiling (see **Techniques, page 36**). The plinths are made one tile height high.

The kitchen system has been designed to be adapted easily. Full instructions for building the kitchens illustrated on pages 78–9, 80–1, and 83 will be found on the following

pages. If you decide to build the complete system, the checklists (below) will help you to compile your own construction schedule.

The elements of each kitchen are listed below for ease of reference:

TILED KITCHEN

Basic Partition Unit and Shelves
Optional extras:
  Back panel
  Floor plinth
  Removable towel rail
  Built-in slatted shelf
  Doors and door handles

Worktop
Tall Partition Unit
Wall-Mounted Shelf Unit
Additional projects:
  Built-in plate rack and drip tray
  Hanging bar for kitchen utensils

ORDER OF WORK CHECKLIST

Tiled base units incorporating shelves, back panels, and floor plinths, and a worktop.

1 Decide depth of worktop.
2 Decide height of worktop (to match tile height and equipment).
3 Decide on thickness of partition units (the thickness of the partition must match the tile width).
4 Decide on spacing of units, and whether you will incorporate shelves or built-in appliances such as a dishwasher.
5 Construct the basic frame unit, including tall partitions if required.
6 Decide on quantity and position of shelves.
7 Mark out position of shelf-support battens.
8 Attach intermediate cross rails.
9 Clad the frame in $\frac{3}{4}$in (19mm) plywood, using common nails.
10 Fit the back panel support battens.
11 Tile the sides of the partition units except for the back and the

bottom rows of tiles (to allow room for scribing the partition unit to fit).
12 Make and attach the shelf-support battens.
13 Put partitions in place, adding any remaining tiles; scribe to fit if necessary, and secure to wall battens and floor with angle brackets.
14 Cut the back panel and slot it into place.
15 Make up and fit the shelves.
16 Make, tile, and fit the floor plinth.
17 Tile the front faces of the partition units.
18 Fit the worktop and any edge-banding.
19 Fit the door frame if required.
20 Construct wall-mounted shelf unit (with shelves if required).

PAINTED KITCHEN

Basic Partition Unit
Knife Rack
Wall-mounted Slatted Shelves
Removable Towel Rail

ORDER OF WORK CHECKLIST

Painted partition units with shelves, and a tiled worktop.

1 Decide depth of worktop.
2 Decide height of worktop.
3 Decide thickness of partition units.
4, **5**, **6**, **7**, **8** as tiled kitchen.
9 Clad the frame in $\frac{3}{4}$in (19mm) MDF, using finishing nails punched in $\frac{1}{16}$in (2mm) below the surface.
10 Make and attach the shelf-support battens.
11 Attach MDF fascia panel to front edge of each partition.
12 Attach partition units in place, supported by vertical battens and angle brackets, and paint as required.
13 Make up and fit the shelves.
14 Install and tile the worktop.

TOOLS

UTILITY KNIFE

STEEL BENCH RULE

TRY SQUARE

CARPENTER'S LEVEL

HAND SAW (or circular saw)

BACK SAW

DRILL (hand or power)

COUNTERSINK DRILL BIT

MASONRY DRILL BIT

HAMMER

NAILSET

SCREWDRIVER (Phillips or slotted, depending on type of screws used)

SANDING BLOCK and SANDING PAPER (or power finishing sander)

TWO C-CLAMPS

PAINTBRUSH $1\frac{1}{2}$in (38mm)

TILING TOOLS

TILE-SCORING TOOL

TILE CUTTER

ADHESIVE SPREADER

TILE SPACERS

GROUT SPREADER

ADDITIONAL TOOLS

POWER SABER SAW for cutting panels and installing sinks and cooktops

ROUTER or POWER CIRCULAR SAW for making cabinet handles

DOWELING JIG for jointing worktops

V-BLOCK to hold doweling for door handles

MATERIALS

Note: All lumber dimensions are finished sizes.
Materials listed are for constructing one base unit with shelves, and a floor plinth.

BASE UNIT — BASIC FRAME

Part	Quantity	Material	Length
FRONT STUD	1	2 × 3in (50 × 75mm) S4S softwood	35in (890mm)
BACK STUD	1	As above	32in (815mm)
TOP RAIL	1	As above	$23\frac{1}{4}$in (592mm)
BOTTOM RAIL	1	As above	$23\frac{1}{4}$in (592mm)
INTERMEDIATE RAILS	As required	As above	$21\frac{3}{4}$in (555mm)

CLADDING (covering for frame and floor)

SIDES	2	$\frac{3}{4}$in (19mm) water-resistant plywood	35 × $24\frac{3}{4}$in (890 × 630mm)
FLOOR	1	As above	$23\frac{1}{2}$ × $24\frac{3}{4}$in (600 × 630mm)

SHELVES

TOP SHELF	1	$\frac{5}{8}$in (15mm) plastic laminate particleboard	$23\frac{1}{2}$in (600mm) wide × $22\frac{3}{4}$in (575mm) deep
INTERMEDIATE SHELF	1	$\frac{5}{8}$in (15mm) plastic laminate particleboard	$23\frac{1}{2}$in (600mm) wide × $22\frac{3}{4}$in (575mm) deep
TOP AND INTERMEDIATE SHELF EDGE-BANDING		$\frac{1}{2}$ × $1\frac{1}{2}$in (12 × 38mm) planed hardwood	$23\frac{1}{2}$in (600mm)

SHELF-SUPPORT BATTENS

TOP SHELF	1	1 × 1in (25 × 25mm) S4S softwood	$24\frac{1}{2}$in (618mm)
INTERMEDIATE SHELF	1	As above	$22\frac{3}{4}$in (575mm)

FLOOR PLINTH

FRONT SUPPORT JOIST	1	1 × 4in (25 × 100mm) S4S softwood	$23\frac{1}{2}$in (600mm)
MIDDLE SUPPORT JOIST	1	As above	As above
REAR SUPPORT JOIST	1	As above	As above

TILES

TILES	As required	$4\frac{1}{4}$ × $4\frac{1}{4}$in (108 × 108mm) white ceramic wall and floor tiles	

CONSTRUCTING THE BASIC PARTITION PANEL

BASIC FRAME

Nail the front stud to the top rail using 3in (75mm) 8d common nails. Make this job easier by nailing against a spare batten clamped to a bench, nailed to the floor, or fixed to a wall, so that there is something solid to nail against. Ideally, the parts will rest on a flat surface while they are being nailed to help hold them flush and keep them stable.

Turn the assembly over and nail the front stud to the bottom rail.

Nail the back stud between the top and bottom rails, 2in (50mm) in from the ends, and nail it in place. This will make it easier to fit the unit to the rear wall later on.

In the case of the partition panel for the laundry area, the back stud should be inset by 4in (100mm), which will allow for a ducting pipe from the clothes dryer.

POSITIONING THE INTERMEDIATE RAILS

Intermediate cross rails coincide with the center line of the shelf support positions, so these must be decided upon at this stage. The finished project will look better if the shelves align with joints between whole tiles. In our basic unit, one shelf is positioned one tile height down from the top, and the other is mid-way between this shelf and the surface of the floor plinth.

On the front and back studs, measure down and mark the shelf top at the required height. Next, mark off the shelf thickness of $\frac{5}{8}$in (15mm) and then the thickness of the shelf support batten, $\frac{3}{4}$in (19mm). The middle of the batten position will be the center line of the internal cross rail. Repeat the procedure for the second shelf.

With the basic square frame resting on edge (support the back stud with a waste piece of 2in [50mm] wood), nail the intermediate rails, correctly positioned, in place.

CLADDING THE FRAME

On the outside edges of the front and back studs, mark the center lines of the cross rails. The sides (which will be nailed to these cross rails) will conceal these rail positions. It is best to mark the center lines of the rails accurately, although the heads of the fixing nails give a rough guide to the positions of the cross rails. Also mark the center line of the back stud on the faces of the top and bottom rails of the frame.

Lay the frame flat, place a side panel cut from $\frac{3}{4}$in (19mm) water-resistant ACX plywood on top (A face uppermost), and align the front edge of the panel with the front edge of the front stud. If you are going to tile the panel, nail it in place *along the front edge only* using 4d common nails, about 6in (150mm) apart. If you are going to paint the panel, use MDF and finishing nails.

You will have made sure that the side panels are cut square, so use these as a guide to getting the basic frame square. Having nailed the front only, pull the rest of the frame into square, if necessary, to align with the edges of the panel, then nail through the panel into the frame, spacing the nails 6in (150mm) apart. To ensure that the nails go into the frame, transfer the center-line marks of the intermediate and back rails on to each side panel.

Turn the partition over and repeat for the other side panel.

TILING

It is best to tile the basic partition panels before they are installed, unless you include a back panel (*see* **Installing a Back Panel, page 88**). Lay the panel flat, mark guide lines to ensure accurate tile spacing, spread tile adhesive, and press the tiles in place, working on a small area at a time (*see* **Tiling Techniques, page 36**). Tile from front to back and top to bottom.

If the floor or wall is uneven where the units are to stand (or if there are pipe runs to cover), leave off the back and bottom rows of tiles until the units have been scribed to fit (*see* **Techniques, page 31**). It is very important that the tiling lines up from one face of the pillar to another. Do not tile the front edge at this stage. When the tiles are dry, grout them. Turn over the units and repeat the process. Make up as many partition panels as you require.

1 **The Basic Frame**
The back stud is inset by 2in (50mm) between the top and bottom rails to make scribing to the wall easier.

2 **First Intermediate Rail**
Shelf batten position is one tile-height down from the top. Rail should coincide with position of the shelf.

3 **Positioning Intermediate Rail for Lower Shelf**
After the first intermediate rail has been nailed in place, the second one should be positioned accurately to coincide with the center line of the shelf-support batten.

TILED SIDE PANEL

TOP SHELF-SUPPORT BATTEN

SHELF EDGE-BANDING

MIDDLE SHELF-SUPPORT BATTEN

FRONT STUD

TILED FLOOR PLINTH

FRONT TILES OVER FRONT FLOOR BATTEN

TOP SHELF

TOP RAIL

SIDE $\frac{1}{2}$in (12mm) PLYWOOD

INTERMEDIATE RAIL

BOTTOM RAIL

● **Cladding the Sides of the Basic Frame**
Mark the center lines of the cross rails on the outside edges of the frames and carefully join up these marks on the $\frac{3}{4}$in (19mm) plywood as a guide for nailing the sides on to the frames.

● **Nailing Down the Side**
Nail the front edges at 6in (150mm) intervals. Pull the frame square, then nail along the guide lines.

● **Tiling the Basic Partition**
Tile from front to back and from top to bottom to keep cut tiles out of sight at the back or at floor level.

MAKING UP PARTITION UNITS

PAINTED PARTITION UNITS

Painted, as opposed to tiled, partition units are shown in the photograph on page 80 and illustrate the versatility of the basic unit design.

The building techniques are the same as before, except that the frames are clad in $\frac{3}{4}$in (19mm) MDF (medium-density fiberboard) instead of $\frac{3}{4}$in (19mm) plywood. For a smooth finish, carefully punch the finishing nail heads about $\frac{1}{16}$in (2mm) below the surface of the board, then fill the holes with a proprietary grain filler. The frame should be sanded down with a sanding block and sanding paper.

Finish the front edge of each partition unit by applying a strip of $\frac{1}{2}$in (12mm) MDF cut to the width of the frame and side panels. Nail in place and smooth in the same way as the side panels. Bevel the front edges of the fascia panels with a sanding block and add the shelf batten. Fit the panels in place (see opposite page) and paint them.

TALL PARTITION UNITS

Tall partition units are required to house eye-level wall ovens, microwave ovens, refrigerators, and so on. Construction is as for low partition units, fixing all the cross rails at the levels required to coincide with the supports. Remember to attach a rail where the worktop meets the partition as this will take a lot of weight.

As the maximum standard length of plywood is 8ft (2440mm) there will be a joint if the units are taller than this. The joint must be at a cross rail so that the cut edges can be nailed down. If there is not a convenient cross rail, then put in an extra one for this purpose.

SHELVES SUPPORTING OVEN RANGES

These shelves must be substantial, to support the weight of the appliance. Use 1×2in (25×50mm) battens for the shelf supports and 1in (25mm) particleboard or MDF for the shelves. The front fascia is cut

from the same material, to the width of the shelf and to the height required – in this case, one tile deep. Either screw or glue and nail the front piece to the front edge of the shelf, and tile the front face.

INSTALLING A BACK PANEL

If a back panel is to be installed on a basic unit (perhaps to hide pipes where there is to be an open shelf), this must be done before installing the shelves and floor plinth, and also before tiling the sides. The front-to-back measurements of the shelves and floor should be reduced to make them fit. If the partition panel unit is to be installed over pipes, scribe the partition around these now to ensure a good fit (see **Techniques, page 31**).

Once all the partitions are sitting in place, correctly scribed, take the first partition and mark a line 2in (50mm) in from the back. Cut two lengths of 1×1in (25×25mm) batten to the height of the partition and attach a batten just in front of the marked line. Glue and nail it in position. Repeat for the second par-

tition. Tile the surface (see **Techniques, page 36**), but only up to the batten. Repeat as necessary.

Make and screw on the shelf-support battens (see opposite page) allowing a $\frac{1}{4}$in (6mm) gap for the thickness of the back. Put partitions back in place and attach to the floor (see opposite page).

Cut the back panel from $\frac{1}{4}$in (6mm) MDF or plywood. The height is the same as the partitions, and the width is as the floor and shelf widths. Slot the panel in place from the top and screw through to the battens using four screws on each side. You may need to undo the shelf-support battens temporarily for an easy fit.

Make up the shelves (see opposite page), adjusting the front-to-back dimension accordingly. Replace the shelf-support battens and fit the shelves.

FLOOR PLINTHS

Each floor plinth is made from $\frac{1}{2}$in (12mm) water-resistant plywood with 1×4in (25×100mm) lumber joists supporting it, assuming you

---

1 Cladding Painted Partition Units
Use $\frac{3}{4}$in (19mm) MDF to clad units. Punch nail heads below surface.

2 Construction of Tall Partition Units
The basic construction method is the same as for the low partition units. Intermediate rails should be included wherever shelves are required or attachments are to be made.

Shelf   Oven Range   Worktop   Microwave   Top Shelf

are using $4\frac{1}{4} \times 4\frac{1}{4}$in (108×108mm) tiles. The front-to-back dimensions are again adjusted accordingly.

Cut the $\frac{1}{2}$in (12mm) plywood plinth panel to size and nail the joists to it at the front, back, and middle. Inset the back one slightly to make scribing easier.

In a utility room or kitchen it is normal to set the washing machine and clothes dryer on the floor, but "built-in" models are also available, and these look better when set on tiled floor plinths as shown in the photograph. If you intend to do this, put in two extra support joists beneath the floor plinth to take the weight of the machines. Pack fiberglass batten insulation quilt between the joists to reduce the noise.

Tile the top from front to back and from the middle outwards, so that any cut tiles are equal at either side (see **Tiling Techniques, page 36**). Grout the tiles to finish. If an appliance is to be placed on a floor plinth, make sure that tiles suitable for floors and walls are chosen as thin wall tiles will crack under the weight and vibration.

SHELVES

We chose easy-to-clean plastic laminated particleboard for our shelves, but you may prefer to use another type of manmade board, such as lumber core or plywood (see **Materials, lumber and boards, page 16**). All shelves are edged at the front with a wooden edge-banding and this thickness has to be allowed for when fitting the shelf-support battens.

ATTACHING THE SHELF-SUPPORT BATTENS

The positions of the shelf supports are already marked on the front and back studs (see **Positioning Intermediate Rails, page 86**). With a pencil, connect the lines on the tiles.

Use 1×1in (25×25mm) S4S for the shelf supports, and cut them to the length required. The top one is the depth of the partition unit, minus the thickness of the edge-banding. The middle one is the partition depth, less half a tile height and the thickness of the edge-banding.

Hold each batten in position on the panel and mark two fixing-screw positions, approximately 2in (50mm) from the ends of each batten, but adjusted so that the screws will not be too near the edge of the tiles.

Using a $\frac{3}{16}$in (4.5mm) drill bit, drill two clearance holes in each batten. Hold each batten in place again and mark the screw positions on the tiles. Drill the tiles with a $\frac{9}{32}$in (7mm) masonry drill (see **Techniques, page 23**) to ensure that the batten-fixing screws will not crack the tiles when they are driven home.

Drill a $\frac{1}{8}$in (3mm) hole through the center of each clearance hole in the partition panel side. Countersink holes in the face of each batten and screw the battens into place using 2in (50mm) No 8 screws. Hide the battens by painting them a suitable color to blend with the tiles you have chosen.

MAKING THE SHELVES

Hold the shelf piece in a vise with the front edge, which is non-laminated, facing upwards.

Glue and nail $\frac{1}{2} \times 1\frac{1}{2}$in (12×38mm) planed wood edge-banding to this edge so that the top edge is flush. The edge-banding must underhang the shelf enough to hide the battens, that is by $\frac{3}{4}$in (19mm). Use 2d finishing nails, blunting the points first so as not to split the wood (see **Techniques, page 23**). Nail carefully, making sure the edge-banding is flush with the surface as you go. Wipe off surplus glue. Punch the nail heads below the surface, then fill the holes and sand down.

Paint, or stain and varnish, the edge-banding. Ours is stained with white oil to match the worktop.

Where a shelf has to fit into a corner, cut off the underhang of the edge-banding where the front of the shelf meets a partition, and screw a batten to the wall, level with the side battens of the partition unit, to support the shelf at the back.

INSTALLING PARTITION UNITS

The partition units are neatly secured to the rear wall with metal angle brackets at positions where

3 Fitting a Back Panel
Scribe partition units around pipes and cut slots. Fit a panel-support batten to the face of the unit.

4 Construction of a Tiled Floor Plinth
Floor plinth comprises $\frac{3}{4}$in (19mm) plywood on 1×4in (25×100mm) S4S lumber battens. The back batten is inset by about 2in (50mm). Front tiles overlap the edges of the top tiles.

5 Fixing Shelves in Place
Hardwood edge-banding attached to the front edge of a shelf (inset) hides support battens screwed to units.

they will be hidden, at the very top and at shelf height. The units are also fitted to the floor with brackets which will be hidden by the floor plinth units when in place.

Position the partition units according to the plans. It is important to have a partition unit where you have to turn a corner, to support the two edges of the worktop.

Do any scribing necessary to secure the partitions to the wall or floor (*see* **Techniques, page 31**).

Where the partition unit is to be installed, screw a vertical batten to the wall. Finish tiling, then push the unit into place over the wall batten and screw it to the batten. Attach the shelves and floor plinth.

Secure the partition to the floor using angle brackets (*see* page 25). Do this by removing the floor plinth and attaching the brackets where they will avoid the joists supporting the floor plinth. Slide the floor plinth back into position.

Fit high partitions to the wall batten, and to the floor and ceiling, if necessary, using angle brackets where they cannot be seen, such as behind the oven range, just underneath the back shelf, or on top of the shelf above eye-level.

When all the partition units are installed, tile and grout their front faces to finish the units.

DOORS

Doors are hinged in pairs and inset within a lumber frame as a neat addition to the basic unit.

MAKING THE FRAME

Measure the opening where the doors are to fit and make a frame to these external dimensions.

Dowel joint the horizontal rails between the uprights with two $\frac{1}{2}$in (12mm) dowels at each frame corner (*see* **Techniques, page 30**). While the glue is setting, the frame should be held square on a flat surface with bar clamps. Alternatively, you can improvise a clamp by resting the frame against a batten temporarily nailed to the bench top. Another batten is nailed to the bench a short distance from the other side of the frame, and then the clamp is tightened by driving folding wedges (*see* **Techniques, page 21**) between the edge of the second batten and the frame side.

From $\frac{1}{2}$in (12mm) hardwood doweling cut eight dowels, the length of which should be twice the thickness of the wood it is going through, plus $\frac{1}{2}$in (12mm). Use a back saw to cut two grooves, $\frac{1}{32}$–$\frac{1}{16}$in (1–2mm) deep, along the dowel length. This will allow the glue and air to escape as the dowel is driven in. With sanding paper, round off one end of each dowel.

With a $\frac{1}{2}$in (12mm) drill bit, drill two holes through each corner joint to a depth of twice the thickness of the wood being fixed. Wrap a band of adhesive tape around the drill bit to indicate the correct depth.

Apply glue to each hole and wipe it around the inside with a small stick. Insert the dowels and hammer them almost home, leaving the ends protruding for the time being. Leave the frames clamped square.

When the glue has set, remove the clamps and saw off the dowel ends flush with the surface.

INSTALLING THE FRAME

Before installing the frame, it must be held square by nailing a batten temporarily across the top and one side of the frame (*see* **Techniques, 3-4-5 method of bracing, page 20** and fig 2 below). After attaching the bracing batten, saw off the ends of the batten flush with the frame to make a neat edge.

Drill and countersink the uprights of the frame and the top and bottom rails. Put the frame in position and screw it to the partition units and to the floor. After fitting, remove the bracing batten from the frame.

MAKING THE DOORS

For a painted finish, cut the doors from $\frac{3}{4}$in (19mm) MDF so that they fit inside the frame with a $\frac{1}{16}$in (2mm) gap all around. There are many different types of door handles which can be fitted to finished doors. Below you will find instructions for making and fitting the handles shown in the illustration. Hinges and catches must also be fitted (*see* **Techniques, page 33**).

1 **Jointing of Frame Corners**
Two $\frac{1}{2}$in (12mm) dowel holes in the ends of the rails are the same length as the thickness of the uprights.

2 **Making the Door Frame Square**
Before fitting the frame, hold it square temporarily by nailing a batten across the top and one side using the 3-4-5 method of ensuring a right-angled corner (see Techniques, page 20 for further details).

3 **Attaching Door Handles**
A right-angled rabbet is cut in 1in (25mm) dowel which is attached to hardwood lipping on the door edge.

MAKING THE HANDLES

To make our handles you will need a router, and a V-block to hold the doweling from which the handles are made (*see* **Techniques, Making a V-block, page 23**). The doweling is placed in the V-block and rabbeted with the router. (You can use a circular saw for this, but it is much more difficult to achieve a good finish.) Cut the doors narrower by the thickness of the lipping, that is, $\frac{1}{2}$in (12mm).

Cut two lengths of 1in (25mm) diameter doweling, to the length of the door plus 2in (50mm) extra to allow the doweling to be nailed in the V-block. The V-block should be a 39in (1000mm) length of 2 × 3in (50 × 75mm) lumber with a 1in (25mm) deep V cut in one face. Nail each end of the dowel in the V-block and mark the finished length. Hold the V-block firmly in a vise.

Working from one end to the other, rout to the depth of the lipping ($\frac{1}{2}$in [12mm]) between the marks. Cut the dowel to final length. Cut two lengths of $\frac{1}{2} \times 1\frac{1}{4}$in (12 × 32mm) hardwood lipping to the length of the dowels. Glue and nail the lipping to the dowel, then sand smooth. Glue and nail the lipping on to the door edges and finish as required.

SLATTED SHELF

Slatted shelves are easy to build and are particularly useful in airing cupboards. In the laundry room (*see* page 83) a slatted shelf has been built-in under the Belfast sink. A number of cross slats are nailed to side rails which rest alongside the same type of shelf-support battens as those used in the basic partition unit in the tiled kitchen.

Cut two pieces of 1 × 2in (25 × 50mm) planed lumber for the side rails to the required front-to-back depth of the shelf. Our shelf is set back about 4in (100mm). Cut the support battens to the same

TOP RAIL

$\frac{1}{2}$in (12mm) DOWELS

BUTT HINGE

UPRIGHT

DOOR

BOTTOM RAIL

HARDWOOD LIPPING

DOOR RABBETED DOWEL HANDLE

HINGED DOOR ASSEMBLY

Doors are hinged within a simple frame assembly which is screwed between partition units.

length and attach in place (*see* **Shelf-Support Battens, page 89**).

Cut the required number of slats (we used seven) from the 1 × 2in (25 × 50mm) planed lumber. The length of these should be the width between partitions, less $\frac{1}{16}$in (2mm) to fit exactly.

Set the side rails in from the ends of the slats by the thickness of the supporting battens. Use offcuts or scrap wood of the same thickness as the support battens. Lay them next to the side rails before laying the front slat across them, so that the battens are at the very ends. Nail the slat in place.

Cut a spacing batten (*see* **Techniques, page 20**) to ensure that the remaining slats are spaced evenly, then nail them in place. Finish the shelf by painting, staining, or varnishing it as required.

④ Making a Slatted Under-sink Storage Shelf

A number of cross rails are nailed to side rails; these rails rest on 1 × 1in (25 × 25mm) shelf-support battens which are then secured at each side to the tiled partition units.

WORKTOPS

There is a wide range of worktops from which to choose. In the tiled kitchen we used 1½in (40mm) thick solid wood, finished with white oil. The worktop in the painted kitchen is 1in (25mm) particleboard which is tiled, and edge-banded at the front with hardwood. A wide selection of laminated worktops is available. The front edges are often rounded (post-formed), or they can be square-edged and edge-banded with hardwood. Most of these worktops are 1¼in (32mm) thick.

If a material like marble or granite is chosen, it will look better if it is made to look thicker at the front edge by bonding a strip of similar material under the front edge. At the back, the worktop's edge will probably be covered by the wall tiles.

Alternatively, the worktop can be attached to the wall by scribing, or by cutting into the wall, although it is easier to cover the gap at the back with a narrow hardwood strip fitted to the wall. If the wall is very uneven, a hardwood strip can be fitted horizontally to the back of the worktop. This strip can be scribed to the wall.

JOINING WORKTOPS

You will probably not need to join worktops end-to-end unless you have a very long run, but you will almost certainly need to turn a corner. Remember that all joins must coincide with a partition.

Joints should be doweled (see **Techniques, page 30**) using a doweling jig to ensure that the surfaces are absolutely flush. You then rout out or drill the surfaces for jointing connector bolts on the underside; there are several types available and they all come with fitting instructions. Alternatively, for corner jointing post-formed worktops, specially shaped metal strips are available to cover the joints neatly.

SECURING WORKTOPS

Fit the worktop to the partitions with knock-down angle plates – two per side of each partition – and screw up through any door frames into the worktop. If you are installing a solid-wood worktop, allow for expansion and shrinkage in the wood by using specially slotted angle plates. Where

a worktop meets a high partition, screw a 2 × 2in (50 × 50mm) batten to the partition for the worktop to rest on. Screw up into the worktop from the underside of the batten (if it is a solid wood worktop, use a slot screw). Angle the front edge of the support batten backwards and set it back from the front edge so it will not be seen. Another method of fitting a worktop is to use a flat metal plate screwed down into the pillar before the worktop is laid over it, and then up into the worktop (fig 2).

If the worktop is to be tiled, do this after fitting, then add a hardwood edge-banding. Seal the gap at the back of the worktop to finish.

SINKS AND COOKTOPS

These are supplied with templates for the required cut-outs. Hold the templates in position and draw around them. Drill ½in (12mm) diameter holes in each corner, inside the line. Put the blade of the Saber saw through one of the holes, and saw around the lines (see **Techniques, Cutting a circle, page 22**).

FRONT CONTROL PANEL FOR COOKTOP

Screw a small length of 1 × 1in (25 × 25mm) batten into the partitions at a depth and distance back to suit your control panel. Screw into the battens following the appliance manufacturer's instruction.

BELFAST SINK

This type of sink sits on a support under a cut-out in the worktop. Make a template of the inside shape of the sink and use this to make the cut-out (see **Sinks and Cooktops, left**). Because the worktop should overhang the sink, the cut-out must therefore be smaller than the inside of the sink. With a router, form a shallow groove on the underside of the worktop, all around the cut-out, about ¼in (6mm) from the edge. This is a drip groove, which will help to prevent water from running under the worktop. Seal around the rim of the sink and the underside of the worktop using silicone-rubber caulking. Make a circular cut-out in the shelf support to allow the waste

① How to Join Worktops
When joining worktops, reinforce the under-surface by fitting jointing connector bolts.

② Fixing Down Worktops
Angle plates (brackets) at top and corner plates at bottom are used for fixing worktops in place.

③ Fitting of Inset Sink or Cooktop
Templates are supplied for marking the top so that a cut-out can be made with a Saber saw. Clips on the underside of the sink or cooktop hold the appliance in place once a hole has been cut.

trap to be fitted into the sink. Stiffen the front edge of the shelf support with 1 × 2in (25 × 50mm) wood edge-banding. Cut a hole, or holes, in the worktop behind the sink to allow the taps to be fitted. Belfast sinks are very heavy, so it may be wise to consult a plumber before attempting to install one yourself.

TILING A WORKTOP

Tiling a worktop provides a very hard-wearing, hygienic surface which is easy to clean and therefore ideal for a kitchen. However, a tiled surface is not suitable for all purposes – for food preparation you need a smooth, wipe-clean surface, such as plastic laminate. For chopping vegetables and meat you need a surface of solid hardwood, such as maple, which is what butchers' blocks are made from. So in a kitchen there is a good case for having a choice of worksurfaces.

When buying tiles for a worktop, be sure to tell your supplier what you will be using them for. Some thin wall tiles will crack when used to work on,

so thicker tiles suitable for both walls and floors are preferable. Some outdoor-type tiles, particularly those with a metallic glaze, are not suitable as a surface for food preparation.

If possible, avoid white grout as it is very difficult to keep clean, although the latest two-part epoxy type is better in this respect. A good choice is a dark-colored waterproof grout. A wide range of colored grouts is available, and coloring powders can be mixed with white grout to your own requirements. If tiles without spacers are used, keep them close together to minimize the width of grouting.

It is essential that the worksurface to be tiled is stable and securely attached before you begin tiling. We recommend 1in (25mm) particle-board. Plywood of the same thickness is also suitable, although more expensive. Try to avoid tiling over solid wood as the wood tends to expand and shrink too much, thus loosening the tiles.

Before starting to tile, tack a batten temporarily to the outer edge of the worktop to give a surface to

tile against. Then lay out the tiles in a dry run to see whether any cutting will be required. This will almost certainly be the case, so keep the cut tiles to the back. If the tiles have to be cut at each end of the worksurface, make sure that the cut ones will be at least half a tile's width. If the initial laying out reveals only thin strips at each end, move all of the tiles sideways by half a tile's width so as to make the end tiles wider.

On the temporary edging batten, mark where the middle tile falls and start tiling from there. Spread tile adhesive over the worktop to cover about 1yd square (1m square) using a notched tile adhesive spreader to ensure an even bed of adhesive. Press the middle tile into the adhesive with a slight twisting motion, then add other tiles to the front edge on each side of this tile. Make sure that they butt against the temporary edging batten. Next, fit whole tiles, working back from the front middle tile towards the back wall. Use a try square and a straight-edge to ensure that this row is straight. Now, working from front to

back again, fill in with tiles on each side of this row to complete the main area of tiling. After this, cut and fit the edge tiles (see **Tiling Techniques, page 36**).

Complete the job by removing the temporary edging batten and re-placing it with hardwood edge-banding, the top edge of which should be level with the surface of the tiles. The edge-banding should be deep enough to cover the entire thickness of the worktop. Grout the joints between the tiles and the space between the tiles and the edge-banding. Finally, seal the tile-to-wall joint with silicone-rubber caulking to make it waterproof.

④ Working out Tile Positions
Tack a batten temporarily to the front edge of the worktop. Set out tiles in a "dummy run."

⑤ Order for Laying Tiles
Lay front tiles from the middle, then work to the back and fill in at each side of the worktop.

⑥ Tiled Worktop
In the painted kitchen shown on page 34, our tiled worktop is finished off with a neat wooden edge-banding to create a functional but attractive surface to work on when preparing food.

WALL-MOUNTED SHELF UNIT

The wall-mounted shelf units are built in a similar way to the floor units. They are neatly mounted to wall battens, so there is no visible means of support. When the units are mounted on a stud wall, extra support is required and so horizontal battens are secured to the wall to support the vertical wall battens. Therefore, the top and bottom rails are thinner in these units, and the sides have cut-outs at the back to slot over the battens on the wall.

MAKING THE PARTITION

Remember that each shelf unit needs a partition panel at each end. Some partitions will support shelving at each side.

Mark out on the walls where you want the shelf runs to be. For the best visual effect, keep the wall shelf partitions above the center lines of the base partitions. Work out what you want to incorporate within the shelves – for example, a stove hood, a plate rack, and a hanging bar for utensils. Decide on the overall height of the shelving. In our case, the partitions are 23½in (600mm) high by 13¾in (350mm) deep.

The basic frame is made from 2 × 2in (50 × 50mm) S4S (smooth 4 sides) lumber clad with ¼in (6mm) MDF (medium-density fiberboard) panels. Two panels are required for each partition unit.

Cut two rails (for top and bottom) 13¾in (350mm) long, and three uprights 20in (510mm) long. Note that for attaching to a stud (hollow) wall, the top and bottom rails will be 1 × 2in (25 × 50mm) and 12¾in (325mm) long.

Nail together the basic frame so that the back stud is set one stud's thickness in. Glue and nail on the side panels, fixing one edge first, before pulling the frame into square so that the other sides line up with the panel. Check that the wall batten slides into the back space.

TOOLS

UTILITY KNIFE
STEEL BENCH RULE
TRY SQUARE
HAMMER
NAILSET
HAND SAW (or circular power saw)
BACK SAW
SCREWDRIVER
SANDING BLOCK and SANDING PAPER (or power finishing sander)
DRILL (hand or power)
DRILL BITS
COUNTERSINK BIT
MASONRY DRILL BIT
PLANE
CARPENTER'S LEVEL
PAINTBRUSH

ADDITIONAL TOOLS

METAL or STUD DETECTOR
SPADE DRILL BIT for drilling partition units for hanging bar

MATERIALS

Part	Quantity	Material	Length
PARTITION UNIT (two required per shelf)			
SIDE PANEL	2	¼in (6mm) MDF	13¾ × 23½in (350 × 600mm)
FRONT FASCIA PANEL	1	¼in (6mm) MDF	As above
TOP RAIL*	1	2 × 2in (50 × 50mm) S4S lumber	13¾in (350mm)
BOTTOM RAIL*	1	As above	As above
FRONT STUD	1	As above	20in (510mm)
BACK STUD	1	As above	As above
WALL BATTEN	1	As above	As above
SHELVES			
TOP SHELF	1	⅝in (15mm) plastic laminate particleboard	12¾ × 23½in (325 × 600mm), or as required
BOTTOM SHELF	1	As above	As above
MIDDLE SHELF	1	⅝in (15mm) plastic laminate particleboard	10 × 23½in (250 × 600mm), or as required
SHELF EDGE-BANDING	3	½ × 1½in (12 × 38mm) hardwood	As above
TOP AND BOTTOM SHELF SUPPORT BATTENS	4	1 × 1in (25 × 25mm) S4S lumber (plane one face down to ⅝in [15mm])	12¾in (325mm)
MIDDLE SHELF SUPPORTS	2	As above	10in (250mm)
*TOP RAIL (for stud wall fixing)	1	1 × 2in (25 × 50mm) S4S lumber	12¾in (325mm)
*BOTTOM RAIL (for stud wall fixing)	1	As above	As above

TOP SHELF-SUPPORT BATTEN

SHELF EDGE-BANDING

MIDDLE SHELF-SUPPORT BATTEN

MIDDLE SHELF

BOTTOM SHELF-SUPPORT BATTEN

BOTTOM SHELF

FRONT FASCIA PANEL

TOP SHELF

WALL BATTEN

BACK STUD

FRONT STUD

BOTTOM RAIL

❶ The Partition Basic Frame
Note that the back stud is inset by the thickness of the wall batten for a neat fit and to make scribing easier.

❷ Cladding the Frame Unit
$\frac{1}{4}$in (6mm) MDF is nailed to the sides, and front fascia is nailed on to cover the edges of the frame unit.

❸ Attaching Shelf Battens
Battens are positioned at the top, middle, and bottom. *Inset*: attaching a batten to make the top flush.

❹ Solid Wall Fixing Method
Batten is securely anchored and screwed to the wall; the partition (cut-away) slots over the batten.

WALL-MOUNTED SHELF UNIT

Measure the total thickness of the partition and cut front fascia strips from $\frac{1}{4}$in (6mm) MDF to that width and $23\frac{1}{2}$in (600mm) high.

Nail on the front fascia and punch the nail heads below the surface (*see* **Techniques, page 24**). Bevel the edges with a plane and sand them down. If the panels are to be a different color from the wall, it is a good idea to paint them before you secure them to the wall.

SHELF-SUPPORT BATTENS

Plane the lumber down to $\frac{5}{8}\times 1$in (15×25mm) to make shelf support battens, and fit these to the partitions before fixing the partitions to the wall. The shelves will look better if they are set back slightly from the front of the partitions. The middle shelf has to be set back even farther – about 4in (100mm).

Decide how many shelves you need and where you want them according to your storage requirements. Ours are flush with the top and bottom of the partitions, with a middle shelf midway between the top and bottom shelves.

① Stud Wall Fixing Method
The wall batten is screwed to horizontal battens that are nailed to wall studs.

Cut the support battens to length, allowing for the edge-banding which is nailed to the front edge of the shelf (that is, the battens are cut to the shelf's depth). Glue, then screw or nail the battens in place.

SHELVES

The shelves are made from $\frac{5}{8}$in (15mm) plastic laminate particle-board with $\frac{1}{2}$in (12mm) hardwood edge-banding. Glue and nail the edge-banding to the front edge. Fill the nail holes, sand smooth when dry and finish according to your decorative scheme.

PLATE RACK

If you are incorporating a plate rack (see opposite page for assembly instructions), it is important to make this up before securing in place the supporting partitions which stand on either side of it.

INSTALLING THE PARTITIONS

Solid walls In most cases the partitions will be secured above a worktop. This should have been fitted level, so measure up from it when marking the positions of the wall battens. Use a carpenter's level to double check that these marks are level. Then, using masonry nails, temporarily fix a straight horizontal batten to the wall on which the wall battens rest while they are fixed. Drill the wall for anchors and screw the wall battens securely to the wall.

Slot the partition unit over the wall battens and glue and screw through the sides into the wall battens with 1in (25mm) No 8 woodscrews, using four either side.

Stud walls Locate the wall studs (*see* **Techniques, Wall fixtures, page 24**) and nail a 2×2in (50×50mm) batten horizontally at the top and bottom of where the partition units will be placed. Screw the 2×2in (50×50mm) upright wall battens to the horizontal battens on the wall for support.

Nail up the frame as before, but use 1×2in (25×50mm) lumber for the top and bottom rails which will be shorter by the thickness of the horizontal battens. Cut out 1×2in (25×50mm) slots on the back corners of the inside panels using a 1×2in (25×50mm) lumber offcut as a template. Nail the panels down, then slot the partitions over the wall battens, screwing through the sides into the wall battens as before. Do not include cut-outs at the ends of the shelf units.

STOVE HOOD

This hood can be the simple recirculating type, which needs only to be attached between two partition panels and connected to a power supply, or it can be the more efficient extractor type. With the latter, you will

USE SHELVES FOR DISPLAY
The wall-mounted shelf unit is ideal for decorative display as well as for practical storage.

need to cut an outlet in a convenient external wall for fumes to escape through. The hood is then either connected directly to the outlet or linked to it with simple slot-together plastic ducting if they are some distance apart. The manufacturer's instructions will have full details.

It will probably be necessary to attach mounting battens to both the wall and the partition units. Fit a narrow shelf at the top to line up with the top of the partition units, but do not fit edge-banding at the front as the stove hood's front panel will conceal this. Attach battens at an angle on each inside face of the partition units to hold the front panel. This can be a sheet of stainless steel or painted MDF. If you use MDF, secure the panel by screwing through into the battens. But if the panel is stainless steel, it is neater to glue it in place with epoxy resin.

You can adapt the fitting of the stove hood according to its design and how it fits into the rest of your kitchen system.

HANGING BAR FOR UTENSILS

This is simply a chrome steel or wooden rod which fits at each end into a wall partition panel. S-shaped meat hooks are hung on the bar to take utensils.

To install the bar, drill holes of its diameter into the sides of the appropriate partition unit so that the bar will clear the bottom rail but will rest on it. Use an offcut of bottom rail as a spacer to mark off the lowest part of the hole on the bottom edge of the partition panel.

Cut the rod to a length equivalent to the distance between two partition panels, plus 4in (100mm).

❷ Positioning the Hanging Bar
Use an offcut of the bottom rail to mark a position on the partition for the hanging bar.

BUILT-IN PLATE RACK AND DRIP TRAY

This is a simply designed storage unit which is intended to be built-in between two wall-mounted shelf units (see opposite page for instructions and page 78 for a photograph of the unit in position). For a perfect result, great accuracy and attention to detail, as well as a pair of helping hands, is called for, but the finished unit is solid, secure, and stylish. Wooden dowels are inserted at regular intervals into three wooden rails which are angled to suit the size of your dishes. Instructions for a drip tray made from plastic laminate particleboard are also included. The drip tray allows you to leave dishes stacked on the plate rack to air dry, and save you valuable time.

TOOLS

UTILITY KNIFE

STEEL MEASURING TAPE

TRY SQUARE

BACK SAW

HAMMER

MORTISE GAUGE

POWER DRILL

DRILL BITS

COMPASS SAW $1\frac{1}{2}$–2in (38–50mm) to suit frame diameter (or use a router)

POWER SABER SAW

MALLET

ADDITIONAL TOOLS

V-BLOCK

DRILL STAND (or home-made drill guide) for accurate drilling

MATERIALS

PLATE RACK

Part	Quantity	Material	Length
FRAME	3	$1\frac{1}{2}$–2in (38–50mm) diameter softwood dowel	As required
RACK SPACERS	As required	$\frac{1}{2}$in (12mm) diameter softwood dowel	$5\frac{1}{2}$in (137mm)
RACK SPACERS	As required	$\frac{1}{2}$in (12mm) diameter softwood dowel	10in (250mm)

DRIP TRAY

Part	Quantity	Material	Length
TRAY BASE	1	$\frac{5}{8}$in (15mm) plastic laminate particleboard	As required
EDGE FRAME	4	$\frac{1}{2} \times 1\frac{1}{2}$in (12 × 38mm) hardwood edge-banding	As required
SUPPORT BATTENS	2	$\frac{3}{8} \times \frac{1}{4}$in (10 × 6mm) S4S softwood	As required

Built-in Plate Rack and Drip Tray

Cut the three large frame dowels to length. To calculate the length of each dowel, measure the distance between the partitions and add 4in (100mm). The 4in (100mm) allows for 1in (25mm) either end to slot into the partitions, and 1in (25mm) excess either end. A nail can be driven into this excess to secure the dowel to the V-block while the holes are being drilled in it (see **Techniques, Making a V-block, page 23**). The excess will be sawn off later.

Position one dowel in the V-block. Draw a straight line along its length using a steel straight-edge resting against one side of the block (fig 1). Starting 2½in (62mm) in from one end, mark off 1⅜in (35mm) centers along it. Use a pencil or mortise gauge to do this.

Using the first dowel as a guide, transfer the 1⅜in (35mm) centers to a second dowel. For the third dowel, mark a line down its length as described above, and continue the line across the end section to the center. Draw a second line, 96° to the first. Continue the second line along the length of the dowel.

Use the first dowel to transfer the 1⅜in (35mm) centers to the third dowel, making the marks between the two lines. Put the first dowel in the V-block with the marked hole-centers vertical. Nail it down at either end to secure it.

Drilling the Holes

Start to drill the vertical holes (see **Techniques, page 23**).

Each hole should be drilled to a depth of ½in (12mm). Use a drill stand, a drill guide set at 90°, or make your own drill guide.

Making a Drill Guide

You will need a block of 2 × 4in (50 × 100mm) lumber. Make a v-shaped cut-out in it so that it will fit neatly over the dowel resting in the V-block. Drill a hole through it vertically (see above).

Thread the drill bit through the hole in the drill guide and place the tip of the bit on the first hole. Pull the guide into position, resting on the V-block, then drill a ½in (12mm) deep hole. Drill all of the holes required in the same way.

Assembly

Cut 1in (25mm) from each end of each of the three frame dowels. (This is the excess used when nailing the dowel to the V-block.)

By tapping gently with a mallet, fit all the 5½in- (140mm-) long dowels into one of the frame dowels (one with a single row of holes) and all the 10in- (250mm-) long dowels into the other frame dowel.

Join the two sections together to complete the assembly. You will need help when aligning the dowels. If the fit is very tight, it will be easier to join the frame if you clamp it together in a woodworker's vise. For an extra-tight fit, clamp the rack in a vise. If the fit is loose, put a little waterproof glue in the holes to fill any gaps.

Look down the length of the rack to check if it is perfectly aligned. If it is not, twist the rack into alignment by getting one person at each end of the rack to adjust it.

Securing the Rack

It is essential that the plate rack is in position before the supporting parti-tions on either side of the rack are finally secured in place.

Lift up the rack to one of the partition sides. Tilt it back until an angle is found in which the plates will sit comfortably. Mark the dowel positions on the partition sides.

Position the wall batten in its correct place at the back of the partition so that this can be drilled at the same time.

Cut out the holes to a depth of 1in (25mm) with a power drill and a spade bit or with a router or with a compass saw.

Fit one partition in place and carefully slot the rack into it. Meanwhile, ask someone to hold the partition against the other end of the rack for you so that the position for the three holes can be marked, and the holes drilled. The partition can then be tapped into the rack to secure it in position. Finally, attach the second partition to the wall batten. You will find ideas and instructions for a variety of wall-mounted plate racks and shelves, hanging bars, and suspended shelves on pages 66–9, 114, and 116.

① Marking Plate Rack Dowel Hole Centers
Rest dowel in a V-block and mark off centers at 1⅜in (35mm) intervals. Transfer all the marks on to the second dowel. On the third dowel draw a second line at exactly 96° to the first.

② Using a Drill Guide
With dowel nailed into a V-block, line up on first hole. Use scrap wood as a drill guide.

③ Drilling the Dowel Holes
A drill guide, which you can make yourself, helps to keep the drill bit vertical. Drill ½in (12mm) holes.

RACK SPACERS (long)

$\frac{1}{2}$in (12mm) DOWELS

FRAME DOWEL

$1\frac{3}{8}$in (35mm) HOLE SPACING

RACK SPACERS (short)

DRIP TRAY

This is removable for easy drying or cleaning. Cut the tray-support battens to the same length as the shelf-support battens, and nail and glue them to the bottom of the partitions.

Make a tray base from $\frac{5}{8}$in (15mm) laminated particleboard. Cut two pieces of edge-banding to the depth of the tray. Saw $\frac{3}{8}$in (10mm) from each to leave them 1in (25mm) high. Glue and nail the pieces of edge-banding to the tray base ends so they are flush with the underside (fig 5). Cut the front and back edge-bandings to the length of the tray plus the end edge-bandings. Nail and glue in place, leaving a $\frac{3}{8}$in (10mm) underhang at front and back. Make small cut-outs at the back to allow the tray to slide over its support battens.

Waterproof the interior edges of the tray with a silicone bath caulking. When using a mastic applicator gun, it is easier to push the trigger away from you to provide an even flow of caulking.

④ Positioning the Plate Rack Between Partitions

The assembled plate rack is fitted between two wall-mounted shelf partition units and slips neatly into three holes that are drilled into each partition side panel for a secure attachment.

⑤ Making the Drip Tray

The plastic laminate particleboard tray, with hardboard edge-banding, rests on two support battens. End edge-banding is fixed first (*top*), then front and back edge-banding.

Back Edge-banding

WALL-MOUNTED SLATTED SHELVES

TOOLS

STEEL MEASURING TAPE

STEEL BENCH RULE

UTILITY KNIFE

TRY SQUARE

BACK SAW

MITER BOX

SCREWDRIVER

DRILL (hand or power)

COUNTERSINK DRILL BIT

MASONRY DRILL BIT

SPADE DRILL BIT

SPACING BATTEN (made from an offcut of wood)

Cut a 45° miter at each end of the 1½in (38mm) diagonal. Glue and screw together the two 1 × 3in (25 × 75mm) pieces. Use two 1in (25mm) No 8 screws.

Lay the L-shaped piece on the workbench and place the diagonal in position. Mark the diagonal's internal shoulder on the L-shape at both ends (fig 1). Continue the lines around the edges on to the backs.

Mark the position for each screw hole, ¾in (19mm) from the pencil line and centrally on the wood. Drill and countersink pilot holes. Lay the L-shaped section on the bench and place a ½in (12mm) thick packing piece in position (fig 2). This is so that the diagonal lies centrally in the 1 × 3in (25 × 75mm) L-bracket. The diagonal can now be repositioned, and glued and screwed in place.

Make up extra brackets as required. Allow one bracket for each 48in (1200mm) of shelf span. If the shelves are likely to be heavily laden, fix the brackets every 36in (900mm).

ATTACHING BRACKETS TO A WALL

The leg of the bracket that is overlapped by the other piece at the top is the one that is fixed to the wall (fig 3). Drill countersunk pilot holes and fix the brackets to the wall by means of a temporary batten, to ensure that they are level.

MATERIALS

Part	Quantity	Material	Length
L-SHAPE BRACKETS	2	1 × 3in (25 × 75mm) S4S lumber	14in (350mm)
DIAGONAL BRACKET	1	2 × 2in (50 × 50mm) S4S lumber	16½in (410mm)
SLATS	5	1 × 2in (25 × 50mm) S4S lumber	As required

Optional: hanging bar of ¾in (19mm) wood dowel or metal rod

HANGING BAR

Drill holes for the bar in the brackets before securing them to the wall. Decide the distance between the brackets and cut the bar to this length plus 1½in (38mm).

Mark on the diagonals the positions for the bar holes according to the size of the objects you intend to hang from it. Drill the holes to the same diameter as the bar and ¾in (19mm) deep. Fit the first bracket to the wall, slot in the bar, then fit the second bracket on the other end and secure it to the wall.

FITTING THE SLATS

Cut the slats to the required length, allowing an overlap of 3in (75mm) at each end. Fit the front slat flush with the front of the brackets. Use a single ½in (12mm) No 6 screw in each bracket. With the back edge of the back slat butted against the wall, space the remaining slats at equal centers for a neat finish.

❶ Marking Brackets for Positioning the Diagonals
Screw the flat pieces of lumber together at right angles. Temporarily fit the diagonal strut. Mark off the internal shoulders and continue the lines on to the back faces of the brackets.

❷ Attaching Diagonal Strut
Use a suitable offcut of wood to give support to the diagonal strut when securing it in place.

❸ Finished Shelf Brackets
The top rail fits on to the wall rail and the brackets are braced by the diagonal strut.

Top

Wall Piece

Wall Piece

Top

Offcut Spacer

Top Rail

Wall Rail

Holes for Wall Fixing

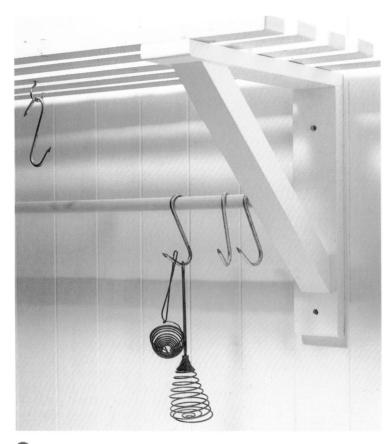

REMOVABLE TOWEL RAIL

Made from $1\frac{1}{2}$–2in (38–50mm) diameter dowel, available from lumberyards.

TOOLS

STEEL MEASURING TAPE
TRY SQUARE
BACK SAW
DRILL (hand or power)
DRILL BITS
HACKSAW
SCREWDRIVER
METAL FILE or EMERY CLOTH
PARING CHISEL or ROUTER

Measure the distance between the base partitions. Cut the dowel to this length. Mark 1in (25mm) in from each end and cut off a disk from each end. Mark center of each disk and the long dowel at either end.

Drill a pilot hole in one end of the dowel, then insert a $1\frac{1}{2}$in (38mm) No 8 woodscrew, leaving just the shank protruding by $\frac{1}{2}$in (12mm). Repeat at other end. Use a hacksaw to cut off the screw heads. File off any burr from the shank ends so about $\frac{5}{16}$–$\frac{3}{8}$in (8–10mm) of shank protrudes.

For the disks, drill a series of $\frac{1}{8}$in (4mm) diameter holes from the center of each disk to the edge to form a slot. The holes should be drilled to the same depth as the protruding screw shanks. To ensure this, stick tape to the drill bit at the correct distance from the tip. Use a chisel to clean out the slot. A much easier method of forming a slot is to use a router with a $\frac{1}{8}$in (4mm) diameter cutter if you have one.

Drill $\frac{1}{8}$in (4mm) diameter screw holes through each disk on either side of the center line. Hold the dowel horizontally in place and mark off the positions of the disks. Then hold each disk in position to mark off screw positions. The holes should be about 3in (75mm) below the worksurface and set back about 2in (50mm) from the front. Screw to partition and slot rail in place.

4 **Fixing Brackets to the Wall and Adding the Slats**
Drill holes for hanging bar and slot it in place before fitting the second bracket to the wall. Nail a batten to the wall temporarily to keep the brackets level. Screw down slats.

5 **Cutting and Shaping Ends**
Use a screwshank to form the rail pivot. For the slot, drill a series of holes in an offcut.

6 **Fitting the Rail in Place**
Use a narrow chisel to form a slot in the disk for the rail pivot. Screw the disks to the partition sides.

Knife Rack

STEEL MEASURING TAPE

TRY SQUARE

HAMMER

BACK SAW

TWO C-CLAMPS

DRILL (hand or power)

COUNTERSINK DRILL BIT

MASONRY DRILL BIT

SANDING BLOCK and
SANDING PAPER

A knife rack is a useful and versatile addition to the kitchen system, and this is a simple project to build.

Working from the back, glue and nail both verticals on to the first slat. Allow each end of the slat to protrude 3in (75mm) beyond the verticals (fig 1).

Fit the remaining slats at $1\frac{1}{2}$in (38mm) centers. Use a spacing batten (see **Techniques, page 20**) to ensure accurate spacing between the slats. Leave a space for the knife slot. Glue the $\frac{1}{4} \times 1$in (6 × 25mm) spacers to the spare slat. There should be a spacer at each end and one in the middle of the slat (fig 2).

Glue the facing piece of the knife slot over the spacers. Secure with C-clamps, allow the glue to set and then sand it down.

Fit the knife-slot section to the verticals in the center of the space remaining, working from the back.

Drill countersunk holes through the front of the rails into the wall at the desired spot. As the load is light, it is not necessary to fix the rack to the studs in a lath-and-plaster wall or a hollow wall.

Materials

Part	Quantity	Material	Length
SLATS	7	$\frac{3}{4} \times 1$in (19 × 25mm) softwood	34in (850mm)
BACK OF KNIFE SLOT	1	1 × 1in (25 × 25mm) softwood	As above
FRONT OF KNIFE SLOT	1	$\frac{1}{4} \times 1$in (6 × 25mm) softwood	As above
SPACERS	3	$\frac{1}{4} \times 1$in (6 × 25mm) softwood	2in (50mm)
VERTICALS	2	$\frac{3}{4} \times 1$in (19 × 25mm) softwood	18in (450mm)

1 **Nailing the Verticals to the Horizontal Slats**
Work from the back and nail the vertical rails to the horizontal slats leaving a space for the knife slot to be fitted. Use a spacing batten to ensure that slats are evenly spaced.

2 **Forming the Knife Slot from Lumber Battens**
The knife slot batten is thicker than the others to accommodate knife handles. The slot is formed from a thin slat laid over three offcuts which act as spacers for the knives.

DRYING RACK

STEEL MEASURING TAPE

STEEL BENCH RULE

TRY SQUARE

SANDING BLOCK, COARSE and FINE SANDING PAPER

SABER SAW or HAND SAW

POWER DRILL

SPADE DRILL BIT

UTILITY KNIFE

Cut the square piece of wood in half diagonally. Round off all the corners with coarse, then fine sandpaper. Paint the wood if required.

Mark the centers for the holes in one end piece. Mark the holes at 4in (100mm) centers and 1¾in (45mm) in from the edge. Drill the six (dowel) holes to 1in (25mm) diameter and the small (rope) holes to ¼in (6mm) diameter. Clamp both end pieces together, then use the first piece as a template to mark the hole positions on the second piece. Drill the holes in the second piece. Locate the dowels in the two end pieces, leaving about 3in (75mm) protruding at either end.

Find the positions of the ceiling joists. If they run at right angles to the rack, then, after fitting the pulleys, adjust the position of each end piece to align with the pulley above it. If the ceiling joists run parallel with the rack, choose the most convenient one to fit the pulleys to. Align the end pieces with the pulleys. Fit the double pulley at the side from which you want to operate the rack.

Screw the cleat to a convenient place on the wall. Tie the rope to the rope hole in the end piece. Feed the rope through the single pulley, across to the double pulley, down to the cleat, up through the double pulley again, and then down to the other triangle. Tie this end in place to form a loop. Take up the slack rope and wind it around the cleat.

Check the rack lowers and raises correctly, then dab aliphatic resin into dowel holes to secure them.

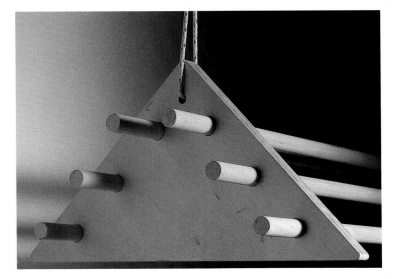

MATERIALS

Part	Quantity	Material	Length
ENDS	1	1in (25mm) plywood (or MDF)	16in sq (400mm sq)
RAILS	6	1in (25mm) diameter hardwood dowel	6ft 6in (2m)

ONE SINGLE PULLEY, ONE DOUBLE PULLEY (screw-in or screw-on type)

A HANK OF SASH CORD, AND ONE CLEAT

❸ Marking Drying Rack End Pieces for Rails
Two triangular end pieces are cut from a 16in (400mm) square of 1in (25mm) plywood. Mark holes at 4in (100mm) intervals on a line 1¾in (45mm) in from the side edges.

❹ Hanging the Drying Rack
A double and a single pulley should be securely fitted into ceiling joists. Fit a cleat firmly to a nearby wall and arrange cords as shown so that the drying rack can be raised and lowered easily.

SERVING AND DISPLAY UNIT WITH MIRRORS

I built shelving similar to this a few years ago in my house in Provence, France; as it has been so successful there it seemed an ideal project for this book. It works on the principle that everybody likes to display their favorite china, bowls, platters, and pans, as these objects create an appetizing backdrop for any kitchen or dining room. The shelving is based on an idea that I first saw in a restaurant in Positano, Italy. The most important aspect of design is the panels of mirror that are slightly angled to reflect the components of the bowls and platters which sit on the shelf. In Positano wonderful bowls of antipasto were displayed and the effect was mouthwatering and demonstrated that, with a little ingenuity, less can be more. The mirror provides an entrancing double vision of a rich arrangement of food and wine, to be enjoyed while sitting at the dining table or working in the kitchen.

The design also incorporates a wide shelf that is waist high and can be used as a serving surface in a dining area. The finish you choose for the shelving unit can be varied to suit your particular decorative scheme. The wide shelf shown here is marble, which, while very effective as a display background for bowls of fruit, vegetables, and seafood, may be substituted for a more economical material if your finances are limited. But don't dispense with the mirrors!

SECTION

strip light

groove in shelf to stop plates slipping

angled mirror

marble shelf

half round shelf

FRONT ELEVATION

strip light

dowels hold plates in place

quadrant shelf supports

Angled mirrors reflect food displays

Center curved shelves for displaying dishes

PLAN

groove

dowel

upper shelves

Cool marble shelf

SERVING AND DISPLAY UNIT WITH MIRRORS

This dining room shelf unit has been designed to be both decorative and practical. The wide serving shelf provides plenty of space from which food can be served and displayed, while the angled mirrors behind reflect the food and flowers, to create a pleasing interplay of color and shape. Above, there are grooved shelves on which to display plates, and there is a shelf below the serving shelf for jugs, bowls, cutlery, and so on. A concealed light behind the valance provides subtle mood lighting at meal times. To maximize impact and storage space, the unit reaches to the ceiling.

The unit can butt up against a wall at one end or fill an alcove, be free-standing or run from wall to wall. The serving shelf can be marble (as here), slate, solid wood, or painted MDF (medium-density fiberboard) or lumber core. If marble is used, any joint *must* lie over an upright so that it is supported.

For the main structure, the vertical partitions are 1in (25mm) MDF; the straight shelves are $\frac{3}{4}$in (19mm) lumber core (for stiffness); and the curved shelves are $\frac{3}{4}$in (19mm) MDF, which is easier to cut into curves than the thicker fiberboard.

The unit is built in two sections. The lower section up to the serving shelf is constructed and secured in place, and then the top section, above the shelf, is added. The whole unit is attached to the wall with angle brackets located in the shelf rabbets, and the shelves are then slotted in to conceal the brackets.

The overall dimensions of the unit are based on the depth of the serving shelf. This one is 18in (460mm) deep, which is ideal. If you prefer a different size, you will have to adjust all the dimensions accordingly. Remember that, for a neat appearance, the depth of the serving shelf should always be equal to the depth of the curved shelves.

Precise vertical dimensions up to the top of the mirror section are given, together with all the shelf depths, so that the angle of the mirror will be exact.

To allow the overall height and width to be varied, the top section above the mirror can be whatever height is required to reach your ceiling. The outer shelf sections can be whatever width is required, but for a balanced appearance make sure that they are of equal measurements either side of the central curved section.

If the unit does not have to fit into a specific width, then just make each outer section twice the width of the central section. This gives the unit attractive proportions.

MATERIALS

Part	Quantity	Material	Length
UPPER VERTICAL PARTITIONS	4	1in (25mm) MDF	As required × 6in (150mm)
UPPER STRAIGHT SHELVES	4	$\frac{3}{4}$in (19mm) lumber core	As required × 6in (150mm)
HALF-ROUND SHELVES	2	$\frac{3}{4}$in (19mm) MDF	$19\frac{1}{4}$ × $15\frac{5}{8}$in (487 × 393.5mm)
VALANCE	3	$\frac{3}{4}$in (19mm) MDF	As required
PLATE-RETAINING RAILS	3	1in (25mm) diameter dowel	As required
SERVING SHELF	1	Optional – minimum thickness 1in (25mm) MDF	As required
SHELF-SUPPORT BATTENS	3	1 × 2in (25 × 50mm) S4S softwood	As required
LOWER VERTICAL PARTITIONS	4	1in (25mm) MDF	6 × 30in (150 × 770mm)
LOWER STRAIGHT SHELVES	2	$\frac{3}{4}$in (19mm) lumber core	As required × 11in (280mm)
CENTER CURVED SHELF	1	$\frac{3}{4}$in (19mm) MDF	$19\frac{1}{2}$ × 18in (500 × 460mm)
LARGE QUADRANTS	4	1in (25mm) MDF	from $49\frac{1}{4}$ × 12in (1250 × 300mm)
SMALL QUADRANTS	4	1in (25mm) MDF	from 5 × $22\frac{1}{2}$in (125 × 570mm)

ALSO: 3 mirrors, strip lights, $\frac{1}{8}$in (3mm) edge-banding, 40 angle brackets $2\frac{1}{2}$in × $2\frac{1}{2}$in × $\frac{5}{8}$in (65mm × 65mm × 16mm)

TOOLS

- HAND SAW
- SABER SAW or COMPASS SAW
- DOWELING JIG
- CLAMPS
- STEEL MEASURING TAPE
- TRY SQUARE
- UTILITY KNIFE
- ROUTER (plus bits)
- TACK HAMMER
- CARPENTER'S LEVEL
- POWER DRILL (plus bits)
- SCREWDRIVER
- HACKSAW
- PLANE
- SANDING BLOCK and SANDING PAPER
- STEEL ROD

UPPER VERTICAL PARTITION (inner)

VALANCE

UPPER VERTICAL PARTITION (outer)

PLATE-RETAINING RAIL

UPPER SHELF (straight)

HALF-ROUND SHELF

GROOVE FOR MIRROR

MIRROR

SERVING SHELF

LARGE QUADRANT

SMALL QUADRANT

LOWER VERTICAL PARTITION (outer)

LOWER VERTICAL PARTITION (inner)

CENTER CURVED SHELF

SERVING AND DISPLAY UNIT WITH MIRRORS

LOWER SHELF SECTION

Using 1in (25mm) MDF, cut four verticals 30in (770mm) – the height of the underside of the serving shelf – by 6in (150mm). For the serving shelf supports, cut out four quadrants from a strip of MDF 12in (300mm) wide and at least 49¼in (1250mm) long, so that the radius of each can be 12in (300mm). Draw the shape of one quadrant before cutting it out with a Saber saw or compass saw and sanding this to a smooth curve. Use this quadrant as a pattern for marking out the remaining three quadrants. For the lower shelf supports, cut out four smaller quadrants from a strip 5in (125mm) wide by 22½in (570mm) long, so that the radius of each can be 5in (125mm). Again, cut out one quadrant and use this as a pattern for the remainder.

FIXING QUADRANTS

Using ⅜in (10mm) dowels, 2in (50mm) long, glue and attach the large quadrants to the front edges of the uprights. Use a doweling jig (or dowel points) to align the holes, ensuring that the top edges of the quadrants and uprights are flush.

Clamp each assembly and allow sufficient time for the glue to set. This will be easier if you leave square notches on the quadrants to clamp against, sawing them off later to complete the curve.

Measure 12in (300mm) up from the bottom edge of each vertical for the position of the top of the smaller quadrants. Fit all four in place as for the large quadrants.

ROUTING FOR SHELVES

The top edge of each lower quadrant aligns with and supports the bottom of each lower shelf. Use a try square and a pencil or utility knife to mark the top of the quadrant on to all of the vertical pieces where a shelf will be supported. Using a router with a ¾in (19mm) straight bit, cut out a groove to the top of the line at a depth of ¼in (6mm). Do the same on the inner faces of the end vertical pieces and then repeat the whole process on both faces of the inner vertical pieces.

Upper Half-round Shelf
Cut from a rectangle of ¾in (19mm) MDF measuring 19¼ × 15⅝in (487 × 393.5mm). Measure 6in (150mm) in from the back edge and draw a line across. At center point of this line draw a semi-circle as shown.

Center Curved Shelf
Cut from a rectangle of ¾in (19mm) MDF measuring 19½ × 18in (500 × 460mm). Mark 11in (280mm) in from the back edge. From this line draw a curve to meet front edge in center. Saw notch as shown.

Lower Straight Shelf
The span of the shelves is flexible, but they must be of equal length on each side. Shelf width is 11in (280mm). Both notches are 6in (150mm) long. The outer notch is ¾in (19mm) wide, the inner ¼in (6.5mm).

---

1 **Assembly of Lower Vertical Partition Panel**
Cut lower vertical from 1in (25mm) thick MDF. Serving shelf support is quadrant of MDF with radius of 12in (300mm). Small quadrant has 5in (125mm) radius. Fix quadrants using dowels.

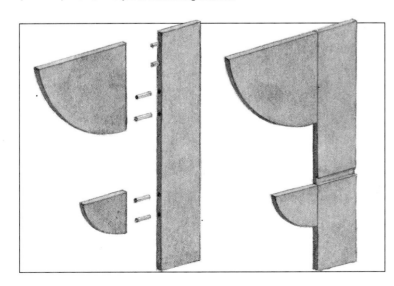

2 **Fitting a Lower Straight Shelf Between Partitions**
Make sure that the shelves at each side are of equal length. The depth of each one should be 11¼in (280mm) including edge-banding. Shelf ends are rabbeted to cover the verticals.

CENTER CURVED LOWER SHELF

For the center curved lower shelf, cut out a rectangle from ¾in (19mm) MDF, 18 × 19½in (460 × 500mm). The 19½in (500mm) dimension will be the width. Mark 11in (280mm) in from, and parallel to, the back edge – this will be the depth of the straight shelf. From this line, draw and cut a curve to meet the front edge in the center. Mark 6in (150mm) in from and parallel to the back edge. Saw out notches from both sides, ¼in (6.5mm) wide and 6in (150mm) long; these locate in the grooves cut in the vertical partitions.

LOWER STRAIGHT SHELVES

Calculate how long you want your ¾in (19mm) lumber core shelves to be on each side of the curved shelf, making sure that they are of equal length. The depth of each one should be 11in (280mm) including a ⅛in (3mm) edge-banding, glued and nailed to the front edge. Cut out the two shelves, then cut notches from each end – 6in (150mm) long, and ¼in (6.5mm) wide on the inner edge; ¾in (19mm) wide on the outer edge. This will ensure that they meet at the center line of the inner verticals with the curved center shelf. The outer edges of the straight shelves cross the outer verticals and finish flush with the outside of the unit.

INSTALLATION

Position one of the uprights against the wall as a guide to marking on the wall the position of the serving shelf. Mark an accurate line for the underside of the shelf along the back wall and any side wall. Using a carpenter's level, ensure that the line is level along its entire length.

Screw 1 × 2in (25 × 50mm) softwood battens along the back wall on the underside of the line to give extra support to the serving shelf. Three battens are needed, cut to fit the distance between the verti-

cal sections. If an end vertical is being attached directly into a return wall, screw directly through the upright and quadrant into the wall. Drill and generously countersink the holes – one near the top edge, one near the bottom of the vertical, and two in each quadrant. Put the upright in place and mark off the positions of the screws on the wall. Remove the vertical and drill holes for 2in (50mm) No 8 screws in the wall. Insert anchors in the holes, replace the vertical, and screw into the wall.

If the end vertical is away from a return wall then it must be secured to the back wall with 2½in × 2½in × ⅝in (65mm × 65mm × 16mm) angle brackets – one at the top and one set into the shelf notch.

The shelf notch bracket will be concealed by the shelf when this is in position. The shelf will have to be trimmed to allow for this bracket. To conceal the top bracket, attach it vertically to the wall so that the top "arm," which protrudes from the wall at a right angle, will rest in a slot cut in the top edge of the vertical partition. The back arm of the bracket should be set into a slotted groove in the wall so that it allows the rear edge of the vertical to be held firmly.

The bottom of the vertical can be secured by using a "dowel" of ⅛in (3mm) diameter steel rod or bolt cut to a length of 1in (25mm) with a hacksaw. Half of the "dowel" should be sunk into the floor and the remainder into the underside of the vertical partition. The difficult part is locating the hole in the vertical partition directly over the "dowel" protruding from the floor. To do this, first secure the "dowel" in the vertical partition, then offer up the vertical in its exact position against, and at 90° to, the wall. Tap the top edge sharply with a hammer so that an impression of the "dowel" will be left in the floor. This indicates the drilling position. The "dowel" can be an easy fit since its function is simply to hold the

base of the vertical partition in place. Protect the top edge of the vertical partition with a block of scrap wood before striking it with a hammer.

Screw the protruding arm of the bracket to the top edge and secure the second bracket into the shelf rabbet and the wall.

Fit the supporting batten in place against the underside of the line, fixing it to the wall with 2in (50mm) No 8 screws at 12in (300mm) centers. Offer up the next vertical and fix it to the wall using the same method as the first. Repeat this process for the remaining two verticals, gluing in the shelves as you work along the wall. The floor "dowel" can be left out of the two middle vertical partitions.

SERVING SHELF

The serving shelf sits on the battens and verticals. If you are using marble or slate, no fixing will be necessary as its weight will be enough. For a wood shelf, use dowels to fix it to the top edges of the uprights and quadrants. If the shelf is to be painted, simply screw down into the uprights.

UPPER SHELF SECTION

Measure the distance from the top of the serving shelf to the ceiling. Measure it in three places – both ends and the middle. Take the smallest dimension, if they differ, and cut four verticals to this length from 1in (25mm) MDF. Each vertical must be 6in (150mm) wide. Measure up 25¾in (655mm) from the bottom

LIGHT
VALANCE
UPPER VERTICAL PARTITION
PLATE-RETAINING RAIL
UPPER SHELVES
HALF-ROUND SHELF
MIRROR
SERVING SHELF
CURVED CENTER SHELF
LOWER SHELF
LOWER VERTICAL PARTITION

Side Section of Display Unit
This section shows how the shelves are spaced, and the positioning of the quadrant supports of the lower shelves. Note that the mirror slopes forward to display items placed on the serving shelf.

Serving and Display Unit with Mirrors

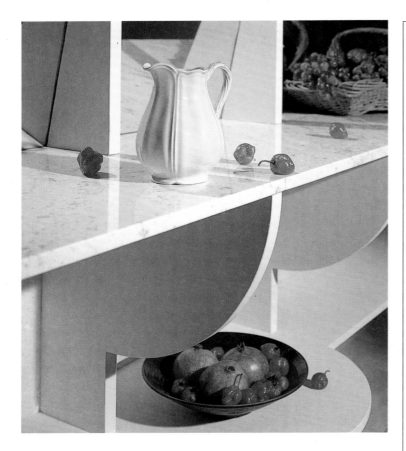

Double the Impact with Angled Mirrors

The angled mirrors behind the serving shelf reflect its contents and create a lush and dramatic display of color and shape. The curved shelves and quadrants add further interest to the composition.

edge. This gives a good size and enables the mirror to rest at a good angle. Divide the remainder of each vertical by the number of shelves required and space them equally.

Routing for Shelves

Using a ¾in (19mm) cutter as before, rout out grooves to a depth of ¼in (6mm) for the shelves on all the inner faces. (Again, do not cut on the outside of the end sections.)

Mirror Section

Use the router with a ¼in (6mm) straight bit to make the grooves for the mirror. Cut ¹⁄₁₂in (2mm) in from the front and rear edges, to make a

¼in (6mm) diagonal groove, as shown (far right). Do this on the inner faces of all four verticals.

Plate-retaining Rails

Mark the centers of the holes to hold the rails, on the inner faces of the verticals, 4in (100mm) up from the shelf rabbets and 3in (75mm) in from the front edges. Bore 1in (25mm) diameter holes, ½in (12mm) deep, using a router or a drill fitted with a spade bit.

Upper Straight Shelves

These are all edge-banded at the front in the same way as the lower shelves, to a total depth of 6in

ROUTING UPPER VERTICAL PARTITIONS FOR SHELVES AND MIRROR

Dowel hole

3in (75mm)

4in (100mm)

Grooves for shelves

Mirror groove

25in (655mm)

25in (655mm)

25in (655mm)

Outer

Inner

(150mm), including edge-banding. Cut the required number, then glue and nail edge-banding to the front.

HALF-ROUND SHELVES

Using ¾in (19mm) MDF, cut out a rectangle for each shelf required, 15⅝ × 19¼in (393.5 × 487mm).

Draw a line across the sheet 6in (150mm) in from the back edge. The center point of this line will be the center point for the circle. Draw and cut out the half circle at the front on each shelf (see page 64).

CUTTING GROOVES

With a router, cut a groove for each mirror in the underside of two of the straight shelves; the groove should be 1/12in (2mm) back from the front edge. It should be ¼in (6mm) deep and the same thickness as the mirror plus a little extra to allow the mirror to slot in. Cut a corresponding groove in the underside of one of the half-round shelves. Measure off from the grooves the exact dimensions for each mirror, making sure you allow for the amount slotted in the top and sides.

① Mirror and Partition Fitting
Top edge of mirror is housed in a groove in underside of shelf. Angle brackets secure vertical panels.

The bottom edges of the mirror should be polished to avoid damage to the serving shelf.

Again with a router, cut plate grooves in the upper faces of all upper straight shelves, ¼in (6mm) deep and wide, and forward from back edge to accommodate plates.

PLATE-RETAINING RAILS

Calculate the lengths for the plate-retaining rails to fit into the straight shelf sections, adding ⅜in (10mm) at each end so they slot into the uprights. Cut the required number from 1in (25mm) diameter dowel.

ASSEMBLY

Put one of the uprights in position (one against a wall first if you have one) resting on the serving shelf, directly above the lower vertical. This upright is secured either to a side wall with screws at 12in (300mm) centers or to the back wall with angle brackets set into the shelf rabbets as with the lower section. Fit an additional bracket in the mirror section, as low as possible behind the groove. This will be hidden by the mirror.

② Fitting of Valances
Valances are cut from ¾in (19mm) MDF. They shield strip lights and are secured with angle brackets.

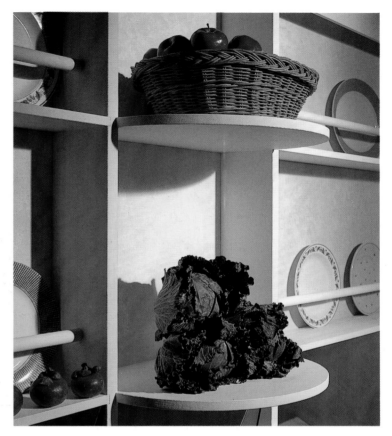

USING THE UPPER DISPLAY SHELVES TO BEST ADVANTAGE
The upper shelves reach to the ceiling for maximum visual impact and to give plenty of storage space. The half-round shelves bring objects on view forward in a dramatic way.

For the next part of the assembly you will need an extra pair of hands. Slot the mirror and rails into place, gluing as you go. You will need to sand the ends of the dowels to fit.

Place the next upright in position. Secure it with angle brackets attached to the shelf rabbets and at the very top, on both sides. You can fit an extra bracket on one side, before the mirror is installed.

Plane or sand the shelves to slot over the brackets, then glue the shelf edges and slot into place.

Position the central mirror, rails, and the next upright, and secure as before. Fit the shelves, then repeat the procedure for the last section.

VALANCE

Measure the internal dimensions between the verticals for the three valances. Cut them to length from ¾in (19mm) MDF. They must be deep enough to shield the strip lights. Fit angle brackets to each end of each valance section, then screw them into the uprights about 3in (75mm) back from the front edge.

At this point you can attach extra brackets from the back of the wall to the top of the verticals to give extra rigidity, but ensure that the valance will conceal these. Fit the tungsten strip lights. Finally, use a filler to cover screwheads before decoration.

DIVIDED SHELVES

CONSTRUCTION

These kitchen shelves are ideal for storing dishes and utensils neatly and safely. The basic shelves and dividers can be made from either $\frac{3}{4}$in (19mm) laminated plywood or from $\frac{5}{8}$in (15mm) laminated particleboard. The lower shelf has a 1in (25mm) deep edge-banding on the front which is glued and nailed flush with the underside.

The upper and lower shelves run to the full width of the unit. Main vertical dividers are installed between them at 45in (1140mm) intervals and at the ends. The center shelves fit between the main dividers. If you are storing plates, glassware, and pans, you can install additional $\frac{3}{8}$in (10mm) dividing leaves between the main dividers.

Dowel joints are used for all of the components in this unit. First, the intermediate shelf units are assembled on the main upright dividers using $\frac{5}{16}$in (8mm) diameter beech dowels $1\frac{9}{16}$in (40mm) long. Then the top and bottom shelves are assembled over dowels of the same size in the top and bottom edges of the main dividers.

Smaller dowels ($\frac{1}{4} \times 1\frac{1}{4}$in [6 × 30mm]) are used to attach the plywood dividers to the underside of the top shelf. The unit is covered at the back with a panel of $\frac{1}{8}$in (4mm) plywood or painted hardboard. The panel is nailed to the edges of the main dividers and shelves, and also to the thin plywood dividers.

To prevent items rolling off the intermediate shelf, you can attach either a deep edge-banding (second bay from left in the main photograph), or a hardwood beading $\frac{1}{4} \times \frac{1}{4}$in (6 × 6mm) to the shelf surface about 2in (50mm) back from the front edge (as in the bay with the dinner-plate rack).

Install the unit by screwing into the walls at each end through the end dividers, and by attaching the main dividers in the rear wall with the brackets used to hang kitchen cupboards. Whichever method is chosen, it is essential that the screws are long enough to pass through the plaster and into the masonry.

❶ The Critical Dimensions
In this exploded view, only two bays are shown, but the unit can be extended to room width. Between the main dividers, plywood dividing leaves can be installed to the undersides of the top and intermediate shelves.

❷ Jointing Main Components
Dowel joints are recommended, although dado joints can be used if greater stength is required.

❸ Mounting Plywood Dividers
These are fitted to shelf undersides using dowels or dado slots, then glued and nailed to the back panel.

Back panel

Top shelf

Main dividers

Intermediate shelf

Edge-banding

Bottom shelf

Edge-banding

HANGING BARS

CONSTRUCTION

Hanging bars for storage make a feature of the rafters in this attic room. The rafters hold the bars a short distance from the sloping ceiling, allowing the space behind to be used for storage. A decorative dado rail above the cupboard front stops anything from slipping down.

If your attic room has a flat, sloping ceiling, then fit false rafters to the ceiling by nailing through the plaster into the real rafters beneath. Alternatively, mount the hanging bars on lumber blocks, or in wardrobe brackets. The hanging bars can be steel piping, such as black-painted electrical conduit, or the hollow tube sold for closet poles in wardrobes. This is available with a chrome, nickel, or brass finish, or with a white plastic coating. Alternatively, you can use copper piping. In all cases, a $\frac{3}{4}$in (19mm) diameter is recommended.

To support the bars, use saddle-type pipe clips screwed directly into the undersides of the rafters. Mount the lowest bars first, about 4in (100mm) above the dado rail. With a long, straight batten, pencil, and carpenter's level, mark the clip positions on the rafters. Mount the clips at each end first. Tie a string line between these to double check that they are level, then start attaching the intermediate clips, loosely at this stage, working towards the middle and using the string line as a guide. Fit the tubing into the clips, then attach the remaining screws. Use twin-thread screws (or particle-board screws) for securing the clips. Attach the second and third rails in the same way, spacing each 4in (100mm) from the rail below. If you have a flat, sloping ceiling and you intend to mount the hanging bars in wardrobe-rail support brackets, first snap a chalked string line on the surface of the ceiling to leave a horizontal line as a guide for positioning the brackets. Next, locate the rafter positions using a small metal detector (ceiling fixing nails will be driven into rafters). Attach the support brackets against the marked line using twin-threaded screws.

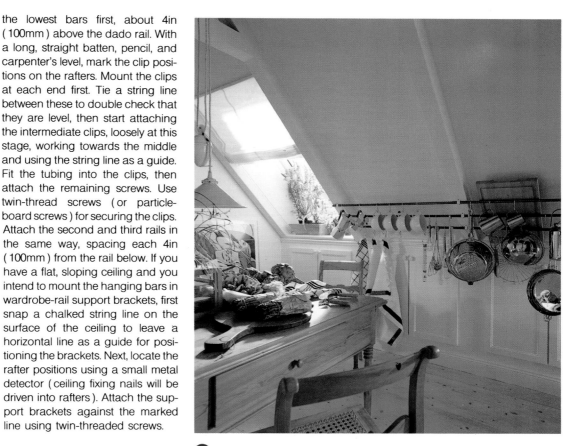

① Attaching the Bars
Support the bars, 4in (100mm) apart, with pipe clips. Align with a carpenter's level. Saddle pipe clips (shown) look most effective, but modern equivalents are suitable. Place beveled wood anchors in the pipe ends.

② Using Hidden Rafters
Where rafters are hidden, mount the bars in wardrobe-rail support brackets attached to the rafters. Alternatively, secure false rafters to the ceiling, or attach the hanging bars to mounting blocks, which are secured to the rafters.

SUSPENDED SHELVES

These shelves suspended over a breakfast bar make excellent use of space that would otherwise be wasted, as well as providing a light and airy divider between the kitchen and the dining area.

The shelves must be suspended securely by using steel piping secured firmly to the ceiling joists. You may be able to get chrome-steel tubing in the required lengths and threaded for attaching into screw-fixed securing plates. Metal fabricators and ships chandlers are likely sources. An alternative is to use lengths of threaded steel rods. These are covered by the steel tubing which is used for wardrobe closet poles and which is ideal for spacing the suspended shelves on the threaded rod. Closet poles are available with a chrome, nickel (matte), or brass finish, or covered with a white plastic coating.

The shelves can be solid hardwood to match the worktop, although it is perfectly acceptable to make them from a hollow lumber frame clad with plywood panels. The panels can have a hardwood ve-

neer to match the worktop. It is important that support battens are placed at regular intervals within the hollow framework.

The upper shelf can be made up and hardwood edge-banding applied around it to hide the edges of the plywood facing panels and to give the appearance of solid wood.

With the lower shelf, it is best to attach the underside facing panel *after* the shelf is in place and the nuts on the suspension rods have been tightened with a wrench.

With the hollow method of shelf building, allow for cut-outs in one edge if you wish to hang glasses by their stems. In this case, the hardwood edge-banding on that edge will have to be increased to at least the depth of the cut-outs.

To hold the shelves in their required positions, they are suspended on lengths of steel threaded rod inside steel tubes which act as spacers. Use $\frac{3}{8}$in (10mm) threaded rod which is commonly available in 36in (915mm) lengths up to 6ft (1830mm). It can be cut to length with a hacksaw, or, where the ceiling

1 The Basic Construction
The shelves can be a simple lumber frame skinned with plywood sheets and edge-banded with hardwood.

2 Support Batten
Lengths of threaded rod hang from a 2 × 3in (50 × 75mm) batten bolted between convenient ceiling joists.

3 Drilled Upper Shelf
Holes are drilled through cross-rails to take threaded rod. Decorative steel tubing spaces the shelves.

DOOR FRONTS

is high it can be extended by joining lengths with extension nuts.

At the top, the rod is bolted through holes drilled in 2 × 3in (50 × 75mm) lumber which itself is bolted (on its side) between ceiling joists above the shelving position. When making the shelf frames, work out where the hangers will be and make sure that there are frame cross-rails at these positions to give additional support.

The ¾in (19mm) steel tubing is passed over the protruding threaded rod before the upper shelf is installed and held with a nut on the rod (use an extension nut if you need to extend the rod). Shorter tubes are slipped over the threaded rod before you fit the lower shelf, which is also bolted in place on the underside. The securing nuts can be recessed into the frame cross-rails before the bottom panel is attached. With a solid wood shelf, the nuts can be fitted in pre-drilled recesses which are filled with matching anchors glued in place. The anchors are then planed and sanded flush with the surface.

❹ Concealed Nut Attachments
Drill recesses in underside of the lower shelf. If solid shelf, anchor the recesses. If hollow, fit a fascia panel.

You can greatly improve the appearance of a kitchen by replacing solid cabinet doors with glazed doors. In this way the contents of the cabinets become a focal point.

It will be virtually impossible to convert the old doors, so remove them, but first noting down their dimensions, and the positions of the hinges and handles. Remove both for use on the new doors.

Make new doors from 1 × 3in (25 × 75mm) S4S lumber (the old doors were probably ¾in [19mm] thick). Cut the side rails slightly longer than required – they can be cut to the correct length later. Cut the top and bottom rails to length to allow for the type of corner joint to be used. For the strongest job, use haunched mortise and tenon joints (*see* **Techniques, page 28**) with the molding mitered to form a neat corner as in the diagram below. After the joints have been made and the doors assembled, the lengths of waste on the side rails can be cut off flush with the top and bottom rails. You will need a router to cut a rabbet along one edge at the back to take the glass. Turn over the frame and round over the front inner edge if required using a router fitted with a rounding over cutter.

If you do not feel confident to tackle a haunched mortise and tenon joint, you can make the door frames using dowel joints (*see* **Techniques, page 30**). These, if properly glued, will be strong enough.

The glass fits into the rabbet from the back of the door. It is bedded on putty and held with glass beading secured by brads. These must be driven in very carefully. Various styles of beading are available. If you do not have a router, use a molding to create a rabbet. Glue and nail it to the inner edge of the frame at the front, creating a rabbet behind for the glass to be fitted, as above. Miter the corners. Replace hinges, apply finish, and add handles.

❶ Fitting Frame and Glass
Use a haunched mortise and tenon joint (below). Rabbet frame; round front inner edge; insert glass.

❷ Alternative Method
Form rabbet by nailing molding to frame's inner edge. Secure glass with putty and beading.

PART 3

LIVING ROOMS AND WORK SPACES

More than any other room, a living room should reflect your personal taste and way of life. It is here that your own ideas of comfort, elegance, style, and decoration can be put into practice. You can dramatically enhance the personality of the room by restoring existing features or introducing character by adding architraves, moldings, and other architectural devices. Shelves in living rooms are normally used for displaying treasures and collections, and exert a strong influence on the room. When you do-it-yourself, shelves can be custom-made to suit the room and your possessions. In addition, an ugly fireplace can be revamped, and wooden floors can be made good by stripping and waxing, staining or painting. The installation of a new lighting system can transform a room.

Workrooms and studies must be both practical and comfortable: with a little planning you can convert a small room (or even a corner of a room) into a purpose-built home office or workroom. With the right shelving, lighting, and display you can make your work area both a delightful place to be in and a truly functional space for your particular requirements.

DESIGN FOR LIVING

The living room is a place where any work you do yourself should be of the highest quality that you are capable, given time and money.

The shelving system in this comfortable cozy living room`(previous page) is well finished and has been cleverly designed to fit wall-to-wall. It also runs around the room at picture-rail height, above the door. The top shelf provides a decorative display area for an attractive and imposing collection of wooden horses. Accent lighting is provided by ceiling downlighters.

DISTINCTIVE DISPLAY

Designing a display unit involves careful consideration of many factors. A fitted unit for storage and display must respond to the shape, character, and decorative scheme of the room as well as to the objects it will house. In a luxurious modern house (right) a designer has created a room of strong, clean lines in which the materials are important. The display unit for contemporary ceramics, books, a television, and a VCR, with useful drawers beneath for hidden storage, has continued this theme. Natural wood has been used for the wide shelf and as edge-banding for the upper shelves, providing graphic lines in a quality material. The positioning of the ceramic pots was of importance in the design, but equally well thought-out was the position of the television. The gray shelves and drawer fronts complement the sofa and blend beautifully with the color-washed wall behind and its striking modern painting.

In a more conventional setting (below left) low closets fill an alcove. The space above has been used creatively and lends character to the room. To provide a large area for plants and bulky objects, there is a gap above the closets and then small pigeon-holes for individual items, with a further section for books.

The equal squares formed by a simple white display unit (below right) echo the design of a glazed door. Such a design suits a collection of treasured objects which require prominent display and which are linked to one another through texture and color.

AROUND THE CORNER

The owner of this room clearly likes to work close to a collection of books. The polished floor and antique furniture ensure that the room (left) retains the atmosphere of a study rather than a home office. In keeping with this character, the custom-made black shelves fit neatly into two corners of the room and are strong and distinctive. Shelves finished in cream or white, and designed to fill rather than edge a wall, would "disappear" into the structure of the room. With this design, the shelves, and the books they contain, are given prominence. Black used so extensively can be very effective, but it has to be linked to the decorative scheme – hence the black chair seat and lampshade.

SMALL SPACES

In an open-plan studio, the kitchen is part of the living room but cleverly separated from it by a small island unit (below left). An upright radiator has been installed to save further space. Because space is limited, there is very little display in the room and the design is utterly plain and easily built by a home woodworker.

In a small awkward corner of a living room, an inventive design for shelves, an alcove, and low closets works on many levels (below right). It uses space effectively, providing neat hidden storage behind plain doors as well as open shelves for books. The alcove also provides an enhancing framed display for a plaster bust, which demands pride of place in the room. By painting the whole structure white to match the walls and avoiding decorative detailing, the unit successfully merges into the room.

ASSESSING THE WORKLOAD

Nothing can rival hand-made, custom-designed, original fixtures and features in a living room. However, this is not a room in which to experiment with your wood-working ability: the standard of work must be as high as you can make it, the quality of the materials as good as you can afford, and the detailing and finishing as perfect as your skills allow.

If, for example, you want a fully fitted closet which is going to add character to the room as well as useful storage, try building a similar structure as a trial run in a less exposed area of the house. If you want some fitted shelves for displaying a treasured collection, think carefully about the design, and, if you are not particularly confident, choose the design which is easiest to construct.

Some of the most effective tasks you can undertake in the living room will, if they are done properly, "disappear" when completed. Wire management is

one of them: remove baseboards and floorboards so that you can channel wires from lights, the television, music equipment, and so on to an area that will be hidden when you replace the woodwork. If this is not possible, box-in wires and any water pipes as necessary. Flat speaker wires can always be run under carpet.

Another effective home improvement task is to dispense with superfluous fixtures. Unwanted shelves attract clutter, so do not think that you must always add fixtures to a room; sometimes taking away unnecessary elements can be equally important and liberating.

The architectural details of a room have a subtle but important impact. By revamping or replacing woodwork such as architraves, dado rails, valances, paneling, baseboards, and so on you will greatly improve the appearance of the room. All of these tasks are relatively simple, but enormously effective.

INSPIRING WORK

The three rooms illustrated here have each benefited from both good design and the work of highly skilled professional craftspeople, who have created well-conceived and superbly finished work.

A broad display shelf (above left) has distinctive and strongly decorative metal supports designed to define the structure and give it, and the objects it carries, handsome prominence in the room.

In a beautifully mellow, welcoming, and elegant room (above right), the distinctive oak baseboard and the fireplace's wooden frame are absolutely made-to-measure.

Magnificent woodwork (opposite) in a Shaker room results from the skills of generations of craftsmen. The simple structures are stunning in their practical beauty. The detailing on joints, handles, and hinges has a charming quality which declares the great pleasure and care with which these fixtures were conceived and constructed.

STRUCTURAL SHELVING

Shelving that is designed specifically for the space that it fills and the objects which it displays is likely to be far better than any that you buy ready-made or in kit form. The crucial point to remember is that shelves should always blend in well with the dimensions and architecture of a room rather than stand out from them.

If you are installing shelves in an alcove, fill the alcove from top to bottom and from side to side. Never run a line of shelves down the center of an alcove, because you will create ugly gaps around it. If you are building a wall of shelves, make sure that they cover the entire wall. Where the wall is interrupted by a door, why not frame the door with the shelving structure.

When a room contains awkward spaces, such as a low or sloping attic wall, consider installing a shelving system which can make excellent use of an otherwise wasted space.

Framing shelves by lining the area to be shelved with wood at the top, bottom, and sides will give them a professional finish and a neat definition. Scribing the frame and securing it to the wall is no more difficult than installing kitchen units; the shelves themselves will then be attached to the wooden frame rather than to the wall, and brackets or supports can be incorporated into the frame. Dividers and shelves can then be made to the same specification as the frame, and act as supports for the shelves as well as giving a pigeon-hole effect.

As as general rule, it is a good idea to use a shelving system that allows brackets to be completely invisible. One of the most effective ways of achieving this is to make the shelves from hollow oblong pieces of wood rather than from single planks, so that brackets can be attached inside the structure. This method of attachment also gives the shelves a strong, sculptural line,

so that they blend in with the walls of the room when painted.

Glass shelves that slot into the two side walls of an alcove look very neat, although achieving this effect is not always possible. Constructing a wooden frame on to which glass shelves can be fitted is a suitable alternative, and also allows you to incorporate wiring for concealed lighting underneath and behind the wooden frame. Glass shelves when lit from above or below look especially attractive.

Sometimes battens or brackets can be used to decorative effect. Specially-made iron brackets can make a very strong feature of shelving in a room.

MADE TO MEASURE
You cannot have the sort of shelving shown on these pages unless they are built specifically for the space into which they fit. Fitted shelves are an important asset in a living room. They provide open storage which is unique to that room and lend an individual character to it. Bought shelves which vaguely fill a space can never complement the shape and dimensions of a room in the same way.

In two of the rooms, whole walls have been shelved to great effect. A large collection of books (opposite) stretches from floor to ceiling and frames an existing window and radiator. A more problematic space has been filled (center) allowing the sloping ceiling to dictate the dimensions of the shelving structure ensuring a strong, architectural quality.

ALCOVE SHELVES
In two modern interiors, alcoves have been specifically created to carry display shelves. These can be easily incorporated into a do-it-yourself scheme using a false wall or building out from an existing wall to form an alcove.

In a large expanse of wall (top) the alcove of shelves breaks up an otherwise flat area and is filled with an informal arrangement of objects. Because of the defined shelf area, the effect remains neat and contained.

A half-wall screens two sections of a room (below) and has been left hollow to carry attractive inset glass shelves.

STORAGE SOLUTIONS

Space is perhaps the greatest luxury a home can offer these days. If you live in a limited space then it is important to stow away as many as possible of life's essentials. Objects and clutter can make even a generous room seem smaller, so make sure that anything you do store out in the open is worthy of the visual attention that it will receive.

If you enjoy being surrounded by personal treasures, private mementoes, ethnic artifacts picked up on travels abroad, and collections of everything from junk to antiques, then provide yourself with the shelf space to carry these objects. Fill alcoves, whole walls, spare corners in halls, free space under stairs and on landings with shelves. The shelves themselves should be simple and not prominent, since the purpose is to display your precious clutter.

A carefully constructed collection of one type of object calls for a quite different approach. If, for instance, you have a collection of 1930s china, rare books, antique bronzes, or model cars discovered over the years then you will want to display these objects as a coherent group. For this purpose, neat, symmetrical shelving placed in a prominent position is the ideal solution.

If you confine yourself to a few very special objects, then give them space and frame them in an alcove of shelves lit from above, or place one object on a handmade shelf. The area around them should be kept empty.

In the living room, there are items other than personal treasures to consider. Books, stereo equipment, records, tapes and compact disks, clocks, plants, and many other objects may require shelving; try to design it so that the objects fit the shelving by spacing and dividing the shelves appropriately. Doing-it-yourself gives you the opportunity to ensure that your shelving units are custom-designed.

If you are creating a special display area, consider incorporating lighting to highlight the objects. Make the shelves themselves as stylish as possible by using good quality materials and a clean, strong design that suits both the room's decorative scheme and the objects on display.

Well-designed shop fixtures, as well as ideas from magazines and the inspiration from these pages, should provide you with an interesting source of ideas.

Finally, be absolutely sure that the shelving you build is strong enough to take the weight you intend to place on it. There is nothing so sad as a sagging shelf.

SYMMETRICAL BALANCE

Simple alcove shelves on either side of a chimney breast (opposite above) carry a large collection of colorful china and objects.

Double doors are completely framed by a shelving structure which fills an entire wall (opposite below left).

On either side of a window (opposite below right) a collection of fine glass is well displayed on shelves which form alcoves. For added character, an attractive old radiator has been restored and painted, rather than hidden.

STRONG SUPPORT

To add interest in a modern room (below left), a wall has been given an alcove to carry shelves which are lit internally. Such a structure can be built out from any partition wall or screening unit.

An asymmetrical wall under sloping eaves has created uneven alcoves (below center) but these have been used effectively to carry strong, broad shelves.

In a home office (below right) a table slots neatly between the natural wood supports of two equal shelving units. Note the use of carrier bags for storage on lower shelves, a neat and cheap solution.

TAILOR-MADE DISPLAY

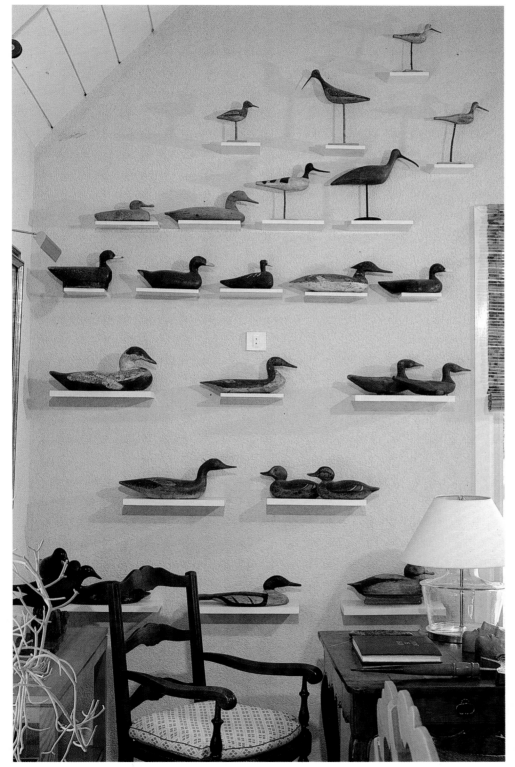

GLORIOUS GLASS

Glass shelves are particularly effective for displays because they are narrow, unobtrusive, and transparent. They can be supported by various means: simple studs support smoked glass (opposite above left) which beautifully displays a collection of fossils. It is easier to use glass in an alcove such as this, or in a sloping recess (opposite below right) formed above a low closet. The glass is not vulnerable to damage by protruding into the room, so it can safely hold delicate objects such as these antique glasses.

Where a glass shelf is not contained within a framework the supports must be very strong. Metal bars (opposite above right) hold thick glass shelves which are also being secured by the back wall into which they have been recessed for added support.

Tough steel wire (available from ships' chandlers) is partially obscured by a hanging ornament (opposite below center), and runs through holes in the glass to suspend these shelves. Give glass shelves a light source from above so that diffused light filters through to illuminate the objects below.

COLOR FOR CONTRAST

The understatement of glass is one way of enhancing a display. A colorful setting can offer another. In an emerald green room (opposite below left) the vivid wall color has been carried on to the shelves to blend them with the room and to provide a stunning background for books and objects. The thick, hollow shelves conceal their supports to give an architectural unity.

PERCHED ON THE WALL

Individual perches have been created for a collection of decoy ducks and carved birds (left) to form a truly original grouping on one wall. A perfect example of an imaginative display, tailor-made for a special collection.

FIREPLACES AND HEARTHS

Fireplaces should be considered in two ways. The first is as a source of heat. If that source of heat is a wood- or coal-burning fire with all the associated warm glow, comfort and well-being, then your living room has a great natural asset. It may be dirty, wasteful of energy, hard work, and highly impractical, but you can only curl up and feel really cozy in front of a *real* fire. Radiators, under-floor heating, electric and gas fires hardly compensate, though some highly realistic coal-effect gas fires are available.

You may want to re-open an existing fireplace that has been blocked off. Tampering with electricity or gas in any way involves checking local codes concerning utilities. It is often safer, and sometimes essential, to leave the removal of gas or electric heating fixtures to professionals. You must also check that a fireplace is unblocked satisfactorily, that the flue is not cracked or damaged (which could lead to the escape of noxious fumes), and that the grate you install is both suitable and efficient for the situation. Get a professional to check the fireplace before you make any changes yourself.

The second consideration of the fireplace is as a focal point for the room and its decorative scheme. A full-fledged fire surround and mantel form a dominating feature in a room. Removing and replacing a surround is often simpler than you may imagine, but the task is a building, rather than a decorating, one. The work will probably involve some brick and plaster work as well as woodwork. Seek professional guidance and do not undertake the task unless you feel confident in your ability to do the work well. When installing a grate and the surrounding fireproof bricks or metal shield, your work should be checked very carefully, since any work which is less than perfect could lead to serious cracks or even an

FOCAL POINTS

A number of inventive design ideas are combined in an outstanding open fireplace (above). The chimney breast is flanked by windows which give added prominence to the fireplace; a magnificent slab of marble forms the raised hearth. The fireplace is a simple square framed in galvanized steel, perfectly suited to the style of the room. Above the fireplace is a clever variation on the traditional mantel shelf. A small shelf has been built into the chimney breast and a pretty arched alcove curves above it.

A more traditional approach (center) is seen in this wooden fire surround and mantel, designed to match the adjoining dado rail and paneling details. The wood is finished with a subtle paint technique that highlights the decorative detailing, while a warm glow from the flames is reflected from the metal fire backing.

PURE AND SIMPLE

A simple but effective design (below) reduces the fireplace to an opening framed in brick and wood. It can be just as important to remove a decorative fireplace from a room as to add one to it, especially if you want the room to have a modern atmosphere. Again, the wooden frame echoes other adjoining woodwork — here, it is the baseboard. The hearth has also been reduced: it is merely a row of heat-resistant stones that abut with the wooden floor.

outbreak of fire. Never underestimate the disruption and mess to the living room which this whole process will involve.

The style of your fireplace will affect the style of the room. A grand installation will add distinction to a period room, but may look ridiculous in more modest surroundings. As a general rule, try to match the period of the fireplace to that of the room. Removing an ugly recent design in a Victorian building and replacing it with an original Victorian fireplace will undoubtedly improve the room, particularly if your overall scheme involves restoring period architectural details throughout the house.

Alternatively, you may wish to reduce rather than enhance the impact of the fireplace. Taking out an overbearing monstrosity and leaving a neat opening, edged, perhaps, with a rim of galvanized steel or with plain white heat-resistant tiles, will suit a more clean-cut and minimal room. You do not have to replace a mantel if you want a plain surround and it may suit your scheme to do away with the fireplace altogether and present a flat-fronted chimney breast. Another option would be to use the hollow chimney breast for built-in shelving and display.

There is an enormous range of period, reproduction, and modern grates available, as well as fireplace surrounds so it may be interesting to design and build your own fireplace. Your work must be of a high quality since a fireplace is such a focal point in a room. You can use exposed or plastered brickwork, or wood to great effect. Marble slabs for a grate and slips for a surround are also a possibility. You can buy period tiles, reproductions of traditional designs, or contemporary tiles. Whatever approach you decide to take, do not begin until you have a clear design to follow or an example to copy.

A PERFECT SETTING

An old setting serves as a reminder of the original architectural character in an otherwise sweeping redesign of an Arts and Crafts villa (above). The chimney has had its adjoining walls removed to open up the ground floor, and it now acts as an impressive screen between living and dining areas. This delightful iron and tile fireplace with its decorative wood mantel could be an inspiration for a home-built fireplace. Alternatively, a period fireplace can be salvaged, or bought from a specialist and installed in a living room. Take care to choose a fireplace which suits the era and decorative scheme of the room.

Another fireplace which perfectly combines with the style of the room is this one in natural brick (center). In a relaxed living room, the warm, mellow tones of the brick match the furnishings and objects. A brick fireplace is not beyond the building capabilities of a good amateur bricklayer.

MODERN AND MINIMAL

A striking design in a minimal modern room (below). The fireplace surround is made from high quality heat-resistant ceramic tiles which carry over from the floor. The energy source is provided by gas, not a real fire, and allows for the use of these exotic, indestructible, volcanic rocks as "fuel." The grate is formed by a basket of galvanized steel, and a panel of specially heat-resistant glass is used for the reflective backing.

FLOORING

In many houses the living room has a variety of roles to play. It is not just somewhere to sit, relax, and entertain: often it has to double as a playroom, a study, a library, a television room, and maybe even a dining area.

All of these functions have to be taken into account when choosing the flooring. One thing is certain: the room will be in constant use, so the flooring must be capable of withstanding a lot of wear.

Although the flooring will run from wall-to-wall in most cases, it can be combined with other floor coverings. For example, a varnished wooden floor with a central square of carpet or a rug laid on it can be most effective.

If you prefer a hard floor, then tiles – whether ceramic, quarry, marble, slate, or stone – can all be used in living rooms if the setting is right. They can be softened by the addition of rag rugs and dhurries.

Wood, of course, is an excellent flooring material. You can lay a new wood-strip or wood-block surface over an existing floor, or you can use the existing wooden floorboards, as long as they are in good condition.

RESTORING A WOODEN FLOOR

Take a good look at the floor to make sure it is suitable for restoration. If it is very badly worn, it may need to be completely renovated, or covered with an entirely new wooden floor.

If there are wide gaps between the floorboards, fill them with wooden strips. These should be planed along their length to form a slight taper. Apply aliphatic resin adhesive to the sides, and then tap the strips into place in the gaps. Allow the glue to set, then plane the strips level with the surface of the floor.

If the floorboards are uneven because of heavy wear that is no more than about $\frac{1}{8}$in (3mm) deep, it may be possible to resurface the floor by sanding it smooth. If the floorboards have worn more deeply, either replace them, or turn the affected boards upside down and re-lay them. Alternatively, cover the floor with plywood and lay a new wood-strip or block floor over the top.

If your floorboards are old, try to replace the worn ones with matching old boards from a secondhand lumberyard or an architectural salvage yard. New boards, even when they are stained to match the old ones, will tend to stand out.

RE-LAYING FLOORBOARDS

If there are damaged boards, or many wide gaps between boards, it will be best to lift the old boards by prying them up, so that the best boards can be relaid without gaps, and replacement boards fitted to fill the empty spaces.

After removing the old boards, pull out the old fixing nails. Re-lay the boards, ensuring that they are tightly pressed together, by using folding wedges (see **Techniques, page 21**) between each block of four or five boards and a scrap of wood temporarily nailed to the joists. Nail boards in place before removing wedges and laying another four or five boards.

BLEACHED WOOD
This impressive wood floor has been bleached, given a pale paint wash, and then varnished for durability. It will not resist heavy wear but can be easily restored, and provides a beautiful background for the room.

LUXURIOUS MARBLE
Marble slips have a splendid impact on a room and can be used effectively in bathrooms and halls as well as living rooms. Marble is a cold and hard substance; however, it is also undeniably luxurious.

PAINTED WOOD
In a large loft space, a wooden floor has been painted pure white. If you are prepared to retouch it regularly, and use existing boards which are less than perfect, this is a simple solution to a broad expanse of floor.

RESURFACING A FLOOR BY SANDING

Make sure that all floorboards are securely nailed down. Any that are split or badly damaged should be replaced. Pull out protruding carpet tacks, and with a hammer and nailset, drive down the heads of the board-fixing nails so that they are about $\frac{1}{8}$in (3mm) below the surface.

You should rent an industrial floor sander for treating the main part of the floor, with a smaller hand disc sander or belt sander for finishing the edges near the baseboards.

The floor sander looks like a giant vacuum cleaner with a revolving drum around which abrasive sheets are attached. Although floor sanders have dust extraction bags, these are not entirely effective, so wear a dust mask and old clothes. Before starting, open the windows in the room and use masking tape to seal around doors leading to adjacent rooms.

The sander should be used along the length of the floorboards, never across them, as this can cause scratches.

Tilt the sander back before switching on, then gradually lower it to the floor and allow it to move forward under its own power, restraining it slightly so that it does not travel too fast. Work forwards and backwards in a line with the boards, overlapping each pass by 2in (50mm).

After the main area has been sanded, sand the edges with the hand machine. Finish corners with a scraper and a hand sanding block. Finally, vacuum the floor and wipe over it with alcohol.

FINISHING TREATMENTS

Staining Any replacement boards that are lighter in color than the rest should be stained darker. With a rag, apply the stain and rub it evenly into the wood to bring out the desired color. Remember that most clear finishes deepen the color of the wood, so test it first in a corner.

Sealing Floorboards can be sealed with several coats of one- or two-part polyure-thane-based varnish/sealer which dries to a clear gloss, satin, or matte finish on the surface. Alternatively, use an oil-based sealer, which will soak into the surface to give a scratch-resistant sheen. To darken the color of the floor, use a varnish stain or simply polish the floor with wax.

Liming This technique involves rubbing a white pigment into the grain of the wood before sealing it. It is easiest to use white paint thinned with turpentine since these materials are readily available, but you can use limed wax or gesso, which is plaster of Paris. Paint the liming mixture along the boards, covering a small area at a time, and wipe the mixture off with rags, leaving a white stain in the cracks. Finally, seal the floor with varnish.

Painting If there are many new floorboards, painting will avoid a patchy appearance. Apply undercoat and two coats of a hard-wearing oil-based gloss paint, or a satin finish paint.

COIR MATTING

The natural quality of coir matting has a similar decorative effect to wood and is often a good alternative. In its own right, it is very popular as a muted, warm background for many styles of room, ancient or modern.

CONTEMPORARY WOOD

Wooden floors are available today in a vast range, and many of them are easily installed by an amateur. They are usually sold in sections. This broad-planked floor in pale wood is especially suitable for a light and airy studio.

PERIOD WOOD

Old wood floors, provided the boards have not been partially replaced and are in a reasonable condition, can be beautifully restored by stripping and finishing. They can be stained or oiled to deepen the tone of the wood.

Rooms to Work In

If you work at home, installing a personal workspace will be a major priority when it comes to designing your home. Equally, you may need a private den or study, a well-equipped workshop, a sewing room or a darkroom. Whatever your requirements, if you have a limited budget, you will achieve something far more comfortable, efficient, and practical by designing and building it yourself than by installing ready-made fixtures.

Few home improvement tasks are more satisfying than creating a room, or a section of a room, which is a pleasure to work in. Unlike the rest of your home, you will probably not be sharing a work space or using it for tasks other than those for which it is specifically designed, so you are free to indulge yourself and create your ideal personal work space.

By adapting the projects in this book, you will find that you can create precisely what you need for a tailor-made workroom, whether it is a wall-mounted unit of pigeon-hole shelving, a simple desk top made from a door, or a bulletin board.

Down to Work

The ultimate Modernist environment for a designer – a pure white minimal room (above) – has a work area separated from the main room by the simple, but highly effective, device of a raised back to a desk unit.

An ingenious use of space on one side of a bedroom (opposite) where high storage shelves are reached by a sliding ladder. A drawing board is fitted into a high-level worksurface partly supported by an attractive stack of drawers. The window is left intact.

HOME OFFICE

Whether you work from home, or merely want a private area for paperwork and home management, for your children to study in, or for your own reading and contemplation, then you must first allocate the amount of space that can be given over to your home office.

A small room is ideal, but if this is not possible or practical, there are many ways to screen off a section or corner of a living room or bedroom, part of a hallway or landing, or even a part of the garage. Work areas should be neither too enclosed nor over exposed. A movable screen may be the answer, so that the room or landing can be easily returned to its original dimensions. Build one in wood, create a Japanese version using stretched paper or fabric, or buy an old or ready-made one, budget permitting. Of course, an effective work area can be made without a partition or screen, but you must define the work space or be prepared for it to spread across the room.

Once the area is defined, plan the office with care and work out precisely what you need to build: a desk or writing surface, shelving, pigeon-holes, display boards, and storage. Keep it simple and remember the practical limitations of wire management, lighting, and comfort.

The desktop can be made from an old door, a plain section of wood, or a bought trestle or desk. Position it close to a natural light source and ensure that all shelves and storage areas are within easy reach when you are sitting at the desk.

We live in the age of the computer. Storing paperwork, files, and notes is no longer any more important than wiring-in the electrical equipment, calculators, personal computer, printer, and keyboard. The development of new technology in the business office has spread across to the home office and the study. Children now use computers to help them study as well as to play computer games for entertainment. These activities are as much a part of their lives as reading or playing with toys.

If you want to build a safe, comfortable workstation incorporating a computer system, then consider the following factors: a surface to carry a keyboard should be lower than a writing desk to ensure that your wrists are not bent and straining when typing; lighting should not interfere with the screen, but should focus on to the desk or writing surface. Invest in a really good office chair rather than risk back injury, and make sure that the room is well-ventilated and adequately heated.

OFFICE STORAGE

The sparse and functional office of a fashion designer has simple adjustable shelving on a standard system of brackets (opposite above). On one wall, the shelves are backed with felt to form a bulletin board.

A unit of closets, with some sliding and some hinged doors (below left), provides ample hidden storage for all office clutter behind a modern desk.

A storage unit which doubles as a screen separating a work area (below right) has access to drawers and cupboards on one side and a fitted desk forms the other.

To display her creative work, a sculptor has suspended glass shelves from strong steel wires (opposite below right) in her home workroom. Hidden storage is cleverly provided by shelves obscured by a Venetian blind.

A PLACE FOR A DESK

In an alcove, a desk is simply a laminated board (opposite below center) offset by two beautiful classic folding chairs.

In a small area adjoining a living room (below center) a wooden structure supports a wide worksurface and extends to form a fitted sofa.

A mezzanine floor has been built-in to a house to create a delightful open office area (opposite below left).

MAKING AN ENTRANCE

There is great potential for home improvements in entrances, hallways, passages, and landings. The front door itself and the area immediately outside it should be welcoming and attractive, perhaps providing shelter and certainly making the transition from outside to indoors as comfortable and convenient as possible.

The entrance hall to any building is important. It sets the scene for what is to come and allows an area for hellos and goodbyes. An entrance that leads directly into a room is rarely ideal, so maintain your hallway at all costs, even if it may appear at first to be a waste of precious living space.

Passages, stairways, and landing are not only the spaces between rooms but are also areas that can be utilized for storage and display, work areas or places to sit.

They should be decorated, planned, and restored with as much care and attention as the living room.

In period homes, the architectural details in the hallways and on the stairs are often neglected or allowed to deteriorate, so concentrate on restoring them to their former glory. In modern buildings, make the entrance as atmospheric as possible and ensure that the lighting is subtle but functional. A common problem, especially for entrance halls, is the clutter that naturally accumulates there – everything from muddy boots, umbrellas, and overcoats, to bicycles, strollers, and unwanted furniture. Create a proper storage area for essential items and discard unwanted objects. Do not forget to buy a large doormat: mud, grit, and moisture can quickly ruin a hall carpet.

FLOOR TO CEILING

An open hall has durable, white ceramic tiles (above left) which reflect the natural light. A fitted closet provides storage.

The hall is defined by a large area of fitted matting (above right). Where walls have been removed in a conversion, a curved wall is a useful and attractive form of transition from hall to living area. Downlighters are suitable for halls and passages. Lights which hang or protrude from the ceiling break up a narrow space and are easily knocked if furniture is being moved.

A wall given over to fitted closets in a passage-way (opposite) provides spacious storage in a compact area. Two types of flooring add to the style of this hall and stairway, with slate used in the entrance and blond wood for the stairs and landing.

Hallways, Passages, and Stairways

Below Stairs

An office has utilized an otherwise dead space below stairs (above) in a hallway. Simple shelves on battens form open storage for books and files. A false back hides wire for lamps and for the personal computer, while a broad shelf forms the desk top.

Open Cloakroom

In a corner of a hall (right), an open cloakroom has been created, reminiscent of a locker room. Across an alcove, the stylish but practical grid of poles provides a useful hanging space and a shoe storage area. Great care has been taken in choosing and mixing pale colors and natural textures to open up and lighten the area. Bleached and white-washed wood paneling is used on some walls and on the ceiling, while other walls have exposed brickwork, painted white. The area is given an added sense of space by the large expanse of mirror.

Building and remodeling projects in halls and passage-ways are dependent on several factors: you may want to restore and highlight moldings, paneling, banisters, dado rails, doors, architraves, or the floor in a period hallway. Ugly gas and electricity meters, wires coming from outside the house, and door bells and alarms may benefit from boxing-in.

You can improve the appearance and character of a dark, tunnel-like hall by replacing a solid door that leads from it with a glazed one, or even by installing an interior window to allow light to enter from another room.

Apart from good restoration and deco-ration, the most important way to improve your entrance and passage-ways is to take a long hard look at the lighting. Such areas often have only an overhead pendant light or two, or unflattering fluorescent strips. Consider installing wall-lights or spotlights on dimmer switches so that a low level of light can be maintained through the night for security reasons. Taking into account the fact that furniture will be moved through the passages and could damage protruding or hanging fixtures, downlighters can be very practical. Decide on your lighting solutions before you undertake restoration or decoration so that you can orga-

TRADITIONAL DISPLAY

The color, style, and impact of a beautifully crafted display unit in a hallway (left) perfectly suits the decorative old tin cans it holds and the architecture of the house. The design, which has been carried up beside the stairs, uses tongue-and-groove paneling and architraves to form separate compartments for the display. In eighteenth- and nineteenth-century houses, pine was painted over, using deep colors rather than left in its natural state.

A HALL OF BOOKS

Beneath the stairs in an ample hallway is the perfect place for extra bookshelves provided they are created to fit precisely the wall they are placed on (above).

nize the wiring and fixtures without disrupting the pristine cleanliness of newly decorated surfaces.

If space is limited elsewhere in your home, take a look around your hall, passage-ways, and landings to see how you can free up extra space for storage and display. All sorts of dead space, empty walls, and under-utilized corners are to be found there. If you follow the guidelines on structural shelving and fitted storage in this book, then rows of book shelves or fitted closets can be built in passages without destroying the dimensions. Designers often integrate floor-to-ceiling closets into halls, with flush doors to give the appearance of a blank wall, behind which all manner of clutter can be conveniently tidied away.

Neat coat hooks can be made into a feature in an entrance hall and a shoe rack can be an attractive addition. Somewhere to place mail, newspapers, circulars, and the many other small items that can congregate near the front door, is also an advantage. A hall table may be the solution but you could consider a unit combining shelves, hooks, and a shoe rack.

If you are desperately in need of a home office space or work area, then do not rule out a corner of the hall or the area under the stairs as a possible solution.

ALCOVE SHELVES AND CUPBOARDS

Many rooms have a chimney breast with an alcove on either side. This design allows you to integrate storage space into an alcove without disturbing the unity of the wall. This is achieved by repeating a triangular molding from the face of the alcove cupboard doors on a decorative panel over the fireplace. Larger moldings of the same shape also form the wall supports for the alcove shelves in the recesses, and for the angled valance which conceals the incandescent strip lights. The repetition of this decorative device provides a unifying element to the design and detailing of the whole wall.

How you decorate the shelves, doors, and panels is dependent on your scheme for the rest of the room. This project is an example of my philosophy that tries to ensure that fixtures which are built-in to the structure of a room blend into the existing architecture and features rather than argue with them.

SECTION OF
CUPBOARD DOOR

top edge of doors
can be beveled
in two ways to
provide a firm
grip

PLAN OF CUPBOARD
& WALL DECORATION

triangular battens
glued & nailed
to door panels —
then filled &
painted.

FRONT ELEVATION.

Triangular shelf-support battens echo the shape of the door & wall decoration

Wall decoration echoes door panels

Concealed lighting at back of shelves.

shelf

triangular shelf-support batten

concealed lighting

light shield grooved into shelf

DETAILS OF SHELF CONSTRUCTION.

ALCOVE SHELVES AND CUPBOARDS

Living rooms always call for a reasonable amount of storage and display space; one way of creating it is to make use of the wasted space on each side of a chimney breast, or in a corner, by installing shelves and a cupboard. A basic design is described below, but the project is easy to adapt to suit your own requirements. You may want alcove shelves and cupboards to house a television, stereo equipment, books, drinks and glasses, or favorite ob-

jects. The function will probably determine the height of your cupboards and shelves, so think about your specific storage needs before you start work. For example, you may want to construct just one cupboard for use as a mini-bar. Alternatively, you may like to vary the number of shelves above a cupboard according to the size, type, and combination of objects you wish to store or display on them.

The "linenfold" decoration which

has been added to the cupboard doors here is echoed on the wall with a panel of the same design, adding an individual and interesting detail. By varying the kind of molding you use on the cupboards and on the wall, you will be able to adapt the overall design to suit your own decorative scheme. Another way of adding a personal touch to the finished project is to vary the cupboard door hardware by using different door handles or knobs.

Whatever the design, it is most important to ensure that all gaps are filled and edges are smoothed so that the cupboards and shelves appear to be part of the structure of the room, even if they are not painted the same color. The shelf battens should be disguised as much as possible to blend in with the wall. In this project, we show how a shelf batten can incorporate a light above a shelf, lending muted tones to the color scheme of the walls.

TOOLS

- STEEL BENCH RULE
- UTILITY KNIFE
- TRY SQUARE
- SCRIBING BLOCK
- CARPENTER'S LEVEL
- HAND SAW (or circular saw)
- BACK SAW
- CHISEL (bench type)
- DRILL (hand or power)
- DRILL BITS
- MASONRY DRILL BIT
- COUNTERSINK BIT
- FORSTNER BIT for fitting concealed hinges
- POWER SABER SAW
- SANDING BLOCK and SANDING PAPER (or finishing sander)
- HAND PLANE (or power plane)
- HAMMER
- MALLET
- NAILSET

MATERIALS For one alcove

Part	Quantity	Material	Length*
UPRIGHTS	2	2 × 2in (50 × 50mm) S4S softwood	As required (ours are 34in [865mm])
HORIZONTAL RAILS	2	2 × 2in (50 × 50mm) S4S softwood	Width of alcove, less 4in (100mm)
BACK SUPPORT BATTENS	2	1 × 2in (25 × 50mm) S4S softwood	Width of alcove
SIDE SUPPORT BATTENS	4	1 × 2in (25 × 50mm) S4S softwood	Depth of alcove, less 4in (100mm)
BASE FRONT- AND BACK-SUPPORT BATTENS	2	1 × 1in (25 × 25mm) S4S softwood	Width of alcove
BASE SIDE-SUPPORT BATTENS	2	1 × 1in (25 × 25mm) S4S softwood	Depth of alcove
ALCOVE SHELF-SUPPORT BACK BATTENS	2	1½in (38mm) triangular section	Width of alcove
ALCOVE SHELF-SUPPORT SIDE BATTENS	4	1½in (38mm) triangular section	Depth of alcove, less 1½in (38mm)
"LINENFOLD" WALL PANEL DECORATION	As required	1½in (38mm) triangular section	Height of wall panel
"LINENFOLD" DOOR DECORATION	12 per door	1in (25mm) triangular section	Door height, less 8in (200mm)
DOWELS	1	Approximately 6ft (1.8m) hardwood doweling	As required
BASE PANEL	1	⅛in or ¼in (4mm or 6mm) plywood	Alcove width × depth, less thickness of baseboard and front frame
CUPBOARD SHELF	1	¾in (19mm) MDF, lumber core, or particleboard	Alcove width × depth of alcove, less 3in (75mm)
TOP PANEL	1	As above	Alcove width × depth
DOORS	2	¾in (19mm) MDF	½ alcove width, less ⅜in (8mm) × front frame height less 1in (25mm)
ALCOVE SHELVES	2	1in (25mm) MDF	Alcove width × alcove depth, less 1in (25mm)
CENTER WALL PANEL	1	¼in (6mm) MDF or plywood	As required

*Approximate lengths only – refer to copy for actual size.

ALCOVE SHELVES AND
CUPBOARD ASSEMBLY

TOP SHELF

TRIANGULAR
BACK BATTEN

MIDDLE SHELF

BEVELED SHELF EDGE

LIGHTS BEHIND
BATTEN

TRIANGULAR
SIDE BATTEN

CUPBOARD TOP

SUPPORTING
BACK BATTEN

TOP RAIL

CUPBOARD
SHELF

SUPPORTING
SIDE BATTEN

DOOR

BASEBOARD
(retained)

BASE SUPPORT
BATTENS

BOTTOM RAIL

TRIANGULAR-SECTION
DECORATION

1in (25mm) GAP

The Cupboards

Making the Frame

Using 2 × 2in (50 × 50mm) S4S (smooth 4 sides) lumber, cut two uprights to the desired height, allowing for the thickness of the top. The height of our cupboards, including the top, is 34in (865mm).

Measure for two horizontal rails so that they fit inside the uprights, and cut these from the same size of lumber as used for the uprights. Before jointing the frame it must be held square with a bracing batten (*see* **Techniques, page 20**). Glue the horizontal rails between the uprights, holding the frame square with bar clamps. When the glue has set, drill into the ends of the horizontal rails through the side rails and insert two lengths of $\frac{1}{2}$in (12mm) dowel into each joint (*see* **Techniques, Dowel joints, page 30**).

Installing the Frame

To fit the frame into the alcove it will be necessary to scribe the uprights to the wall (*see* **Techniques, page 31**). If there is baseboard around the walls of the alcove, the side rails should be scribed around it. Alternatively, remove small sections of baseboard, using a back saw and a chisel, where the side rails will fit. Another option is to remove the baseboard entirely, although this rarely looks satisfactory.

Set the frame about 1in (25mm) back into the alcove, attaching it in place with two screws and anchors on each side (*see* **Techniques, page 24**). Countersink the screwheads so that the holes can be filled and painted over.

Attaching the Supporting Battens

The supporting battens for the cupboard top and for the cupboard shelf are made from 1 × 2in (25 × 50mm) S4S lumber.

Using a carpenter's level, mark a line all the way around the alcove from the top of the frame. Cut the back batten to the full width of the alcove and attach it to the wall, under the line at the back, using screws and anchors to secure it.

Cut two side battens to fit between the back batten and the front frame.

Attach the battens to the wall at the marked lines as before.

Decide on the height of the cupboard shelf or shelves, and cut and fit the supporting battens at the appropriate height, making sure that they are level.

Installing the Base

The cupboard base panel is made from $\frac{1}{8}$in (4mm) or $\frac{1}{4}$in (6mm) plywood and is supported at the edges on 1 × 1in (25 × 25mm) battens.

At the front, glue and nail a supporting batten to the inner face of the bottom rail of the front frame. Attach it $\frac{1}{8}$in (4mm) or $\frac{1}{4}$in (6mm) down from the top (depending on the thickness of plywood you are using) so that the base panel will sit flush with the frame.

At the back, glue and nail a similar batten to the baseboard. Use a carpenter's level resting on the bottom rail of the front frame to mark the height of the base panel at the back, and measure down $\frac{1}{8}$in (4mm) or $\frac{1}{4}$in (6mm) to mark the height of the rear base supporting batten so it can be fitted accurately.

Using lumber of the same size, cut side supporting battens to fit between the front and rear battens, and glue and nail these battens to the baseboard at each side.

Cut the plywood base to size, and use brads to attach it to the supporting battens at the front, back, and sides of the frame. Use a plastic filler to fill the join between the base and the frame, and sand it smooth when dry.

Installing the Top

Measure the width of the alcove and the depth from the back wall to the front edge of the frame. If the wall is very uneven, increase these measurements to allow the top to be scribed to the wall.

Cut out the top from 1in (25mm) medium-density fiberboard (MDF), lumber core or particleboard. If using lumber core or particleboard, it will need to have a molded front edge for protection and neatness.

Scribe and fit the top in place and attach at the front by screwing up through the frame. At the back, screw down through the top, and do

1 **Assembly of the Cupboard Framework Using Dowels**
The cupboard frame is made simply by butt-jointing top and side rails. Joints are reinforced with dowels, two per joint. Protruding ends are cut off flush once glue has hardened.

2 **Installing Cupboard Base**
Battens are placed at front, rear, and sides (not shown). The base is nailed to the top.

3 **Installing the Top Section**
The frame is set back 1in (25mm) from front of alcove. Screw up into top panel.

the same at each corner, countersinking the screwheads so that the holes can be filled and painted over neatly when you have finished.

If you are using MDF, plane and sand the front edge flush with the frame. Fill and sand this joint flush.

INSTALLING THE CUPBOARD SHELF

Cut the cupboard shelf from $\frac{3}{4}$in (19mm) MDF, lumber core, or particleboard (with a molded front edge). Make sure it fits, and rest it on supporting battens.

MAKING AND INSTALLING THE DOORS

Using $\frac{3}{4}$in (19mm) MDF, cut two panels to fit the front, flush with the top, but leaving a 1in (25mm) gap at the bottom. The size of the gap at the sides of the doors is determined by the hinges used – consult the manufacturer's instructions. We have used concealed self-closing hinges, and the doors overhang the inner edges of the frame by an amount specified in the manufacturer's instructions (usually about $\frac{5}{8}$in

[15mm]) so that the hinges will operate correctly (see **Techniques, page 32**).

To create a finger-grip, bevel the top edge of each door panel to 45° through two-thirds of its thickness, leaving about $\frac{3}{16}$in (5mm) flat on top.

The "linenfold" front detail is created with 1in (25mm) triangular-section birch or pine (fig 4). Measure and mark a square on each door for the "linenfold", leaving a suitable border around the edge (ours is 4in [100mm] at top and bottom, and about $3\frac{1}{2}$in [90mm] at each side). Cut sections to length and bevel the ends to 45° (fig 4).

Mark a center line vertically down the door, and, working outwards from this, glue each length on to the surface, nailing through the side faces in about three places. Continue in each direction until the required number of triangular-shaped sections are attached, with an equal border at each side.

Install the doors using the concealed hinges according to the manufacturer's instructions (see **Techniques, page 33**).

④ **Making and Decorating Cupboard Doors**
Left Top edges of doors are beveled to provide a fingergrip. **Inset** Attaching "linenfold." **Center** First "linenfold" attached. **Right** Cut a triangular section and bevel the ends to 45°.

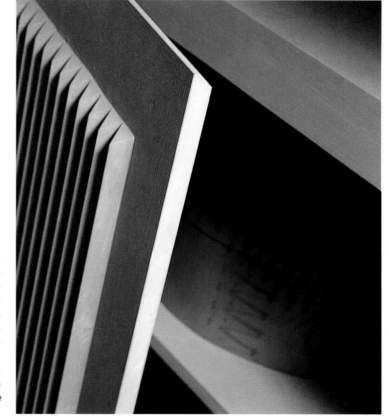

DETAIL OF "LINENFOLD" DOORS

This photograph shows the full effect of the "linenfold" door decoration, together with the neatly beveled fingergrip. You can vary the kind of decoration you use on the door front according to personal taste.

ALCOVE SHELVES AND CUPBOARDS

THE SHELVES

The shelves are made from 1in (25mm) MDF boards supported by 1½in (38mm) triangular battens which are secured to the back and side walls of the alcove.

CUTTING THE TRIANGULAR BATTENS

If you cannot find suitable triangular lumber moldings at your local lumberyard, you can cut them yourself from 2 × 2in (50 × 50mm) S4S lumber using a circular saw.

Tilt your circular saw blade to 45° and cut the lumber diagonally along its length so that it is split into two equal triangular sections. If your saw blade is not large enough to cut right through in one pass, cut partway through and complete the cut with a hand saw. Finally, clean up the sawn faces with a smoothing plane for a neat finish.

If you do not have a suitable circular saw, your lumberyard should easily be able to make this cut for you.

INSTALLING THE TOP SHELF

Decide on the height of the top shelf. From the triangular battening, cut a back batten to span the width of the alcove and secure it to the wall.

Cut the side battens to length, which should be the distance from the back of the alcove to 1½in (38mm) in from the front edge. Use triangular battens, and cut a 45° bevel on the front end so that the batten will tail away from the front edge of the shelf. Bevel the back end of the batten in the same direction so that it fits snugly into the corner against the back batten. Attach the side battens in place.

Cut out the shelf from 1in (25mm) MDF to the width of the alcove and to a depth whereby it is set back into the alcove by 1in (25mm). Bevel the front edge of the shelf through the bottom half of its thickness to allow the front edge of the beveled side batten to run flush into the bevel and create an unobtrusive support for the shelf. Screw shelf down into battens. Fill all joints and gaps, and when the filler is hard, sand smooth.

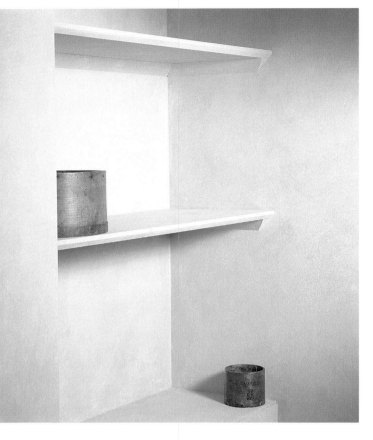

THE SHELVES IN PLACE
The shelves (above) are 1in (25mm) thick MDF boards which are screwed down to the battens.

SHELVES AND BATTENS
The beveled support battens blend neatly with the beveled front alcove shelves (below).

❶ Cutting the Triangular Battens Yourself
Tilt your circular saw blade to 45° and cut down length of lumber to split it.

❷ Installing the Shelves
Top and middle shelves secure on to triangular battens that are screwed to the walls. One batten hides a light.

INSTALLING MIDDLE SHELF

Decide on the height of the shelf and cut the back batten to fit into the alcove. In this case the back batten is secured about 3in (75mm) out from the wall so that a light can be installed behind it. Do not attach the batten securely at this stage.

Cut the side battens so that when beveled at front and rear they will be 3in (75mm) away from the wall at the back, and $1\frac{1}{2}$in (38mm) in from the front. Attach the side battens in place, screwing and anchoring them tightly to the alcove wall so that they are both level.

Cut the shelf to size from 1in (25mm) MDF and place it on the side battens, beveling the front as before. Screw it down on to the side battens, countersinking and filling the screwheads.

The back batten, which is cut square at the ends, is positioned under the shelf behind the ends of the side battens. It is secured by screwing down through the shelf. This provides a cover for the light fixtures and also acts as a beam to support the shelf and prevent it from sagging. Countersink the screw holes and fill after inserting the screws. Sand smooth when dry.

LIGHTING

For the concealed lighting under the middle shelf we used three 12in (300mm) long tungsten tube lamps secured behind the back batten.

THE CENTER WALL PANEL

Although not essential to the project, we fitted a center panel on the chimney breast to give a unified look by continuing the theme of the door decoration. The panel is $\frac{1}{4}$in (6mm) MDF or plywood on which $1\frac{1}{2}$in (38mm) triangular-section lumber is glued and nailed. The panel is screwed into the chimney-breast wall using masonry anchors, filled, smoothed, and painted to match the general decoration.

SOFT LIGHTING IN ALCOVES
When lighting is needed, built-in incandescent strips (above) offer a good alternative to the more commonly used fluorescent version.

CONCEALED LIGHTING
The concealed lighting under the middle shelf throws a muted shadow into the alcove and creates a softer atmosphere in the room. Taken from below, this photograph (left) shows the position of the concealed incandescent strip lighting. When viewed from straight on, the lighting is hidden behind the back shelf batten.

WALL OF DISPLAY SHELVING

The simplicity, style, and sheer practicality of a wall of shelves with no visible means of support is what I set out to achieve with this design.

I realized that if steel brackets were inserted into the wall and secured, I could then construct hollow-core shelves to slide over the brackets and hide them.

A great advantage of this construction method is that all of the wiring for audio-visual equipment, telephones, and lighting can be contained in the cavity of the shelf rather than trailing around on the surface in an untidy, spaghetti-like mess.

They also give the room a horizontal emphasis as there are no uprights dividing the shelves, which are necessary with conventional shelving to stop the shelves sagging in their lengths.

To complete the shelves I painted them the same color as the wall so that they had a sculptural quality and became part of the fabric of the room.

METAL SUPPORTS

Various metal supports for shelves either grouted into a brick wall or screwed to the surface

when you secure the metal supports to the wall, ensure that they are perfectly aligned to fit the shelf by tying them firmly to a pre-notched length of lumber.

LONGITUDINAL SECTION

plywood skin

metal support inserted into shelf frame

ALIGN YOUR SUPPORTS

metal support

EXPLODED SECTION OF SHELF

plywood skin

Front edge-banding of shelf attached after assembly.

The shape can be changed to suit your decorative scheme

Metal support

space for concealed wiring

Leave plywood skin extended by ½" (12mm) to allow for easy scribing to uneven walls

If you want to make a thicker shelf, add an extra wooden slat

A THICKER SHELF
surface of shelf can be veneered plywood, painted, or even tiled

Drill shelf and rabbet back edge to accept metal shelf support

Metal shelf support screwed to wall

Metal shelf support grouted into wall

A THINNER SHELF WITH INVISIBLE SUPPORT

WALL OF DISPLAY SHELVING

This project features shelving without any visible means of support, giving clean lines without any ugly brackets. It is all done by making a hollow box-section shelf unit comprising top and bottom plywood-skin panels over a sturdy lumber framework, creating the appearance of a thick, solid shelf.

For added strength on long shelf runs, protruding steel rods are drilled into the rear wall. They slide into the box frame of the shelf. Battens-only attachment can be used for a run of shelving up to 8ft (2440mm) long and 18in (450mm) deep. It is important to note that steel rods should only be driven 3in (75mm) into walls, whether they are solid or hollow. For cavity walls, the rods should not bridge the cavity. If the walls are plasterboard, stud walls, or lath and plaster, then, for strength, the steel rods should be inserted directly into the main vertical timber studs within the wall.

CONSTRUCTION

Decide on the height of your shelves and, using a carpenter's level, mark their position on the wall; continue these lines on to the end walls. Measure for the length and required depth, and for each shelf cut two pieces of $\frac{3}{8}$in (9mm) thick plywood, or $\frac{1}{2}$in (12mm) MDF or particle-board. If the shelves are to be longer than 8ft (2440mm), you will have to butt-joint the lengths and position a batten inside the shelving to support the cut ends.

From 1 × 2in (25 × 50mm) S4S battening, cut one piece to the length of the shelf for the front batten. Cut two end wall battens to the depth of the shelf, less the thickness of the front batten. Cut two back battens to the length of the shelf less twice the thickness of the end battens so that they will fit between the latter. Cut further battens to the shelf depth, less three

batten thicknesses, to fit between the front and back shelf battens at each end and at about 24in (610mm) intervals along its length.

Lay out all the pieces in place on the top panel of the shelf to make sure that they fit together.

Attach some scrap pieces of wood to the underside of the top shelf panel for the steel rods to rest on. These pieces should be of a suitable thickness (about $\frac{3}{4}$in [19mm]) to allow the rods to fit roughly midway in the edges of the back battens. Cut the pieces, if necessary, to fit in between the cross battens inside the shelf, and glue them to the top panel. They will need to be at intervals of about 24in (610mm) to coincide with the steel rod positions (16in [400mm] if you are fitting into a stud wall).

Draw a guide line the thickness of the scrap wood on to the back batten to help positioning when you are drilling steel rod back battens.

The rods should be spaced about every 24in (610mm) (16in [400mm] if drilling into wood studs) roughly midway between the cross battens. They should run the width of the shelf from front to back, butting up against the inner side of the front batten and going into the wall about 3in (75mm) beyond the thickness of the plaster. Cut the required number from $\frac{1}{2}$in (12mm) steel rod.

Clamp the two back battens together, and using a drill bit slightly larger in diameter than the steel rod (an approx. $\frac{9}{16}$in [13mm] drill bit and $\frac{1}{2}$in [12mm] diameter steel rod), drill through the two battens together in the appropriate places. Use a pencil to number the battens.

Nail up the internal frame of the shelf, marking the side to be fixed to the upper panel. Spread glue on the top side of the frame and lay the top shelf panel in place. Draw a line around the edges of the frame and the shelf panel to mark a center line

TOOLS
STEEL MEASURING TAPE
CARPENTER'S LEVEL
TRY SQUARE
SMALL HAND SAW (or power circular saw or Saber saw)
HACKSAW
POWER DRILL or HAND BRACE
TWIST DRILL BIT, SPADE BIT, or AUGER BIT
MASONRY DRILL BIT
HAMMER
SCREWDRIVER (Phillips or slotted, according to screws used)
TWO C-CLAMPS
NAILSET
SMOOTHING PLANE
POWER FINISHING SANDER (or hand-sanding block)
METAL FILE

MATERIALS

Part	Quantity	Material	Length
SHELF PANELS	2	$\frac{3}{8}$in (9mm) plywood or $\frac{1}{2}$in (12mm) MDF or particleboard – width as required	As required
FRONT BATTEN	1	1 × 2in (25 × 50mm) S4S lumber	As shelf length
END WALL BATTENS	2	1 × 2in (25 × 50mm) S4S lumber	Width of shelf, less thickness of front batten
BACK BATTENS	2	1 × 2in (25 × 50mm) S4S lumber	Length of shelf, less twice the thickness of end battens
INTERMEDIATE BATTENS	As required to fit at 24in (610mm) intervals along shelf length	1 × 2in (25 × 50mm) S4S lumber	Shelf width, less three batten thicknesses
ROD SUPPORT BLOCKS	As above	1 × 2in (25 × 50mm) S4S lumber	About 12in (300mm)
STEEL ROD SHELF SUPPORTS	One per 24in (610mm) length of shelf run	$\frac{1}{2}$in (12mm) diameter mild steel rod	Distance from inner side of front batten to back of shelf, plus plaster thickness, plus 3in (75mm)
SHELF FRONT EDGE (rounded)	1	2 × 3in (50 × 75mm) S4S lumber	As shelf length

BASIC ASSEMBLY

SHELF PANEL
(upper)

BACK BATTEN (shelf)

BACK BATTEN (wall)

STEEL ROD

SHELF FRONT EDGE

INTERMEDIATE BATTEN (shelf)

FRONT BATTEN

END WALL
BATTEN

of the inset battens to give a nailing line. Nail the panel in place, punch in nail heads and fill the indentations. Repeat for the other shelf panel.

To make a rounded edge at the front, cut a piece of 2 × 3in (50 × 75mm) lumber to the length of the shelf. Glue and nail it (along the

center line) to the front edge, and punch the nail heads well below the surface. Mark a half-round curve on the ends using a suitable plastic cup or carton. Continue rough guide lines on to the top face so that you can use a circular saw to take off the corner edges before planing.

INSTALLING THE SHELF

Screw and anchor the rear-wall batten in place. Then, using a $\frac{1}{2}$in (12mm) diameter masonry drill bit, drill through the pre-drilled holes in the wall batten, making the holes in the bricks or blocks about 3in

(75mm) deep. Screw the end battens against the rear-wall batten.

Bevel both ends of the steel rods with a metal file, then push the rods into the holes in the wall. Slot the shelf on to the protruding rods and slide it over the end battens and on to the rear-wall batten.

① Stages in Assembling the Box-section Shelf Unit
The basic framework nailed up; holes for steel rods between battens.

② The rear-wall and side battens fit neatly into the recess created by insetting the side and back shelf battens. Holes for rods match up.

③ The lower shelf panel is attached and the upper shelf panel exploded away to show how the softwood frame is neatly recessed.

④ Front edge is attached to front batten and it is rounded off. Through-section (5) shows steel rod resting between support blocks.

1

2

3

4

5

HOME OFFICE

Whether you need a place in which to do your household accounts and other domestic paperwork or whether you earn your living from home (a growing trend in this age of computerization), you will need a quiet, well-organized space that encourages you to get down to work. This design for a home office provides the essential work area, although it cannot, unfortunately, guarantee the necessary peace and quiet.

I have used conventional steel filing cabinets as pedestals for the desk. The cabinets are well engineered to allow the heavy drawers to run smoothly and to lock securely. The wall unit is pigeon-holed with adjustable shelves on "magic wires" so all your files, ledgers, and office equipment can be neatly stacked away.

Because the unit is attached away from the wall with beveled battens, there is enough space behind it for wiring-in power points; these allow for the increasing amount of electronic equipment that modern life deems necessary.

It is important to have light on the worksurface: it allows you to see what you are doing and also invites you to concentrate and work industriously. The light is provided here by a concealed incandescent strip across the full width of the worksurface, illuminating the bulletin board and its memory-jogging messages.

FRONT ELEVATION.
Adjustable shelving

standard metal filing cabinets

Fiberboard or cork bulletin board

SIDE ELEVATION.
Uprights screwed through backing board

Concealed strip lights illuminate the work surface

space for electrical wiring

Desktop is a simple door blank covered with sheet vinyl

Horizontal beveled battens

SECTION.
Electrical outlets

HOME OFFICE

This project offers an easy way to create office space in the home. The desk could not be simpler — it is just a flush door laid across a couple of two-drawer filing cabinets. At the back of the desk a bulletin board is fixed to the wall, and above it is a boxed unit of adjustable pigeon-holes. These are very adaptable as they are supported by Swedish-type shelf supports. This means their heights can be altered easily and sections can be removed or interchanged to take office equipment, materials, books, and so on.

To give a good, general-purpose working light, strip lights are concealed behind a valance fitted to the bottom of the shelf unit. Electrical outlets and a telephone jack can be installed in the bulletin board section to allow a desk lamp, word processor or typewriter, telephone, and other equipment to be connected. Also incorporated in the design are two conduit covers, drilled through the center of the bulletin board to take cables serving the keyboard and printer through to the back of the unit where they will be hidden.

There is quite a bit of wiring behind this unit. Therefore, both the wall unit and the bulletin board are mounted on beveled battens, which not only give a strong support, but also form a gap for the wiring.

If you do not want to hide the wires behind the unit, and the backing wall is solid, with sound plaster, then you can mount the wall unit and the bulletin board directly on the wall by screwing through the back panel into anchors. In this case, the screwheads will show, so for neatness either fit screw cups under the screwheads or alternatively fit screw covers over them.

The main benefit of this wall unit is that it can be attached to any wall to create an instant study or office, whether in the corner of a living room or in a spare bedroom.

TOOLS

STEEL MEASURING TAPE

STEEL BENCH RULE or STRAIGHT-EDGE

TRY SQUARE

ADHESIVE SPREADER

UTILITY KNIFE

POWER CIRCULAR SAW (or power Saber saw)

DRILL (hand or power)

MASONRY DRILL BIT to suit size of anchors used

TWIST DRILL BIT for clearance holes

TWIST DRILL BIT for pilot holes and shelf support wire location

COUNTERSINK BIT

COMPASS SAW (if Saber saw not available) for cutting recesses for electrical outlets

ROUTER and ROUTER BIT

SCREWDRIVER (Phillips or single-slot, depending on the type of screws used)

ORBITAL SANDER (or hand-sanding block)

PAINTBRUSH

MATERIALS

Part	Quantity	Material	Length
DESK UNIT			
BASES	2	Two-drawer filing cabinets	
DESK TOP	1	Plywood-faced interior door blank	As required
BULLETIN BOARD			
BACKING BOARD	1	$\frac{1}{2}$in (12mm) plywood or lumber core, 12in (300mm) wide	As desk top
FACING BOARD	1	$\frac{1}{2}$in (12mm) medium fiberboard, 12in (300mm) wide	As desk top
MOUNTING BATTENS	2	1 × 3in (25 × 75mm) S4S lumber	As desk top
WALL UNIT			
BACK PANEL	1	$\frac{1}{2}$in (12mm) plywood or lumber core, $34\frac{1}{2}$in (870mm) wide	As desk top
SIDE PANELS	2	$\frac{3}{4}$in (19mm) plywood or lumber core, 13in (330mm) wide	$34\frac{1}{2}$in (870mm)
MAIN DIVIDERS	2	$\frac{3}{4}$in (19mm) plywood or lumber core, 13in (330mm) wide*	Distance between top and bottom panels
TOP AND BOTTOM PANELS	2	$\frac{3}{4}$in (19mm) plywood or lumber core, $13\frac{1}{2}$in (330mm) wide*	Distance between side panels
MIDDLE DIVIDERS	3	$\frac{1}{2}$in (12mm) plywood, 13in (330mm) wide*	Distance between top and bottom panels)
CENTRAL SHELVES	12	$\frac{1}{2}$in (12mm) plywood, 13in (330mm) wide	8in (200mm)
SIDE SHELVES	6	$\frac{1}{2}$in (12mm) plywood, 13in (330mm) wide	Distance between main divider and side
MOUNTING BATTENS	2	1 × 4in (25 × 100mm) S4S lumber	As desk top
VALANCE			
FRONT PANEL	1	$\frac{1}{2}$in (12mm) plywood, 3in (75mm) wide	As desk top
SIDE PANEL	2	$\frac{1}{2}$in (12mm) plywood, 3in (75mm) wide	6in (150mm)
CORNER BLOCK	2	1 × 1in (25 × 25mm) S4S lumber	3in (75mm)

*Approximate lengths only — refer to copy for actual size.

BASIC ASSEMBLY

TOP PANEL

SIDE PANEL

MAIN DIVIDER

SWEDISH-TYPE
SHELF SUPPORTS

ANGLE BRACKET

VALANCE FRONT PANEL

MIDDLE DIVIDERS
MAIN DIVIDER
BEVELED
BATTENS

BACK PANEL

SIDE SHELVES

BOTTOM
PANEL

CORNER BLOCK
VALANCE
SIDE PANEL

BULLETIN BOARD
BACKING BOARD

BULLETIN BOARD
FACING BOARD

DESK TOP

THE WALL UNIT
*This compact unit contains
everything you might need for
working at home: an adjustable
storage-shelf unit and bulletin
board section above a door-blank
desk top resting on twin two-drawer
filing cabinets (not shown).*

HOME OFFICE: DESK AND WALL UNIT

DESK

Position the filing cabinets about 40in (1015mm) apart. Place the desk top across them. This can be a plywood-faced interior flush door, finished as required *(see* **Techniques, page 32** *)*. We covered our door with a sheet of thick sheet vinyl which makes a good writing surface. To stick it in place, use a contact adhesive applied to the upper surface of the door with a serrated spreader. Cut the vinyl slightly oversized, position it carefully, then weight it down overnight to allow the adhesive to harden. Finally, with a utility knife trim off the surplus vinyl at a slight angle to leave a neatly beveled edge.

BULLETIN BOARD

Cut the backing board for the bulletin board from $\frac{1}{2}$in (12mm) plywood or lumber core to the length of the desk top. Our board is 12in (300mm) high, but you can adjust this to suit your requirements.

1 Bulletin Board Assembly
Bulletin board is medium fiberboard screwed to plywood or lumber core and hooked over beveled battens.

Cut out the bulletin board itself to the same size. We have used a brand-name finished fiberboard, but you can use any material that will take thumb tacks, such as cork or felt-covered fiberboard. In the latter case, the felt covers the board, front and sides, and is stapled or glued at the back.

Screw the bulletin board to the backing board using flat head wood screws fitted into screw cups for neatness. About four screws at both the top and bottom will be sufficient.

ATTACHING THE BULLETIN BOARD TO THE WALL

The bulletin board on its backing board is mounted on two pairs of beveled battens. Each pair of battens is made from 1 × 3in (25 × 75mm) S4S (smooth 4 sides) lumber cut to the full length of the bulletin board. Cut through the middle of each length with a circular-saw blade set at 45° to make a pair of beveled battens *(see* **Techniques, page 25** *)*. Beveled battens allow the bulletin board to fit snugly against the wall, but leave enough

space to conceal wiring for lamps, a telephone, and a word processor which sit on top of the desk.

Place the pairs of beveled battens on the back of the bulletin board to position them and screw the upper ones to the back of the bulletin board.

To attach the bulletin board to the wall, first rest it in place at the back of the desk top. This is important as the desk gives extra support for the things above. Hold the lower battens in place under the two fitted ones, and with a pencil mark their positions on the wall.

Take the bulletin board away and, using anchors, screw the lower battens to the wall. Hang the bulletin board on the battens, making sure that the two sets of battens interlock neatly and securely.

WALL UNIT

The unit shown here is made from $\frac{1}{2}$in (12mm) lumber core, with an edge-banding applied to the front. Alternatively, you could use ordinary veneered particleboard, with either a

wood or a plastic finish, left natural or painted black or a color to suit your decorative scheme.

Using $\frac{1}{2}$in (12mm) plywood, lumber core or veneered particleboard, cut out the back panel to the same length as the desk top and to the desired height; ours is 34$\frac{1}{2}$in (870mm) high, which allows for four shelves in the center with a depth of 8in (200mm) each.

Using $\frac{3}{4}$in (19mm) plywood or lumber core, cut out the side panels, the top and bottom panels, and the two main dividers. The side panels should be the height of the back panel, the top and bottom panels fit between them, and the two main dividers fit between the top and bottom panels. The depth of all these panels is as required – in our case it is 13in (330mm). Add a hardwood molding edge-banding to all the front edges of these panels *(see* **Materials, page 18** *)*.

Lay the back panel on a flat surface, and place the top, bottom, and side panels in their positions on top of it. Mark these positions on the front of the back panel.

2 Spacing the Middle and Main Vertical Dividers
Put central divider in place, exactly in center. Use two shelf panels to position the next dividers on each side of the central one. Position all of the dividers in this way.

POSITIONING THE DIVIDERS

Your starting point for positioning the dividers will be the position of major items, such as a word processor, that need to be incorporated. Otherwise, you can start with the pigeon-hole section in the middle. This has been planned to provide 16 pigeon-holes 8in (200mm) square – four across by four high.

Cut three middle dividers to the same dimensions as the main dividers, but from $\frac{1}{2}$in (12mm) plywood, lumber core, or veneered particleboard. From the same material, cut 12 shelves, in our case measuring 8×13in (200×330mm). Add edge-banding to the front edges of all the shelves and dividers.

Put the central divider in place, exactly in the center, and mark its position on the back panel. Use two of the shelves to position the next divider on either side of the central one. Then repeat the procedure to position the main dividers. When you have done this, the positions of all the dividers will be marked on the back panel.

SHELVES

Measure the space between the main divider and the side of the wall unit on each side. Using $\frac{1}{2}$in (12mm) plywood, cut shelves to these dimensions and add edge-banding to the front edges. We have three shelves on each side of the main divider.

Position all the shelves with equal spacing between them. Even if some of the shelves are to be left out to accommodate tall books and office equipment, it is still worth buying supports for all of the shelves in case extra shelf space is needed later. When the shelves are correctly positioned, mark their positions on to the sides of the panels and then on to the dividers.

DRILLING THE BACK PANEL

Remove all the panels and shelves, and pilot-drill the back panel through from the front, along the center of the lines marked for the top, bottom, and side panels, and for all the dividers. Turn the panel over and countersink the holes from the back (see **Techniques, page 23**).

3 **Attaching the Dividers in the Wall Unit Framework**
Mark center line of each divider to ensure accurate positioning. Drill, countersink, and screw the divider in place, attaching it securely through the top and bottom panels.

DETAIL OF HOME OFFICE

The bulletin board includes an electrical outlet and a metal disk to house wiring for office equipment. The position of the pigeon-hole shelves can be adjusted to accommodate large items such as a word processor.

HOME OFFICE: WALL UNIT

DRILLING SIDE PANELS AND DIVIDERS

Allowing two per shelf, buy the required number of Swedish-type shelf supports of the appropriate length. Pre-drill the side panels and dividers to take the shelf supports. Positioning the drill on the *center* of the lines marked for the shelves, use a $\frac{1}{8}$in (3mm) twist drill bit to drill through the dividers, but drill only $\frac{3}{8}$in (9mm) into the side panels. Make sure that the holes at the front of the unit are set back a little from the edge so that the front of the shelf will conceal the shelf support wires. The holes at the back are spaced according to the length of the shelf support wires, to allow the wires to be pushed into the holes.

ASSEMBLING THE OUTER FRAME

Install one side panel by gluing and screwing it from the back.

Drill and countersink holes in the end of the side panel to attach one of the long panels (top or bottom). Glue and screw this panel in place.

Pull the back panel over the edge of the workbench, then screw up from the back into the long panel. Repeat the procedure for the other side panel of the outer frame.

After gluing the ends and rear edge of the other long panel, put it in position and screw through the side panels into the ends. Do not insert screws at the back until you have attached the dividers, so that small adjustments can be made if necessary when the dividers are positioned.

ATTACHING THE DIVIDERS

Apply glue to the ends of the central divider and put it in place, checking with a try square that it is square to the frame and vertical. To ensure accurate positioning of the screws in the ends of the divider, draw a line from the center line of the divider, over the front edges of the long panels, and then across them. Drill, countersink, and screw the divider in place through the long panels. As one panel is not yet attached, it is possible to make adjustments, if necessary, to ensure that the front

edges are flush. Repeat the procedure with the other dividers, working from the center outwards.

Turn the unit over and, working from the back, screw the remaining long panel in place. Finish by screwing through this panel into each of the dividers.

INSTALLING SHELVES

Position the shelf support wires in the dividers. Using a router, make $\frac{1}{8}$in (3mm) grooves $\frac{3}{8}$in (9mm) deep in the edges of the shelves, so that the shelves will be able to be slotted over the shelf support wires. Make sure that the grooves stop short of the front edges of the shelves, so that the grooves and the wire supports will not be seen.

FINISHING

Fill the screw holes, rub down the filler when dry, and apply your chosen finish (*see* **Techniques, page 20**). The finish should be selected so that it suits the style of the home office and blends in with the decorative scheme you have planned for the room.

ATTACHING THE UNIT TO THE WALL

The unit is hung using two pairs of beveled battens, in the same way as the bulletin board, but with 1 × 4in (25 × 100mm) battens (*see* **Techniques, page 25**). Place the two pairs of battens on the back of the unit to position them, and attach the *top* battens to the back of the unit. It is important to ensure that the fixing screws go through into each upright panel and divider, to give sufficient strength to hold the unit.

To attach the unit to the wall, hold it in place on top of the bulletin board and mark off the positions of the lower battens on the wall, as you did with the bulletin board. Take the unit away and screw the lower parts of the battens to the wall using anchors. Hang the unit in place, making sure that the battens interlock to give a secure fixing.

PIGEON-HOLE SHELF UNIT

The shelves offer ample storage space and are secured firmly to the wall with beveled battens.

1 **Hidden Shelf Support**
Swedish-type shelf supports "plug"
into holes drilled in wall unit
dividers; shelf slots over wires.

VALANCE

Using $\frac{1}{2}$in (12mm) plywood or lumber core, cut out the valance front to the length of the unit and about 3in (75mm) wide. Cut two side pieces to the same width and about 6in (150mm) long.

Miter the front corners and fit a 1 × 1in (25 × 25mm) batten, cut to the valance depth, to the inside of each corner. Glue and screw it in place to the front and side pieces.

Attach the valance in place to the underside of the bottom of the wall unit using steel angle brackets behind the valance – one at each end and one in the middle.

Install lights behind the valance. We used four tungsten-tube strip lights. The wiring for the lights can be run in the space behind the units created by the bevel of the battens.

It is easy to cut recesses in the bulletin board with a Saber saw or a compass saw to take electrical outlets and a telephone jack. Conduit covers with the centers drilled out can be installed to take the cables for office equipment.

② The Valance Attachment
Valance panels are neatly mitered
and screwed to corner blocks.
Brackets attach valance to unit.

BACK PANEL

BEVELED BATTEN (attached to unit)

BEVELED BATTEN (attached to wall)

CAVITY

WALL

BEVELED BATTEN
(attached to backing board)

CAVITY
(use for wiring runs)

BACKING BOARD

WALL UNIT
SIDE PANEL

VALANCE
SIDE PANEL

BULLETIN BOARD

DESK TOP

TWO-DRAWER
FILING CABINET

SIDE VIEW OF HOME
OFFICE

RADIATOR COVER

Radiators are often an eye-sore, particularly modern ones. This design offers a solution that screens a radiator from view but still allows a free passage of air and heat; it will look good in a modern or a traditional interior in any room in the house. The design is adaptable for any size of radiator. The front panel, which lifts off easily for maintenance or adjustment, can be made from vertical or horizontal wooden slats. The wooden cover may be left as natural wood or finished in any color or texture to fit in with your chosen decorative scheme.

If the radiator is a low one, then an excellent alternative design is to make the frame deep enough so that a cushion can be added on top, thereby transforming the radiator cover into a seat. This is particularly effective if your radiator is below a bay window.

FRONT ELEVATION.

SECTION

hot air

cold air

Vertical slats provide a screen that lifts off easily.

Beveled battens

A low radiator can be made into a WINDOW SEAT. This one uses a different configuration of slats for the front screen.

Beveled battens allow front cover to lift off easily

cushion

Bottom half fitted to end of frame

RADIATOR COVER

The radiator cover can be adapted in size to suit any shape of radiator. With low radiators in an alcove or bay, the shelf and sides can be widened to form an attractive seat. In all cases the front panel is easily removable for decorating, bleeding air from the radiator, or adjusting the valves. Heat-reflecting foil should be attached to the wall behind the radiator with double-sided adhesive tabs. The advantage of a radiator cover is that it can hide an ugly feature of a room. Think about small children when building this project; if there are children in the home, make sure that the front panel of the radiator does not contain gaps that are wide enough for small arms and legs to get caught in.

TOOLS

STEEL MEASURING TAPE

CARPENTER'S LEVEL

HEAT-RESISTANT ADHESIVE

CONTOUR GAUGE

SMALL HAND SAW

CIRCULAR SAW

POWER DRILL (and suitable drill bits)

SABER SAW

SANDING BLOCK and SANDING PAPER

SURFORM

SCREWDRIVERS

MATERIALS

Part	Quantity	Material	Length
SHELF	1	1in (25mm) particleboard or MDF	As required
SIDES	2	1in (25mm) particleboard or MDF	As required
BACK HORIZONTAL BATTEN	1	1 × 3in (25 × 75mm) S4S lumber	Distance between vertical battens
BACK VERTICAL BATTENS	2	1 × 1in (25 × 25mm) S4S lumber	Height of sides
BEVELED BATTENS	4	1 × 4in (25 × 100mm) S4S lumber	Distance between side panels
SLATS	As required	1 × 3in (25 × 75mm) S4S lumber	As required
DOWELS	4	¼in (6mm) dowel	1¼in (30mm)

MAKING THE FRAMEWORK

To calculate the overall dimensions of the cover, measure the length of the radiator to just beyond the valves and measure the height, allowing an extra 2in (50mm) clearance between the top of the radiator and the shelf. Mark these positions on the wall with a pencil.

The side panels should be cut so that they protrude 2–3in (50–75mm) in front of the radiator. The top should overhang the sides by about 2in (50mm) at both ends and protrude 1in (25mm) at the front. Use 1in (25mm) particleboard or MDF (medium-density fiberboard) for the sides and the top.

ATTACHING THE SIDES

Cut two 1 × 1in (25 × 25mm) lumber battens to the same height as the sides. If there is a baseboard, the sides of the radiator can be scribed to fit neatly over the baseboard, so that they blend in well with the walls (see **Techniques, page 31**). Similarly, make sure that the battens are cut so that they stop above the baseboard for a neat finish.

1 Marking Top Shelf Batten
Batten is centralized on underside edge of shelf panel, and fixing screw depth is marked.

2 Counterboring Screw Hole
Mark drill bit with tape to depth required and drill holes larger than screwhead.

3 Attaching Sides and Top
Side panels are screwed and anchored to walls. Top shelf attaches to sides on dowels.

4 The Beveled Battens
Using 1 × 4in (25 × 100mm) lumber cut to internal width, saw lengthways at 45° in ratio of ⅔ to ⅓.

BASIC ASSEMBLY

DOWELS

VERTICAL BATTEN

SIDE PANEL

HIGHER BEVELED BATTEN

HIGHER BEVELED BATTEN

SLATS

TOP SHELF

TOP SHELF BATTEN

VERTICAL BATTEN

LOWER BEVELED BATTEN

SIDE PANEL

LOWER BEVELED BATTEN

FRONT PANEL

RADIATOR COVER

Drill and countersink the battens on two adjacent faces. Glue and screw them to the inside faces of the sides, flush with the back edges.

For easier access when adjusting the radiator valve, cut a 5in (125mm) diameter hole at a required place in the appropriate side. Drill a hole in a pre-marked circle, then cut around it with a Saber saw. Smooth the edges with sandpaper.

Attach the sides to the wall by screwing through the battens. Check that the sides are plumb.

MAKING THE TOP SHELF

To round off the corners, use a suitable object – a saucer, for example – to mark arcs on them. Cut away the waste with a Saber saw or a coping saw. Round the edges by sanding by hand. This is best done by holding a sheet of sandpaper over the edge with both hands and pulling both sides alternately. Use a sanding block on the corners.

Alternatively, use a router with a $\frac{1}{2}$in (12mm) rounding-over cutter attached to cut the top of the edge and then the bottom of it. Smooth by

sanding down with a block and sandpaper. You may prefer to leave the corners square and to glue a $\frac{1}{2}$in (12mm) half-round molding to the front of the shelf. Tape the molding in place until the glue has set.

Cut a 1 × 3in (25 × 75mm) horizontal batten to fit between the vertical side battens. Lay the shelf upside down on the bench and place the horizontal batten on it so that its ends are equidistant from the ends of the top.

Position a screw by the side of the batten and the back edge of the top shelf, holding it so that the tip is about $\frac{1}{4}$in (6mm) short of the top surface of the shelf. This is to ensure that the screw will not break through to the shelf's surface. Mark off the position of the screwhead on the batten (fig 1, page 168).

Find a drill bit slightly larger than the screwhead. Hold this against the batten with its tip against the position of the screwhead. Fix a piece of tape around the drill bit to indicate the depth to which you should drill. Drill downwards until the tape is at the top edge of the batten (fig 2,

page 168). Glue and screw the batten in place using three equally spaced screws.

THE TOP SHELF

The shelf is doweled to the sides using $\frac{1}{4}$in (6mm) dowels, $1\frac{1}{4}$in (30mm) long (fig 3, page 168). Drill two $\frac{1}{4}$in (6mm) diameter holes in each top edge of the sides. The hole depths should be half the length of the dowels. Transfer the hole positions exactly to the underside of the shelf and again drill $\frac{1}{4}$in (6mm) holes to half the dowel length.

Glue the dowels and the top edges of the sides and place the shelf in position.

THE FRONT PANEL

Measure the length between the sides. Calculate how many 1 × 3in (25 × 75mm) equally spaced vertical slats are required. The width of the spacing is optional, but it is very important that the spaces are not wide enough for a child to get his or her hands, feet, or head accidentally stuck between the slats of the radiator cover front panel.

Measure for the height of the slats, allowing for a 2in (50mm) gap at both top and bottom. Cut the slats to this dimension.

Battens should be cut to the width between the side panels. Cut two from 1 × 4in (25 × 100mm) lumber. To bevel them, use a circular saw set to 45°, cutting lengthwise through each batten to divide it into two portions, one twice the size of the other (fig 4, page 168). The wider portions will be attached between the sides of the cover. The narrower portions will be attached to the slats.

FRONT PANEL ASSEMBLY

Lay out the slats on the bench using a spacing batten between them (*see* **Techniques, page 20**). Lay the pairs of beveled battens in place across the slats so that they are flush with the top and bottom. Make sure that the battens are the right way around – that is, the narrower one is at the top in each case – and lying at the correct angle (fig 1).

Remove the wider battens. Mark the top edge of the bevel on to the back face of the batten, so that you do not screw over this line (fig 2).

Screw the battens to the first slat, using two screws at each end. Continue to screw down the remaining slats using the spacing batten for accurate distribution.

Mark the wider battens where they are to be screwed to the side panels. Either measure down from the top of the side panels or lift up the gate to its correct position.

Drill clearance holes through the sides, then countersink and screw the battens in place.

① Assembling Slats and Beveled Battens of Front Panel
Use a spacing batten to place the slats an equal distance apart with the same space at each end. The battens line up neatly with top and bottom edges of the front panel slats.

② Attaching the Slats
Scew top (narrow) batten to each slat using two screws. Line on back of slat is screw guide.

BLENDING A RADIATOR COVER WITH ITS SURROUNDINGS

Cool, luxurious stone has been used wall-to-wall in this Mediterranean-style setting (left) to box-in and cleverly disguise a radiator cover. The result is a stylish, low-level storage or seating area which enhances the painting on the wall above it.

INCORPORATING A RADIATOR IN A DIVIDING WALL

Here two radiators have been built-in to a wall of windows (below left) which divides a porch and a hall. Building-in a radiator cover in this way complements the clean lines of the walls.

SMALL-SPACE LIVING

Many radiators are situated under windows (below center). Here, where space is limited, a shelf has been added above the radiator cover for an extra storage and display area. The cover slats echo the design of the wooden platforms that support the sofa beds.

HIGH CEILING AND TALL WINDOWS

This light and spacious living room (below right) contains two radiator covers which, with the addition of cushions, are adapted to form comfortable window seats.

WORKROOM IDEAS

ADJUSTABLE SHELVING

To be efficient when working at home you need to be well-organized and comfortable, and that requires careful planning. For both the examples shown here the bulletin board, shelving, and furniture harmonize well with the decorative treatment of walls and floor.

Adequate storage is essential – there is nothing more frustrating than being swamped by paper and unable to find anything. Drawer storage will probably be required and is ideally provided by a deep filing-cabinet-type drawer. You will also need cupboards and lots of shelves, as shown on the right. Here, a sturdy, adjustable shelf system has been combined with bulletin boards for messages and memos.

The shelves are ordinary $\frac{5}{8}$in (15mm) laminated particleboard on adjustable steel shelf supports spaced about 24in (610mm) apart to ensure that the shelves do not sag when heavily loaded.

At the bottom of the adjustable tracks, wide shelf supports are fitted to carry a laminated worktop which provides extra space for storage and working. This standard 24in (610mm) wide worktop, $1\frac{1}{4}$in (30mm) thick, has a hardwood edge-banding and rests on $18\frac{1}{2}$in (470mm) wide supports to which it is screwed from the underside.

Bulletin boards are constructed from $\frac{3}{8}$in (9.5mm) thick medium fiberboard panels cut to fit between the adjustable shelf uprights. The panels are covered in felt which is stapled at the back.

PLAN STORAGE

A simple storage idea is shown in the photograph of the office (opposite). U-shaped brackets support half-round gutters, which store plans and drawings.

Temporarily attach a vertical batten to the wall to align the brackets, and use a carpenter's level to mark horizontal lines for their heights. Space them all equally, marking screw holes on the wall. Drill and anchor to the wall.

1 Marking Height of Shelving
Cut uprights to equal length. Hold upright on wall and mark position of the base.

2 Attach Batten to Wall
Temporarily nail a batten to the wall to align with marked line. Check that it is level.

3 Mark Screw Fixing Holes
Rest upright on temporary batten, check it is vertical, then mark screw hole positions on wall.

4 Cut Bulletin Board to Shape
Fit two brackets and double-check they are level. Measure between them; cut bulletin board to fit.

Bottom level of uprights

Temporary batten

HOW TO ATTACH ADJUSTABLE SHELVING

When attaching the shelving to a solid wall, measure the wall and decide how many uprights are required. You will need one at each end and intermediate uprights spaced a maximum of 24in (610mm) apart.

Allowing for wider brackets to be attached at the base of each upright to support the worktop adequately, decide how high you need the shelving supports and cut all the adjustable shelving uprights to this length. Using a hacksaw, cut through at a solid part of the uprights between two pairs of slots.

Hold an upright against the wall at one side and decide at what height it should be. Mark the bottom of the upright on the wall and remove it. Use a straight batten and carpenter's level, or a chalked string line, to draw or snap a straight horizontal line at this height.

Tack a straight batten temporarily to the wall with the batten's top edge level with the marked line. Mark along the batten where the uprights will be attached. Use a metal detector to check that there are no electric cables or water pipes in the wall at these points.

Rest one of the slotted uprights on the end batten and, holding a carpenter's level against the upright to ensure that it is vertical, use a pencil to mark the screw fixing points.

Drill the wall at the marked points, insert anchors, and screw the upright in place. Repeat for the other uprights. Make sure that the slots are exactly in line with each other.

Measure the spaces between the uprights and cut the bulletin board panels to fit. Cover them with felt and fit the panels by screwing to the wall, using screw cups under the heads for neatness. For an invisible fixing, glue the panels in place with panel adhesive or hang them using keyhole plates attached to the backs of the panels and hooked over woodscrews inserted in anchors.

Finally, slot the brackets into place, fit the shelves, and screw them to the brackets from the underside.

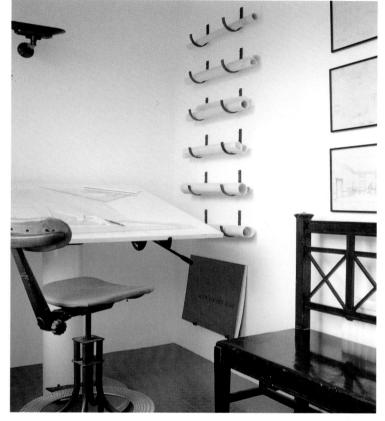

5 Bulletin Board Panels
Fit bulletin boards by screwing through using screw cups or by hanging on keyhole plates.

6 Screwing Bracket and Shelf
Slot brackets into place and attach shelves to the brackets by screwing through from the underside.

7 Attaching to Hollow Walls
On hollow walls screw three horizontal battens to wall, screwing through into the main wall studs.

8 Installing Plan Brackets
Temporarily attach vertical batten to wall to align brackets. Drill, anchor, and screw them to wall.

REPLACING BASEBOARDS

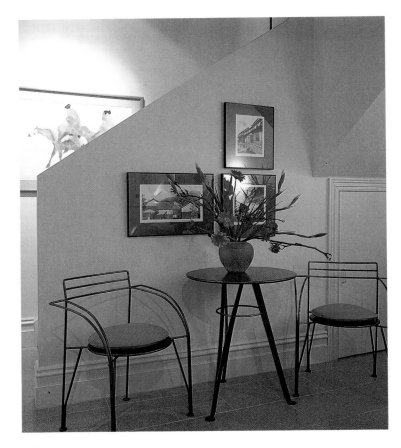

It is attention to detail that adds the finishing touch to a room. In this hallway (left) the traditional handrail and balusters of a half-turn staircase have been boxed-in to give a clean line to this previously dominant feature. A staircase feature like this can be made simply by cladding a sawn lumber frame with $\frac{1}{2}$in (12mm) MDF. The nails should be punched flush with the surface, and the MDF then painted.

The basis of the lumber framework should be the newel posts. They are an integral part of the staircase construction and should be retained.

BUYING AND MAKING BASEBOARDS

In the examples shown here, the baseboards provide the elegant finishing touches.

The type of baseboard shown may be available ready-made from a good lumberyard. The size normally available is 1 × 9in (25 × 225mm). Made from softwood, it can be stained with wood dye if required.

If you cannot find a ready-made baseboard, try a specialist lumberyard, which may have a milling machine capable of producing the exact molding you require.

There are two ways in which to produce an elaborate molding yourself. The easiest is to build one up as shown (fig 2) by combining plain planks with suitable ready-made moldings or beadings. This may not produce exactly what is required, but will provide an acceptable match.

For an exact match you need a router and one or two cutters from a specialist router bit manufacturer. First, draw the outline of the molding on to lined tracing paper. If you are copying a molding, a contour gauge makes this an easy task. By studying the outline you will be able to break it down into its various shapes, which you can match up to router bits from the range available. You can then build up the molding by making several passes with the router, changing router bits and/or the angle of wood as necessary.

1 Modernizing a Staircase by Boxing it in
A staircase can be boxed-in by simply nailing sheets of MDF to a lumber frame so that the MDF panels will then appear to be an extension to the surrounding walls.

2 Making Baseboard
To match an existing baseboard yourself, build up one with suitable planks and moldings.

3 Attaching to Plastered Wall
Nail the baseboard to wood blocks and a batten which is screwed and anchored to the wall.

Panel molding

Scoop molding

Batten

Mounting block

GLASS SHELVES

ATTACHING BASEBOARDS AND ARCHITRAVES

When attaching baseboards to a firm, flat base of MDF, the molding can be nailed in place using finishing nails. Punch the nail heads below the surface and fill the indentations, rubbing down the filler before painting.

When attaching a baseboard to a plastered wall, nail it to wood blocks of the same thickness as the plaster layer. The blocks are screwed and anchored to the wall.

At external corners, the edges of the baseboard should be mitered. At internal corners, one baseboard is cut square and is attached to the corner. The end of the adjacent baseboard is scribed to the outline of the first and simply butts against it.

Architraves, the moldings around door frames, are mitered at 45° at the top corners, and at the bottom are cut square with the floor. They are held in place on the surface of the plaster around the door by nailing through them into the door frame.

④ Dealing with Corners
Baseboards and architraves at external corners can be mitered. At internal corners butt join and scribe.

Glass shelves are excellent for display, but the glass must be sufficiently thick to take the load to be placed on it. The supports must be well attached, too.

Ideally, use tempered glass or laminated safety glass, although ordinary float glass can also be used. The important thing is to ensure that the glass is thick enough to carry the load likely to be placed on it, and that the shelf supports are also spaced with this in mind. Ask your glass merchant's advice.

The minimum thickness of glass to be used for shelving is $\frac{1}{4}$in (6mm). This is suitable for light loads only and brackets spaced no further than 16in (400mm) apart. For normal loading, increase the thickness of the glass to $\frac{3}{8}$in (9mm) and the brackets can be spaced up to $27\frac{1}{2}$in (700mm) apart. If the shelves are likely to be heavily loaded – with books, for example – use $\frac{3}{8}$in (9mm) glass, but reduce the bracket spacing to a maximum of $19\frac{1}{2}$in (500mm). For safety, ask the supplier to polish the edges of the glass.

In the photograph here, the glass shelves rest on shelf support studs attached to the side walls of the alcove. There is a wide range of these neat studs in metal and plastic. Sometimes the studs simply screw to the sides of the alcove, but more commonly the studs are pushed into pre-drilled holes, allowing the shelves to be adjustable if a series of holes is drilled. Another way to have adjustable glass shelves is to install a slotted-upright adjustable shelving system for which special glass shelf holding brackets or adaptors are available.

For an "invisible" method of attachment, there are cantilever supports, where a narrow bracket to the full width of the shelf is attached to the rear wall, and the glass shelf is slotted into the bracket.

For bathrooms, there is a wide range of glass shelf support brackets, usually with a chrome finish.

⑤ A Selection of Supports
A selection of support brackets for glass shelves; some for permanent shelves; stud types are adjustable.

⑥ Cantilever Shelf Support
For an "invisible" attachment, a cantilever bracket to shelf width is attached to the rear wall.

PART 4

BATHROOMS AND BEDROOMS

The bathroom is not a simple room to renovate, restore, or redecorate. Often, a new bathroom seems to be an expensive luxury when compared with other home improvements which appear more urgent. Besides, any undertaking in the bathroom can turn into a major task if new plumbing is involved. However, as the hand-built bathroom and other projects featured in this book show, remodeling the bathroom can be as easy and satisfying to carry out as work in any other room. Leaving the bathtub, basin, shower, and lavatory in place, you can completely transform your bathroom by tiling walls, by laying a new floor, and by adding shelves and cabinets, towel rods and mirrors to your existing layout.

In the bedroom, doing-it-yourself gives you the opportunity to create clothes storage that meets your exact requirements. You can make the room more comfortable and practical by constructing your own built-in wardrobes, building a bed, or even creating a work area. A folding screen can quickly and efficiently modify a spare room from a study or a place for storage to a cozy guest bedroom.

People are often put off attempting alterations to the bathroom because they feel that it inevitably involves complex plumbing tasks. However, there is an enormous amount that can be done which is simple and effective. With today's easy-to-use, flexible plumbing and piping accessories, even some plumbing can be undertaken by the amateur. But always check that it is legal for you to tamper with plumbing and that you are insured for any leaks and damage. Never undertake this kind of work unless you are confident of your ability.

Also, before you plan your new bathroom or revamp an existing one, make sure that you plan the workload carefully in advance. The relocating of bathroom fixtures is not always possible given existing water pipes, and moving the main drain which serves the lavatory can be particularly difficult. Local codes may impose significant restrictions on this for obvious reasons. Remember that wiring must be completely waterproofed and that only pull-cord switches and approved electric razor outlets can be placed in the bathroom. Overflows and drainage in floors are also important, given the likelihood of water spillage on the occasions when faucets are accidentally not turned off, or when bathtubs or showers leak.

BELOW THE SURFACE

A false wall hides plumbing and wiring, and provides an alcove for recessing a radiator (previous page). Getting the "workings" of the bathroom out of the way so that the surface materials are uninterrupted is the most important aspect of a successful bathroom. Here the material is magnificent marble used in the form of slips (solid marble tiles) which cover almost every surface, including the floor.

In a small house or apartment where space is limited, the bathroom is often the ideal place to plumb in a washing machine; again, there may be restrictions on this, so make sure you are within the law and the safety regulations and seek expert advice before you start work.

Using wooden stud partitions, or brick or concrete block, it is not difficult to build your own bathtub and basin surrounds, perhaps incorporating storage and a vanity unit. Finished surfaces can be made from tiles, wood paneling, marble slips, or laminates. A fitted closet, perhaps a variation on your bedroom clothes storage, can be installed for storing tow-els, linen, and bulk purchases of toilet rolls, as well as soaps and lotions.

It can be a good idea to make a feature of attractive jars and bottles, bowls of small soaps, shaving equipment, and other bathroom accessories. They are often appealing enough to display on open shelves. Installing mirrors, towel rods, new faucets, and other features can enhance the style as well as the practicality of your bathroom. By changing these small features, it is sometimes possible to transform the look of a bathroom eco-nomically and without a complete re-ordering of the plumbing system: think carefully about *your* particular needs.

MIRRORS AND TILES

A sophisticated white bathroom is simplicity itself (opposite) with its perfect grid of tiles. The floor-to-ceiling mirror gives a sense of space and reflects light. Chrome faucets and shower fixtures, together with a long chrome rod for towels, unify the decorative scheme.

A do-it-yourself bathroom (above), finished with ceramic tiles and white linoleum floor, has mirror on two facing walls to add light and space, with glass shelves neatly fitted into a recess. Brightly colored accessories lend a cheerful air.

LIGHTING AND HEATING

Safety first is essential when considering how to heat, ventilate, and light your bathroom. Any electrical installation in a bathroom should be carried out by a professional electrician.

Lighting a bathroom is a challenge but with the range of fixtures and types of bulbs available today, you can achieve excellent results. If your bathroom has no window, invest in good lighting to compensate for the lack of natural light.

Avoid fluorescent lights. The effect this light gives is too dull and even, and does nothing to flatter either the attractive surfaces in a bathroom, or the person using it. An overhead, central pendant is rarely necessary or useful in a bathroom and once again will limit the attractiveness of the whole room. Consider the many other possibilities. Incandescent strip lights can give a warm glow to an alcove or a shelving system. Incandescent strips or bulbs can also be used around a mirror for a Hollywood effect. Low-voltage fittings with tungsten halogen bulbs will make your bathroom sparkle – especially if it is modern and features chrome and ceramics. Remember to incorporate lights so that they are angled to reflect off mirrors but do not produce an unpleasant glare.

If your bathroom is to be styled as a comfortable and relaxing room – perhaps with easy chairs, warm natural woods, and softer decoration – then the lighting should enhance this. You cannot install side lamps or pretty wall lights, but ensure that what lighting you do incorporate is easily adjusted with dimmer switches (placed outside the bathroom) and is subtle, rather than glaring, light. Candles can be used if you really want to indulge yourself in your bathroom

You may want to read while soaking in the bathtub, so ensure that a light is suitably placed to make this possible, and that you have incorporated space to place your book out of water's reach while you are in the tub.

Showers can present lighting problems. Closing the shower curtain or installing a unit in an enclosed space could make it very dark. Avoid this by strategically placing light fixtures or consider installing an outdoor waterproof light in the shower. It is essential to plan your lighting before you undertake any tiling.

Daylight is always an added pleasure in a bathroom. Blinds can lend privacy to the room; but if the window does not look out on to a neighbor's house, it can remain bare. A skylight is very pleasing in a bathroom and is often a good addition if the room is without a window.

Undue condensation is unpleasant and can damage the decoration or fabric of the room. Both heating and ventilation are important if condensation is to be avoided. It is usually illegal to have an internal bathroom without a window, unless you have adequate air extraction and circulation which remains switched on for a certain time whenever the room is used. Seek professional advice on this.

The heating will depend upon the system in your house or apartment but try to incorporate heated towel rods. Radiators are now available which are shaped as towel rods and are specially designed for bathrooms; alternatively, you can install electrically heated rods with a safe bathroom switch.

WARM ILLUMINATION

Reflected in a wall of mirror above the bathtub in this warm and elegant bathroom (opposite above) is a false wall which hides pipes and wiring. It also provides a recess into which a basin, mirror, and shelf as well as a discreet closet have been fitted. Incandescent strip lighting has been incorporated into the wood cornice of the room, providing a general soft illumination. The radiator is stylish and contemporary, and fits neatly beneath the window. Wooden blinds and a chrome bar, stretching across the width of the room for hanging towels, are excellent accessories.

STRONG ACCESSORIES

In a small bathroom (opposite below left) a metal grid provides a durable radiator cover to keep it flush with the line of the wall.

A heavy-duty, waterproof, industrial-type light fixture hangs above a basin (opposite below center) to great effect. Its grid design is reflected in the vertical radiator which heats the room.

Another method of waterproofing is to install outdoor lights in the bathroom, shown here (opposite below right), giving a strong, concentrated light above a basin.

BATHROOM MATERIALS

The bathroom should, of necessity, be a room of resistant, durable surfaces. Marble, mirror, slate, glass, laminate, chrome, plastic, vitreous china, treated wood, and water-resistant paint are the tough, elegant materials that bathrooms are made of. Softness can be provided by towels, bathrobes, comfortable easy chairs, cotton shower curtains, and bath mats.

Soften a bathroom considerably with accessories, or turn it into a stark interior — the level of sleek functionalism is up to you. For example, if you decide to tile the room, the type of tiles you choose can have dramatically different effects. Brick-shaped tiles in white ceramic with a border of a contrasting dark color produce an old-fashioned and traditional appeal. Expensive marble slips are a pure luxury; decorated or textured tiles will have their own impact, while plain white squares will provide a simple harmony.

The materials you choose will depend largely on your budget. Marble or granite is not easily affordable or simple to install. Tiles are also a relatively expensive way to decorate large areas, although not difficult to apply if the wall surface is flat. Wooden paneling can be highly effective and is available by the yard. Tiles can be used for areas where water will often be splashed, and other wall surfaces can be painted with water-resistant paint.

Floor coverings must be practical, resilient, and preferably waterproof. The drawback to using ceramic or marble tiles, or other hard surfaces, for flooring is that they are cold, whereas sealed cork and inexpensive sheet vinyl provide warmth. Carpet is best avoided, but rugs, especially if made from washable cotton, are a good alternative. Any bathroom floor should be able to withstand dampness; vinyl tiles and wood block will rise easily if water penetrates the surface, so carefully choose your flooring.

MIXING MATERIALS

Small white tiles, a clear plastic shower curtain, and a pretty porthole window (above) create a bright, airy bathroom in a small space.

Exposed brick forms a partition wall between bedroom and bathroom (center). The strong texture of the brick is offset against the clean and smooth white tiles.

Glass bricks are an excellent choice for a bathroom (below) as they are easily wiped clean and allow light to shine through them. Here they have been effectively combined with a steel sink with exposed pipes and a dramatic black Venetian blind.

DECORATIVE FINISHES

A showerhead has been recessed into marble slips above a bathtub (opposite left) and a deep alcove allows for generous shelves. The elements of the bathroom are unified by the pale gray marble to stylish effect.

Black and white tiles form a decorative checkerboard frieze (opposite above right) in this lively bathroom. The black slats on the white blinds continue the duotone theme. Other strong features include the chrome supports for the double basins and the "dressing room" lights around the mirror.

Unusual finishes give this bathroom originality (opposite right center). The basin unit is made from black-stained wood, and is topped with marble-chip terrazzo to produce a dramatic and luxurious effect.

The rolled top of an old-fashioned bathtub (opposite below right) and the traditional contrasting strip of tiles at "picture rail" height set the scene for a bathroom styled in the past. A basin has been set into an old wood cabinet and the mirror has a wooden frame.

BATHTUBS AND SHOWERS

Deciding upon the type of bathtub or the brand of shower unit to use is perhaps the most daunting aspect of planning a bathroom, since there is such a wide range available. Your do-it-yourself skill lies in placing the bathtub and shower in an attractive, practical, and water-tight unit.

A bathtub is best placed in a niche or alcove and if one is not ready-made in the room, you can create one with a hand-built partition made from wooden paneling, brick, concrete blocks, or glass bricks. A separate shower unit can be placed against this panel. The whole area is finished in the same material for unity.

Shower units can be placed above a bathtub if space is limited, and a screen or curtain hung around the tub to avoid water spillage and to provide privacy. Consider using a cotton curtain, if it can drip dry, as an alternative to plastic. A glass screen is also an attractive option and can be hinged so that it is turned away when not in use.

Ready-made shower units that come as a separate shell to install in your bathroom can be effective but will not harmonize nearly as well as a unit built yourself. The shower head, faucet, and mixing valve should be all that protrudes from the wall, but make sure you have access to the mechanism and pipework if necessary, in case of problems. Using a stud partition makes this a lot simpler. Similarly, with a casing for the bathtub, make sure you can gain easy access to the area behind and beneath the faucets. When building a partition for a bathtub, consider including a small alcove or niche in the wall as a decorative feature, and remember that you can vary the width of the shelf surrounding the tub.

You can give the effect of a sunken bathtub in a reasonable-sized bathroom by building a generous frame around the tub in wood, which is then tiled.

LOW-LEVEL LIGHTING

A false step raised above the floor creates the impression of a sunken bath (above). The luxury of this is heightened by the use of soft gray mosaic tiles, an edging of beech wood, and a wall of mirror. Heating is situated below the raised step and escapes through a vent.

TWO-TONE CHECKERBOARD

The most effective shower unit is built-in to a bathroom (opposite) with a raised shower base, and is part of the overall design rather than an added extra. Link all the elements with the facing material – here a dramatic use of black and white tiles.

BASINS AND VANITY UNITS

There are two basic alternatives for basins: freestanding designs, often on a pedestal, or basins fitted into a framework, commonly known as a vanity unit. What you build around your basin will to some extent depend upon this choice.

A vanity unit can be a very simple but highly effective home-built project. It consists of a broad shelf or top into which a basin is set; the unit is supported by open shelves or a closet. By building it yourself you can ensure that the unit fits the dimensions of your bathroom precisely, is integrated into the decorative scheme, and contains storage space according to your needs.

If you are reconstructing or building a completely new bathroom, then your decision on how to construct the vanity unit will be decided as part of the overall bathroom design. Vanity units can, of course, also be installed as part of an overhaul of an existing bathroom.

The frame, in wood or brick, can be tiled or painted, with plastic-laminate shelves underneath, and doors placed over them if required. Any material that is hard and waterproof – such as solid marble, plastic laminate, ceramic tiles, or natural but treated wood – can be used for the top surface of the unit.

Another example of a false wall creating an attractive recess for a basin (above) beautifully finished in sleek, cool terrazzo tiles.

An interesting idea for double basins in a spacious bathroom (below left) has them on either side of a central column faced in mirror.

A '30s-style bathroom (below right) with traditional decorative elements has a vanity unit with a marble top and an elegant mirror.

You can embellish both fitted and freestanding basins with all manner of bathroom accessories. A vast range of ready-made accessories is available – shelves, toothbrush mugs and holders, mirrors, and cabinets – which can coordinate with toilet-paper holders, towel rods, soap dishes, and clothes hooks. Alternatively, you can combine handmade shelves and accessories with bought items. For an original approach, especially in a period house, you could install antique or second-hand pieces such as a hanging shelf unit with fitted mirrors from the Victorian era, a mirror with an attractive frame, or old shop fixtures converted to wall cabinets.

Make sure that you have ample room over the basin to bend over without banging your head or splashing water over shelves and surrounds. A basin that is too small is often a major problem in a bathroom. You could consider using an old-fashioned kitchen stone sink if you want a more generous basin.

Changing or installing new faucets has a dramatic effect in the bathroom. For the hand basin it is far more practical to have a dual faucet which combines hot and cold water so that you can rinse your hands comfortably and quickly.

This stylish modern bathroom takes the design for its vanity unit from a fitted kitchen (above). A white laminated top has an inset basin with a range of drawers and cupboards below.

A stone "Belfast" sink, usually the preserve of the country kitchen, has here been incorporated into a bathroom (below left). The unit which surrounds it has deep open shelves for towels and forms a screen to hide the lavatory.

In a tiny cloakroom (below right), the black rim of the small sink is continued in the window-sills. A curved laminate front hides plumbing.

BATHROOM STORAGE

What you keep in the bathroom apart from essential items depends upon the size of the room. A large bathroom can accommodate a spacious closet, which you can build yourself, for storing linen, towels, bulk supplies of toilet paper, and anything else you want out of the way. A tiny bathroom should be more minimal, with just the fixtures and sufficient supplies of toiletries in evidence. Towels and bulk supplies can be stored elsewhere.

Closed closets and open shelves are the ideal combination for bathroom storage. Open shelves can carry jars, flowers, towels, and other objects, but remember that whatever you display in a bathroom has to be regularly washed and dusted. It is easy to be seduced into displaying rows of pretty bottles and lotions as seen in endless magazine articles, but in reality a relatively bare bathroom is much more practical. The area above the basin and the shelf around the bathtub is the favorite place for such displays. When planning yours, take into account which items you need close by and which would look better behind closed doors; build your units accordingly.

On open shelves, store items neatly in containers. Large wicker baskets can add an attractive and softening dimension to a white-tiled bathroom.

Shelves may be tiled if they are built as chunky hollow constructions rather than made of single planks of wood. Glass shelves are always well-suited to bathrooms. You can create a unit incorporating glass shelves in the design so that they rest within a frame of wood. Cabinets are also reasonably easy to construct and can have mirrored or painted doors.

Design the whole area above the basin with care, taking into account the amount of display space you want and how much hidden storage you need there. If you have children, you should store razors and medicines in a lockable cabinet that is out of reach of tiny hands.

A built-in cupboard can be extremely useful. In a limited space, closet-space can be part of a vanity unit but in a larger bathroom, design a closet to fill an entire wall. Doors can be made of wooden louver slats or painted MDF (medium-density fiberboard), they can be laminated or glazed. Either of the wardrobe designs illustrated on pages 36 and 54 can be adapted for the bathroom.

If kitchen space is limited, washing machines and clothes dryers can be installed in the bathroom, but make sure there is adequate ventilation and that the machines can be easily reached for maintenance. In some instances, it is illegal to install washing machines in the bathroom, so check local codes first.

The area of exposed pipes behind a toilet can be attractively concealed behind a wooden housing which will also provide a useful shelf along the top. If you have a bidet, this can be installed in a similar way for a neat appearance. Whenever you box-in pipes, always consider turning the wooden box itself into something useful such as a shelf or even a seat.

If you are building your own bathtub surround, consider incorporating a hinged shelf if there is room at the end of the tub, so that the otherwise dead space beneath can be used for storage.

Soiled clothes and linen are often kept in an overflowing and rather untidy basket or plastic container which does nothing to enhance a bathroom. If you are creating your own bathroom, consider building a box for dirty linen. In an existing bathroom, one could be incorporated into a cupboard. A broad shelf could have a boxed-in support and be hinged along its length, or in part, to act as a lid; in addition, you could turn the lid into a seat using a loose cushion.

BATHROOM STORAGE

This vanity unit is styled for storage (top) with its practical drawers and cupboards.

In a high but narrow Edwardian bathroom (above), the dead space near the ceiling has been used for pine storage closets, housed in a false wall.

A glossy stylized bathroom (opposite) has ceramic-tiled, steel-faced partitions to hold glass shelves. Further storage is provided on metal carts which are pushed into the recess when they are not in use.

Given adequate storage space, the bathroom is
an excellent location for a spacious, fully fitted
closet when you require extra storage. This
elegant fitted unit (opposite above right) is
given a graphic black trim.

The area around the basin is easily utilized for
extra storage (opposite below right). Here the
closets are situated above and below the basin
to hide bathroom clutter.

BEDROOM POTENTIAL

The bedroom is a private haven for relaxation and sleep. Here you can concentrate on building projects which will heighten your enjoyment of the room and enhance it.

There are still practical considerations to think about before starting work – clothes storage, lighting, and comfort are all important factors – but what you put in your bedroom, and the style you create there, is completely up to you. There is enormous potential here and doing-it-yourself can make all the difference between an untidy, uncomfortable, and unrelaxing room and a well-appointed, stylish, and appealing one.

Wardrobes are an obvious and worthwhile project to undertake, since good fitted storage will add enormously to the tidiness and convenience of the room. They can also vastly improve its appearance. By designing and building them yourself you can ensure that they fit the dimensions of the room precisely and are in keeping with its decorative scheme and architectural details.

There are many other things to build in the bedroom. Window seats are a delightful addition if you want somewhere to read and relax, have a room with a view, and need some extra storage, since the area below the seat provides capacity for bedding, linen, and clothes.

Of course, you can also build a bed. There is a spectacular bed project with spacious built-in storage later in this book, but a simpler model could be created instead. A platform for a mattress is all you need. It could be a platform under which you can stand in order to make the best use of very limited space. Below it you can create a storage area, install a desk, open shelves, or a second bunk bed.

You can embellish a hand-made or store-bought bed in many ways. Add a headboard as something to rest against, as a decorative feature, and as protection for the wall behind. A simple frame with four posts, one at each corner of the bed, connected at the top, will transform any simple divan into a magnificent and luxurious four poster.

The materials you use in the bedroom are not going to have to endure too much wear and tear so it is here that you can indulge yourself with more expensive materials; they will not need to be replaced as often as those used elsewhere. Natural wood or painted cheaper wood is always effective. In small bedrooms, mirror can be used for door fronts to increase the sense of space.

SEATING SOLUTIONS

The broad sweep of a bay window (opposite above) has been turned into a sunny place to sit with an easily-constructed wooden window seat. Low level radiators fit below the center seat. In a smaller bedroom (opposite below right) a padded window seat has filled the gentle curve of a bay window.

In the narrow corner of a bedroom (below center), a television has been placed on an angled bracket above a built-in storage box. Plump cushions on top turn it into a seat.

INSPIRING IDEAS

Romantic muslin drapes (below left) are hung above a bed from wooden poles bound together and suspended from the ceiling by chains.

A flat-fronted, wall-to-wall fitted wardrobe has been given glamorous mirror doors (below right). The wall of glass reflects and doubles any light source in the room, adds depth and space, and is stunning in a room which is dedicated as much to dressing as to sleeping.

Dramatic decorative detailing has been added to a bedroom (opposite below left) by uplighters placed on columns. These highlight a curved architrave which frames a door. On either side are fitted wardrobes.

Providing practical bedside shelves, a unit in mellow wood (opposite below center) has been built at the head of a bed, situated beneath an attractive sloping window. The wide shelf which sits on top of the unit offers display space and the lower shelves can carry books, radio, lights, and other essentials.

BEDROOM STORAGE

Clothes are the major item for storage in bedrooms. You may also want rows of bookshelves, a linen chest, a vanity-unit for make-up and toiletries, a display area for a treasured collection, or a corner fitted as a home office. These are, however, added extras. We all have to store clothes. A dressing room is undoubtedly the best solution but one that is only possible with adequate space.

Doing-it-yourself not only allows you the freedom to design and build a fine wardrobe in keeping with the room but also to customize it to meet your individual needs. You can decide the length of shoe rails, the depth and number of drawers for underwear, accessories, socks, and scarves, the length of a closet pole for bulkier garments, and the number of shelves and how they should be divided for sweaters, t-shirts, and jeans.

There are many ready-made storage accessories for fitting out cupboards, and some of the most effective are made from wire mesh and plastic; they include drawers and containers. Alternatively you can construct fixtures from wood. Attach mirrors to the inside doors of wardrobes so that you can check your appearance. Visit a few stores which you consider to be well-designed, see how they display

Linking a bedroom with a bathroom (above) is a passage which has been transformed into a walk-in wardrobe with ingenious wooden fixtures.

A false wall has created a deep and beautifully detailed recess for a window and allowed for low subtle closets to be added on either side (center).

their clothes, and use this as inspiration to design your changing room.

A dressing room or dressing area can be made even in quite limited space by building a partition in the bedroom, utilizing a passage, or using a box room. Line it from top to bottom with pigeon-holes, rails, shelves, and drawers to create a neat, orderly storage area.

You can incorporate lighting into a wardrobe or as part of the dressing room by installing it under shelves. In addition, make sure you have adequate light in front of the mirror.

Low closets or high shelves can be equally effective in a bedroom – as discreet storage or display areas for any kind of item from linen and towels to personal mementoes.

In a very small bedroom, a studio room for living in, or a box room for guests, built-in storage is particularly important. Use every spare inch of space to the best possible advantage, filling whole walls with shelves and cupboards, building units rather than using freestanding wardrobes or tables. Make the bed into a storage area by choosing a mattress or divan that can be placed on a storage platform. Place shelves above or below the bed rather than use bedside tables.

A magnificent built-in wardrobe, everybody's dream (below and opposite), is fitted with superb clothes storage – a closet pole, suspended open drawers, and neat shelves. The folding doors are faced with mirror.

TILED BATHROOM

Traditionally, bathrooms tend to be rather badly organized rooms, in which a collection of pipework and bathroom equipment is arranged, so it seems, to suit the convenience of the plumber rather than the bather.

This design tries to organize the various elements of a bathroom so that plumbing work, which can often look rather brutal, is hidden from view. The bathroom is uncluttered and easy to clean – requirements which I think are essential, given that the whole point of a bathroom is hygiene.

The bathroom system is remarkably easy to construct once you have mastered the simple art of cutting, laying, and grouting wall tiles. The cavity behind the bathtub, shower, and washbasin allows for pipework and drainage to be hidden. The large mirror behind the bathtub, while not essential, gives a sense of scale to a small space.

Tile colors and patterns can obviously be selected to suit your own particular preferences. I think that plain white tiles combined with white baths, basins, bidets, and showers are particularly pleasant in bathrooms; they have light, reflective qualities, that induce an atmosphere of cleanliness and hygiene.

Tiled frame for a
Simple vanity
unit

Mirror

light under tiled shelf

Recessed Basin in
tiled top, with wood
Shelf & towel rod.

FRONT ELEVATION

wall of mirror

Bath tub

recessed lighting

mirror

Thick glass shelf

removable tiled panel for access to plumbing

Shower tray

Towel rod
Wooden shelf
Basket for dirty laundry

PLAN

false wall makes a duct for all pipework & plumbing

tiled surround to Bath tub

shower curtain & rail

Basin let into tiled top

TILED BATHROOM: BATHTUB UNIT

This project shows how to make a tiled bathroom with the fixtures set into hollow panel frames so that all the pipework is kept out of sight. The dimensions of the frames are based on those of your bathroom suite and your wall tiles. Obviously, the layout will have to be adapted to suit your particular bathroom.

It is strongly advised that you make a sketch of the proposed bathroom and discuss it with your plumber and electrician so that they can suggest the exact positioning of pipes and wiring, where access will be needed, and the sequence in which the work will be carried out. Coordinating your tasks with the installation of the plumbing and wiring will have to be carefully worked out between the three of you, since it is easier to put in the pipes and cables as the elements of the bathroom are built. Of course, this is not a problem if you are doing your own plumbing. This is now feasible, thanks to the availability of a wide range of easy-to-fit modern plumbing components, such as plastic supply and waste pipes, and push-fit joints. However, by building the frames and fitting some of the panels temporarily, it should be possible to do all the plumbing in one session.

Before starting, it is important to spend some time working out the dimensions carefully so that the minimum of tiles will need to be cut, and so that any cut tiles can be located where they will be least noticeable. Try to use only whole tiles. Tiles which overlap the edges of others should be positioned so that their flat surface is uppermost and the joint is at the side. This will occur at the top of the shower tray and where the bath and wall tiles come on to the bathtub. Always think about how water will run off the tiles. Wherever possible it should not run down into a joint, but off one tile and on to another to avoid unnecessary water penetration.

MATERIALS

Part	Quantity	Material	Length
BATHTUB FRAME			
TOP AND BOTTOM RAILS	4	2 × 3in (50 × 75mm) S4S softwood	Bathtub length, plus width of two tiles
UPRIGHT RAILS	8	2 × 3in (50 × 75mm) S4S softwood	Internal distance between top and bottom rails
END FRAME TOP AND BOTTOM RAILS	4	2 × 3in (50 × 75mm) S4S softwood	Internal distance between inside faces of front and back panels
END FRAME UPRIGHT RAILS	4	2 × 3in (50 × 75mm) S4S softwood	Internal distance between end frame top and bottom rails
END SHELVING STRIPS	2	$\frac{1}{2}$in (12mm) water-resistant plywood; cut to tile width	Distance from back wall to front face of bath panel
BACK SHELVING STRIP	1	Plywood as above; width as above	Length of bathtub
FRONT SHELVING STRIP	1	Plywood as above; cut to tile width, less a tile thickness to allow shelf tiles to overlap edge of facing tiles on bathtub panel	Length of bathtub
BATHTUB PANEL	1	Plywood as above; width as height of front frame	As front frame and to overlap end panels (if any)

The entire framework is made from 2 × 3in (50 × 75mm) S4S (smooth 4 sides) softwood, skinned with $\frac{3}{4}$in (19mm) or $\frac{1}{2}$in (12mm) water-resistant plywood. Our tiles are 4$\frac{1}{4}$in (108mm) square, which works well with this framework.

BATHTUB

Measure for the frames to fit each side of the bathtub, allowing for $\frac{1}{2}$in (12mm) plywood to be attached on top. This will be exactly level with the rim of the bathtub, and will allow the tiles to rest on the tub rim for an easily sealed joint.

Using 2 × 3in (50 × 75mm) lumber, nail the frames so that the top and bottom rails run the full length of the bathtub recess and the uprights fit between them — one at each end and two spaced inside them at equal distances.

The bathtub will either rest in a cradle or will be supplied with adjustable legs. The manufacturer's assembly instructions should be carefully followed. To spread the load across several floor joists, the bathtub feet should be rested on 2 × 3in (50 × 75mm) battens laid on their sides on the floor, and allowance should be made for these when measuring the height of the tub. The bathtub should be carefully positioned lengthwise and widthwise to ensure that water drains properly to the waste outlet.

BATHTUB FRAME ASSEMBLY

TOP RAIL

SHELVING STRIPS

END FRAME

BACK FRAME

TILES OVERLAP BATHTUB PANEL

UPRIGHTS

FRONT FRAME

BATHTUB PANEL

DOME-HEAD SCREW

End frames are made up in the same way as the front and back frames, and are made to fit between them. Allowance is made for the thickness of the front panel ($\frac{1}{2}$in [12mm]). If you are installing the bathtub tight to the wall or partitions at the foot or head, these end frames can be dispensed with, although you will need to cut top rails at the ends to support the shelving strips.

INSTALLING FRAMES

Screw the back frame to the wall, shimming underneath it if necessary to ensure that it is level. Screw through the end frames into the back frame uprights and into the wall or partition at each end if there is one there. Put the bathtub in place and level it for correct drainage.

Position the front frame, screwing it into the end frames and the side walls or partitions where appropriate.

ATTACHING THE PLYWOOD SHELF STRIPS

Measure for these strips using $4\frac{1}{4}$in (108mm) wide (or tile width if different) $\frac{1}{2}$in (12mm) water-resistant plywood to the width of the frame to the outer edges of the front frame, so that they fit across the bathtub at the head and foot, overhanging on the inside edges of the top rail.

Measure the spaces along the sides of the frame between the end shelves and cut two more lengths of plywood to fit between them. Note that the front shelf will be slightly narrower than the others as the tiles on this shelf will overlap the edges of the tiles used to cover the front panel of the bathtub unit.

Apply clear silicone-rubber caulking to the inside edges of all of the shelves and screw them down into the frame on all sides so that the plywood butts against the bathtub exactly level with the rim. The join between the bathtub and the shelves must be sealed with caulking to prevent water getting under the edging tiles. These strips make a good surface for tiling.

INSTALLING FRONT PANEL

Cut out the front panel from $\frac{1}{2}$in (12mm) water-resistant plywood and fit it over the frame and any end panels, if required. The front panel must be removable to make access easy in case you need to adjust or repair the internal plumbing. The panel is secured with dome-head screws inserted through the tiles once these have been fitted.

TILED BATHROOM: SHOWER UNIT

Part	Quantity	Material	Length
SHOWER PARTITION			
FRONT STUD	1	2 × 3in (50 × 75mm) S4S softwood	Floor to ceiling height
TOP AND BOTTOM RAILS	2 per side	2 × 3in (50 × 75mm) S4S softwood	Back of front stud to back wall
BACK STUD	1	2 × 3in (50 × 75mm) S4S softwood	Internal distance between top and bottom rails
MIDDLE RAILS	As required	2 × 3in (50 × 75mm) S4S softwood	Internal distance between front and back studs
SIDE PANELS	2 per side	¾in (19mm) water-resistant plywood	Length and width as overall dimensions of lumber partition frame
SHOWER BASE			
TOP AND BOTTOM RAILS	4	2 × 2in (50 × 50mm) S4S softwood	Width between side partitions
SIDE STUDS	4	2 × 2in (50 × 50mm) S4S softwood	Height of shower tray, less 4½in (112mm)*
FRONT PANEL	1	¾in (19mm) water-resistant plywood; width as distance between side panels	Height of base frame
TOP PANEL	1	As above; width as above	Width from front of base panel to shower tray
SHOWER CEILING			
CEILING PANEL	1	¾in (19mm) water-resistant plywood; depth as width of recess	Depth of shower recess
FRONT PANEL	1	As above; depth as above	Height of tiles
FRONT PANEL SUPPORT RAIL	1	2 × 2in (50 × 50mm) S4S softwood	Width of ceiling panel
CEILING FIXING BATTENS	2	2 × 2in (50 × 50mm) S4S softwood	Depth of ceiling panel, less 2in (50mm)*

*Approximate lengths only – refer to copy for actual size

SHOWER PARTITIONS

Measure the floor-to-ceiling height for the front stud in exactly the place where it will be positioned. Then measure for the top and bottom rails to be positioned behind the front stud, having previously worked out the front-to-back depth of your shower recess (dependent on size of shower tray – ours is the depth of the tray plus one tile height). Cut them to length from the 2 × 3in (50 × 75mm) S4S lumber. Next, cut the back stud to fit between the top and bottom rails, that is, to the length of the front stud, less the combined thickness of the top and bottom rails (approximately 3in [75mm]).

BASIC FRAME

Nail the front stud on to the top rail with 10d common nails, driving them in with a support behind (*see* **Techniques, page 24**). Nail the bottom rail in place at the bottom, then insert the back stud ½in (12mm) in from the ends, to make scribing easier when the partitions are attached to the wall. (If pipes have to be run along the back, this back stud can be positioned even farther in.) Nail the back stud in place. Repeat the process for a second partition, if one is required.

MIDDLE RAILS

These brace the basic frame to make it sturdier, and are also used to make attachments to any adjacent support battens and fixtures. They should therefore be placed at heights which coincide with the locations of these fixtures, such as faucets and shower heads.

In our case, a rail is needed where the basin and shelf supports meet the side. You may need additional support for the shower spray head, depending on the type of shower used (fig 1, page 24). Another cross rail would be needed where you have to make any joints in the plywood panels to make up the full height of your room. Space other cross-rails at intervals of about 24–36in (610–900mm).

It is a good idea to include a small removable access panel opposite the shower fixtures in case there is

1 **Assembly of the Shower Partition Basic Frame**
Assemble basic framework from S4S lumber as shown, using common nails. Nail front stud to top rail, then bottom rail, and add the back stud, insetting it by ½in (12mm) to aid scribing.

Back stud

Bottom rail

Top rail

Front stud

SHOWER UNIT ASSEMBLY

CEILING FIXING BATTEN

CEILING UNIT

TILED FRONT PANEL

ASSEMBLED PARTITION

SHOWER TRAY POSITION

SHOWER BASE UNIT

TOP PANEL

TILED FRONT PANEL

TOP RAIL

PLYWOOD SIDE PANEL

FRONT PANEL SUPPORT

BACK STUD

MIDDLE RAILS

FRONT STUD

TILED SIDE PANEL

TOP RAIL

SIDE STUD

BOTTOM RAIL

ever a problem with the plumbing. This is done by making a panel to coincide with whole tiles (fig 2). The panel is attached to additional rails inside the frame. You may prefer to make one large panel to give access to the shower mixing valve and the spray head. If you are using a plumber, ask his advice.

ADDING THE SIDES

When both frames are nailed up, measure for the side panels to finish flush with all the edges. Then cut out the required number of panels from $\frac{3}{4}$in (19mm) water-resistant plywood, making suré that you cut them all square. Mark the center lines of all the studs on the edges of the frames as a guide for nailing the side panels.

Lay the frame flat and lay the *inner* plywood panel on top. Line up the edge of the panel accurately with the *front* stud. Glue together and then nail down into the stud about every 6in (150mm), using 4d common nails. Use the center marks on the edges of the frame as an accurate guide for the nail positions,

to ensure that they are driven centrally into the rails.

Having nailed the front stud, pull the rest of the frame into square to align with the other edges of the plywood. Mark on the face of the plywood the center lines of the rails and back stud so that you have guide lines for nailing.

Continue nailing down along the top and bottom rails, the back stud, and the middle rails, checking as you do so that the frame is still square. Do not install the other side panel at this stage.

Repeat for the other partition.

INSTALLING PARTITIONS

Put the partitions in place, spacing them by the width of the shower tray. Use a carpenter's level and plumb bob to check that the partitions are standing plumb. Do any scribing necessary to fit the partitions to the wall (*see* **Techniques, page 31**). This does not have to be very accurate as the final joint between the partition and the wall will be achieved with the tiles. Install the partitions by screwing through the

back stud and shimming any gaps between the back stud and the wall where the screws are positioned.

Screw through the top rail into the ceiling. If possible, screw into the ceiling joists. You can find these by using a metal detector to locate the nails securing them (*see* **Techniques, page 24**). If the partitions fall between two joists (as is likely where the partitions run parallel with them), secure a blocking of 2 × 3in (50 × 75mm) lumber between the joists and screw into this. Depending on the location of your bathroom, you may have to go into the attic to do this, or it may be necessary to lift a few floorboards in the room above the shower position. It is a good idea to get an electrician to install the ceiling light at the same time.

Finally, screw the bottom rail into the floor, shimming under it if necessary to ensure that it sits square.

Temporarily attach the other plywood panel with a few nails only, not fully driven home. This will allow easy removal later, during plumbing, and will allow you to finish your framework first.

SHOWER BASE

Put the shower tray in place temporarily and adjust its legs so that the top of the tray is the height of whole tiles. Make a frame for the "step" at the front from 2 × 2in (50 × 50mm) S4S lumber to the width of the recess by the height of the shower tray, but allowing for the thickness of the plywood panel ($\frac{3}{4}$in [19mm]) which rests on top. The rails run the full width between the partitions, with the uprights between them. Butt the panel to the front of the shower tray and screw through the uprights into the sides of the partitions.

Make up an identical frame to the first, to be positioned in from the front edge of the partition by the thickness of the plywood. Screw through the uprights into the side partitions as before. If, as in our case, the total width of the step is only one tile, the two frames will almost touch each other. Cut a piece of $\frac{3}{4}$in (19mm) plywood to fit the front of this frame, flush with the top edge. Cut a top piece to rest on top of the frame, flush with the front of the

① Adding Sides to Frames
Middle rails are required at fixing positions for the bathtub or basin unit, possibly for the shower fixture, and also where it is necessary to join plywood panels. Nail down every 6in (150mm).

② Installing an Access Panel
It is wise to include an access panel opposite the shower fixture. Panel should coincide with whole tiles.

frame and butting up to the shower tray. Do not fit these pieces yet, so that you will have access for fitting the shower tray and installing the pipework *(see* **Plumbing and Wiring, page 206** *)*.

Refer to the manufacturer's instructions on how to assemble and install the shower tray. Some trays have to be rested on sturdy lumber battens to spread the weight of the tray when it is in use: if this is the case with yours, you may have to adjust the height of the support legs to accommodate the thickness of the support battens.

When attaching bathroom fixtures into the lumber frame, use a caulking gun to insert a generous line of caulking between the fixture and the framework. This acts as a second line of defense should water get under the tiles owing to the breakdown of the caulking which will be used between the fitting and the tiles *(see* **Tiling, page 36** *)*.

SHOWER CEILING

Measure the recess in the shower area and cut out a ceiling panel from ¾in (19mm) water-resistant plywood. Cut a front panel to rest on top of it, so that the total depth is sufficient to house a shower downlighter, while the panel lines up with a joint line in the tiled partitions and the wall. It is best to work out exactly where the tiles will lie. Alternatively, tile the partitions up to where you require the ceiling. Make up the ceiling unit and continue tiling.

Use a 2 × 2in (50 × 50mm) batten, glued and screwed in place, to join the ceiling panel and the front panel together at right angles. Assuming it is safe, cut a hole in the middle of the ceiling panel, and install the downlighter according to the manufacturer's instructions.

Cut two lengths of 2 × 2in (50 × 50mm) lumber to be attached horizontally to the inside faces of the partition panels, to allow the ceiling unit to be attached to the sides. Cut these battens so that they will fit behind the front batten, but do not secure them or the ceiling unit yet, as the plumbing must be completed.

Buy a shower rail the width of the shower recess and screw in place.

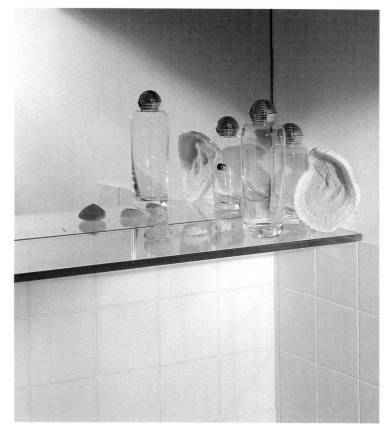

③ Making Shower Base to Height of Shower Tray
The base comprises two frames, covered by a front panel and joined by a top panel which is cut to the width of one tile. If shower tray is only one tile height high, top and bottom rails of frame will almost touch.

④ Shower Ceiling Assembly
Cut ceiling panel to fit between partitions. Front panel must be deep enough to hide shower downlighter.

GLASS SHELF

A sleek glass shelf sits above the basin unit (see page 207 for instructions).

TILED BATHROOM: BASIN UNIT

MATERIALS

BASIN FRAME

Part	Quantity	Material	Length
PARTITION FRAME FRONT STUD	1	2 × 3in (50 × 75mm) S4S softwood	Height of basin, less $\frac{1}{2}$in (12mm)
TOP AND BOTTOM RAILS	2	2 × 3in (50 × 75mm) S4S softwood	Distance from inside face of front stud to back wall
BACK STUD	1	2 × 3in (50 × 75mm) S4S softwood	Height of basin, less $\frac{1}{2}$in (12mm), less 4in (100mm)*
MIDDLE RAIL	1	2 × 3in (50 × 75mm) S4S softwood	Distance between inside faces of front and back studs
SIDE PANELS	1 or 2	$\frac{3}{4}$in (19mm) water-resistant plywood; width as overall width of frame	Height of frame
FRONT PANEL	1	Plywood as above; width to give sufficient depth to hide underside of basin	Distance between partition panel and side of shower partition
TOP PANEL	1	$\frac{3}{4}$in (19mm) water-resistant plywood; width as depth of recess	Width of alcove
FRONT PANEL SUPPORT RAIL	1	2 × 3in (50 × 75mm) S4S softwood or 2 × 2in (50 × 50mm) S4S softwood	Width of alcove
BASIN SUPPORT BATTEN	1	2 × 2in (50 × 50mm) S4S softwood	As top rail of basin partition frame
UNDER-BASIN SHELF PANEL	1	$\frac{1}{2}$in (12mm) laminated particleboard (or plywood if to be tiled); width as depth of recess, less about 5in (125mm)	Distance between inside faces (after tiling) of shower and basin support partitions
EDGE BANDING	1	1 × 2in (25 × 50mm) pine	As above
SHELF-SUPPORT BATTENS	2	1 × 1in (25 × 25mm) S4S softwood	As width of under-basin shelf panel
GLASS SHELF	1	Tempered glass as recommended by supplier. Width as required, plus $\frac{1}{2}$in (12mm) to be inset in rear-wall plaster	Width of basin alcove, plus 1in (25mm)
REAR-WALL GLASS SHELF-SUPPORT BATTEN	1	$\frac{1}{2}$ × $\frac{1}{2}$in (12 × 12mm) hardwood (or as plaster thickness)	Width of basin alcove, plus 1in (25mm)
SIDE-WALL GLASS SHELF-SUPPORT BATTEN	2	$\frac{1}{2}$in × $\frac{1}{2}$in (12 × 12mm) hardwood (or as plaster thickness)	Width of glass shelf, less $\frac{1}{2}$in (12mm) (or batten thickness, if different)
VALANCE PANEL	1	$\frac{3}{4}$in (19mm) plywood; width as tile depth	Width of basin alcove
VALANCE SUPPORT BLOCKS	2	1 × 2in (25 × 50mm) S4S softwood	As valance depth, less 1in (25mm)

*Approximate length only – refer to copy for actual size

BASIN

The basin is set into a tiled surface with a shelf underneath. The frame is installed between the shower partition and another low-level partition. Alternatively, you can make the fitting between two low-level ones.

BASIN PARTITION

Work out how high you want your basin, and how far out from the wall you want to extend, allowing a generous space around the basin.

Make up the partition frame in the same way as for the shower, but only one middle rail will be required. This will be at the level you want to attach the shelf supports. Note this level as you will need to know where it is once the sides are in place.

Mark the center line of all the rails and studs on the edges of the frame as before, as a guide for nailing on the side panels. Cut these out. If the partition is to be attached to a wall it will need only one side panel. Do not install it at this stage. If it is *not* going against a wall, attach only the outer one (the farthest from the basin) by following the procedure described for the shower partition on page 200 (attach the front stud first, and pull it into square to complete nailing). Secure the partition panel in place as described above.

If the partition is to be attached to a wall, stand the framework $\frac{1}{2}$in (12mm) away from the wall, checking that it is plumb, and shimming the bottom rail level if necessary. Use shims between the frame and the wall at the point where the screws go in. If the distance between the frame and the wall varies because the wall is uneven, make the $\frac{1}{2}$in (12mm) gap between the frame and the wall the maximum width. This will avoid any need for scribing to fit the frame to the wall, and will still allow for whole tiles to fit the front edge of the partition. Fit the inner side panel in place and temporarily nail to frame.

BASIN UNIT ASSEMBLY

BASIN TOP UNIT
SUPPORT BATTEN

SHOWER
PARTITION

SECURING PIECE

SHELF-SUPPORT
BATTEN

BASIN RECESS
(cut to shape of
template supplied
with basin)

FRONT
PANEL

TOP PANEL

TOP RAIL

FRONT PANEL
SUPPORT RAIL

BACK STUD

SHELF
EDGE-BANDING

MIDDLE RAIL

FRONT STUD

BASIN
PARTITION

SHELF
(adjust position to suit
storage requirements)

TILED BATHROOM

FRONT PANEL

Measure the width of the recess from inside the basin partition to the side of the shower partition and cut a piece of $\frac{1}{2}$in or $\frac{3}{4}$in (12mm or 19mm) water-resistant plywood to fit across this width. The depth of this piece should be enough to hide the underside of the basin. Work it out so that the total depth will coincide with whole tiles, after allowing for the thickness of the top panel.

TOP PANEL

Measure for the top panel to fit the width and depth of the alcove, and to finish flush with the front of the low partition. Cut the panel from $\frac{3}{4}$in (19mm) water-resistant plywood. Use a 2 × 3in (50 × 75mm) or a 2 × 2in (50 × 50mm) batten cut to the length of the front batten to join the top and front panels together at right angles. Make sure that the front panel rests under the top panel, and that there is a space at the end to slot over the end partition. Glue the batten in place and screw through the panels into it.

INSTALLING THE BASIN FRAME ASSEMBLY

To support the basin unit at the shower partition end, cut a 2 × 2in (50 × 50mm) batten to length and screw it to the side of the shower partition, screwing into the cross-rail inside the partition. It must be fitted exactly level with the top of the low partition. Rest the unit in place, but do not secure it yet as it will need to be removed for plumbing.

Cut the aperture for the inset basin by using the template supplied by the basin manufacturer. Use a power Saber saw to cut this hole, or do it by hand with a compass saw. Check that the basin fits in the hole, but do not install it until you have tiled the top panel.

Screw scrap pieces of 2 × 2in (50 × 50mm) lumber to the back of the front panel to secure it to the partitions at each side.

PLUMBING AND WIRING

At this stage the plumber can install the basin, shower tray, and bathtub, and the supply and waste pipes.

Inset showers can be installed now, and the pipework can be put in place for surface-mounted types, although the fixtures themselves are installed after tiling in both cases.

Also, have the wiring put in at this stage, with tails left protruding for lights, electric razor outlets, heaters, electrical showers, and so on to be installed later.

PERMANENT SECURING OF THE SIDES, BASIN, AND SHOWER UNITS

Attach all of the second sides to the partitions by nailing into the studs and rails. Screw the basin unit in place through the top panel into the partition and the support batten and through the scrap pieces to secure to the partitions at each side.

For the shower base, screw the front panel in place on to the front frame, and screw the top piece down on to the front and back frame. Insert silicone-rubber caulking between the frame and bathroom fixtures, where appropriate.

For the ceiling unit, screw the 2 × 2in (50 × 50mm) battens into

the plywood sides for the ceiling to fit correctly, and screw through the ceiling panel into the battens. However, if you prefer to do most of the tiling on a flat surface, do not secure the ceiling panel until it has been tiled, leaving off the tiles at the edges, at the points where you will be screwing through into the battens. Attach the ceiling panel in place, then tile over the screws.

TILING

Protect the bathroom fixtures while you are tiling, as they can be spoilt by adhesive and grout. If they are in wrappings, keep these on for as long as possible. Begin tiling (see **Techniques, page 36**); below are some tips relevant to this project.

Tile the sides of the partition first, but note the middle rail positions before, so you know where to fit the shelf supports. Work from the front edge to the back so that any cut tiles will be at the back, against the wall.

Apply the shower ceiling tiles before securing the ceiling panel in place. Leave off the edging tiles so that you can screw the ceiling panel

---

1 **Assembly of Basin Top Unit from $\frac{3}{4}$in (19mm) Plywood**
Cut the top panel to the width and depth of the basin alcove. Glue and screw the top panel and front panel to a square batten so that they are at right angles, the front panel resting beneath the top panel.

2 **Making up the Under-basin Shelf Assembly**
Shelf is cut to inside width of recess and set back slightly from front of side partitions. Wooden edge-banding, glued and nailed to the front edge of the shelf, hides the shelf-support battens which are screwed to the partition units.

to its fixing battens. If you have already attached the ceiling panel, tile the partition walls up to it.

Tile the front surfaces next, that is, the front edges of the partitions, the front panels of the basin, shower tray, and bathtub panel.

Tile the top surfaces, that is, around the bathtub, basin, and shower. Around the bathtub, where a lot of water is likely to lie, put some extra thickness of adhesive around the outer sides of the tiles so they slope very slightly towards the tub.

Tile the walls and remaining partitions next. If you are fitting a glass shelf, apply tiles up to one tile's height below the level of the shelf on those walls where the shelf will be fitted. Fit the glass shelf (see below), then complete the tiling.

Finally, if you previously tiled the shower ceiling while it was flat, you can now attach the remaining tiles to the partition sides. These were initially left off in order to screw the ceiling unit to its fixing battens; they can be held in place with masking tape while the tile adhesive sets. If the shower ceiling has already been installed, tile with the aid of a simple home-made lumber T-support. This is lightly wedged in place between the ceiling and the floor to hold each row of tiles in place while the adhesive sets. The support will be needed for about 15 minutes on each row.

After a minimum of 12 hours the joints between the tiles can be grouted with a waterproof grout, and the tiles can be polished clean.

Attach the bathtub panel, and any access panels, with dome-head screws. You can drill clearance holes with a masonry drill bit. Do not press too hard, and make sure that your electric drill is *not* switched to hammer action. Put a piece of masking tape on the tile where you want to drill the hole, to prevent the drill bit from skidding across the surface.

Finally, apply a silicone-rubber caulking to all joints between the bathroom fixtures and the ceramic tiles and to all internal corners where partitions meet the original walls. Caulks are available in white, clear, and a range of colors, and are supplied with full instructions. To eject a bead of the caulk, you usually press a plunger with your thumb, although trigger-operated aerosol packs are also becoming popular.

GLASS SHELF

Setting a glass shelf in a wall is an unorthodox method of fitting, but, if properly done, the effect of having no visible means of support is well worth the effort. However, for an easier solution, rest the glass on rubber door stops screwed into the wall – two stops at each end – after the wall or partition has been tiled.

For a concealed attachment, ask your supplier what thickness of tempered glass you need for your span. Ours is $\frac{1}{2}$in (12mm) glass spanning 43in (1100mm). The glass must be cut to size and the edges polished.

Stop the tiles one tile's height below where you want the shelf. Cut a slot into the wall at the back and each end to the thickness of the plaster and about 1in (25mm) or so wide. Fix in place a thin batten to the thickness of the plaster, minus the thickness of the shelf.

Where the shelf meets the shower partition, you must cut a slot to the thickness of the glass in the facing panel. Do this either by drilling a row of overlapping holes with a diameter the same as the shelf's thickness, and chisel out the waste to make a straight-sided slot, or use a Saber saw or router to cut a neat slot.

Slot the shelf into place. This can be difficult and it may be necessary to cut away a little extra plaster above where the shelf has to go. Fill any gaps with wall filler or tile adhesive, then complete the tiling up to the shelf. Above the shelf you can add a mirror, or tile the wall.

UNDER-BASIN SHELF

This is made from $\frac{1}{2}$in (12mm) plastic laminate-faced particleboard, but you can use plywood if you are going to tile the shelf. Cut the shelf to the width of the recess and to the required depth. It will look better if it is recessed back from the front edge a little way – $4\frac{1}{4}$in (108mm) (one tile's width) in our case.

Cut edge-banding from 1 × 2in (25 × 50mm) pine. Hold the shelf in a vise and glue and nail the edge-banding to the shelf's front edge so that the top edge of the edge-banding is flush with the shelf surface and the bottom edge hides the support battens. Punch the nail heads below the surface, fill holes, sand smooth, and apply a finish.

SHELF-SUPPORT BATTENS

These support the shelf at each side from behind the edge-banding to the back wall. Cut two pieces to length from 1 × 1in (25 × 25mm) lumber. Drill two clearance holes in each batten, then drill the sides at the marked levels. Countersink the holes and screw battens in place.

MIRROR

Attach the mirror to the wall with dome-head screws if it is drilled for these. If it is not, use corner fixing mirror plates. When using dome-head screws, put a tap washer over each screw behind the mirror to keep it slightly away from the wall. Whichever type of attachment you use, be careful not to over-tighten the fixing screws as you may crack the glass; ask your glass supplier for the correct screws and washers.

VALANCE

To conceal the overhead lighting, attach a valance above the mirror in the basin recess. Make it from $\frac{3}{4}$in (19mm) plywood cut to the width of the recess and to the depth of one tile. Cut two support blocks from 1 × 2in (25 × 50mm) lumber, about 1in (25mm) less than the valance depth, to fit behind the valance strip at each end. Screw these into the wall and the side partition in order to fit the valance in place.

③ Securing a Glass Shelf Using Hidden Supports
The wall is chaneled to the thickness of the plaster for a batten which is attached at the back and sides of the alcoves. The shelf is made of tempered glass and rests neatly on the batten. After fitting, fill any gaps and finish tiling.

PANELED BATHROOM

Often, the best ideas are the simple ones. Very few things in life are more unpleasant than trying to dry yourself with a damp towel, so if you install this room-width rod combined with a radiator you can remedy this forever. The rod here is made from chromed tube, but could be finished in colored enamel or be made in wood like the spar of a yacht.

All of the pipework in this bathroom has been hidden neatly behind a false wall which is simply constructed from painted tongued-and-grooved pine boarding. This is a particularly good solution, as a section of the paneling can be mounted on a batten frame to create an access panel which can be easily removed if you have any plumbing problems.

Chrome or wooden bar spans the entire bathroom wall to allow plenty of room to hang & dry towels

Wall heater or radiator helps towels to dry
Tongued-&-grooved boarding provides a false wall & a duct for unsightly pipework.

PANELED BATHROOM

Building a false wall is a clever way of concealing ugly pipework in the bathroom. The job is relatively easy if you are installing a new bathroom suite. However, if a suite is already installed, you may have to move one or more of the fixtures to make space for the new wall. Check that this is possible, bearing in mind the position of pipes and drains.

The false wall is made by attaching battens to the existing wall and covering them with lumber boards. These are normally tongued and grooved, and can range from plywood strips faced with an attractive veneer to solid lumber such as pine. Normally, they are attached vertically over horizontal battens.

The battens need only be of rough-sawn softwood, and should be at least 2 × 2in (50 × 50mm) if you intend to run pipes behind them. They should be fixed at centers of about 24in (610mm). There is no need to strip off any of the wall decoration before attaching the battens.

The spacing of the battens is determined largely by the thickness of the boards to be used, but also by the degree of rigidity required. It is important for the paneling to be more rigid in places where it may be leant against. As a guide, ⅜in (9mm) boards should have battens at centers of 16–20in (400–500mm), while ½in (12mm) boards need battens set 20–24in (500–610mm) apart.

Always begin and end battens a short distance from corners or ceilings so that nails do not have to be driven into the last few fractions of an inch (millimeters) of the boards, as this can cause splitting.

In order to bring all the battens flush with each other, plywood or hardboard shims may have to be used behind some of the screws. This will certainly be necessary with an undulating wall. Check the battens carefully with a long straight-edge, for unless they are completely flush, you will not be able to attach the boards to them properly.

The 2in (50mm) battens should provide enough space to conceal most bathroom pipes. If not, use thicker battens. Screw the battens to the wall, cutting out sections to accommodate pipework where necessary. However, if the wall is perfectly flat, you can secure the battens with masonry nails, provided they are long enough to go at least ½in (12mm) into the masonry.

Should you want to attach boards of random lengths for effect, then additional horizontal battens will be needed, spaced to suit your board lengths. Position boards so that the cut ends meet in the center of a batten and those at either end are both a similar width.

You can attach the boards with nails or with special clips which slot on to the tongue and are then nailed to the battens. Nailing through the face of the boards is the simplest and quickest method, but the nail heads must be punched below the surface and the holes filled with a matching wood filler. It is not necessary to match the wood exactly if the boards are to be painted.

MATERIALS

Part	Quantity	Material	Length
WALL BATTENS	As required	2 × 2in (50 × 50mm) (minimum) softwood	Width of wall
BOARDS	As required	⅜in or ½in (9mm or 12mm) thick boards	As required
TOWEL ROD	1	1½in (38mm) diameter aluminium, chrome, or wooden pole	As required
SUPPORT DISKS	2	¾in (19mm) MDF disks	As required

Nailing through the tongues with very thin brads provides an invisible attachment. These are driven at an angle into the tongue and are hidden by the groove of the next board. You may find that the wood splits in some cases, since dry pine is rather brittle. Do not worry if this should happen. Just break off any splinters; the splits will be covered by the groove of the next board, which is slotted over the tongue.

If the boards are to be nailed, attach the first with its groove in the corner, and check with a carpenter's level that it is standing plumb. Adjust the board as necessary before securing it in place by driving brads through the grooved edge. These are the only surface brads used and should be sunk below the surface of the board with a nailset. The holes should be filled with a matching wood filler.

TOOLS

STEEL MEASURING TAPE

CARPENTER'S LEVEL

STRAIGHT-EDGE

SCREWDRIVER

NAILSET

HAMMER

SMALL HAND SAW

BACK SAW (fine toothed)

SABER SAW (or compass saw)

TONGUE-AND-GROOVE CLIPS

MITER BOX

POWER DRILL

SPADE BIT

COUNTERSINK BIT

MASONRY BIT

① Attaching Tongued, Grooved, and V-jointed Boards with Nails
First board, left, is scribed to side wall, ensuring board is vertical. Nail to batten, driving nail at an angle through grooved edge. Tap next board, right, over tongue and nail through tongue. Repeat for all succeeding boards.

Nail the other side of the board, angling brads through the tongue. Fit a brad into each wall batten.

Tap the next board over the tongue to hide the brads. Protect the edge of the board from the hammer with a piece of scrap wood.

Clips are easy to use and provide a stronger attachment than brads, but are more expensive. They lock into the lower part of a groove.

The tongued edge of the first board goes into the corner you are starting from. Cut off the tongue with a fine-toothed back saw. Position the cut edge in the corner and nail it in place or use a special starter clip. Then secure the grooved edge with a clip. This is hidden by the next board inserted in the groove.

If boards of random length have to be butt-jointed at their ends, use a miter box with a right-angled slot for very accurate saw cuts. Do not fill the gaps between the joints.

The boards used in our bathroom were stopped short of the floor, giving an attractive finish. The lower edge was decorated with beading. To do this, attach a temporary batten at the bottom at the required height above the floor, to serve as a finishing guide for the bottom edge of each board. When it is removed, the bottom edges of the boards will be flush with each other.

Glue and nail the beading in place along the lower edge of the boards. Also, fit the beading in the corners and along the ceiling line to hide gaps. It should be nailed to the walls or ceiling and not to the boards. Again, the heads of the brads should be sunk below the surface and the holes filled with a matching wood filler. If you prefer to avoid nail holes, fit the beading with an aliphatic resin glue.

It is advisable to provide easy access to pipework and joints for maintenance or repair. Therefore, attach a few strategic boards with screws rather than brads, cutting off the tongues, so that the boards in question can be lifted out easily. Make a feature of the screws by using dome-head or brass screws.

Although lumber boards provide an excellent way of covering up old or unsightly walls, they must never be used on damp walls. The cause of the dampness should be traced and eliminated. The only form of dampness that they will cure is condensation, since the new wall surface will be warmer.

If an insulating blanket is to be applied between the battens to increase the heat retention of an outside wall, first cover the wall with vapor barrier (either polyethylene or building paper) and attach the battens over it. Although this will ensure that no dampness from the bathroom seeps through to the wall, it is not a cure for dampness or the structural damage that it can cause.

Finally, remember that all lumber can move with changes in moisture. Therefore, all boards should be conditioned before use by keeping them in the room in which they are to be used for about a week beforehand.

TOWEL ROD

A feature is made here of the towel rod, which runs the width of the bathroom. A $1\frac{1}{2}$in (38mm) diameter anodized aluminium pole was chosen, although chrome or wood can be used instead. If the pole is very long, a couple of intermediate supports will prevent it sagging.

If you have to make your own support disks, use $\frac{3}{4}$in (19mm) MDF. To mark out a circle for a disk, draw around an object of a suitable size, such as a coffee mug. Cut the circle with a Saber saw or compass saw.

Mark off the circumference of the pole in the center of each disk and cut it out with a spade bit, or with a Saber saw or coping saw. Repeat for the other disk.

Countersink two holes in each disk, attach the disks to the pole, and get a helper to hold the pole level while you mark off the screw hole positions on the wall. Remove the pole and disks while the holes in the wall are drilled and anchored.

Replace the disks on the pole and get a helper to hold the pole while the screws are inserted. Use 2in (50mm) No 8 screws.

Fill the screw holes, sand down when dry, and apply a finish to the disks to match the pole or the wall.

2 **Using Clips**
Saw off tongue. Push the board over a starter clip and secure grooved edge with clips.

3 **Finishing the False Wall with Beading at the Bottom**
Boards are attached to 2 × 2in (50 × 50mm) wall battens, or whatever thickness necessary to hide pipes. For neatness stop the boards short of the floor and nail a beading here.

4 **Towel Rod Support Disks**
Make support disks from $\frac{3}{4}$in (19mm) MDF and cut hole in center for rod using a Saber saw or a coping saw.

WARDROBE
WITH HINGED DOORS

I suppose the dream that most people want to realize when furnishing their bedroom is to be able to afford a complete and well–fitted wall of clothes storage units. Although very expensive to buy, these fitted units are relatively easy to build yourself.

Wardrobes never seem large enough to allow all your clothes to hang properly without being crushed, and there is always the problem of last season's clothes, which are not being worn but still have to be stored; bulky items such as bags and suitcases must also be considered. This simple but solid wardrobe has ample storage space for everything and will add value to your home should you wish to move in the future. Its simple wooden frame can be scribed to the wall, floor, and ceiling if they are uneven or sloping.

The main doors have framed panels, and the panels could be easily replaced with mirror if you prefer a reflective wall. The upper doors are hinged and fitted with a stay so they will remain open when you stow away your luggage.

The interior can be fitted with closet poles, shelves (either solid or slatted), and a shoe rail. A full–length mirror could be attached to the inside of one door.

A shoe rail is fitted into the bottom of the wardrobe

Wooden framework of wardrobe

flap door

slatted shelf

closet pole

door

W·A·L·L

shoe rail

SECTION

door stay mechanism

top flap door lifts easily for storage of luggage and out-of-season clothes.

additional shelf above closet pole if required

Front elevation of wardrobe with masses & masses of space for clothes!

Wardrobe with Hinged Doors

This wardrobe is comprised of three independent double-wardrobe sections linked together. Each section is designed as a free-standing unit to which you fit end panels if necessary. You can build as many sections as you wish, and the design allows for a single section to be built easily should your storage needs or available space require it. You can fit one or both end frames to the wall. In either case, an end panel is not needed to fit the frame at the end(s) adjoining the wall.

Buy the doors ready-made from a do-it-yourself store or lumberyard. The style is optional, but check that either a small version is available for the top cupboard, or that you can make smaller doors to match.

To make the doors, laminated particleboard panels can be used, to which moldings can be nailed to give a paneled appearance. The size of the doors governs the overall dimensions of the framework. They should extend from floor to ceiling, with an equal allowance of just over 1in (25mm) at the top and bottom, and where the main doors and the top doors meet. The doors are recessed about ⅜in (10mm) from the front edge of the frame for neatness.

Alternatively, cut down a standard door to make small top ones.

The other important dimension is the inside depth of 24in (610mm), since this is the optimum for hanging and storing clothes.

TOOLS

STEEL MEASURING TAPE

ADHESIVE

CARPENTER'S LEVEL

HAND SAW

BACK SAW

DOWELING JIG

POWER DRILL (with twist drill bits)

ROUTER

CHISEL

MALLET

BAR CLAMP

SCREWDRIVER

TACK HAMMER and BRADS

ANCHORS (or cavity-wall fixings)

OPTIONAL TOOLS FOR SCRIBING

SABER SAW

COMPASS SAW

SURFORM or RASP

MATERIALS

Per *double* wardrobe section unless otherwise stated

Part	Quantity	Material	Length
DOORS			
2 large and 2 small to fit from floor to ceiling with an allowance of 1in (25mm) at top, middle, and bottom. Width of doors governs overall width of wardrobe			
FRAMES	(Quantities given are for one frame. Three frames required per double wardrobe)		
POSTS	2	2 × 4in (50 × 100mm) S4S softwood	Floor to ceiling height
CROSS RAILS	3	As above	16in (410mm), plus 2in (50mm) if using tenon joints
END PANELS	(Quantities given are for one end frame. Two end frames required per free-standing wardrobe)		
END PANELS, TOP AND BOTTOM	2	¼in (6mm) laminated or plain plywood; width is distance between posts, plus 1in (25mm)	Height between top and middle rails, and middle and bottom rails, plus 1in (25mm)
BEADING		½ × ½in (12 × 12mm) S4S softwood	Sufficient length to fit around perimeter of end panel
CLOSET POLE			
CLOSET POLES	2	1in (25mm) diameter dowel or broom handle	Distance between frames, plus 1½in (38mm)
SPACING RAILS			
SPACING RAILS	12	2 × 2in (50 × 50mm) S4S softwood	Width of door, plus 5/32in (4mm), plus 1½in (38mm) if using tenon joints
SLATTED SHELF			
SHELF SLATS	7	1 × 2in (25 × 50mm) S4S softwood	Length of wardrobe, plus 1in (25mm)
TOP SHELF			
TOP SHELVES	2	¾in (19mm) plywood; 22¾in (580mm) wide	Distance between frames, plus ¾in (19mm)

TOP DOOR

MAIN DOOR

END PANEL

BEADING
STRIP

MORTISE

SPACING RAIL

TOP CROSS-RAIL

TOP SHELF

SPACING RAIL

SHELF SLATS

MIDDLE CROSS-RAIL

CLOSET POLE

POST

SPACING RAIL

BOTTOM CROSS-RAIL

THE BASIC FREE-STANDING DOUBLE WARDROBE UNIT
*Each unit is designed as a free-standing section which can be linked to
other sections if required. End frame can be left open, or paneled-in.*

WARDROBE WITH HINGED DOORS

BASIC ASSEMBLY

FRAME ASSEMBLY

FRONT SPACING RAIL

TOP DOOR

TOP SHELF

MIDDLE CROSS-RAIL

MAIN DOOR

POST

END PANEL

BOTTOM CROSS-RAIL

TOP CROSS-RAIL

REAR SPACING RAIL

SLATTED SHELF

CLOSET POLE

Mortise and Tenon Joint
(used to join cross-rail
to posts)

❶ Components of the Wardrobe Shown in Cross-section
The depth of the wardrobe is 24in (610mm) which is optimum for clothes
storage. Note that bottom rear spacing rail is set forward as shoe rack.

❷ Joining of the Cross-rails to the Posts
Wardrobe frames are made by attaching three cross-rails between two posts
using glued mortise and tenon joints as shown, or dowel joints.

FRAMES

Measure for the height of the frames. If your floor or ceiling is uneven, make all the frames to the largest measurement and scribe them to fit.

To make the posts, cut two lengths of 2 × 4in (50 × 100mm) softwood to the required measurement. Side rails are fitted between the posts at the top, bottom, and at the height of the closet pole using glued mortise and tenon joints or dowel joints *(see* **Techniques, pages 28 and 30** *)*. The tenons or dowels need only be about 1in (25mm) long.

Measure for the required length of the rails to fit between the posts (and add 2in [50mm] for the tenons, if you are using them) and cut three rails from the 2 × 4in (50 × 100mm) softwood. The top and bottom rails fit flush with the ends of the posts. The middle rail supports the closet pole bar.

In the center of the middle rail drill a 1in (25mm) diameter hole for the closet pole. This can be cut from 1in (25mm) dowel or a broom handle.

Decide how high you want the closet pole to be as this will determine the height at which you fit the middle rail. The height of the pole is governed by the configuration of the main doors and on the length of your longest item of clothing, when it is on a hanger.

Make up the required number of frames but do not drill the holes right through the end frames – these should be drilled to only half the thickness of the rail. Before drilling the holes, mark out their centers very accurately to ensure that the closet pole fits easily.

END PANELS

Measure for the two end panels. They should be cut to the height between the top and bottom rails and to the width between the posts, plus ½in (12mm) all around. Cut them from either veneer-faced particleboard or plywood, for a wood finish, or from plain plywood if you want a painted finish rather than a varnished effect.

Use a router to make a rabbet ½in (12mm) wide and ¾in (19mm) deep

③ Attaching Spacing Rails to Wardrobe Frame

Mortise and tenon joints are used to join the spacing rails to the wardrobe frames. Each tenon is half the thickness of the lumber that is used for making the posts and the cross-rails.

④ Attaching the End Panels

End panels are secured in rabbets cut inside the frames and held with beading (below).

FRAME AND END PANEL

Detail inside the wardrobe (above) shows spacing rail shoe rack and frame scribed around baseboard.

WARDROBE WITH HINGED DOORS

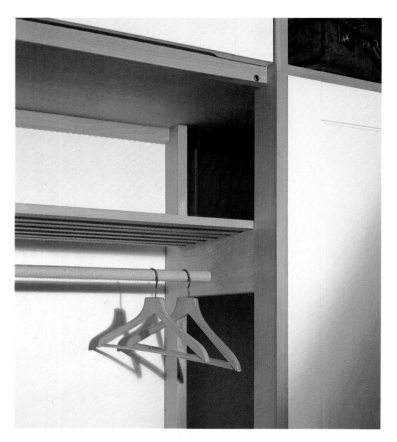

WARDROBE INTERIOR
Generous storage space is provided by a slatted shelf (above) and a sturdy wooden hanging bar.

around the inside of the frame. Do not fit the panels yet as you will need to fit a bar clamp through the frames when assembling them later. Repeat the process to fit the other end panel if your chosen design calls for a second one.

SPACING RAILS

The 2 × 2in (50 × 50mm) rails fit between each frame at the top, the bottom, and between the two rows of doors. They are also fitted using either mortise and tenon or dowel joints *(see* **Techniques, page 28 and 30** *)*. Each tenon should be half the thickness of a post so that one tenon each side will meet the other in the middle of a post.

Cut each spacing rail to the width of the door, plus $\frac{1}{8}$in (4mm) for clearance all around the door, plus the depth of the tenons if you are using them. Cut the required number of spacing rails to length, allowing for six between each frame.

The three front rails are set back from the front face of the posts by the thickness of the doors plus $\frac{3}{8}$in (10mm). The bottom back rail is set

forward about 9in (225mm) from the back edge to act as a shoe rail. The top and middle back rails are set forward about $\frac{1}{2}$in (12mm) to allow for easy scribing of the frame to the wall.

CLOSET POLES

Cut the required number of closet poles to the same length as the spacing rails, including an allowance for tenons so that they will meet in the middle of the posts, as with the spacing rails. If you plan to secure the rails with dowels, you must still remember to allow extra length on these poles, so that they meet in the middle of the posts.

INSTALLING THE FRAMES

Position one frame at a time and scribe it to fit at the wall, floor, and ceiling *(see* **Techniques, page 31** *)*. Ensure that each frame is level with the next.

Scribe around the baseboard or remove it and replace it later. Mark where each frame will sit and identify each so that its position will not be interchanged. Fit the first end frame

1 **Assembly of Slatted Shelf**
Slats form shelf on middle cross-rails. Cross-rails are drilled to take the closet poles.

2 **Top Door Hinging and Handle Detail**
Top doors hinge on a door lift mechanism which is screwed to the tops of the side frames. Note the rabbet on the bottom of the door edge to create a finger-hold for easy access.

in place using corner brackets at the ceiling and floor on the inside (*see* **Techniques, page 25**). Ensure that the frame is plumb. If you are fitting it to the wall at the end, allow a 1in (25mm) gap. This will be covered later with a scribing fillet. Otherwise, screw into the wall, placing a 1in (25mm) spacing batten between frame and wall.

ATTACHING THE SPACING RAILS

Glue and fit the spacing rails and the closet pole in position into the first end frame. Position the next frame with the joints already glued. Secure the two frames with bar clamps across the width and allow time for the glue to set. Repeat this operation for as many frames as you are using, fitting each frame as you go.

ATTACHING END PANELS

Fit each end panel into the rabbet in each end frame. To secure the panel, use beading nailed on the inside to finish flush with the frame.

SLATTED SHELF

The slats run the whole length of the wardrobe, resting across the middle rails of the frames. The outer ones butt against the posts and the others are spaced equally between them. If you have to join lengths, butt-join them at a frame. Nail the slats down to each rail.

TOP SHELF

Each $\frac{3}{8}$in (10m) plywood top shelf rests on the middle spacing rails. It is set back a little from the front edge to conceal it, or, better still, rabbeted into the rail. Cut each shelf to meet its neighbor in the middle of the center post. Cut out notches in the corners to fit around the posts. Nail down the shelf to the spacing rails at the back and front. Repeat for each shelf.

MAIN DOORS

Hang the main doors using 3in (75mm) brass butt hinges (*see* **Techniques, page 32**). Fit the hinges so the doors are set back $\frac{3}{8}$in (10mm) from the front edge. This will mean that you must not pull your doors open by more than 90° or the hinges will be weakened or pulled out. If you feel it necessary (if children will use them, for example), attach stops to ensure this will not happen.

Finally, fit handles of your choice and any form of paneling or applied decoration to the front of the doors.

TOP DOORS

These are hinged at the top. It is well worth buying a special hinge called a "door lift mechanism" which acts as a combined hinge and stop (*see* **Techniques, page 33**). A spring action allows the door to be raised and remain in an open position.

Rout out a rabbet or bevel to create a handle along the bottom edge of each door. Fit magnetic catches to all the doors (*see* **Techniques, page 33**).

SCRIBING FILLET

If you are attaching the frame to a wall at one or both ends, use a scribing fillet to fill the gap between the wall and the end frame; this will ensure a neat and secure fit. Set the fillet back from the frame the same amount as the doors. It can then be painted to match either the doors or the wall.

BASEBOARD

If there is a baseboard already in position against the wall, it will be necesary to remove the baseboard from between the frames. Cut a piece of baseboard to length so that it fits exactly the space between each frame.

3 Hinging of Main Door
Brass butts are used to hinge main doors which are set back from edge of frames.

WARDROBE STORAGE SPACE
With doors open, the wardrobe gives access to solid top shelf, slatted shelf, and closet pole.

FOLDING SCREEN

Screens have many uses in the home, subdividing space both physically and visually, and defining different areas.

This screen has a second use as a clothes horse for a bedroom or hall. With the addition of a hanging rail, wooden knobs, and a shelf, it can quickly become an elegant and simple wardrobe for use in a spare room, for a weekend guest, or in a student's or child's bedroom.

The geometric grid of wooden slats can be rearranged to make the particular pattern of your choice. The slats can either be painted, stained in a variety of colors, or left simply as natural wood. Alternatively, each panel of the screen can be covered on one side with a light fabric to provide a more private room divider. The traditional and ingenious webbing hinge allows the panels of the screen to fold flat when not in use.

Dovetail joint on corner of frame

Woven fabric webbing connects screen frames

The screen can be transformed into a temporary wardrobe

Fabric hinges allow screen to fold in a variety of ways

Shelf & hanging knobs for clothes are slotted into frame grid.

Hanging rail slots through frame to lock screen at right angles

Hanging knob with back-plate slots into frame grid

FOLDING SCREEN

You can use a folding screen to divide space in a room or to hide ugly corners and unsightly features in various rooms in the home. If you nail lightweight gauze to one side of an open frame, it will provide a screening effect without reducing light transmission too much. Alternatively, you can nail or staple an opaque material to one side to form a solid screen. For our screen, we created a trellis.

MATERIALS

Note: Quantities are for one frame; three frames required

Part	Quantity	Material	Length
OUTER FRAME UPRIGHTS	2	1 × 2in (25 × 50mm) S4S softwood	5ft 8in (1730mm)
OUTER FRAME TOP AND BOTTOM RAILS	2	1 × 2in (25 × 50mm) S4S softwood	28in (710mm)
HORIZONTAL FRAME CROSS BATTENS	15	1 × 1in (25 × 25mm) S4S softwood	Approximately 26in (660mm)
VERTICAL FRAME CROSS BATTENS	6	1 × 1in (25 × 25mm) S4S softwood	Approximately 5ft 6in (1680mm)
BATTEN FIXING DOWELS	42	$\frac{1}{4}$in (6mm) dowel	1$\frac{3}{16}$in (30mm)
HANGING RAILS	As required	1in (25mm) dowel	Distance between screen frames, plus approximately 1$\frac{1}{2}$in (38mm)
HANGING RAIL ENDS	6 (2 per rail)	3in (75mm) or 2$\frac{1}{2}$in (63mm) diameter wooden ball	
SHELF	1	$\frac{1}{2}$in (12mm) plywood, about 12in (300mm) deep	Approximately 30in (760mm)
KNOB BACK PLATE	1	1in (25mm) S4S softwood, about 3in (75mm) wide	Approximately 5in (125mm)
KNOB STOPPER BATTEN	1	1 × 1in (25 × 25mm) S4S softwood	Approximately 5in (125mm)
KNOB DOWEL	1	1in (25mm) dowel	3in (75mm)
KNOB END	1	2in (50mm) diameter wooden ball	

Using traditional fabric hinges which fold in both directions allows the screen to be used in either a Z-shape, or in a U-shape so that rails can be hung across its width for a temporary wardrobe. Additionally, a detachable shelf can be added. It fits neatly above the hanging rail. Also, wooden knobs can be slotted into the screen wherever required for hanging clothes. When not in use, the screen can be simply folded flat for easy storage.

The screen can be made from as many panels as you require. Ours comprises three, each 5ft 8in (1730mm) high by 28in (710mm) wide. The cross battens within the outer frame create spaces 3in (75mm) square. Each frame is made with dovetail joints at the corners for strength. However, you may prefer to use dowel joints (see **Techniques, page 30**) at the corners. These are perfectly reliable if glued securely with an aliphatic resin glue.

MAKING THE SCREEN PANELS

The outer frame of each panel is cut from 1 × 2in (25 × 50mm) S4S (smooth 4 sides) lumber and is assembled flat. For each panel, two uprights and two rails (top and bottom) are required. Our uprights are 5ft 8in (1730mm) long and the rails are 28in (710mm) long.

FABRIC HINGE

SHELF

HANGING
RAIL

HANGING
KNOB

OUTER FRAME
TOP RAIL

DOWELS

DOVETAIL
JOINT

HORIZONTAL
FRAME
CROSS
BATTEN

VERTICAL
FRAME
CROSS
BATTEN

OUTER
FRAME
UPRIGHT

DOWELS

OUTER FRAME
BOTTOM RAIL

FOLDING SCREEN

DOVETAILING THE TOP AND BOTTOM RAILS

A full description of how to make a basic dovetail joint is given elsewhere in the book (see **Techniques, page 29**); included here are instructions specific to this project. Set your marking gauge to the thickness of the rail and mark off this distance from the end of the short rail, continuing the line around both faces and edges. Repeat for each end of the top and bottom rails.

Mark off the approximate pin shape on to the end of a piece of scrap wood of the same stock size, and work out the correct setting for your marking or mortise gauge.

Using the gauge, mark off the lines of the top of the pin on to the outer face of the rail. Then, using the sliding bevel, mark out the pin on to the ends of the rails using a pencil sharpened to a chisel point. Continue the lines of the bottom of the pin around on to the inner face, using a try square (fig 1). Repeat the procedure for each end of the top and bottom rails of each frame.

Hold the rail upright in a vise and saw down through each pencil line to the depth of your marked line, using a dovetail saw or a fine back saw. Then hold the rail horizontally in the vise to remove the shoulders of the tail, to leave only the "pin" (center part), sawing down to the marked line of the tail. Repeat for each end of the top and bottom rails.

DOVETAILING UPRIGHTS

Using the marking gauge as before, set it to the stock thickness and mark off the ends as before, continuing the lines right around the rail. Number each joint to ease assembly later.

Lay a short rail lengthwise on top of a long one to mark off the thickness of the pin. Then stand the short rail upright at the end of the long one to mark the cut-out to house the pin on to the long rail, which will be the "post" (fig 2).

Repeat for each joint, making sure that you number them as you go, as they will not be interchangeable. Extend the marks on to the ends with a try square. Mark each end of the uprights in this way.

To make the vertical cuts, the post must be held firm. It is best to place it upright in a vise, supported with long shim pieces clamped on either side, and then to stand on steps to reach it. Cutting *inside* the pencil lines (the waste side), make angled cuts to the marked line.

To remove the waste from the post, use a coping saw to cut down the center and out to each side, being sure to stay a little way inside the marked lines. Pare down to the sides with a paring chisel. Repeat for the other ends of the uprights and fit the joints together, matching the identification numbers. Identify the faces of the rails and uprights as well as their pins and tails. It is a good idea to do a practice joint first on a piece of scrap wood.

CROSS BATTENS

With the frame dry assembled, measure the internal dimensions and cut the cross battens from 1 × 1in (25 × 25mm) S4S to these measurements. In our case, there are 15 horizontals and 6 verticals per panel. Dismantle the frame.

We used $\frac{1}{4}$in (6mm) diameter hardwood dowels, $1\frac{1}{4}$in (30mm) long to attach the cross battens to the outer frame. (This is about the right size. If your dowel sizes are different, you will have to adjust the dimensions accordingly.)

Using a doweling jig, drill the ends of all the battens in their centers to a depth of about $\frac{3}{4}$in (19mm), using a $\frac{1}{4}$in (6mm) diameter centerpoint or brad-point drill bit (also called a lip-and-spur drill bit).

MARKING DOWEL HOLES

Take the vertical battens and bunch them up together on the top and bottom rails, against the shoulders of the dovetail joints. Measure to the other shoulder and divide this figure by the number of spaces. This will give you the gap between all the battens. Measure this distance in from the shoulder, plus half the thickness of the batten. The first dowel hole center will be on this line. From then on, mark the dowel hole center lines according to the spacing measurements already calculated. The final distance should be

---

1 **Dovetailing the Rails**
Depth marked all around; top of pin marked. Dovetail marked on end; bottom of pin marked.

2 **Marking the Frame Uprights**
Depth and thickness of rail pin marked; then shape of pin marked on frame upright.

3 **Completing the Outer Frame Dovetail Joints**
Top rail pin is cut with a fine back saw or dovetail saw. Frame upright post is cut with dovetail and coping saws. Clean up the joint with a paring chisel for a good, secure fit.

Pin

Top rail

Frame upright

Frame top rail

Frame upright

the same as the first. Transfer the hole marks to all the other top and bottom rails.

To mark the dowel hole positions widthways, find the center of the rail width and measure out from it exactly half the thickness of the vertical batten. (This will be nearer $\frac{3}{4}$in [19mm] than the nominal 1in [25mm].) Draw a line down the rail. Where it crosses the dowel hole lines will be the dowel hole center points.

Repeat the above procedure for the horizontal battens on the upright posts, spacing them apart by the same distance as you did for the vertical battens. Space one of the battens down from the top, and then the rest of them up from the bottom. This will create a larger gap between the top horizontal batten and the next one down, which is where the removable shelf fits.

To mark the dowel hole positions widthways, measure exactly half the batten thickness out from the center, but in the opposite direction to that of the vertical battens. This ensures that the horizontal battens are fitted *exactly* in front of the verticals.

Drill all the marked holes to a diameter of $\frac{1}{4}$in (6mm) and a depth of $\frac{1}{2}$in (12mm).

ASSEMBLING THE PANELS

To assemble a panel, put a small amount of glue in each dowel hole in the top and bottom rails. Insert the dowels. Put a small amount of glue into the hole on each end of the vertical battens and push them into all the dowels.

Take one of the posts and glue and assemble both of the dovetail joints on one side. Then glue and dowel all of the horizontal battens into the upright post. Glue and join the second post, the dovetails, and the dowels simultaneously.

Use bar clamps (or a band clamp or folding wedges) across the panel to pull the joints together. Then, using a spacing batten, check that all the spaces are equal, and nail the battens to each other where they cross, using the spacing batten as you go. Repeat the procedure for the other two panels and paint, stain, or varnish to finish according to your decorative scheme.

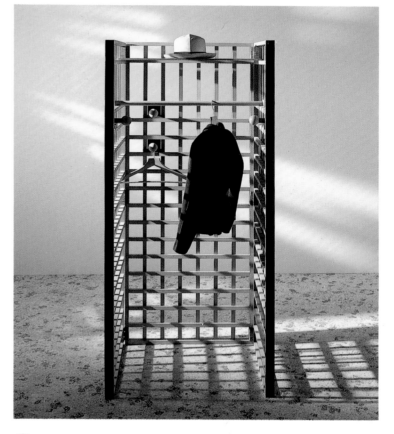

4 **Working Out Dowel Hole Spacings for Vertical Battens**
Bunch the vertical battens together on top and bottom rails against shoulders of the dovetail joints. Measure gap to other shoulder and calculate spacing of battens.

5 **Vertical Batten Assembly**
Mark and drill dowel holes in rails. Apply glue and insert dowels. Glue holes in battens and attach dowels.

TEMPORARY WARDROBE
The screen can be easily converted to a wardrobe for hanging clothes. Useful when guests come to visit.

FOLDING SCREEN

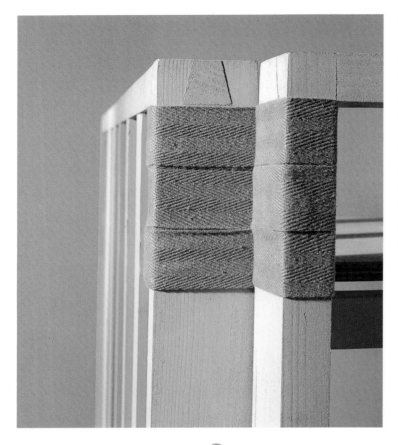

FABRIC HINGES

The three panels are joined together with fabric hinges at the top, bottom and middle. Each hinge comprises three separate strips of 1in (25mm) wide webbing the color of which matches the finish of your screen.

The two outer strips are identical and are attached first, leaving a space for the middle one, which is fitted the opposite way around. The outer strips are about 12in (300mm) long, and the middle one about 11$\frac{1}{4}$in (280mm). Cut the webbing overlength, try it in place, and cut off the excess. Follow fig 3 to attach the first strip, by stapling or tacking it on to one panel and joining it to the next by winding round in a figure eight to cover the ends. Put temporary staples in to hold the webbing firm while winding it around. Staple the last face to the panel and push the end through on to the next face to conceal the staples on both panels. Repeat for the other outer strip.

Follow fig 3 to fit the middle strip. You will not be able to take this one around as far as the others, concealing only the first set of staples. Push the end through on to the next face as before. Make three hinges each between adjacent panels.

outer strips

middle strip

DETAIL OF SCREEN HINGE
The fabric hinge (above) enables the screen to fold in two directions. Fabric matches screen color.

① **Assembling Horizontals**
Apply glue and push first upright post into dovetails of top and bottom rails. Glue and dowel.

② **Assembling the Second Upright Post on the Assembly**
Glue and join dovetails and dowels at same time. Batten left out at top.

③ **Making the Hinges**
Wind webbing fabric around the panel uprights in the direction of the arrows to form a secure hinge.

HANGING RAILS

Set the screen up in a U-shape and measure across for the hanging rails from the outside edges of the cross battens, plus $\frac{3}{4}$in (19mm) at each end to go into 3in or $2\frac{1}{2}$in (75mm or 63mm) diameter wooden knobs. Cut the required number of rails from 1in (25mm) dowel. Each rail will be about 30in (760mm) long if made to our dimensions.

Put each knob in turn into a vise and drill into it to a depth of $\frac{3}{4}$in (19mm) using a 1in (25mm) spade bit. Assemble the rails by gluing the dowel and knobs together and slot them into place where desired.

SHELF

Use $\frac{1}{2}$in (12mm) plywood to make a shelf, if required. This rests on top of the cross battens and is easily removable when you want to fold the screen. Cut the shelf to fit (about 12in [300mm] deep). As it is intended as a temporary shelf it should not be used to store heavy items, although it is perfectly adequate for lightweight clothing.

HANGING KNOBS

To make a back plate, use a piece of 1in (25mm) S4S softwood as high as one section of the outer dimensions of the horizontal battens and of a width to fit easily between the vertical battens.

Using a 1 × 1in (25 × 25mm) offcut, cut a piece as long as the outer dimensions of one upright batten to the next. This is the stopper. Put the back plate into position in one square and the stopper in place to the front of it, to mark where it will fit on the back plate.

Drill a 1in (25mm) diameter hole in the back plate, its center about 1in (25mm) up from the top of the stopper position, to a depth of $\frac{1}{2}$in (12mm). Cut a piece of 1in (25mm) dowel to a length of 3in (75mm) and glue it in the hole. Glue and nail the stopper in place on the back plate.

Drill a 1in (25mm) diameter hole to a depth of $\frac{3}{4}$in (19mm) into a 2in (50mm) diameter wooden knob and glue it in place on top of the dowel. Hanging knobs can be slotted into any square.

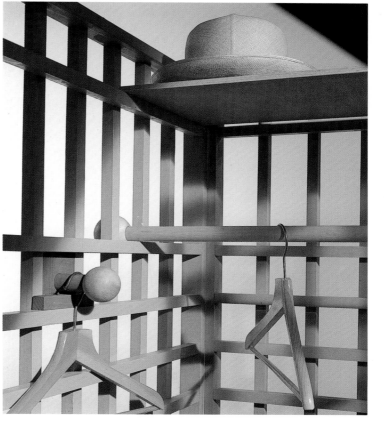

④ Nailing the Battens
Clamp frame, and, with an offcut to check the exact dimension of the spacings, nail battens together.

⑤ Making the Hanging Rail and Hanging Knobs
Hanging rail is 1in (25mm) diameter dowel with wooden knobs at ends. Hanging knobs comprise batten across back plate on which wooden knob on short dowel is attached.

DETAIL OF WARDROBE

As a wardrobe, the screen is a stylish addition to any bedroom or spare room.

JAPANESE WARDROBE

Although this particular sliding screen has been designed as a wardrobe in a bedroom, the same construction would look equally stylish in a living room. To me, there is nothing more serene than a traditional Japanese room and I have tried to echo this serenity in this project.

The frame that holds the screens must form a rectangle, with every corner an exact right angle. For this reason you will notice that there is a scribing fillet around the edge of the screen's frame to take up the inevitable inaccuracies of your floor, walls, and ceiling.

The screens are simply constructed to a rectangular module which will vary according to the exact size of the wall you wish to screen. I have used a tough, natural, creamy cotton rather than traditional Japanese paper to back the screen, but you could alter the material to suit your own decorative scheme.

One of the great bonuses of this screen wall, apart from its storage potential, is that a light inside the wardrobe will be gently diffused by the fabric, to provide an elegant, soothing background to your bedroom or living space.

PLAN OF WALL
FIXING—
Block to take up
unevenness between
Wall, ceiling & frame

WALL anchor

sliding door track

sliding
Door
cloth backing
held in place
by fillet

scribing fillet
painted the same
colour as Wall and
Ceiling

SIDE ELEVATION OF
CEILING FIXING

CEILING

scribing fillet

sliding door
track

fabric covering

incandescent
strip light
mounted on
back of
frame
produces
diffused
LIGHT

FRONT ELEVATION OF JAPANESE WARDROBE.

Gap between wall
and wardrobe frame
filled with scribing
fillet.

PLAN

closet
pole

shelves

sliding doors

uprights secured
to sides of chimney
breast to form side
of shelving unit.

Japanese Wardrobe

The lightweight sliding doors of this fitted wardrobe are divided with a narrow trellis-like framework and backed with fabric to produce a Japanese-style "wall". The doors are designed to fit wall-to-wall across a room with (or without) a chimney breast and alcoves. Lights are installed behind the doors to light the inside of the wardrobe and to throw a diffused light into the room when the doors are closed – an excellent way to create a restful atmosphere in a bedroom, for example.

In our design, the doors slide in front of the chimney breast, completely hiding it. Vertical partition panels are fitted to each side of the chimney breast, protruding a short distance in front of it and allowing narrow shelves to the width of the chimney breast to be incorporated.

If you are building this wardrobe on a flat wall, you will still need to include two internal partition panels to support the closet poles and the deep shelves. However, in this case all the shelves will be deep, and three closet poles can be attached instead of two.

For neatness, where there is no chimney breast, make the vertical partition panels as two narrow, plywood-covered box sections.

MATERIALS

Part	Quantity	Material	Length
PARTITIONS	2	$\frac{3}{4}$in (19mm) plywood, lumber core or particleboard. Width as inside depth of cupboard; 21in (530mm) in our case	Room height
DEEP SHELVES	4	As above; $20\frac{1}{2}$in (518mm) wide to allow for thickness of edge-banding	Distance between partition panels and side walls
SHALLOW SHELVES	6	$\frac{3}{4}$in (19mm) plywood, lumber core or particleboard. Width as distance from chimney breast to front of partition panels, less $\frac{1}{2}$in (12mm)	Distance between partition panels
SHELF EDGE-BANDING	10	$\frac{1}{2} \times 1\frac{1}{2}$in (12 × 38mm) S4S pine or hardwood	As shelf lengths
DEEP SHELF REAR SUPPORT BATTENS	4	1 × 1in (25 × 25mm) S4S softwood	As shelf length
DEEP SHELF SIDE SUPPORT BATTENS	8	1 × 1in (25 × 25mm) S4S softwood	Shelf depth, less $1\frac{1}{2}$in (38mm)
SHALLOW SHELF REAR SUPPORT BATTENS	6	1 × 1in (25 × 25mm) S4S softwood	As shelf length
SHALLOW SHELF SIDE SUPPORT BATTENS	12	1 × 1in (25 × 25mm) S4S softwood	Shelf depth, less $1\frac{1}{2}$in (38mm)
CLOSET POLES	2	Chrome pole or 1in (25mm) diameter dowel	Alcove width
RAIL SUPPORT BATTENS	4	1 × 3in (25 × 75mm) S4S softwood	2 at 21in (530mm) 2 at 24in (610mm)

DOOR FRAMES

Part	Quantity	Material	Length
TOP AND BOTTOM RAILS	2	2 × 4in (50 × 100mm) S4S softwood	Room width, plus 6in (150mm)*
UPRIGHTS	2	As above	Room height*
TOP SCRIBING FILLET	1	1 × $1\frac{1}{4}$in (25 × 32mm) S4S softwood	Room width*
SIDE SCRIBING FILLET	2	As above	Room height*

DOORS (quantities are for one door. Our project uses three doors)

Part	Quantity	Material	Length
STILES (side rails)	2	2 × 2in (50 × 50mm) S4S softwood	Internal height of door frame, less clearance for door hardwear
TOP RAIL	1	2 × 2in (50 × 50mm) S4S softwood	One-third of internal width of frame
BOTTOM RAIL	1	2 × 4in (50 × 100mm) S4S softwood	As above
HORIZONTAL TRANSOMS (central bars)	3	1 × 1in (25 × 25mm) S4S softwood	Internal width of door frame, plus 1in (25mm)
VERTICAL MULLIONS (central bars)	2	1 × 1in (25 × 25mm) S4S softwood	Internal height of door frame, plus 1in (25mm)
SIDE FABRIC FASTENING BATTENS	2	$\frac{3}{8} \times \frac{3}{8}$in (9 × 9mm) S4S softwood	Internal height of door frame, plus 4in (100mm)
TOP AND BOTTOM FABRIC FASTENING BATTENS	2	$\frac{3}{8} \times \frac{3}{8}$in (9 × 9mm) S4S softwood	Internal width of door frame, plus 4in (100mm)

*Dimensions are oversize to allow for trimming later.

JAPANESE WARDROBE

Assembly Drawing

234/235

COMPONENTS OF THE MAIN ASSEMBLY

DEEP ALCOVE SHELF

SHALLOW SHELF

EDGE-BANDING

END BATTEN

DOOR GUIDE

DOOR TOP RAIL

MULLION (vertical bar)

TRANSOM (horizontal bar)

STILE

WHEELS

CHIMNEY BREAST

PARTITION PANEL

SHELF-SUPPORT BATTEN

TOP RAIL

CLOSET POLE

SHELF-SUPPORT BATTENS

SIDE RAIL

RUNNERS

BOTTOM RAIL

PLAN VIEW

WALL

WALL

CHIMNEY BREAST

END BATTEN

CLOSET POLE

SCRIBING FILLET

FRAME

DOORS

Japanese Wardrobe

Tools

STEEL MEASURING TAPE

STRAIGHT-EDGE (or a straight, planed batten)

CARPENTER'S LEVEL

PLUMB BOB AND CHALK

TRY SQUARE

UTILITY KNIFE

MARKING GAUGE

CIRCULAR POWER SAW or SABER SAW (or small hand saw and back saw)

DRILL (hand or power)

TWIST DRILL BITS $\frac{1}{8}$in (3mm) for pilot holes $\frac{3}{16}$in (5mm) for clearance holes

SPADE BIT

COUNTERSINK BIT

MASONRY DRILL BIT to suit anchors being used

POWER ROUTER and ROUTER BITS

SET OF CHISELS

SCREWDRIVER

HAMMER

NAILSET

SMOOTHING PLANE

POWER FINISHING SANDER (or hand sanding block)

ONE PAIR OF FRAME CLAMPS (minimum 8in [200mm] jaw opening)

ONE PAIR OF BAR CLAMPS or BAND CLAMP to hold doors during assembly

PAINTBRUSHES

MORTISE GAUGE

MITER BOX (optional)

SCRIBING BLOCK

Layout

Decide on the internal layout of the wardrobe: the height of the closet poles, the position of the shelves, etc. Our shelves are spaced at 14in (350mm) centers down the chimney breast, with closet poles in the alcoves at either side and two deep shelves above the main closet pole.

Mark the internal depth of the wardrobe (ours is 24in [610mm], which is a good width for hanging clothes). Mark all the way around: on walls, floor, and ceiling. Start by marking a point 24in (610mm) out from the rear wall at each end and mark on to the side walls just above the level of the baseboard. Hang a chalked plumb line on each wall to align with these marks and snap the line to mark a vertical line on each wall. Snap a chalked line on to the ceiling to join these two lines. Finally, repeat for the floor. This line will be the inside of the door frame.

If you are working in an old house where the room is not square, you may not be able to measure out from the end wall to fix the position of the door frame. Instead, you may have to use the 3-4-5 method (see **Techniques, page 20**) to get the frame at right angles to one, or both, of the side walls. Mark the frame position on the floor, then snap vertical lines on the side walls and finally snap a line on the ceiling. Also, in an old house the floor, walls, and ceiling may slope a lot. If so, you may have to use shims under the floor rail and scribe wide shims between the sides and top of the door frame to fill odd-shaped gaps. It is vital that the door frame is square, regardless of how much the walls, floor, and ceiling are out of true.

After marking the inside of the door frame line, measure back 3in (75mm) and snap another line around the walls, floors, and ceiling parallel with the first line. This inside line marks the front edge of the shelves and partition panels.

Partitions

Cut partition panels to the height of the room from $\frac{3}{4}$in (19mm) plywood, lumber core, or particleboard. These are fitted to each side of the chimney breast. Their width is the distance from the rear wall to the inside line (21in [530mm] in our case).

Position the panels, check that they are plumb (shim them if necessary), and screw and anchor them to each side of the chimney breast.

If there is no chimney breast, make and install two partition panels as follows: each partition is made from two panels of $\frac{3}{8}$in (9mm) plywood on a 1 × 2in (25 × 50mm) S4S lumber framework. The panels should extend from floor to ceiling, and should be slotted over 1 × 2in (25 × 50mm) battens which are screwed to the rear wall, floor, and ceiling to give a strong, invisible support. Within the panels, position cross battens to provide extra support at levels which coincide with the shelf and closet pole positions when these are installed.

Shelves

On the back and side walls mark the positions of the undersides of the shelves, using a pencil, carpenter's level, and straight-edge (or a planed length of lumber batten).

Cut shelf-support battens from planed pine to run along the back and side walls, allowing for the thickness of the edge-banding on the front of the shelves. The battens are 1 × 1in (25 × 25mm) (see **Materials list, page 234**).

Drill and screw the battens to the rear walls, side walls, and partition panels, ensuring that they are level with one another, and level on each side of the partition panels. Anchors will be required where the battens are attached to masonry walls.

Use a filler to cover the screwheads. Paint the battens.

Cut the shelves to fit from $\frac{3}{4}$in (19mm) plywood, lumber core, or particleboard. Nail $\frac{1}{2}$ × $1\frac{1}{2}$in (12 × 38mm) edge-banding to the front edge of each shelf, flush with the top edge of each shelf. The edge-banding will overhang to hide the support battens.

Closet Poles

Use proprietary chrome rails and end supports, or 1in (25mm) diameter wooden dowels, cut to fit the widths of the alcoves. The dowels are fitted to 1 × 3in (25 × 75mm) end battens cut to fit the width of the cupboard from the frame to the back wall in the case of the end battens, and from the front edge of the partition panels to the back wall for the inside battens. To form the closet pole, the inside battens are drilled centrally to hold the dowels and the end battens drilled to match. To fit the pole, screw the end batten to the wall, slot the inside batten on to the dowel, then put the dowel in the attached batten, and finally screw the other batten in place, checking with a carpenter's level that the pole is level. Make sure that the poles on each side are level with one another, at the desired height.

Sliding Door Frame

The frame is built to give a $1\frac{1}{4}$in (30mm) gap at the top of the frame and at each side, to allow for scribing for a neat finish while coping with baseboard and irregularities in the wall and ceiling surfaces. When you measure, allow for these spaces and make the frame to these external dimensions.

The frame is made from 2 × 4in (50 × 100mm) S4S (smooth 4 sides) lumber and is constructed with dado joints (to be precise, rabbet-and-dado joints) at the corners. This type of joint is very strong, but the short grain on the outside of the grooves is a weakness and therefore the top and bottom rails are left about 6in (150mm) overlength to form "horns" which are sawn off after the joint is made.

Put the top and bottom rails side by side and clamp them together. Mark the external width of the frame on to them. Rest a frame upright across the top and bottom rails to mark off the internal dimensions and then mark this line square on the top and bottom rails using a try square and a utility knife. Set a marking gauge to half the thickness of the uprights and mark off from the internal face, squaring across as you go with a try square and a utility knife (*see* **Techniques, page 20**).

Use a router to cut out the dado (or groove) as marked, or saw along the inside (waste side) of the dado lines using a fine-toothed back saw and then chisel out the waste wood.

Cut the frame uprights to length. (Note that these fit into the bottom of the dados.) Using the marking gauge as set for marking out the dados, mark off for the rabbets at the ends of the rails which will fit into the dados.

Cut out the waste with a back saw so that the rabbets fit securely in the dados.

Dry assemble the frame to check that the external dimensions are accurate enough to fit the room size with approximately 1¼in (30mm) spaces at the top and at each side of the frame. These will be filled by the scribing fillets, which will ensure a neat fit.

Take the frame apart and install the sliding door hardware. The method of fitting depends on the type and you must follow the manufacturer's instructions. It is very important to choose door hardware in which the wheels run along a bottom track, rather than hang from a top rack, otherwise our frame will not be suitable. It is much easier to fit this bottom-running track and the guide track at the top before the frame is finally assembled.

Assemble the frame, gluing the joints and screwing through the top and bottom rails into the uprights. At this point the frame must be braced square before the glue sets. Do this by nailing two diagonal braces on opposing corners following the 3-4-5 method of bracing (*see* **Techniques, page 20**).

INSTALLING THE FRAME

Lift the frame into position, ensuring that the upright rails are centralized between the side walls, with a 1¼in (30mm) gap at each side. Use a carpenter's level to check that the bottom rail is absolutely level, and if necessary adjust it with shims. With the diagonal braces still in position, screw the bottom rail to the floor after scanning the floor with a metal detector to ensure that the screws will not puncture pipes or wiring just beneath the floorboards. Use 3in (75mm) No 10 woodscrews, and, if possible, try to coincide the screws with the positions of the floor joists (floorboard fixing nails will indicate their location).

Check that the frame is vertical, then drill the side rails and wall at about 24in (610mm) intervals so that the frame-fixing screws complete with anchors already threaded part of the way can be inserted through the frame and into the wall. Before tightening the screws, insert shims between the uprights and the wall at the attachment points, keep-

ing the shims 1in (25mm) back from the front edge of the frame so that the scribing fillets can later be fitted between the frame and the wall. Check that the frame is still square by measuring across the diagonals, to ensure that they are of an equal length. If necessary, adjust the shims on either side.

Drill and screw the top rail to the ceiling, using 4in (100mm) No 12 screws, and screwing into the ceiling joists where possible. As with the uprights, at the screw positions, insert shims between the top of the rail and the ceiling before finally tightening the screws.

Check again that the frame is square, and then remove the bracing battens.

Between each side and the walls, and between the top rail and the ceiling, scribe a fillet made from ¼in (6mm) plywood to the wall and to the ceiling to fill the space. Attach the fillet by screwing into the shims.

Fill over the screwheads and, when dry, paint the frame the same color as the wall so that it blends with the rest of the room.

1 Shelf Construction and Attachment of Shelf-support Battens
Shelves have edge-banding on front edges to hide the support battens and to stiffen the shelves to help prevent them from sagging. Remember to allow for the thickness of the edge-banding by setting back the side battens.

2 Shelf Edge-banding
Plywood, lumber core, or particleboard shelves have hardwood edge-banding on front edge.

3 Rabbet-and-Dado Joints
Rabbet-and-dado joints are used at the corners of the frame. Note the horns which are cut off later.

JAPANESE WARDROBE

SLIDING DOORS

Work out the external dimensions of the doors. For the door height, measure the height of the internal frame, allowing for the clearance specified in the instructions supplied with the sliding door hardware. For the width, divide the internal width of the frame by the number of doors required (we use three), allowing for doors to overlap each other by the thickness of the door stiles.

Using lumber as specified in the Materials list (page 56), cut the door stiles (vertical side members) slightly overlength and mark on them the positions of the top and bottom rails. Haunched mortise and tenon joints are used to joint the door components at the corners (*see* **Techniques, page 29**).

Cut the top and bottom rails to length and chop out the mortises in the stiles, then cut the tenons on the rails. The stiles are left overlength at this stage to avoid breaking out the end of the mortise while cutting it.

Dry assemble the door frame and check that the joints fit well.

Repeat the procedure for the other doors.

To make the transoms (horizontal internal bars) on each door, measure the internal width between the stiles, and cut three transoms to this length, plus 1in (25mm). (The number of transoms can be varied according to the size of the doors you are making.) Measure the distance between the top and bottom rails and cut two mullions (vertical bars) to this length, plus 1in (25mm). (Again, the number can be varied to suit the door size.) The bars are joined to the frame with bare-faced mortise and tenon joints, and where they overlap they are joined with cross-lap joints.

Take the frame apart and cut the mortises for the sliding door wheels in the bottom edge of the bottom rail (see the manufacturer's instructions).

TOP RAIL
2 × 2in (50 × 50mm)

BARE-FACED
MORTISE AND
TENON JOINT

STILE 2 × 2in (50 × 50mm)

CROSS-LAP JOINT
1 × 1in (25 × 25mm)

HAUNCHED
MORTISE AND
TENON JOINT

MULLION (vertical bar)
1 × 1in (25 × 25mm)

TRANSOM (horizontal bar)
1 × 1in (25 × 25mm)

BOTTOM RAIL

SLIDING DOOR ASSEMBLY
Three different joints – haunched tenon, bare-faced tenon, and cross-lap – are used in assembly.

Work out the spacing for all the internal bars and mark them on the inside faces of the frame. Set the mortise gauge to the full thickness of the 1 × 1in (25 × 25mm) bars, and gauge a line from the back of the door frame to mark the front positions of the bars.

Using a square-edge chisel (a mortise chisel is ideal, although an ordinary firmer chisel will do), or a router cutter, chop out, or rout, mortise slots to $\frac{1}{2}$in (12mm) depth, and to half the thickness of the square bars by their full width.

Set the marking gauge to the width of the chisel or router cutter that you have used for cutting the

mortises, and using this setting, mark off the thickness of the tenons on the ends of the internal bars. Reset the gauge to $\frac{1}{2}$in (12mm) and mark off the lengths of the tenons on both ends of each bar. Cut the (bare-faced) tenons. When fitted, the back of each bar should lie flush with the back of the door frame.

Cut cross-lap joints at the intersections of all of the bars (*see* **Techniques, page 26**).

Start assembly by gluing the cross-lap joints and assembling the bars carefully, as they are easy to break. Assemble the top and bottom rails into the mullions, gluing all the joints beforehand.

Apply glue to the mortises and shoulders on one side of the doors and assemble the stile on this side of the tenons of the top and bottom rails and transoms simultaneously.

Repeat the procedure to attach the second stile.

Put bar clamps across the doors in line with the transoms, or put a band clamp right around the door. Check that the door is flat and square (the diagonals should be equal).

When the glue has set, remove the clamps and cut the excess lumber off the door stiles. Use a sharp plane to skim the faces of the doors to ensure that all the joints are flush.

JAPANESE WARDROBE

With the lights switched on, this wardrobe becomes an interesting trellis-like framework. The diffused light behind the fabric panels creates a restful backdrop in any room.

Repeat for the other doors. If you find these joints too hard to make, or too time-consuming, the door could be doweled together *(see* **Techniques, page 30** *)*. Dowel joints are perfectly secure when glued with an aliphatic resin glue.

To fit the fabric behind the door, a groove is formed in the back of the door frame, and the fabric is laid in the groove, where it is then held in place with a batten pressed into the groove. Use a router to make the groove, which should be $\frac{3}{8}$in (9mm) wide and the same depth. The groove is cut in the back of the door frame, its outer edge 1in (25mm) from the inside of the frame.

Cut a $\frac{3}{8}$in (9mm) square batten and check that it is a tight fit when slid into the groove. If necessary, plane it to fit. Cut lengths of batten to fit the groove, mitering the corners.

Following the door hardware manufacturer's instructions, fit the wheel into the mortises previously cut in the bottom of the doors, and fit the guides to the tops of the doors.

Try the doors in place and check that they run correctly. If necessary, adjust the door hardware according to the manufacturer's instructions. Paint or finish the doors as required.

For the fabric we used 50% polyester/50% cotton sheets. Cut and fit the fabric by laying the door

1 Attaching the Fabric Behind the Door Using Battens

To fit the fabric neatly, it is held in a groove in the back of the door by a batten which fits into the groove, holding the fabric taut. Miter the corners of the battens for a neat effect.

frame down and draping the fabric over it. You will need a helper to keep the fabric taut. Fit one long edge, screwing the batten in place to hold the fabric down. Pull the fabric taut to fit the opposite edge in the same way. Fit one end like this, and finally fit the opposite end in the same way. Screw the battens in place rather than nail them, as this allows the fabric to be removed and cleaned.

Fit the doors in place *(see* **Techniques, page 32** *)*.

Wire in the internal lights at the back of the door frame. However, check the relevant codes to ensure that wiring regulations are compatible for use in enclosed wardrobes.

BED WITH TRUNDLE DRAWER

A lack of adequate storage space for blankets and unseasonal clothing is a perennial problem in bedrooms.

This generous bed provides storage space under the mattress, in a pull-out trundle drawer, and beneath the head-board, which is padded to make sitting up in bed and reading a book a real pleasure. The bed is designed so that it is easy to dismantle should you wish to move house, something that is quite often a problem with conventional double and king-size beds.

The loose covers of the headboard and footboard are easily removable for cleaning and can be made from fabric to coordinate with the other soft furnishings in your bedroom.

Generous storage space at the head and in the foot of the bed

Angled back provides comfortable support for reading in bed.

pull-on loose covers fit over 1" (25mm) foam glued to the foot & head-boards

Velcro fastening

pull-out drawer on castors slides underneath foot of bed.

SIDE ELEVATION OF BED

Mattress

slatted mattress support
rests on sides of bed.

storage.

Storage drawer
on castors

cross rails.

pivot for
head board

Head board pivots
forwards.

EXPLODED
ISOMETRIC

pullout
drawer with
footboard loose
covered in
fabric

Cross rails must
be firmly fixed
as they are
fundamental
to the solidity
of the bed.

Bed with Trundle Drawer

The bed should be assembled in the room for which it is intended. However, it can be taken apart and reassembled if necessary – when moving to a new house, for example.

Firstly, decide how large the bed is to be. The length will be determined by that of a standard mattress – 6ft 6in (2m) – plus 14in (350mm) for the headboard section. When the bed is positioned in the room, there must be sufficient space between its end and a wall or furniture for the trundle drawer to be pulled out by means of the footboard. The drawer shown is 24in (610mm) long.

The width of the bed is again determined by the size of the mattress. The "king size" mattress here is 6ft (1.8m) wide, but the bed can be made for one of 5ft (1.5m) or 4ft 6in (1.35m). It can also be adapted for a single-width mattress. The bed's height is also optional. Ours is 18in (450mm), offering plenty of storage space below.

The angled headboard provides comfortable support when you are sitting up in bed, and the upholstered top panel is readily removable to give access to ample storage space in the headboard section.

Further long-term storage space – for duvets and other bedding, for example – is available below the bed. This is reached by removing the mattress and the central slatted section of the mattress support.

The main components of the bed are constructed from ¾in (19mm) plywood, MDF (medium-density fiberboard), or particleboard. The edges of the latter will need an edge-banding of hardwood molding, which must be allowed for when calculating the dimensions. The Shaker-style pegboard shown in the photograph on page 242 is simple to construct. It consists of a lumber batten attached around the room at picture-rail height which is attached with hanging pegs at regular intervals. The pegs are used for storage, to hang curtains or pictures.

Materials

Part	Quantity	Material	Length
THE BASE			
SIDE PANELS	2	¾in (19mm) MDF or particleboard	Length of mattress plus 14in (350mm) × required height
CROSS DIVIDERS	2	As above	Width of mattress × height of sides less 4in (100mm)
CORNER BATTENS	4	2 × 2in (50 × 50mm) S4S softwood	Height of cross dividers
HEADBOARD			
TRIANGULAR HEADBOARD SUPPORTS	2	¾in (19mm) plywood, MDF, or particleboard	23 × 45in (575 × 1125mm), divided diagonally into two pieces
TRIANGULAR FILLERS	2	As above	As required to fit
CROSS RAIL	1	1 × 3in (25 × 75mm) S4S softwood	Width of mattress
HEADBOARD SECTIONS	2	¾in (19mm) plywood, MDF, or particleboard	Width of mattress (see text for height)
STRENGTHENING BATTEN	1	2 × 2in (50 × 50mm) S4S softwood	Width of mattress less 1½in (38mm)
MATTRESS SUPPORT SECTION			
SIDE RAILS	2	2 × 3in (50 × 75mm) S4S softwood	Length of mattress, plus approximately 3in (75mm)
END RAIL	1	As above	Width of mattress
CENTER RAIL	1	As above	Length of mattress, plus approximately 3in (75mm)
SLATS	As required	1 × 3in (25 × 75mm) S4S softwood	Width of mattress
CROSS BATTENS	4	1 × 3in (25 × 75mm) S4S softwood	Internal distance between cross dividers
TRUNDLE DRAWER			
FOOTBOARD	1	½in (12mm) MDF	Width of bed less ½in (12mm) × height as required
DRAWER SIDES	2	As above	Height of sides of bed less 6in (150mm)
BACK	1	As above	Height of drawer sides × width of mattress less 2in (50mm)
BASE	1	As above	Internal dimensions of trundle drawer

BED ASSEMBLY AND MAIN
COMPONENTS

HEADBOARD CROSS RAIL

TRIANGULAR HEADBOARD
SUPPORT

TRIANGULAR
FILLER

UPPER HEADBOARD SECTION

STRENGTHENING BATTEN

LOWER HEADBOARD SECTION
CORNER BATTEN

SLATS

FILLER
PIECE

DOWELS

CENTER RAIL

END RAIL

CROSS DIVIDER

SIDE RAIL

SIDE PANEL

THE BASIC CONSTRUCTION OF THE BED
*All the main components of the bed are shown
here, except for the cross battens which fit under
the slats, and the trundle drawer which fits
under the bed end.*

BED WITH TRUNDLE DRAWER

TOOLS

STEEL MEASURING TAPE

TRY SQUARE

SPACING BATTEN

HAND SAW

POWER DRILL

BACK SAW

ROUTER

SCREWDRIVER

CLAMPS

HAMMER

PUTTY KNIFE

PLANE (or sanding block and sanding paper)

THE BASE

Cut two side panels from $\frac{3}{4}$in (19mm) plywood, MDF, or particleboard to the mattress length plus 14in (350mm) × required height. This one is 7ft 8in × 18in (2.35m × 450mm).

You will also need two cross dividers and four corner battens. Measure 24in (610mm) in from each end of the side panels and mark the positions of the cross dividers. Drill and countersink the corner battens on one face. Check that they are square with a try square. Then glue and screw them to the sides, inside the positions for the cross dividers and flush with the bottom edge.

Put the cross dividers in position against one of the sides, flush with the bottom edge (and outside the four corner battens), then drill, countersink, and screw through the dividers into the corner battens (fig 1). Do not reinforce this fixing by gluing, since it can then easily be taken apart should the need arise.

Put the other side panel in place and fit in the same way.

HEADBOARD

By dividing diagonally, cut two triangular headboard supports from one rectangle measuring 45 × 23in (1125 × 575mm).

HEADBOARD CROSS RAIL

This supports the headboard at the top. Cut one length from 1 × 3in (25 × 75mm) lumber, to the width of the mattress.

MAKING THE FRAME

Lay down one of the triangles and stand the cross rail on end, flush with the front edge of the triangle at the top, and as far to the point as it will go without overhanging the back. Mark its outline on to the end of the triangle. Repeat on the other triangle (fig 2).

Using a back saw or a Saber saw, cut inside the marked lines to remove the waste. This will then create a notch for the headboard cross rail to sit on.

Fit the two triangular supports inside the sides, at the head end, flush with the ends of the sides. Drill and countersink the inside of the triangles in at least four places each side, and screw one to each of the side panels (fig 3).

Put the cross rail in place. Drill and countersink the cross rail and screw it into the triangle's notches, keeping the screws low in the cross rail. Make sure that the ends of the cross rails are flush with the outside of the triangles (fig 4).

For the triangular fillers (fig 5), position a piece of MDF on the side panel. Line it up with the back edge of the triangular support and mark the triangle on to it. Cut out this triangle and repeat for the other side. Fit the fillers in place by drilling, countersinking, and screwing from the inside of the triangular supports. Use three screws on each side.

The headboard consists of two pieces, one above the other, cut to the width of the mattress. For the height of the lower piece, measure up the triangular support from the floor to about three-quarters of the

---

1 Attaching the Cross Dividers to the Side Panels
Glue and screw the corner battens to the side panels, then position the cross dividers against the battens, flush with the bottom edge, and screw in place through the dividers and into the battens.

2 Headboard Cross Rail
Hold the cross rail on end at the top of the triangular support and mark out the notch.

3 Attaching the Triangular Headboard Support
Headboard supports are screwed to the insides of side panels.

way up the thickness of the mattress, with the mattress in place. The higher piece measures the distance from that point to the top of the triangle plus ½in (12mm). The extra portion serves as a fingergrip for access to the storage below.

STRENGTHENING BATTEN

The strengthening batten is cut from 2 × 2in (50 × 50mm) softwood to the width of the mattress minus the thickness of the two triangular supports (1½in [38mm]). Glue and screw the lower headboard section to the front edges of the triangular supports. Put the strengthening batten at the top of the lower headboard section on the underside, and clamp it in place half-way up its thickness, thereby creating a ¾in (19mm) rabbet for the top part of the headboard to locate in. Drill, countersink, and screw through the lower headboard section into the batten. Try the top headboard piece in place, then remove it for covering. The upholstery will bring it flush with the sides of the triangular fillers for a tidy finish.

Hold a piece of 1 × 1in (25 × 25mm) softwood batten against the gap between the top of the lower headboard section and the side panel. Mark off the top and bottom and cut with a back saw. The bottom will be at an angle to fit the side of the bed. Glue and nail or screw the batten in place to each side (fig 1, page 248). Plane, then sand off completely flush. The batten acts as a filler to give a clean line, and will be filled and painted with the rest of the bed.

The top edge of the side panels should be rounded over either with a router and a round-over cutter, or by planing and sanding. Alternatively, glue and nail a half-round molding to the top edges for a professional-looking finish.

PADDED HEADBOARD

The padded and upholstered headboard pulls forward to reveal additional storage space at the bed head.

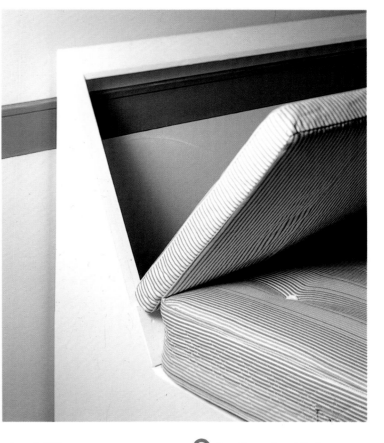

4 **Attaching the Headboard Cross Rail in Place**
Headboard cross rail is attached with two screws kept low in cross rail.

5 **Attaching the Triangular Fillers at each Side**
Triangular fillers are made from the same material as the side panels, and give a flush finish at each side. Cut the fillers to fit exactly and screw through from the inside of the triangular supports.

6 **Headboard and Batten**
Screw lower headboard section in place. Clamp the strengthening batten to top edge and screw down.

BED WITH TRUNDLE DRAWER

PADDED FOOTBOARD

REMOVABLE CENTRAL
SLATTED SECTION

PADDED HEADBOARD

UPPER HEADBOARD SECTION

HEADBOARD
CROSS
RAIL

STRENGTHENING BATTEN

MATTRESS

END RAIL

TRUNDLE DRAWER
STORAGE

CROSS DIVIDER

CORNER BATTEN

LONG-TERM
STORAGE SECTION

LOWER
HEADBOARD
SECTION

CROSS-SECTION OF BED
SHOWING STORAGE AREAS
This cross-section clearly shows the various storage areas which are a feature of the design. The trundle drawer is particularly easy to reach.

① Adding the Filler Piece
Use a piece of softwood to fill the gap between the side and lower headboard section.

② Attaching the Mattress-support Side Rails in Place
Cut the headboard ends of the mattress-support side rails at an angle to fit neatly against the lower headboard section. Note that the top edge of the side panel is rounded to give a neat finish.

③ Joining the End Rail
End rail is joined to side rails using end-lap joints; end rail laps on top and is screwed to side rails.

MATTRESS SUPPORT SECTION

The side rails are cut to the length of the mattress, plus a little overlength so that the angle can be cut into the headboard. Place their 2in (50mm) face on the cross dividers alongside the sides, and scribe one end of each rail to the angle of the headboard. Cut this angle and push them against the headboard, then mark them off flush with the ends of the side panels and cut them square.

The end rail is cut to the width of the mattress. Cut end-lap joints *(see* **Techniques, page 26** *)* to join the side and end rails (fig 3).

Glue and screw the side rails in place, screwing through the rails and into the side panels. Fix the end rail in place by inserting small screws through the end-lap joints.

The center rail is cut from 2 × 3in (50 × 75mm) softwood to the length of the mattress plus a little overlength. Rest it on the cross dividers, and scribe to the angle of the headboard, as before. Cut the center rail to length to butt tightly

A unit of the mattress support section (above) lifts out for access to ample but unobtrusive storage space under the bed.

against the inner face of the end rail. Screw it down into the cross dividers.

Drill through the end rail into the end of the center rail in two places, to a depth of between 3–4in (75–100mm) and dry-dowel the joint

using ½in (12mm) doweling *(see* **Techniques, page 30** *)*.

Work out how many slats you need by dividing the length of the mattress by 4in (100mm) – the total of one slat plus a gap. Cut all the

slats to the width of the mattress. The area between the cross dividers is a slatted unit which can be lifted out to give access to storage below.

The softwood cross battens hold the slats together on the slatted unit. Measure the internal distance between the cross dividers and cut four lengths of 1 × 3in (25 × 75mm) to this dimension.

Using a spacing batten *(see* **Techniques, page 20** *)*, space the slats equally and mark the position of the cross battens on to the first slat. The two outermost slats should be positioned in from the ends by the thickness of the side rails – that is, at least 1½in (38mm). Screw the ends of the outer cross battens in place to the first slat. Continue along the cross battens, spacing and screwing down the rest of the slats. Then space the innermost two cross battens equally in between and screw them in place (fig 5).

Place this panel on the center section and screw the remaining slats into the side rails, spacing them equally. Make sure that there is a slat flush with each end (fig 6).

4 **Joining End and Center Rail**
Center rail butts against end rail. Drill through end rail and hammer dowels in place.

5 **Making the Under-mattress Lift-out Slatted Unit**
The slatted unit between the cross-dividers can be lifted out. Slats are screwed to four cross battens. The outer two cross battens are inset so that they clear the side rails.

6 **Spacing the Fixed Slats**
Place lift-out unit over the center section and screw remaining slats, equally spaced, to side rails.

BED WITH TRUNDLE DRAWER

FOOTBOARD

DRAWER SIDE

BACK

BASE

CASTER

Trundle Drawer Assembly
Note that sides are set in from the footboard and that the back sits within the sides.

THE TRUNDLE DRAWER

The bed should be finished before you make the drawer. The footboard is cut from one piece of MDF to ½in (12mm) less than the overall width of the bed. Its height is as required – ours is 35in (890mm).

Preferably, the height of the two MDF drawer sides should be at least 6in (150mm) lower than the sides of the bed. This allows the drawer to run underneath the end rail and accommodates casters. Our sides are therefore 12in (300mm). The length is 24in (610mm).

For the back, cut one piece of MDF to the height of the drawer sides. Its width should be that of the mattress minus 2in (50mm). Glue and screw through the sides into the back edges, then glue and screw through the footboard into the sides, ensuring that the footboard overlaps the sides equally.

Measure the internal dimensions of the rectangle for the size of the drawer base, and cut it to size from MDF. The base should be spaced 1in (25mm) up from the bottom edges of the sides and back. To fit it firmly in place for screwing, lay the base on scrap battens 1in (25mm) thick, then place the carcass over the base. This will ensure an even 1in (25mm) spacing up from the bottom edges of the carcass.

Screw through into the edges of the base on all four sides, having marked the height of the center line

of the base around the outside of the carcass. Finally, screw 2in (50mm) casters to the four corners of the base to allow easy movement.

UPHOLSTERY FOR THE BED

THE PADDING

The padding is expanded-polystyrene foam of three different thicknesses, covered with Dacron. Cut the foam with an electric carving knife or any blade with a serrated edge.

HEADBOARD

Cut a piece of 2in (50mm) foam to the size of the headboard's upper section. Spray one face of the headboard with latex spray adhesive and stick the foam to it, smoothing it down carefully.

Cut a piece of 2in (50mm) foam to the length of the top edge and stick it in place, positioning it carefully, with spray adhesive.

Use 1in (25mm) foam for the sides. Cut two pieces, each to the

length of the headboard's side, plus the thickness of the foam covering the top, and stick one on each side.

Stick a thin layer of Dacron over all the foam with the spray adhesive and leave to dry.

FOOTBOARD

Cut one piece of 1in (25mm) foam to the width of the footboard, to run from the top of the drawer sides up and over the top of the footboard and down to the bottom edge.

Draw a line on the inside face of the footboard in line with the top of the drawer sides and spray adhesive on the wood down to this line, and on to the outside face.

Stick down the foam, starting at the line and smoothing it on to the wood. Ease it over the top and down the other side of the footboard.

Cut two pieces of 1in (25mm) foam to fit the small sections either side of the drawer, on the inside face of the footboard, and stick in place as shown (fig 3).

Cut two pieces of ½in (12mm) foam to the size of the side edges and stick one to each edge.

Padding the Headboard
Stick 2in (50mm) thick foam to upper headboard section and top edge; 1in (25mm) foam at sides.

Padding the Footboard
One piece of 1in (25mm) foam covers front/back of footboard, plus 1in (12mm) foam at sides.

Put a layer of Dacron over the foam, stick in place and leave to dry.

THE COVERS

The bottom edges of the covers are folded under and joined to the bases of the padded headboard and footboard with Velcro to allow easy removal for cleaning.

If you use a large-patterned fabric you will need to piece together three same-sized widths of fabric, and match the pattern along the seams. Plain fabrics are simpler to use, since no pattern-matching is necessary and you can use one long length of fabric rather than three widths to cover the large area.

If you lack the confidence to make separate border panels to go around the sides of the covers, you can achieve good results by skipping that step and joining the front panel directly to the back panel.

HEADBOARD COVER

Cut two panels – one for the front and one for the back of the padded headboard, allowing extra fabric at the edges for the seams. If you are

piecing together widths, cut them oversized (allowing extra fabric for internal as well as edge seams) and match the internal seam positions of the front and back panels.

Fold the front and back panels in half across their width and make a notch at the center of each top edge, to match up the front, border, and back panels later when sewing.

Next, measure for the long border panel that will go around the top and sides and under the bottom edge by 3in (75mm). Cut the border panel, allowing extra fabric on each side for the seams, and then fold it in half widthways and make notches on both edges – in the center and where the panel corners will be.

With right sides together, place the edge of the front panel to the edge of the border panel, matching the notches. Pin, baste, and then machine-stitch the seam, working from the center notch outwards, first in one direction and then the other, along the top and down each side until you reach the bottom corners; this ensures that the panels are sewn together evenly.

Attach the back panel to the other edge of the border panel, right sides together and with notches and corners matching. Pin, baste, and machine-stitch as before, down to each bottom corner.

Hem by machine all the remaining edges of the cover. Cut a strip of Velcro to the length of the long panels and machine-stitch it in place to the bottom edges of the front and back panels, so that the bottom edge of the front panel wraps around to the back panel. Fold in the two border pieces first, and join the panel flaps together with the Velcro for a neat finish.

FOOTBOARD COVER

Measure the padded footboard from edge to edge and cut one panel for the inside face, allowing extra all round for the edge seams, plus about 3in (75mm) at the bottom to enclose the padding. If piecing together widths, follow instructions for headboard cover for extra seam allowances. Cut the panel for the outside face, allowing extra fabric all round for edge seams

plus enough at the bottom to fold the edge under. Cut the material for the long border, allowing extra fabric for the edge seams and for folding under the bottom edge.

Make the cover as for the headboard cover and attach the outside panel to the border panel. For the inside panel, sew down as far as the drawer sides, then attach a small piece of fabric on each side to cover the narrow border on either side of the drawer. Machine-stitch these pieces to the cover with right sides together. Cut the fabric so that it fits neatly around each drawer side turning the edges under and then machine-stitching. Turn under all the bottom edges and machine-stitch.

On the outside, fold in the ends and hem along the bottom edge. Fit the bottom edge to the footboard with Velcro, using the soft part on the fabric and the hard part on the wood. To attach Velcro to the wood, glue, nail, or staple it in place, or use self-adhesive Velcro.

On the inside face, secure the bottom edge and side flaps to the footboard with Velcro as before.

4 Making the Cover for the Headboard
Cut the front and back panels allowing extra fabric all around for seams and (if necessary) piecing together widths, plus about 3in (75mm) to fold under the bottom edge. Pin, baste, then machine-stitch seams.

5 Making the Cover for the Footboard
Make up as for the headboard, carefully cutting and fitting around drawer sides. At the narrow sides of the drawer, attach thin strips of fabric. Secure with Velcro along the bottom edge and along side flaps.

Notches in center match up

Pinned in place

Velcro covering hem edge

CUPBOARDS WITH ARCHITRAVES

Many old houses have plain chimney breasts which protrude into the room, forming alcoves on each side. In such cases, cupboard doors with decorative architraves (door casing) can be installed to create a stylish feature. The same effect can be achieved if there is an entrance door on the side of the chimney and an alcove on the other, as here.

To increase the depth of the cupboard, the doorway can be brought forward by a small amount (as with the doorway on the left of the picture) without detracting from the overall effect.

A straightforward architrave can be formed simply by attaching various boards and moldings on to the wall surface around the door. If you want to hang the doors forward, as on the left in this example, then you need to build a column-like box section architrave.

DECORATIVE ARCHITRAVE

To form an architrave on the door surround itself, simply attach the moldings to the wall around the door. Visit local lumberyards for suitable moldings, bearing in mind that larger moldings can often be formed by joining two or three smaller moldings together.

The edges of the boards can be rounded off, grooved, or otherwise shaped with a suitable cutter in a hand-held router.

Attach the first (widest) molding to the wall using screws and anchors, and, where possible, nail it directly to the door frame. The other pieces of molding can then be glued and nailed in place.

BOX-SECTION ARCHITRAVE

In this case a simple lumber box is formed on each side of the door opening. The front piece is joined to the sides using a bare-faced rabbet and dado joint, or with dowels (see **Techniques, pages 27 and 30**). A pilaster effect can be achieved by cutting grooves with a flute cutter in a router on a second piece of lumber attached to the face of the front piece. Glue and screw blocks behind the box section at the top to box-in the architrave at the top of the frame.

MAKING A CORNICE

Glue a batten behind the lower edge of a cornice molding. Glue and nail another, smaller, cornice molding between the larger one and the architrave (fig 3, left). Form the cornice above the box section by fitting battens behind the molding; for the molding underneath use coving. Add triangular fillers at ends and shape with a coping saw.

① Fixing a Decorative Architrave
A wide decorative architrave can be built-up by attaching moldings around a door frame.

② Built-out Box-section
A built-out architrave can be made by attaching a box-section around the door opening.

③ Finishing the Built-out Architrave at the Top
The box is completed at the head of the door and the space between the box-section and the ceiling is filled with a wooden cornice molding. Cross-section on right shows cornice molding attached to architrave above a door.

PANELED BATHTUB

The basic framework is made from 1 × 2in (25 × 50mm) S4S softwood. The wall battens and vertical studs, six of each, are cut to the distance between the floor and the underside of the bathtub rim.

You will also need two end rails, the same width as the bathtub, less about 5in (125mm); two side rails to the same length as the bathtub, less about 3in (75mm); and the intermediate stud to the distance between the side rails.

For the paneling use $\frac{1}{2}$ × 4in (12 × 100mm) TGV (tongued, grooved, and V-jointed) pine boarding, the same length as the vertical studs. Use as many pieces as are necessary to clad the side and end of the bathtub.

The removable panel section consists of two cross rails made from a $16\frac{3}{4}$in (425mm) length of 1 × 3in (25 × 75mm) S4S softwood.

Cut the wall battens and vertical studs to length. Mark where the wall battens will be installed. They should be inset by about $\frac{1}{2}$in (12mm) from the edge of the bathtub rim.

Cut rabbets 3in (75mm) wide by about $\frac{1}{2}$in (12mm) deep in the edges of two vertical studs, 6in (150mm) down from the top, and 6in (150mm) up from the bottom. These house the cross rails of the removable panel. The panel provides access to the pipes.

Screw and anchor the wall battens to the wall. Attach a vertical stud temporarily to each wall batten. Temporarily screw two uprights together in an L-shape to form the corner studs. Wedge these under the tub rim at the external corner.

Measure between the studs and cut the end and side rails to length. Remove studs and assemble side and end frames by butt-jointing cross rails to vertical studs, gluing and nailing each joint. For ease, set the upper cross rails 1in (25mm) down from the top of the vertical studs. Nail an intermediate stud between the side frame cross rails.

Hold the frames flat and square while the glue sets. To fit, screw the frames to the wall battens, and to each other at the external corner.

Cut the TGV boarding to tuck under the bathtub rim. Cut off the tongues from two lengths and joint these together at the external corner, either by mitering their edges, or by butting them to a quarter round molding (fig 2). Attach them to the frame by carefully screwing through from the back. Attach subsequent lengths using fixing clips (see **Panelled Bathroom, page 211**).

Fit the last four sections of TGV boarding to the 1 × 3in (25 × 75mm) cross rails, leaving a short length protruding to catch behind the permanent paneling.

① Building a Timber Tongue-and-Groove Clad Bathtub Panel
Nail together a simple frame using 1 × 2in (25 × 50mm) lumber. Screw the frames together at the corner, and to wall-attached battens at each end. Note removable panel for access to bath waste pipes and tap connections.

② Bathtub Panel Corner Detail
Frame is clad in TGV boards. External corner edge is mitered or finished with quadrant molding.

Wall batten — Vertical stud — End cross rails — Cross rail — Intermediate stud — Cross rail — Rabbet for rail — Fixing clip — Removable section — Cross rail — Vertical studs — Miter joint — Quarter round

INTRODUCTION
TO GARDEN PROJECTS

If you have a garden, the chances are that you already "do it yourself." Planting, seeding, mowing, turfing, fencing, and paving are tasks that the majority of gardeners do themselves, since few people today have either the space or the means to justify a full-time gardener.

This book is a logical extension of that established tradition of working outdoors in the garden. It contains a range of projects, from the simple to the more complicated, and shows you how to make a variety of structures, including containers, seats, trelliswork, and even a summer house. All of these are classic garden accessories, the design of which is too often overlooked.

Achieving success with these projects has to do with confidence. Once you have completed a simple project, this will give you the confidence to move on to a more complicated piece. If you are a novice woodworker, choose the simplest item in terms of design and progress gradually as your skills and dexterity develop.

If the garden is a good place to practice and refine your remodeling skills, you can also get away with a lower standard of finish: precision and perfection are not really at home in the garden, where a weathered, rustic appearance can be a positive attribute. Materials need not be expensive and what you make will usually have cost less than the retail product in the garden center, although this is not invariably the case. You can buy lattice, for example, for far less than the wood you would need to make it, so to economize by doing-it-yourself you must examine what is commercially available from the garden center and make the proper comparisons.

The great benefit of building things for the garden, however, is the degree of satisfaction it affords – the pleasure of making something that has been tailored to suit your own space and needs. What you make will often be better designed than its equivalent in the garden center; more importantly, it will reflect your own taste and sense of style.

Terence Conran.

PLANNING A GARDEN

In the words of Sir John Soane, good design should contain an element of "hazard and surprise." Although Soane was talking about interior design, this important principle applies equally to the disposition and arrangement of outdoor space. Nothing is less memorable than a garden which can be surveyed in a single glance: you want to be able to move through a garden and be surprised by what you discover around each corner.

Fortunately, "hazard" in gardening is easy to create. Changes of direction, with paths leading around structures which divide and separate different areas within the garden, immediately generate interest. Forms can be created very simply with trelliswork over which climbing plants are trained, providing a sort of growing "veil" through which to walk.

Even more important are changes in level. In this, as in so much of garden design, there is a great deal to be learned from Japan. Different levels give a sense of movement, transforming even the dullest

patch of ground. And because plants like falling over edges or trailing over walls, a change in level provides endless opportunities to blend architectural form with planting, thereby softening the lines of the design.

Trellising, planters adjacent to the house, fast-growing creepers and climbers grown up the walls can all help to blend a house in with its setting, anchoring it to its environment and creating an established garden within a short space of time. One great advantage of building garden accessories is that if your house has distinctive architectural details, such as decorative bargeboarding, it is easy to incorporate these features into the design of your structures. Something as simple as picking out a color from a door to use on seating or containers can help to unify the overall design and visually link the house to the garden.

Because the garden is an organic place where things grow, the materials you use for structures and accessories should be

natural ones as far as possible. Plastic has no affinity with plants: the two simply do not go together. Artificial materials always stand out in a garden because they do not weather in the way that natural ones do. Wood, stone, terracotta, brick, and – for some reason – metal all work well in the garden, harmonizing with one another so that you can vary the textures and surfaces in an interesting way. What is particularly appealing about all of these materials is the way they age and weather, oxodizing, bleaching, staining, and acquiring lichens and mosses so that they meld into the garden. Show gardens, because they have not had time to mature, always look too new and clean for my taste. You can encourage aging if your garden is looking too new by scrubbing salt or domestic bleach into wooden decking to achieve a weathered look or by painting non-pasteurized milk, houseplant food, or manure made into a slurry onto concrete or terracotta surfaces to speed up the growth of lichen.

THE OUTDOOR ROOM

Good garden design is a question of creating an outdoor space that reflects your needs, style, and preferences, and is at the same time compatible with the materials, structures, and details of your house. The garden should be a natural extension to the house, rather than a jarring contrast. Sources of inspiration for garden designs include the ever-popular informal look of the English country cottage, the architectural terraces of modern urban gardens, and the contemplative beauty of Japanese landscape settings.

If the garden needs an element of wilderness and a certain lack of precision to be truly inviting, it is also the place for color. Far too often, people play safe with garden accessories, sticking to the traditional shades of white or a dark green which fades into the background. Splashes of bright color are an attractive and appealing feature of Mediterranean gardens and, contrary to popular belief, such vivid accent shades also work in countries where summer light is not as intense. Color makes a strong positive statement, and is also extremely cheerful in the winter when the garden is least interesting. Yellow, for example, goes equally well with the fresh greens of summer and the grays of winter. Blue (either dark blue or blue-gray) is another good garden color. If you make your own garden accessories, you can decide for yourself what color you want to paint them, rather than having to accept the limited and uninspiring shades that are offered commercially.

Finally, a garden, in the same way as a room, needs a focus of interest: the path must lead somewhere; the view through the pergola must reveal something at the other end; a formal layout of beds demands a centerpiece. Whatever you base your design around should look positive and well-considered, not half-hearted. A large terracotta pot tumbling with colorful plants, an inviting garden seat in a shady place, a patio under a striped awning, a garden pond full of fish or a collection of strange, disparate containers all make good focal points as long as they are properly complemented by their environment. There are many excellent ideas illustrated in this book to stimulate your imagination, but the important point is that these are merely a starting place for your own plans and ideas. Your garden is the place where you can express your own personality and idiosyncrasies to create the kind of outdoor room you want to live in, whether it is formal or rustic.

PRACTICALITIES

A new garden should start with a plan which takes into account practical as well as aesthetic considerations. A camera is a useful tool in the planning process: take photographs of the views from the house to the garden (and from upper levels, too) as well as from the garden to the house. A simple sketch of the plot annotated with rough dimensions will help you to decide on the layout of paths, beds, and patio. For a formal design you may wish to work out a strong controlled grid or a symmetrical framework of beds and connecting paths. For a more informal, natural arrangement, it is still important to think about where the paths will go and what shape beds they will create: too often, paths are laid without due regard to the shape of the beds, with awkward and ill-judged results. You should also work out any changes in level required or note existing slopes or steps, as well as features such as mature trees and garden sheds.

PLANNING A GARDEN

Although the climate of your garden cannot be altered radically, it can be tempered. Exposure to strong winds can be limited to some extent by the filtering effect of boundary hedging, fencing, or trellis. In a dry area, a damp microclimate can be created by the addition of a pond, around the perimeter of which moisture-loving plants can flourish. Shade can be supplied by a variety of means, both manmade and natural, including awnings, arbors, and vines or climbers trained over trellis or wire frameworks. Too little light poses another problem. You cannot, of course, reorientate a garden which faces the wrong way, nor do much about the deep shade cast by high walls. But you can clear out overgrowth, take down fencing, and drastically prune overhanging branches to let in as much light as possible. Unfortunately if the sun doesn't shine, there is little you can do about it.

Many other factors will have a bearing on the eventual design:
- The siting of a compost heap, a tool shed, and utility area
- Access to water
- The position of eating or sitting areas
- Barbecues
- Areas in which children can play and in which to site play equipment
- Permanent fixtures such as mature trees, existing walls, and boundaries
- The presence of any eyesores which may need to be camouflaged
- The need for privacy or security
- Noise from neighboring gardens
- Special requirements such as the extreme climate of a roof garden
- The amount of time you can spend
- Your budget

All gardens benefit from careful organization. Planting stands a greater chance of success if the basic framework is right.

DESIGN AND DETAIL

Gardens thrive on an element of surprise, hidden corners, and changes of level. Decking is a harmonious outdoor surface, and can be planned in advance to provide different seating and eating levels, and beds for planting (above). Strategically placed, arbors or trelliswork can act as a focal point in the garden, directing the eye to splashes of color (above left and opposite).

COLOR IN THE GARDEN

Color has long been a neglected element in the garden as far as structures, accessories, and garden furniture are concerned (overleaf). Containers, seats, trellises, fences, and walls can all be painted to give a positive lift to the overall design of a garden.

PART 5

SEATING AND EATING

In every garden there should be a place where you can sit down, look with pleasure at what you have achieved, and think about all the hard work that remains to be done. Any seating area, whether it is a bench in a shady corner or a patio equipped with table, chairs, awning, and barbecue, becomes a focal point in the garden's design; its position, accordingly, is part of that initial process of architectural planning. Should it be in sun or shade? In view of the house or in a more secluded location? If you intend to eat outdoors, at least partial shade will be required. Eating outside, preferably in dappled sunlight, is one of the great pleasures of life.

You can sit in the garden to read a book, have a drink, watch the children play, eat a meal, or simply take stock of your surroundings, and there are as many styles of garden seat as there are functions for them to fulfil. Which type of seat you choose should reflect the general plan and style of your garden. The quality of light and shade is a very important consideration, not only for personal comfort, but also for good growing conditions and for intrinsic interest.

SEATING AND EATING

Seats and table tops must be designed so that water does not sit on the surface and rot or rust them away. A fractional tilt to a seat or table top will ensure that water drains off; slats or drainage holes fulfil the same function and there are also new outdoor paints which protect garden furniture to a much greater degree than traditional undercoat and gloss.

Much garden furniture, particularly the cast-iron or painted metal variety, is too ornate for my taste. Tables and seats which are clean-lined, whether they are curved or rectilinear, look more confident and suit outdoor living much better. Simple garden furniture allows the focus of attention to remain on the planting. This is not to dismiss wrought-ironwork entirely. Benches with wrought- or cast-iron ends, but plain slatted backs and seats, can be attractive and are more comfortable than all-metal versions which heat up in the sun.

Garden seats can also be amusing. In the nineteenth century, rough-hewn tree branches were nailed together to create whimsical Gothic benches, a kind of visual joke. In a similar vein are sections of tree trunk used as bench supports, a chimney pot filled with sand as a table base, or a stone slab inset into a clipped box hedge, with the foliage making a living upholstered back. One of the most irresistible designs is the tree seat, almost a ground-level tree house, which forms a platform around the base of a tree.

In addition to semipermanent garden furniture, there are many varieties of ready-made garden seating which work equally well indoors. Painted wooden benches, wickerwork, rattan and basket chairs, folding canvas chairs, and metal park chairs suit their location and are generally light enough to move easily.

With garden tables, there is the same choice between permanent fixtures and tables which can be set up as required. Stone, marble, and ceramic tiles are excellent materials for table tops; folding

OUTDOOR LIVING

Stepped wooden seating (above) provides interesting and versatile changes of level in a garden. A terrace of herringbone paving and shaded by mature plane trees (right) makes a delightful outdoor eating area.

Overleaf A range of garden seating ideas.

SEATING AND EATING

metal tables, traditionally associated with French parks are more economic.

Seating areas are almost always more pleasurable and useable if there is a degree of shade. If your patio is exposed to the full force of the sun, there are many ways of creating shade that look appropriate as well as stylish. In this area, the yachting world is a fruitful source of visual ideas. Sail-like canvas awnings, varnished wooden frameworks for climbing plants, and canvas in bright clear colors eyeletted and lashed to a simple metal frame all have a faintly nautical flavour. A simple metal armature or framework with a vine trained over it is a particularly Mediterranean solution to the problem; narrow gauge trellis overhead breaks up sunlight into a small square grid, taking the power out of it. Shop blinds fitted with a retractable mechanism, canvas clipped on to a wood and wire frame, or a large market umbrella are other effective ideas. For a more theatrical effect, a bright, patterned fabric can be knotted and tied to poles like an oversize scarf, or you can borrow ideas from tent design. Plain canvas (perhaps painted on the underside) or broad blue-and-white stripes are crisp, fresh, and appealing.

Most people today want their outdoor eating area to be a cooking area as well. A barbecue area is particularly easy to build, a good project to build in the garden. Brick or stone are the best materials for construction and you will probably also need to pave around and beneath the barbecue to make cleaning easy. At the simplest level of design, you can buy a mass-produced, cast-iron barbecue and simply set it on a brick or stone slab. If you are building the barbecue as well as its setting, it is best to line it in firebrick as a precaution against the intense heat.

Barbecues should be sited with care. Not only do they generate a great deal of heat, they are also smoky. Avoid positions where smoke and cooking smells will drift into the house – or worse, through your neighbor's windows. Overhanging plants are likely to be singed or even incinerated; adjacent walls will be blackened by smoke, although this is not necessarily unattractive.

You can extend the potential of outdoor eating areas by the addition of good garden lighting. Outdoor lighting calls for a degree of sensitivity, since obvious, glaring fixtures will immediately rob your garden of whatever charm it possesses; on the other hand, subtle, diffused light sources create an instantly magical atmosphere. Garden lighting should be as unobtrusive as possible, with fixtures built into walls or shielded in some way.

When you furnish a garden, what you choose should be simple, so as not to compete with the planting; practical, for obvious reasons; and architectural, to contribute to your overall plan or design. You can use this opportunity to go one step further and think about the way you furnish your home indoors as well: a continuation of the same basic attitude will bring the house and garden closer together, to the benefit of both.

OUTDOOR SEATING AREAS

If you intend to use a seating area as a place for outdoor meals you will need to provide a degree of shade or shelter. Sitting in the full glare of the hot midday sun is very unpleasant for any length of time; on the other hand, you do not necessarily want to have to move indoors on account of a few drops of rain. Solutions include integrated terraces and balconies, awnings, and trellises supporting a canopy of vines or climbing plants. Perhaps the most appealing of all in fine weather is a table and chairs placed in the dappled shade under a tree, a natural shelter which filters the light to just the right degree.

GARDEN BENCH

When it comes to garden furniture, people tend to have rather conservative taste. Although they might tolerate modern and even occasionally avant-garde pieces in the home, these are less welcome for outdoor living, where the emphasis has generally been on the traditional. Wrought-iron seating typically has a Victorian flavor, and, in recent years, the designs of Sir Edwin Lutyens have been enormously influential, with their classically inspired curves.

This garden bench with its upright railed back and plain, flat seat and legs owes something to the strict functional beauty of nineteenth-century Shaker furniture. Extremely simple by comparison with much of what is commercially available for the garden, the bench is nevertheless one of the more demanding projects to make. This is partly because garden furniture must be finished to a higher standard than other garden structures, as it will receive closer inspection.

Even if you move your garden furniture indoors for the winter it will have to take some degree of weathering. Allowing water to collect on a surface is the quickest way of causing deterioration and decay. Here the seat slopes slightly so that water drains off and, similarly, where the back joins the seat a narrow gap has been left to allow water to flow down. The straight edges of the legs are beveled so that accidental knocks by the lawnmower do not cause too much damage.

The height of the back is a critical factor in the design. Equally distinctive is the back's reeded quality. This is, perhaps, not a bench for lounging, although, supplied with a long cushion, it would work very well indoors.

Don't be afraid to let color make a positive statement in the garden. Yellow and various tones of blue look as good in winter as they do in summer and are more eye-catching than the more sedate shades of dark green or white.

GARDEN BENCH

The garden bench is perhaps the most familiar piece of garden furniture. Building one yourself will almost certainly be cheaper than buying one, and will give you a real sense of satisfaction. If need be, you can adapt the design shown here to suit the size and proportions of your garden and your individual requirements. Choose the site for your bench with care, positioning it to serve as a focal point that draws the eye in a certain direction; alternatively, you could place it to provide a place of sanctuary in a tranquil, shady corner of the garden where you can retreat to sit in peace, quiet, and comfort.

This garden bench could be made from hardwood, but it will be considerably cheaper and more environmentally acceptable if you make it from good-quality softwood. In the latter case, it is important that you treat the lumber with good-quality wood preservative at all stages of construction to ensure that it will give you many years of service. A clear wood preservative should be applied to the lumber after the component pieces have been cut, but before the joints are assembled; the strength of the joint will not be affected if you allow about 24 hours for the preservative to dry thoroughly before applying the glue. A second coat of preservative should be applied after construction, before the application of the final finish.

Using clear preservative will allow you to keep your options open regarding whether you finish the bench by painting or by applying a water-repellent wood stain of the type used widely on wood window frames. If you finish the bench by painting it, it is a good idea to use an exterior gloss paint or microporous (satin sheen) system. Such paint often contains a penetrating preservative wood primer, and this should be used in preference to a second coat of clear wood preservative.

The ideal way to construct the bench to ensure many years of service is to use traditional mortise and tenon joints for the main frame and dowel joints for the back rest slats and the seat boards. However, if you feel that you do not possess the necessary skills to cut accurate mortise and tenon joints, then the entire bench could be made using dowel joints throughout. If you do use only dowel joints, however, it will be more important than ever to apply a good-quality waterproof woodworking adhesive to each joint before assembly, and to keep each joint firmly clamped until the adhesive is thoroughly set.

MATERIALS

Part	Quantity	Material	Length
BACK LEGS	2	3 × 4in (75 × 100mm) S4S softwood	41in (1035mm)
FRONT LEGS	2	3 × 3in (75 × 75mm) S4S softwood	17in (430mm)*
SIDE FRAME RAILS	4	2 × 3in (50 × 75mm) S4S softwood	19in (480mm)
FRONT RAIL	1	As above	70½in (1790mm)
LOWER BACK RAIL	1	1¼ × 6in (32 × 150mm) S4S softwood	70½in (1790mm)
UPPER BACK RAIL	1	2 × 3in (50 × 75mm) S4S softwood	74in (1880mm)*
BACK SLATS	32	1 × 1½in (25 × 38mm) S4S softwood	Distance between back rails
SEAT BOARDS	4	1¼ × 6in (32 × 150mm) S4S softwood	73½in (1865mm)
DOWELS (seat to lower back rail)	5	From ½in (12mm) hardwood doweling	Approx. 3¾in (95mm)
DOWELS (to join seat boards and fit back slats)	As required	From 5/16in (8mm) hardwood doweling	Approx. 1½in (40mm)

* Overlong and then cut to size after affixing – see text

TOOLS

WORKBENCH (fixed or portable)

UTILITY KNIFE

STEEL MEASURING TAPE

STEEL BENCH RULE

TRY SQUARE

SMALL CROSSCUT SAW (or circular power saw)

BACK SAW (or power saber saw)

CHISELS

MARKING GAUGE

MORTISE GAUGE

POWER DRILL

BRAD-POINT DRILL BIT – (5/16in) 8mm

SPADE BIT

DOWELING JIG

ONE PAIR OF BAR CLAMPS (or band clamp)

SMOOTHING PLANE

POWER ROUTER and BEADING BIT

MALLET

ORBITAL SANDER (or hand sanding block)

Garden Bench Assembly

Back Leg

Back Slat

Dowels

Seat Board

Front Leg

Front Rail

Upper Back Rail

Lower Back Rail

Top Side Frame Rail

Lower Side Frame Rail

Back Leg

Seat Boards

Top Side Frame Rail

Front Leg

Lower Side Frame Rail

Side Elevation

GARDEN BENCH

1 Shaping the Back Legs
Lay front leg at an angle on back leg and mark its position. Measure 1⅜in (35mm) from the back at the top and join marks with top of front leg marks. Cut out around marked lines, curving the shape at the back. Mark off seat thickness parallel with top of front leg position.

SEAT SIDE FRAMES

SHAPING THE FRONT LEGS

Cut the front legs overlong – at least 17in (430mm) long in total – and measure 15¾in (400mm) up from the bottom to mark off the finished length. Square a line around the leg on all faces (see **Techniques, page 396**). Put the front legs aside for the time being.

SHAPING THE BACK LEGS

The back legs are shaped from 3 × 4in (75 × 100mm) lumber. Mark out the legs by laying one of the front legs on the wider face of one of the back legs, sloping at an angle but touching at the bottom and side edges (fig. 1). Remember that the front leg is overlong at the top, so align with the finished leg line. Mark around the shape of the front leg onto the back leg.

At the top of the back leg, measure 1⅜in (38mm) from the back face on both sides and join these two points to the top points of the marked front leg position, giving the shape for the back leg (fig. 1).

With one back leg marked, cut out around the marked lines, with straight lines at the front face of the leg, but rounding off the angle at the back of the leg to produce a gentle curve. Plane the face edges at the front straight and square to the sides as the joints are measured from this edge.

Use the cut-out back leg to mark the other one and cut it out. When both legs are cut, mark off the seat thickness, parallel with the top of the front leg position, using a seat board and a try square.

MARKING UP THE MORTISES AND TENONS

Take one of the front legs and line one of the side rails (wide face against the leg) to the top marked line (fig. 2), taking into account the excess length at the top. Mark off the position of the bottom of the rail onto the leg. Working from this line, mark off the length of the mortise 2in (50mm) up. Square the lines around to the two inside faces *(see* **Techniques, page 396** *)*.

For the bottom joint, measure 2⅜in (60mm) up from the bottom of the leg on the back face, then another 2in (50mm) up for the top of the mortise. Transfer all of these lines to the back of the other front leg using a try square. Square the lines of the top mortise around to the inside face of the second front leg.

Using a try square, transfer the length and position of the mortises from the front legs onto the front face of the back legs.

Take a ¾in (19mm) chisel and set a mortise gauge to this width with the stock set so that the mortise is centered on the edge of the side rails (*not* centered on the legs).

Mark off the top mortises on the front faces of the back legs, and on the two inside faces of the front legs. Measure from the *outside* edge in each case so that the front and upper side rails will be flush.

On the ends of all four side rails, mark off the tenons (fig. 3) and also mark off the tenons on the ends of the front rail.

Re-set the stock on the mortise gauge so that it is centered on the legs and mark off the lower mortises centered on the inside faces of all the legs for the lower side rails.

Measure 2in (50mm) in from each end on one of the side rails, and mark the shoulder of the tenon. Square around all faces. Using a try square, transfer the lines onto all the other side rails. Measure 2in (50mm) in from each end of the front rail and square around as before. To ensure a strong construction, it is important that all the lengths between the shoulders on the side rails are accurately marked. Mark the widths of the top tenon 2in (50mm) from the bottom edges of all the *top* rails so that the tenons are bare-faced to the lower edge.

The tenons are centered on the two *lower* side rails, so measure ⅜in (10mm) up from the lower edge, then 2in (50mm) for the width of the mortise (fig. 3).

CUTTING THE JOINTS

Cut the mortises slightly deeper than 2in (50mm) (*see* **Techniques, Mortise and Tenon Joint, page 402** *)* and then the tenons.

Dry assemble the parts to check the fit. The ends of the tenons on the front rail and the ends of the front tenons of the top side rails will all need to be cut at a 45° angle to ensure a tight fit (fig. 4).

Cut off the "horns" (protruding ends) at the tops of the front legs to leave the front legs flush with the upper side rails.

THE BACK

FITTING THE LOWER BACK RAIL

Take a chisel about ½in (12mm) wide and set a mortise gauge to exactly this width. Set the stock so the tenon will be offset to the back on the lower back rail, making a bare-faced tenon joint (fig 1, page 276). Mark the mortise on the inside faces of the back legs, working from

the front faces. Mark the bare-faced tenons on the lower back rail.

Align the lower back rail with the mark for the seat at the front so that it is square to the top front face of the back leg (fig 1, page 276). Mark off the position of the rail, and mark a ⅝in (15mm) shoulder at the top and bottom.

On the lower back rail, mark 2in (50mm) in from the ends and ⅝in (15mm) in from the edges for the shoulders. Before cutting the tenons, check that the length between the shoulders is the same as the front rail. Cut the tenons and then chisel the mortises to a depth of 2in (50mm).

FITTING THE UPPER BACK RAIL

Mark 2in (50mm) down from the top of the back leg and square around using a try square. Transfer these lines to the other leg. With the mortise gauge still set to ½in (12mm) set the stock so that it is centered on this shoulder line, working from the front face (fig 2, page 276). Now mark off the tenon on both legs.

② **Front Leg Mortises**
Mark rail positions on leg. Mortise centered on edge of front and top side rails, centered on lower side rail.

③ **Front and Side Rail Tenons**
Top **Cut bare-faced tenons for front and top side rails.** *Bottom* **Tenon is centered on lower side rail.**

④ **Dry Assembly of Front Legs to Front and Side Rails**
Left **Position of cut mortises on front leg.** *Inset* **Plan view shows front rail and upper side rail flush with outside edges of front leg.** *Right* **Ends of tenons are angled on front and upper side rails.**

GARDEN BENCH

The upper rail should be cut over-long by 2in (50mm), but use the lower rail to mark the exact length between the shoulders and square around the upper rail at each end. From these lines mark 2in (50mm) to the outside (toward the ends).

With the mortise gauge still set for the width of the tenon, mark the mortises on the bottom edge of the rail, working from the front face (fig. 2). Mark the width of each tenon to 2in (50mm) from the inside face of the legs so that the tenons are bare-faced.

Cut the mortises to 2in (50mm) deep, and cut the tenons. Dry assemble the back legs to the upper and lower rails to check the fit and cut off the "horns" (protruding ends) flush with the outer face of the legs.

SHAPING THE UPPER RAIL

The upper rail has to be shaped at the back to follow the taper of the back legs (fig. 3). Strike a line up each back leg to continue the taper onto the rail and then join up these lines by marking a line along the top edge of the upper rail.

Remove the rail and cut off the waste with a power plane or by using a crosscut saw. This is a long rip cut and will need care. Finish the taper by planing the surface of the upper rail smooth.

FITTING THE BACK SLATS

The width and spacing of the back slats are matters of preference. We used 1 × 1½in (25 × 38mm) slats, spaced about ¾in (19mm) apart.

The easiest way to fit the slats is to use two dowels top and bottom, positioned by means of a doweling jig. We used ⁵⁄₁₆in (8mm) dowels, 1½in (40mm) long. For an even stronger fitting you can use mortise and tenon joints top and bottom, but without a mortising machine it would be a very time-consuming task to make all the necessary joints.

Measure on the back leg the distance from the top of the lower rail to the underside of the upper rail, and cut the slats to this length if you will be affixing them using dowels. Cut the slats about ¾in (19mm) longer at each end if you intend to use mortise and tenon joints.

DETAIL OF THE GARDEN BENCH

For decorative effect, the outside edges of the legs, frame rails, seat boards, and so on are beveled before final assembly.

1 **Fitting Lower Back Rail to Back Leg**
Lower back rail fits square and flush with slope of front face of back leg and will align with back edge of seat boards. Mark mortises on inside faces of back legs and cut bare-faced tenons on lower back rail.

2 **Fitting Upper Back Rail to Back Leg**
Mark mortise on ends of upper back rail (remember it is overlong) and cut out. Mark rail position on top of back legs and cut bare-faced tenons on legs. Cut excess from ends of rail to fit flush with back legs.

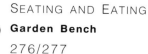
Mark up the ends of the slats for the two dowel holes (fig. 4) and, using a doweling jig, drill the ends of the slats to a depth of $\frac{7}{8}$in (22mm) using an $\frac{5}{16}$in (8mm) dowel (brad-point) drill bit.

Mark a center line along the top edge of the lower rail and the bottom edge of the upper rail for the center line of the dowel holes.

Work out the positions of the slats along one of these, adjusting as necessary to give an even spacing between the slats. Mark the centers of the dowel hole positions all the way along.

Clamp the two rails together and transfer the dowel center marks to the other rail. Drill the dowel holes to a depth of $\frac{7}{8}$in (22mm).

ASSEMBLING THE FRAME

Dry assemble the whole bench. Bevel the edges of the front and back legs, the lower side rails, the underside of the upper side rails, the edge of the lower back rail, and the underside of the front rail using either a router with a beveling bit or a power plane.

Sand all the components to smooth the faces and edges, and to clean off any pencil marks. Glue up the end frames using a gap-filling waterproof glue such as epoxy resin, clamping it tightly until the glue has thoroughly dried.

At this point, an adjustment has to be made to the height of the back legs to allow the seat to angle back slightly to assist rainwater drainage. This is done by standing the end frame on a flat surface, such as the workbench, and shimming the front edge of the front leg by $\frac{5}{8}$in (15mm) using a scrap piece of wood (fig. 5).

Using an offcut of the same thickness, scribe the back leg and the side and back of the front leg to the correct angle. Cut off the bottoms of the legs to these lines. Repeat for the other end frame. Glue the front rail and the lower back rail into the end frames, then glue all the dowels and slats into the lower back rail. Apply glue to the tops of the slats and to the dowels and seat-back tenons, then tap the upper back rail into place. You will need someone to help you with this.

THE SEAT

CONSTRUCTION

The seat is a solid piece formed by doweling together a number of narrow lengths of wood. Use a doweling jig and join to the frame with $\frac{5}{16}$in (8mm) dowels, 1$\frac{1}{2}$in (40mm) long, spaced about 6–9in (150–225mm) apart.

After doweling, glue the lengths together using a gap-filling water-proof wood adhesive, such as epoxy resin, and hold the assembly together with bar clamps or folding wedges against a fixed board nailed to a worktop.

When the glue has dried, sand the surface flush and position the seat on the seat bench frame, leaving a $\frac{1}{8}$in (4mm) wide gap at the back for drainage. Mark around so that there is a $\frac{3}{4}$in (19mm) overhang at each end and at the front, then trim the seat to this line.

Cut a $\frac{1}{2}$in (12mm) chamfer on the top edges at the front and sides using either a router with a beading bit or a power plane.

INSTALLATION

Secure the seat in place using galvanized shrinkage plates – two at each end and three along the front – and screw into the seat rails and underside of the seat.

To keep the seat rigid so it will not bow in the middle, drill through the back rail into the seat in five places using a $\frac{1}{2}$in (12mm) spade bit. Drill about 2in (50mm) into the seat. Cut five lengths of $\frac{1}{2}$in (12mm) dowel about 3$\frac{3}{4}$in (95mm) long. Use a tenon saw or the point of a nail to cut two grooves $\frac{1}{16}-\frac{1}{8}$in (2–4mm) deep along the dowel lengths to allow glue and air to escape as the dowels are driven into position.

Apply waterproof adhesive to the holes and hammer the dowels into position using the mallet. After the glue has set, saw off the protruding ends flush with the seat rail.

Bevel the bottom edges of the legs so the wood will not split if the bench is dragged on the ground. To prevent the legs from rotting, affix large, metal hammer-in glides to the bottoms of the legs.

3 **Shaping Upper Back Rail**
Mark sides and back of back rail to follow taper of back face of back leg. Remove waste and plane smooth.

4 **Fitting the Back Slats**
Mark slat and dowel positions on rails. Fit slats between back rails using two dowels each end.

5 **Angling the Legs**
Above Stand bench frame on a flat surface and shim front leg with scrap wood. Scribe legs as necessary.

6 **Cross-section of Seat**
Below Seat boards are butted up and joined using dowels. Longer dowels affix seat to lower back rail.

OCTAGONAL TREE SEAT

Even in the smallest garden, a tree seat makes an inviting point of interest. Any type of seating really makes a garden look furnished, but a seat which encircles a tree is particularly appealing. Children enjoy playing on, under, and around the shady platform and seem to gain endless amusement sitting on opposite sides from each other or their parents.

Although this seat looks complicated, it is actually fairly simple to make.

Nevertheless, it is a time-consuming project. Because the back leans inwards, cutting the back slats could have been quite a difficult proposition. To prevent unnecessary complication, a gap has been left between the slats to accommodate any discrepancies.

Other design simplifications were made. There is a simple bold structure for the frame underneath rather than mortise-and-tenon joints.

Softwood is an easy material to work with and contributes a great deal to the ease with which a structure like this can be made. But softwood does need to be protected in some way, by treating with preservative, and then by applying a final finish of wood stain or, as in this case, paint. Depending on where in your garden the seat is positioned, you might like to choose a brighter color: a strong blue would be very effective.

OCTAGONAL TREE SEAT

TOOLS

- WORKBENCH (fixed or portable)
- STEEL MEASURING TAPE
- STEEL BENCH RULE
- TRY SQUARE (or combination square)
- SLIDING BEVEL
- PROTRACTOR
- CIRCULAR POWER SAW – preferably bench-mounted (or small crosscut saw)
- BACK SAW
- POWER DRILL
- DRILL BIT – approximately $\frac{1}{8}$in (3mm) diameter
- COUNTERSINK BIT
- SCREWDRIVER
- CLAW HAMMER
- NAIL PUNCH
- PINCERS
- SMOOTHING PLANE (hand or power)

MATERIALS

Part	Quantity	Material	Length
BACK LEGS	8	2 × 3in (50 × 75mm) S4S softwood	42in (1050mm)
FRONT LEGS	8	As above	20in (500mm)
SEAT FRAME RAILS	32	1 × 3in (25 × 75mm) S4S softwood	21in (530mm)
SEAT SLATS	48	As above	As required
APRON BOARDS	8	As above	As required
BACK SLATS	72	$\frac{5}{8}$ × 2in (16 × 50mm) S4S softwood	As required
APRON BACK-UP BATTENS	8	1 × 1in (25 × 25mm) S4S softwood	6in (150mm) shorter than apron boards

Also required: waterproof woodworking adhesive; $1\frac{1}{2}$in (38mm) No. 8 galvanized countersunk wood screws

The size of this eight-sided tree seat is governed by the size of the tree you wish to surround. Remember, you must leave room for the trunk to expand as the tree grows! Some trees grow faster than others: we built our seat around a small walnut tree, which is a slow-growing species, but even so we allowed an internal diameter of 24in (600mm) at the very top of the back support. Quite large tree specimens are available from good garden centers, so it could be worth planting a small "standard" tree (that is, one with a long trunk) just as the focal point around which to build this seat.

The basic construction consists of eight separate frames on which the seat and backrest slats are affixed. The frames are of a predetermined size, but the length of the slats is varied according to the internal diameter of the seat.

The seat is made in two sections, dry assembled to each other, so the two halves can be easily unscrewed to install around the tree.

SEAT FRAMES

Cut the components of the seat frames to length.

Bevel the front face of each back leg at an angle of $22\frac{1}{2}°$ from the center line of one of the 3in (75mm) faces (fig. 1). It is best to do this using a circular saw canted over at the correct angle – use a sliding bevel aligned on a protractor to set this. Finish off using a hand or power plane for a smooth finish.

1 Beveling the Back Leg
Draw a line down middle of front face of each back leg. Bevel legs at an angle of $22\frac{1}{2}°$ from this line.

2 Making the Spacing Template
Cut a spacing template from a scrap piece of board to the dimensions shown below. The template is used for accurate positioning of the front and back legs and the seat frame rails to make up the seat frames.

OCTAGONAL TREE SEAT ASSEMBLY

BACK SLAT

BACK LEG

SEAT SLAT

SEAT FRAME

APRON BOARD

SEAT FRAME RAIL

FRONT LEG

SEAT FRAME RAIL

OCTAGONAL TREE SEAT

Using a scrap of hardboard or plywood to the shape and dimensions shown (fig 2, page 280),make up a template for attaching the seat frame rails to the front and back legs to make up the seat frames.

Temporarily nail a batten to your workbench to give a flat surface to rest the feet of the legs against. Lay the front and back legs of one frame on the bench with two seat frame rails on top and the spacing template between them (fig. 1). The

back leg must be angled to align with the back of the template and the front leg should be exactly flush with the front edge of the template. The bottom of the legs should be resting against the batten nailed to the workbench.

The bottom seat frame rail is positioned so that it overlaps the front leg by ½in (12mm), while the top frame rail should be flush with the front and top of the front leg.

If a suitable flat workbench is not

DETAIL OF SEAT LEGS
Gravel-filled holes around the front and back legs of the seat frames make leveling easier and keep the legs off water-logged ground, reducing the risk of the wood rotting.

❶ Making Up the Seat Frames
Lay the front and back legs of one frame on a flat surface so they are flush with template. Top frame rail rests on template and is flush with the top and front of front rail; bottom frame rail overlaps front leg by ½in (12mm).

❷ Finished Construction of the Seat Frames
Above **Glue and screw seat frame rails to legs, then trim overlap at the back so it is parallel with slope of back leg and protrudes ½in (12mm).** ***Below*** **Finished frame shows frame rails screwed in position to front and back legs.**

available for this setting out, the pieces can be laid out on a flat floor, with the legs resting against an adjacent wall, so that the wall aligns the base of the legs.

Glue the top of the seat frame rail in place using a waterproof wood-working adhesive (ideally an epoxy resin), then drill pilot holes and screw it to the front and back legs using two screws at each end. Glue and screw the bottom seat frame rail to the legs in the same way.

Turn the frame over and position the other two seat frame rails in the same way, top and bottom. It is very important that these rails are exactly square to the ones on the other side so that the rails will be flush across the top where the seat slats will be fixed (fig. 2).

To complete the construction of the frames, the seat frame rails are trimmed off in line with the back leg, but leaving a $\frac{1}{2}$in (12mm) overlap (fig. 2). Strike a line at this position, and then trim off using a small crosscut saw or circular saw.

Repeat the construction for the remaining seven frames.

SEAT SLATS

The seat slats are cut from 1 × 3in (25 × 75mm) S4S (smooth 4 sides) softwood. The dimensions of the seat frames are predetermined, so that the number of slats required will not vary, no matter how large the finished seat. What you will have to calculate yourself, however, is the length of each slat. This will depend upon the internal diameter of the seat, itself dependent on size of the tree trunk around which you assemble the project.

To measure for the seat section, stand the eight frames around the tree roughly in position and spaced at the required distance from the tree, allowing for growth and depending on how large you want the diameter of the tree seat.

MAKING THE SEAT SLATS

When you are satisfied with the spacing of the seat frames, measure the distance between the centers of the back legs at seat height and calculate the average ("x" in fig. 3).

This will be the length of the inside edge of the innermost seat slats (ours are 15in [380mm] long).

Mark length "x" onto the back edge of a piece of the slat wood and draw $112\frac{1}{2}°$ angles off at either end using a sliding bevel. You can then use this slat to help draw up a full-size plan of a seat section (fig. 4) which will enable you to cut the remaining five seat slats to the correct length.

To make the full-size plan, mark off the back measurement using the innermost slat as a guide for the angles. Extend the angled lines outwards, using the sliding bevel to double check that the angle is $112\frac{1}{2}°$. Returning to the seat frame, mea-sure the distance from the center of the back leg to the front of the frame ("y" in fig. 3). On a full-size plan, mark the length "y" on the angled lines, and add $\frac{3}{4}$in (20mm) to allow for the approximate thickness of the apron board at the front of the seat. Join up the two marks "y plus $\frac{3}{4}$in (20mm)" at the front of the plan, parallel with the back line, to give the front edge of the seat.

You can now work out the necessary spacing for the slats. Place the innermost slat in position on the full-size plan and roughly cut five more slats, making sure that they are overlong. Bunch the slats together against the innermost slat, measure the remaining distance to the front line of the seat, and divide by five to give the amount of space to be left between each slat. If you want to increase the spacing, at this stage plane the edge of the inner-most slat to reduce its width.

Using one of the slats and a spacing batten or spacing blocks cut to the width of the calculated space, draw out all six slats in position on the full-size plan. You will then be able to measure off the plan for the exact lengths of all the slats in each section of the seat.

Cut out all the slats for one seat section, but cut about $\frac{1}{16}$in (2mm) inside each marked line in order to create a deliberate gap between the ends of the slats. You can use the slats cut for the first seat frame as templates for cutting the seat slats for the other sections.

3 **Measuring up for the Seat Slats**
Measure distance between centers of back legs at seat height ("x") to calculate length of innermost slat. Measure distance between center of back leg and front of frame ("y") to calculate spacing between slats.

4 **Drawing up Full-size Plan of Seat Section**
Mark length "x" and draw lines "y plus $\frac{3}{4}$in (20mm)" either end at $112\frac{1}{2}°$ angle. Bunch six slats on plan, measure remaining distance to front and divide by five to calculate spacing. Cut spacers to size, then mark slat positions.

OCTAGONAL TREE SEAT

AFFIXING THE SEAT SLATS

Affix the innermost slats first. Place the first slat across the back of two seat frames, spaced about $\frac{1}{16}$in (2mm) in from the center of the back legs, then glue and screw the slat to the top seat frame rails with one screw at each end (fig. 1).

Take another seat frame and innermost slat, and space in the same way. Glue and screw in place as before.

Continue in this way for two groups of three sections each. It is very important that you only dry assemble two sections opposite one another, as you will need to remove the slats on two opposite sides of the structure in order to install the seat frames around the tree.

To affix the subsequent slats, line up the next shortest slat with the innermost slat (fig. 2). With the spacing batten (or blocks) between the slats, align one end of the new slat with a batten held against one end of the previously affixed slat. Glue and screw into the top seat frame rail at each end.

Continue with this second size slat all the way around, remembering only to dry assemble where you did before. Continue in this fashion, one row at a time, assembling without glue those slats in the two sections that are dry assembled.

Before the frontmost slats are fitted, the apron boards must be assembled (fig. 3). Cut a piece of 1 × 3in (25 × 75mm) wood to the longest length of the frontmost slat and bevel back the edges at each end so they are in line with the angles of the seat slat. Cut a 1 × 1in (25 × 25mm) back-up batten about 6in (150mm) shorter than the apron board and glue and screw it centrally in place to join the apron board to the frontmost slat. The front edge of the slat must be flush with the front face of the apron board. Repeat the process to make the other apron boards.

Round off the front edges of the frontmost slats to give a smooth finish. Glue and screw into place at the front edges of the frames, remembering not to glue the dry assembled sections.

THE BACK SLATS

The back of each seat section is comprised of nine slats, cut from $\frac{5}{8}$ × 2in (16 × 50mm) S4S (smooth 4 sides) softwood. However, because the back legs of the frame are angled, the slats are not all the same length; instead, they get shorter as they reach the top.

Decide on the spacing of the back slats, and use scrap pieces of wood of the required thickness as spacing blocks. Lay the spacing blocks at seat level so that you start with a space, then lay the first slat, left overlong for the time being, in position. Mark off the ends in line with the centers of the back legs (fig. 4). Set a sliding bevel to this angle, and cut the back slat to the marked length. Use the sliding bevel to mark off the correct angle and cut the first slats for the remaining back sections to length. Glue and screw the first back slats in place to the front of the back legs of all the seat sections, but leave the slats dry assembled in the same sections as you did before on the seat slats.

Use the spacing blocks to position the next length of slat (fig. 4), mark off the ends as before, and cut to length. Repeat for the other seven slats in the row around the seat, and affix as before.

Continue in this way, row by row, until the seat back is completed (nine rows in our case). If the back legs protrude above the top slats they can be cut flush with the top of the slats for a neat appearance.

Dismantle the dry joints so that the seat is in two "halves" (actually, two three-eighths).

ASSEMBLY

Take the two "halves" of the seat to the tree and partially reassemble it without glue so you can mark on the ground where the legs are positioned. Dismantle the seat again.

At the leg positions, dig holes for each of the 16 legs, 6in (150mm) in diameter and 6in (150mm) deep, and fill them with gravel. The gravel provides good drainage, reducing the risk of the legs rotting, and allows you to level the seat easily.

1 Affixing the Innermost Seat Slats
Use plan as guide but cut slats about $\frac{1}{16}$in (2mm) short both ends. Space slat about $\frac{1}{16}$in (2mm) in from center of back legs; affix between two top frame rails. Work around frames, but *dry assemble* slats on two facing sections.

2 Affixing Subsequent Slats to the Frame
Align next shortest slat with innermost slat: put the spacers or spacing battens in position, align ends of slat with innermost slat, and affix to frame rails. Continue around frame, then repeat for next size slats.

FINISHING

Before painting, it is important to treat the seat with a good-quality wood preservative which can be painted over when dry – most clear sealers available fall into this category. We applied two coats, allowing each to dry thoroughly, and stood the legs in dishes of preservative for a couple of days.

Once the wood preservative is thoroughly dry (allow at least a week), the seat can be painted. We used a microporous paint which needs no primer (apart from preservative) and is intended for outdoor use. The seat can be treated with a water-repellent preservative stain if a natural finish is preferred.

After finishing with paint or wood stain, the seat can be finally assembled around the tree. Make sure the seat is well-bedded in the gravel and stands level on the ground. You can glue all joints at final assembly, or leave two sections of slats "dry" to allow easy removal of the seat should the need arise.

3 **Making the Apron Board**
Above Use batten to attach apron board to frontmost slat. *Below* Front edge rounded over.

4 **Spacing and Affixing the Back Slats**
Back slats are initially overlong. Use spacing batten or spacing blocks to position back slat, and mark off ends of slat to line up with centers of back legs. Cut slats to length, then reposition and glue and screw in place.

BARBECUE

Most barbecues, whether they are home-made or ready-made versions, have a number of design problems. One common fault is that they are generally too low to work at comfortably, which means the cook spends most of the time crouched awkwardly over the grill. The second problem is that grilling areas are often too small, providing food for only a limited number of people at a time.

This barbecue area corrects both of these typical defects, as well as providing a carefully considered series of spaces and surfaces for serving the food, storing fuel, and keeping pans and dishes.

The generous grill area can be temporarily reduced in size if you only want to cook a small amount of food by placing bricks in the middle and confining the space in that way. The grill supports consist of several strips of angle iron cemented into place and these hold the grill tray. The entire structure is built up against a brick wall. With time, the wall will blacken with smoke, but this is not an unattractive effect. If you do not have a similar site for the barbecue, you can build a small brick wall at the back instead or leave the barbecue free-standing.

One particular advantage of this construction is the spaces it provides at either end of the grill area as well as beneath. On top, two quite extensive surfaces can be used as a place for resting pans and dishes of food in preparation. Underneath, wood can be stored. If you use the barbecue often and for long enough, the whole structure will warm up and the timber will be "kiln-dried."

BARBECUE

Few pleasures are equal to that of sitting outside on a warm, summer's evening, eating food in the company of family and friends. If you build a barbecue, it will add a second focal point to your sitting-out area, but be careful to site it away from overhanging plants and any other vegetation that might catch fire while you are cooking.

The barbecue here is built from reclaimed bricks which match the wall against which it is built. Second-hand bricks are marginally larger than new bricks, but the dimensions here are calculated in courses rather than specific measurements, and you can use either sort of brick for building this project. The grill area is large enough to cook a substantial amount of food, but you could build the ends closer together if preferred.

The barbecue can be built against an existing wall or it can be free-standing. You can either build it on top of concrete pavers, or you can lay the pavers around the barbecue once it has been built. If you choose the latter option, you will

have to cut the pavers to fit, and you will also need to construct a foundation before laying the first course of bricks. The foundation will need to be at least 6in (150mm) deep and 8in (200mm) wide around the outline of the barbecue. Lay 4in (100mm) of gravel in the trench, ram it down, and then cover it with a 2in (50mm) layer of concrete. Check that the surface is level, and then leave the base to dry out and harden for a day or so.

As long as the pavers are level and are correctly laid on a firm base, however, it will be easier to build the barbecue on existing pavers. It is a good idea to protect the paving on which the barbecue is to be built with a sheet of thick, heavy-duty polyethylene. Simply lay the polyethylene sheet over the pavers, build up the barbecue on top of the polyethylene, and then cut away the protruding sheet afterwards. The polyethylene will protect the surface of the paving from staining with wet cement while you are building, and will keep the brickwork at the base clean and dry.

CONSTRUCTION

Lay the bricks following the course-by-course plans (figs. 1–3; *see also* **Techniques: Bricklaying, pages 404/5**). You will find it helpful to lay out this project to ensure that the side walls are built exactly at right angles to the rear wall. A builder's square is quite easy to make from three battens with lengths in the proportion of 3:4:5. These should be nailed together to form a right-angled triangle – a useful size of square to make is a triangle with a base measuring 18in (450mm), a height of 24in (600mm) and a hypotenuse of 30in (750mm). Leave all of the battens slightly overlong, then nail or screw them together to form *exactly* these dimensions. Saw off the surplus afterward.

Using a tight string line and the builder's square, make sure that the bricks in each course are straight and, using a carpenter's level, make sure that each course is vertical.

When the seventh course is reached, set angle irons across the

central section to support bricks forming the firebed. Do *not* lay these bricks for the time being.

Lay the eighth to eleventh courses, and on the eleventh course bed mild steel strips across the side walls to support the "table" tops.

Spread the mortar on the strips, then lay the twelfth course. Finally, lay bedding mortar on the angle irons in the central section and lay the firebed bricks edge on.

After the mortar has dried out, drill the bricks in the eleventh and twelfth courses to take steel supports (lag screws with the heads cut off are ideal) which will hold the food grill tray above the firebed. Measure the size of the central opening and get a local steel fabricator to make a grill tray by welding an outer frame of mild steel strips, braced with mild steel strips and fitted with mild steel rods welded at intervals about 1in (25mm) apart.

To protect the bricks of the firebed from excessive heat and to keep them clean, at the same time that the grill is made, a steel tray can be made up to cover the firebed.

TOOLS

BRICKLAYER'S TROWEL

POINTING TROWEL

BRICKLAYER'S HAMMER

BRICKLAYER'S CHISEL

SHOVEL

BUCKET

BUILDER'S SQUARE

CARPENTER'S LEVEL (long)

MATERIALS

BRICKS – 231 new or second-hand

MORTAR – from cement and builder's sand in the proportion 1:6

STEEL ANGLE IRONS – 4 pieces, 40in (1016mm) long

MILD STEEL STRIPS – 6 pieces, 4 × 12in (100 × 300mm)

MILD STEEL – for grill; measure finished barbecue for exact dimensions

1 *Above* **Plan View of 1st, 3rd, 5th and 7th Courses**
Lay bricks as shown; bed angle irons to support firebed on 7th course only.
Below **Plan view of 2nd, 4th and 6th Courses**
Cut three-quarter length bricks to enable courses to be staggered.

SEATING AND EATING
● **Barbecue**
288/289

BARBECUE ASSEMBLY

FOOD GRILL TRAY

$2\frac{1}{2}$ BRICKS

FIREBED

STEEL REINFORCEMENT STRIPS

ANGLE IRON

12 BRICKS

12 BRICKS ON EDGE

❷ *Above* **Plan View of 8th Course**
Two rows of 12 bricks are laid edge on above angle irons to form firebed
Below **Plan View of 9th and 11th Courses**
From 9th course, bricks only laid at ends; steel plates above 11th course.

❸ *Above* **Plan View of 10th Course**
Lay six bricks each end as shown.
Below **Plan View of 12th Course**
Ten bricks each end are laid above steel strips to form top.

Wall

Wall

Steel reinforcements

Wall

Wall

Steel reinforcements

AWNING

An awning over a patio or terrace area gives privacy and allows you to use the area in most weather. The awning here is an optional addition to a simple pergola attached to a house wall. It rests on the pergola and can be brought out in sunny or warm showery weather, yet is simple to remove when not required.

You can make the pergola more or less any size to suit your patio or paved area. The structure is made from planed stock; western red cedar is ideal, but ordinary preservative treated softwood coated with a water-repellent wood stain is a very serviceable alternative.

The supporting posts are made from 4 × 4in (100 × 100mm) lumber of sufficient length to give headroom of at least 7ft 6in (2.3m) under the pergola structure. The posts are positioned about 8ft (2.4m) apart and are linked to the house wall by 2 × 8in (50 × 200mm) roof joists. At the front, the posts are steadied and separated at the top by a fascia board measuring $1\frac{1}{2}$ × 4in (38 × 100mm) which runs the entire length of the pergola.

In the example shown, where there is a wall at the end of the terrace, there is no need to position a post and roof joist against the house wall. Instead, a length of 2 × 4in (50 × 100mm) lumber is bolted to the wall so that the top of this length of lumber is at the same level as the tops of the roof joists. Use expansion bolts to ensure a secure attachment.

On the main wall of the house, the roof joists can be supported in galvanized steel joist hangers, which are screwed and anchored to the house wall; the roof joists are then screwed into the joist hangers. An alternative method for supporting the roof joists is to rest them on a 2 × 4in (50 × 100mm) wooden beam (called a wall plate) which is fixed horizontally to the wall, using expansion bolts, so that it supports the roof joists at the correct height. In this case, the roof joists can be affixed to the wall plate by nailing at an angle through the sides of the roof joists and into the top of the wall plate (see **Techniques, Toe-nailing, page 399**).

An unusual but practical feature of this pergola is the covered roof section close to the wall of the house. This provides permanent shelter and shade at the back of the seating area, and also strengthens the pergola, prevents sideways movement in high winds, and keeps rain off the house window frames.

The removable awning is made from deck chair canvas and is intended to be fitted during the warmer months of the year. It is draped across the roof joists and is held in place by tapes that loop around the roof joists. The tapes are secured by Velcro fasteners. The awning is stiffened at each end by being folded over and tacked to a $\frac{3}{8}$ × $\frac{3}{4}$in (9.5 × 19mm) strip of hardwood such as yellow birch.

CONSTRUCTION

Start by cutting the support posts to length. You need to take into account that the roof joists are affixed at a slight downward slope, and that you might not have a great deal of flexibility over the height at which you can affix the joist hangers or wall plate to the wall of your house. You also need to decide how the posts will be secured at the bottom. The easiest method is to slot them into socket-type supports which can be screwed to the surface of the patio (fig. 2). Alternatively, each post can be fitted over a protruding bolt or bracket cemented into the surface of the paving. Yet another option is to chip a hole through the surface of the patio using a hammer and cold chisel so that the bottom of the post can be concreted in place.

Once the length of post has been decided, the top can be angled and the joint cut to accommodate the roof joist. Saw down to form a slot to suit the width of the roof joist – its actual width will be less than 2in (50mm). Most of the waste can be removed by sawing, and the joint (a form of mortise and tenon joint) can be cleaned up using a chisel.

If the roof joists will be affixed to the house wall using joist hangers, these are installed next. Make sure that they are level by lining them up with a line drawn along the wall.

 Detail of Top Section
The roof joists are supported by 4 × 4in (100 × 100mm) posts at the front and by the main wall of the house at the back. Shade is provided by the permanent covered section and the removable canvas awning.

2 **Socket-type Post Supports**
Metal support is screwed or bolted to ground. Post slots in support and is secured by tightening screws.

Canvas awning

Fascia board

Bolt

Velcro fastener

Post

Roof joist

Permanent covered section

Check that the line is horizontal using a carpenter's level and affix the joist hangers using galvanized screws into anchors. Alternatively, affix the wall plate in place using expansion bolts. Slot the roof joists in place between the post and joist hanger or wall plate, and secure with a bolt through the post, and by screwing through the joist hanger. Toe nail the joists if they are resting on a wall plate (fig. 3). Nail the fascia board to the top of the support posts.

All that remains is to install the permanent covered section (fig. 4). Nail $\frac{1}{2} \times 1\frac{1}{2}$in (12 × 38mm) cedar or stained softwood slats across the joists finishing with a 1 × 1$\frac{1}{2}$in (25 × 38mm) batten which is notched at intervals to accept the roof joists and is fitted vertically against the lowest slat. The top is covered with a 36in- (915mm-) deep sheet of $\frac{3}{4}$in exterior grade plywood which is then covered with roofing felt or shingles. The roof-to-wall joint is sealed by pressing a strip of self-adhesive flashing across the entire length of the joint.

3 **Affixing the Joists to the Wall**
Left Joist hangers are aligned at correct height and screwed to wall; joists sit in hangers and are screwed in place. *Right* 2 × 4in (50 × 100mm) wall plate secured horizontally to wall; joists toe nailed in place.

4 **Permanent Covered Section**
Softwood slats are nailed to roof joists. Batten at front of slats is notched at intervals to accept joists. Section is then covered in exterior-grade plywood and building paper and shingles. Seal roof-to-wall joint with flashing strip.

Joist hanger

Roof joist

Roof joist

Wall plate

Flashing strip

Building paper and shingles

Plywood

Slats

Notched batten

Roof joist

WOODEN TABLE

This sturdy garden table makes an attractive feature in any outdoor setting. The table shown is only 15in (375mm) high, but by increasing the height of the base on which it is built you can make it to any height required. If you make it about 30in (750mm) high, for example, you will be able to sit around it on garden chairs and use it as an outdoor dining table.

Apart from the brick base, the table is made entirely from solid wood. Preservative-treated quality softwood is ideal; hardwood could be used, but because of the large quantity of lumber required, its cost would be prohibitively high.

The table top is made from 2 × 3in (50 × 75mm) lumber, in the form of 12 square frames which become progressively larger from a central block. There is a gap of about $\frac{1}{2}$in (12mm) between each square, which is created by using 2in (50mm) wide S4S (smooth 4 sides) lumber for the table top. S4S lumber is sawn to its nominal width – in this case 2in (50mm) – and then each face is planed about $\frac{1}{2}$in (12mm) so that the actual width is about 1$\frac{1}{2}$in (38mm).

CONSTRUCTION

Start by building a base from brick, stone or reconstituted stone-and-concrete blocks (see **Techniques, page 404/5**); the base should measure 22 × 22in (560 × 560mm) and it should be about 9in (225mm) high if you want to make the table as shown in the photograph. The height could be increased to as much as 24in (600mm) if an outdoor dining table is required.

The table top is fixed on two diagonal supports which are fitted to the base plinth to form an "X." Cut cross lap joints (see **Techniques, page 400**) at the point where the supports intersect (fig. 2). For neatness, the ends of the supports are sloped as shown in the side view

(fig. 2). The last 12in (300mm) is sloped from the nominal depth of 3in (75mm) to 1in (25mm) at the end. Assemble the supports by gluing the cross lap joint with waterproof woodworking adhesive and then clamp the supports until the glue sets, checking first that the supports are exactly at right angles.

If you are unable to buy preservative pressure-treated lumber, then at this stage it is wise to treat the supports with a good quality water-repellent preservative; apply a second coat of preservative 24 hours later.

The supports are fixed down to the base plinth using expansion bolts into holes drilled in the base plinth and recessed into the supports. Before tightening these bolts, check that the supports are absolutely level using a carpenter's level and put shim pieces underneath them to adjust as necessary.

FORMING THE TABLE TOP

The table top consists of concentric "frames" which fit one inside the other down to the solid block

MATERIALS

Part	Quantity	Material	Length
PLINTH	As required	Bricks or concrete blocks	As required
TABLE-TOP SUPPORTS	2	2 × 3in (50 × 75mm) S4S softwood	67in (1700mm)
TABLE-TOP FRAMES	4	2 × 3in (50 × 75mm) S4S softwood	48in (1200mm)
	4	As above	44in (1100mm)
	4	As above	40in (1000mm)
	4	As above	36in (900mm)
	4	As above	32in (800mm)
	4	As above	28in (700mm)
	4	As above	24in (600mm)
	4	As above	20in (500mm)
	4	As above	16in (400mm)
	4	As above	12in (300mm)
	4	As above	8in (200mm)
	4	As above	4in (100mm)

ALSO: about 48ft (15m) of $\frac{3}{8}$in (9.5mm) diameter hardwood dowel to be cut into 4in (100mm) lengths for joining corners; 4 expansion bolts for securing table-top supports; waterproof woodworking adhesive.

① Brick Plinth Base
Table rests on brick or stone plinth built to required height. Fill middle with rubble topped with concrete.

② Making the Table-top Supports
Cut cross lap joints in the supports so that they meet to form an "X," with the supports exactly at right angles. The ends of the supports are sloped on the underside through the last 12in (300mm).

formed of four pieces in the center. Although the stock is 2 × 3in (50 × 75mm), the "frames" are formed just like giant picture frames, with the corners mitered at 45°. The easiest way to cut these miters is to use a power saw with the blade tilted to a 45° angle. You can use an ordinary portable circular power saw with the lumber held securely in a vise, but it will be even easier to make the cuts if you hire or buy a miter saw, a radial arm saw, or a circular saw table for the purpose.

Cut the largest frame so that it gives external dimensions of 48 × 48in (1200 × 1200mm). Apply waterproof woodworking adhesive to the mating parts of each joint, then draw them together with frame clamps before drilling into the joint with a ⅜in (9.5mm) drill bit, keeping the bit at a 90° angle to the joint. Drill two holes in each joint and then drive ⅜in (9.5mm) long wooden dowels into the holes, after coating the dowels with waterproof woodworking adhesive. Before applying the adhesive, make a shallow saw cut along the length of each dowel, which will help to ensure that not all of the glue will be driven out when the dowel is inserted. At this stage, make sure that the dowel is long enough to protrude from the hole at each end; when the adhesive has set, the ends of the dowels can be sawn off close to the sides of the frame and the surface then neatly planed smooth to give an unobtrusive fixture. Make up the remaining frames in the same way to the dimensions specified in the Materials chart (opposite).

The central block is formed by cutting four pieces of 2 × 3in (50 × 75mm) lumber sections which are joined by dowels to form a square block. The frames are treated with two coats of water-repellent wood preservative before being assembled on to the wooden supports.

The table-top frames are attached to the table-top supports using waterproof woodworking adhesive and dowels inserted into holes drilled vertically down into the supports and vertically up into the undersides of the table-top frames.

③ Affixing Table-top Supports to Plinth
Use expansion bolts to affix the supports at each corner of the plinth. Drill the plinth to accept the bolts and drill 2in (50mm) deep holes to recess the bolts in the supports. Check supports are level before final attachment.

④ Forming Table-top Frames
Cut 45° miters at corners and affix using waterproof adhesive and dowels through the sides.

⑤ Affixing Frames to Supports
Drill corresponding holes down into supports and up into corners of frames. Join using dowel joints.

PART 6

GARDEN HOUSES

The garden house is a subject in itself. At one extreme, garden houses can be supremely romantic, providing a true retreat from the world; at the other, they can be as mundane as a shed. In between come summer garden houses, gazebos, pavilions, follies, greenhouses, workshops, playhouses, studios, offices, and garden rooms. One could even include dovecotes, pigeon lofts, rabbit hutches, dog kennels, and chicken coops, since animal houses so often accompany human ones. But whatever their ultimate function, there is something uniquely appealing about buildings on such a small scale. For the garden designer, they are places where wit and imagination, as much as practicality, can come into play.

Children have inspired some of the most charming versions of the garden house, while animal houses, when they are decorated rather than strictly functional, also tend to be designed to amuse and appeal to children. More than any other type of garden structure, the many varieties of garden house offer the opportunity to use bright paints, providing a much-needed splash of year-round color to the garden.

GARDEN HOUSES

The summer house or garden retreat has a long tradition in Europe and an even longer tradition in the Far East. As a pavilion or gazebo it was essentially built to provide a platform from which to view a garden or, in Eastern terms, to contemplate nature. However, from the eighteenth century onward, the nature of the garden house evolved from being a viewing place to a kind of architectural attraction in the garden. Chinese pavilions, Japanese tea houses, miniature thatched cottages, classical temples, and Gothic grottoes were some of the styles that were enthusiastically embraced.

As a rule, follies of this kind really need acres of parkland to act as a foil for their charms; today, however, garden houses are usually simpler in design, reflecting their essentially practical nature. Nevertheless there are many attractive "ordinary" buildings to act as inspiration, including bathing huts, lodges, and gypsy caravans. Painted wood, clapboarding, shingle, and exterior-grade plywood are all good basic construction materials. Roofs can be tiled, shingled, or made of corrugated metal; for a truly rustic look, you could seek out a thatcher, or have the roof covered in turf. Building a garden house can be an exercise in creative salvage and recycling for those with that kind of imagination and skill.

The degree of finish depends on the ultimate use of the house: a building which must function as an annex for overnight guests obviously needs to be completed to a higher standard of comfort than one which merely serves as a place to read a book or escape from the rain. If you are going to use the house as a studio or office, for example, you will need to put in electricity; in other cases, having a supply of water might be a distinct advantage. Similarly, building permission may have to be sought from your local government department, depending on the intended size, function, and location of your structure.

Site is an important issue. A summer garden house or pavilion plays an obvious role in the layout of the entire garden. If you are going to sit there and admire nature, the view must be worthwhile.

HOME AWAY FROM HOME
The garden house – shed, pavilion, workshop, or summer garden house – is innately appealing (left and far left). Part of the charm of these small-scale buildings is their forthright style and use of simple materials.

Ample garden storage is an invaluable asset (above). Wall-mounted racks are generally a good idea; hanging tools saves floor space and prevents tines and blades becoming damaged. Ceiling hooks can be used to suspend baskets.

GARDEN HOUSES

Paving and planting should be planned taking into account the site of the building as far as possible. You could arrange for a pavilion to be set at the end of a walkway to give impact to a formal design, placed on a higher level to offer a view, or secreted in a sheltered corner to add a sense of mystery and surprise.

Although there is nothing mysterious or romantic about a garden shed, with a little thought it need not be the unlovely and somewhat blatant feature common to so many gardens. A garden shed which functions as a true garden room for maintenance of tools, potting, and storing seeds and bulbs is an invaluable resource in any household.

Storage is one of the main requirements. You will fill a shed very quickly with outdoor and garden equipment, so it is important to build or buy one which is big enough for your needs. The first consideration is likely to be providing an efficient system for storing garden tools, seeds, bulbs, fertilizer, and so on.

In addition to tool storage, you will need floor space for big items, which may include a lawnmower, bicycles, garden furniture, awnings and umbrellas packed away during the winter, portable barbecues, and large toys. You will also need somewhere to put bags of compost and charcoal, as well as a dry, high shelf for storing fertilizers and pesticides out of the reach of children and animals. Ceiling hooks can be used to accommodate baskets and buckets; shelves will take pots and seed trays. It is also useful to have somewhere cool and dark for storing bulbs or root vegetables during the summer or after the harvest.

One advantage of a well-planned storage system is that you can see at a glance if anything has not been put back. But the benefits are not merely practical. As well as providing an efficient area to work, a carefully organized garden room or shed, with its array of traditional garden tools and equipment, can be as pleasant a place in which to spend time as a kitchen.

As far as site is concerned, there is no reason why a shed needs to be in full view. You may not have all that much choice when it comes to position, but it is a good idea to place the shed out of the way, near a compost heap or bonfire site. Alternatively, you can create a utility area by positioning the shed near an existing garage or greenhouse and screen the view by adding trellis panels or fencing and climbing plants.

Off-the-shelf sheds, which come in ready-to-assemble packs, are rarely as attractive as those you design and build yourself. But there are ways of improving the appearance of the standard shed which are especially useful if you have little choice about where the shed is positioned. Many examples look better if they are simply painted. Good quality brick pavers laid around the base, plant tubs filled with flowers, and trellis with plants trained over will all help to connect the shed to its surroundings, making it look less brash and out of place.

GARDEN RETREATS

A garden house can provide a secluded spot for sitting and watching the world go by (far left, center and far right). If you want to disguise a structure or hide an ugly shed from view, fast-growing climbers are the answer.

ANIMAL HOUSES

Coops, dovecotes, birdhouses, and the like can be the excuse for wit and decorative flair to come into play. These structures provide a good opportunity to practice remodeling skills.

SUMMER GARDEN HOUSE

Most people could use the extra space that a summer garden house provides. And although this is the perfect place for storing tools, bulbs and seeds, or for potting plants or a variety of other garden chores, you need not necessarily put it to horticultural use. A workshop, an artist's studio, a guest annex, the ultimate play-house – it is easy to think of a host of functions for this kind of structure to fulfil. It could prove invaluable as a home office or study, and it is substantial enough to serve as a pavilion on a village green. However, the use it is put to can mean that you will have to seek approvals and permits from local authorities. It is best to check during the planning stages, well before you start building.

The house may appear a daunting prospect for all but the most ardent enthusiast; but the skills you require are well within the average range of ability and there is no need for the kind of refinement demanded by furniture-making. There is no sophisticated joinery and there are few techniques which should not already be familiar. The cost of materials, all readily available, is roughly the same as a family vacation, which makes it fairly reasonable, unless you put a high price on your own time and labor. The major commitment is time. Working alone during the evenings and weekends, it should take about three months. Full-time, with a few willing assistants, it might take only a couple of weeks.

As far as the design is concerned, there were a number of influences. The idea to use corrugated metal for the roof came from the houses of the Australian out-back. The shape of the roof was suggested by the roofline of the traditional English cricket pavilion. In different color combinations, the house acquires quite different aspects: green and white for a cricket pavilion; pale pastels for a seaside look; bright blues and pinks for the Caribbean.

The project is a major undertaking. We would recommend that you attempt most of the other projects in the book before tackling this one. But if the demands are high, so are the rewards. What could be more satisfying – or useful – than building your own garden house?

SUMMER GARDEN HOUSE

A summer garden house, somewhere in a secluded part of the yard, is a delightful retreat to be savored when you want to relax away from the bustle of the house. This design captures all the magic, charm and intrigue required from a garden hideaway and just invites you to explore inside. The size of the room is about 8 × 12ft (2.4 × 3.6m) which is a comfortable size to furnish with wicker chairs yet remains cozy and intimate. The extended roof covering over the veranda gives the impression of greater size while providing a 39in (1000mm) deep protected area on showery days when you want to sit outside. The size of the base is critical in determining whether you need building permission; location within your yard and the use for which the building is intended are also important. Check codes with your local authority during the planning stage.

The red-and-blue color scheme chosen here not only accentuates the design and materials but is fun, too. By changing the color combinations you can substantially alter the finished look of the building; a few suggestions for alternative colors are illustrated on page 67.

The basic structure rests on a level base of concrete pavers which in turn supports the joists. The veranda is pressure treated wooden boards, while the interior floor is exterior-grade plywood finished, in this case, with floor paint, although you could equally well use carpets, tiles, or boards. It is possible to extend the walls to include the veranda area if you require more indoor floor space. The interior walls are also clad with plywood to give the structure rigidity – between this and the exterior boarding is a layer of insulation. The level ceiling is covered in tongue-and-groove

boards and is also insulated. You could leave the roof structure exposed if you wanted, although you would lose a lot of heat in cold weather as a result. If you require heating, a paraffin heater or a fan heater are the best options.

The chains leading down from the gutter at the four corners of the building act in the same way as the drainpipes, conducting water down to the ground, where four drywells are dug: a feature of traditional Japanese houses.

The illustrations below and opposite give an overall impression of the construction of the front, back, and side walls and of the roof. However, in addition to the project text and illustrations, you may also need to refer to the sections on Materials and Techniques (pages 394–5 and 396–405) when further guidance is needed on individual stages of the construction.

(pages 394–5 and 396–405)

TOOLS

PORTABLE WORKBENCH
STEEL MEASURING TAPE
STEEL BENCH RULE
TRY SQUARE or COMBINATION SQUARE
ADJUSTABLE T-BEVEL
SMALL CROSSCUT SAW (or circular saw)
POWER DRILL
DRILL BIT – $\frac{1}{2}$in (12mm) and $\frac{1}{8}$in (3.2mm)
WRENCH
HAMMER
NAILSET
PLIERS
CHISEL
MALLET
TIN SNIPS

CAPPING PIECE

CORRUGATED SHEET

FLASHING

GUTTER

FASCIA BOARD

POST

EXTERIOR CLADDING

TONGUED-AND-GROOVED BOARDS

JOIST

EXTERIOR CLADDING

ROOF CAPPING

FLASHING

EXTERIOR CLADDING

POST

PAVERS

CEILING JOIST

RIDGE PURLIN

MAIN ROOF TRUSS

RAISED ROOF PURLIN

INTERMEDIATE PURLIN

JACK RAFTER HEAD PLATE

END JACK RAFTER

GUTTER

SHORT CEILING RAFTER

BLOCKING

INSULATION

POST

PLYWOOD FLOOR

JOIST

SUMMER GARDEN HOUSE: BASE ASSEMBLY

FACING BOARD

POST

PLYWOOD FLOOR

TRIMMER

JOIST

PAVER (24 × 24 × 1½in)

HALF PAVER (24 × 12 × 1½in)

BASE ASSEMBLY

① Setting Out Position of Base
Use pegs and stringline to set out base outline. Two sizes of paver are used
– 24 × 24in (600 × 600mm) and 24 × 12in (600 × 300mm) – to support joists
centrally while leaving a narrow border around house perimeter.

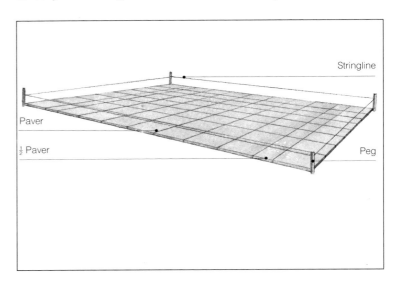

FOUNDATION AND BASE

Lay out the site to be covered by the complete base using four corner pegs and a string line (fig. 1). Choose a sheltered part of the garden: this will minimize the risk of structural damage in storms and high winds.

Make sure you choose a flat site – sloping terrain would need a great deal of excavation work to enable a level base to be laid.

The base can be laid using either concrete pavers or poured concrete. If you choose pavers, then you will need 72 pavers measuring $24 \times 24 \times 1\frac{1}{2}$in ($600 \times 600 \times 38$mm). You will also need 16 half-size pavers (24×12in [600×300mm]). These are required to ensure that only a narrow border remains around the walls of the house while the joists rest centrally on the pavers (Base and Floor Assembly).

The pavers should be laid on a 1:5 mix of cement to sand. You need to build in a slope of $\frac{1}{4}$in per foot from front to back to ensure that rainwater drains away and does not lie alongside the joists and cause them to rot away.

Alternatively, if you use concrete you will have to dig out about 5in (125mm) of soil and lay a foundation of well-compacted gravel covered with a 2in (50mm) layer of concrete mixed from one part cement to five parts ballast.

You will have to set up a form (wooden frame) of lumber to retain the concrete, again having first staked out the site. The forms should be held in place using stakes driven into the ground. Old floorboards, or similar, are ideal for forms. Do not forget to build in a slight slope in the formwork from front to back.

When the base is completed you can lay out the joists. Use 2×4in (50×100mm) members for the floor joists, making sure that they have been thoroughly treated with preservative. Ideally, pressure-treated stock should be used. There are 13 joists in all, with a double row being support the end walls. The outer joists support the veranda floor at each end.

Each joist should be laid on a strip of bituminous felt to serve as a vapor barrier and to prevent moisture seeping up through the base. Since the base has a slight slope built into it from front to back, you will need to lay small shim pieces about every 24in (600mm) under each joist to bring it level. This is important since you want to have a level floor.

Next lay the summer garden house floor (fig. 3). This is $\frac{3}{4}$in (19mm) exterior-grade plywood and the area is nominally 12×8ft (3.6×2.4m). The sheets should be affixed to the joists using $1\frac{1}{2}$in (38mm) No. 8 screws at 16in (400mm) centers around the edge. Affix the middle sheet first and then a sheet either side, cut to fit as needed. Next lay $\frac{3}{4} \times 2$in (19×50mm) strips of plywood on which the front and back walls will sit.

The end joists, which support the veranda floor, can be removed temporarily since they will be a hazard while the summer garden house frame and roof are constructed.

2 **Setting Out and Leveling Floor Joists**
Wood joists are laid down at 24in (600mm) centers. A double row is needed to support the end walls. Since the pavers are laid to a slight fall, shims are needed below the joists to level them.

3 **Laying the Plywood Floor**
The floor is formed from $\frac{3}{4}$in (19mm) thick exterior-grade plywood screwed to the floor joists using $1\frac{1}{2}$in No. 8 screws. Lay the middle panel first and then one other panel on each side.

Indicates fall required in slabs

Joist

Concrete paver

Shim

SUMMER GARDEN HOUSE: WALL ASSEMBLY

WALLS

The inner faces of the walls are made from ½in (12mm) exterior-grade plywood. Cut out the pieces needed for each of the four walls. The window openings, front and back, are about 27½ × 23½in (700 × 600mm) and the doorway is about 78 × 32in (2000 × 810mm). If you buy the door ready-made, then tailor the door opening to size – remember to allow for the dimensions of the door frame.

Taking each wall by turn, lay out the 2 × 2in (50 × 50mm) studding at the centers shown (fig. 1). Note also that the short horizontal blocking is intentionally slightly misaligned in order to stagger the screws in the wall panels.

Lay the plywood panels on the studding with the inside surface uppermost – these will form the internal walls of the house (fig. 2). Use 1½in (38mm) No. 8 screws to secure the panels to the studs at 16in (400mm) intervals. Countersink and fill all of the screw heads.

The door and window openings are all framed with 1 × 2in (25 × 50mm) trimmers toe-nailed to the studs using 2in (50mm) nails.

The walls are joined together using 5in (125mm) long ½in (12mm) diameter bolts. If you position all four walls (fig. 3) using a helper and temporary supporting struts, you can drill bolt holes at the corners through adjoining vertical studs. Clamp each corner before drilling the holes and securing the bolts, leaving a little "play" at this stage for final adjustment of the four walls. Four bolts are needed at each corner at the approximate positions indicated (fig. 1, back wall). The order of assembly is to form one corner with the front wall to one end wall and bolt together; then bolt the back wall to the other end wall; finally, bolt the two remaining corners together.

When all the walls have been joined and are square, the sole plates of each wall (fig. 2, front wall) can be nailed through to the joists using 4in (100mm) nails at about 16in (400mm) centers.

1 **Assembling Framework for each Wall**
The illustrations show the arrangement of the 2 × 2in (50 × 50mm) studding for each of the four walls. *Top* Front frame with allowance for the door and windows. *Middle* Rear frame with a window opening. *Below* Solid end walls.

Sole plate

WALL FRAME ASSEMBLY

2 Adding Inner Walls to Frames
The inner walls are formed from ½in (12mm) thick plywood. The front wall is made from five pieces with cut-outs for the windows in the side sections. The sheets are affixed to the frame using 1½in No. 8 screws.

3 Joining the Four Frames Together
Each studding framework is joined together using 5in (125mm) long bolts. Using a helper, supporting struts and clamps, keep the frames aligned at the corners. Drill holes for four bolts at each corner and bolt together.

Summer Garden House: Roof Assembly

LAYOUT OF ROOF

WALL PLATE PURLIN

MAIN ROOF TRUSS

INTERMEDIATE PURLIN

SHORT CEILING JOIST

RIDGE PURLIN

PURLIN

RAISED ROOF PURLIN

END JACK RAFTER

CEILING JOIST

HIP RAFTER

EAVE PURLIN

40in   48in   48in   48in   40in

18ft 8in

SECTION ACROSS LENGTH OF ROOF

MAIN ROOF TRUSS

JACK RAFTER HEAD PLATE

SHORT CEILING RAFTER

POST

ROOF

The striking, veranda-covering roof of this summer garden house is a fundamental part of its design. It consists of a pitched roof clad with sheets of corrugated metal and with a "hip" at either end projecting out to cover the sides of the veranda. It is quite complicated, so it is strongly recommended that you spend a little while studying the plans, and then tackle the construction one step at a time as described here. The positions of the rafters and purlins will become much clearer as you start to put the pieces together.

MAIN TRUSSES

Start by making the four main roof trusses. Each truss, a triangular-shaped frame mitered at the top, is made from two 2 × 3in (50 × 75mm) angled rafters each about 8ft 8in (2.6m) long (allowing for them being overlong), reinforced with a triangular plywood gusset at the top, and braced with a ceiling joist at the appropriate level.

The rafters are cut at an angle at the top, butted together and held at the correct angle by being nailed to a $\frac{1}{2}$in (12mm) thick triangular plywood gusset. Each triangular plywood gusset is pitched at 26°, and this controls the angle of all the rafters. The rafters are prevented from spreading by the ceiling joists, which are bolted to them toward the bases of the rafters.

All the main trusses are the same, except that the two end trusses have double rafters, formed by bolting pairs of rafters together using $\frac{1}{2}$in (12mm) lag bolts with steel connectors on the bolts sandwiched between the two members. Similar bolts and connectors are used to bolt the ceiling joists to the rafters.

Ensure that the four main trusses are cut and nailed at the same angle: nail the first truss on a flat surface, and use this truss as a template for nailing subsequent trusses.

Make all the rafters about 8in (200mm) overlong; they can then be cut to the correct length after they have been installed. Nail the top furring in place.

AFFIXING MAIN TRUSSES

Lift the main trusses onto the walls, spacing them approximately 48in (1200mm) apart. Do not forget to position the double rafter trusses at each end. Make sure that all the trusses are square and vertical, and then nail them down to the top plates of the front and back walls, using 6in (150mm) round head nails which should be toe-nailed into the top plates (*see* **Techniques, page 399**).

Temporarily hold the trusses in place so that they are vertical: nail long boards diagonally across the rafters to act as bracing (fig. 1, below). Position the boards carefully so that there is enough room to affix the purlins at the ridge, wall plate, and eave levels.

AFFIXING PURLINS

Cut and affix the ridge purlins (horizontal members) in place. These are the same overall length as the front and back wall structure and are secured to the furring on either side of the apex of the main trusses.

Cut the eave purlins (positioned at the front and back to support the outermost edges of the pitched roof covering) 8ft 2in (2.5m) overlong to give an overhang of 49in (1250mm) at each end (fig. 2). Affix in place by nailing into rafters.

Next cut the front and back wall plate purlins (the ones above the eave purlins), approximately 25$\frac{1}{2}$in (650mm) overlong at each end to allow for trimming later. Nail in place on the rafters (fig. 2). Remove the diagonal bracing and cut and secure the two intermediate purlins (one each side) midway between the ridge and wall plate purlins. These butt up against the ends of the furring pieces, which should now be cut to length. The intermediate purlins are about 12in (300mm) overlong each end for cutting back at an angle later.

MAKING THE RAISED ROOF SECTION

The furring acts as a shim over the rafters. Fit a second purlin close to the lower end of the furring pieces to form the raised roof section.

① **Construction of Main Roof Trusses**
Each truss is formed by nailing it to a pre-cut $\frac{1}{2}$in (12mm) thick plywood gusset pitched at 26°, and then braced by a ceiling joist for stability. End trusses have double raters. After positioning, rafters are braced by purlins.

② **Affixing the Purlins to the Roof Trusses**
With trusses spaced along the top plates on the walls, and held upright by temporary diagonal braces, cut and nail the ridge purlins in place. Note that eave, wall plate and intermediate purlins are left temporarily overlength.

Plywood gusset

Furring piece

Diagonal brace

Ceiling joist

Ridge purlin

Raised roof purlin

Intermediate purlin

Wall plate purlin

Eave purlin

SUMMER GARDEN HOUSE: ROOF ASSEMBLY

SETTING OUT HIP ROOF AT EACH END

Measure 39in (1000mm) along the top outer edge of the eave purlin, measuring from the outer face of the outside truss. Tack a line from this point (string will do) to where the end lean-to roof meets the end truss. This should form a roof pitch at the ends of about 36° (8½-in-12). Make up a triangle of plywood or scrap wood to this angle and use it to check the roof pitch during all stages of construction (fig. 2).

Tie another string line from the top of the first eave purlin (39in [1000mm] from the face of the end truss) to the top of the corresponding eave purlin on the opposite side (39in [1000mm] out from the end truss). From this point, take another string line up to where the end lean-to roof meets the end truss. With these string lines in place, 39in (1000mm) out from the end truss, the general arrangement of the roof hips and pitch down to eave level on the lean-to roofs at each end of the building will become apparent.

Cut the end jack rafters (four at each end) overlong, and also the short ceiling joists for the ends (again, four at each corner). Both are cut from 2 × 3in (50 × 75mm) stock (fig. 6).

Cut the jack rafter top plates (which support the jack rafters against the end trusses). Nail or bolt these to the end trusses as shown (fig. 3), and after affixing trim the ends of the top plates to the slope of the main roof rafters.

Use an adjustable T-bevel set to the angle required for the ends of the jack rafters where they butt against the end trusses, and trim the ends of the jack rafters to this angle. On the underside of each rafter cut a birdsmouth (notch) so that the rafter will sit neatly on the top plate. The eave ends are left overlong for the time being.

Nail the four jack rafters and the four short ceiling joists in place at each end. Check that the top of the rafters are aligned and slope in line with the previously set string guidelines. Make sure that the undersides of the short ceiling joists

are horizontal and are in line with the undersides of the ceiling joists at the front and back of the building.

Note that in the center of the ends there are two rafters set 3in (75mm) apart (fig. 4). Later these will be bolted to the central veranda support post.

Cut the 1 × 6in (25 × 125mm) hip rafters (boards) overlong and hold them as close to their final position as possible so that the correct angles can be marked on the ends of the front and rear purlins which rest against the hip boards and which are now cut to length. Again, an adjustable T-bevel is used to mark these angled cuts, which are angled in two directions to ensure that the ends of the purlins fit tightly against the hip rafters when these are affixed in place.

At the top, the hip rafter is notched to fit over the jack rafter top plate (fig. 3), and the end of the hip rafter is angled so that the hip rafter fits tightly against the main end truss. This angle needs careful marking with an adjustable T-bevel to ensure an accurate fit, particularly

of the support notch at the top end. The top surface of each hip rafter should be carefully lined up with the top of the purlins.

The hip rafters can now be fitted and held in place by nailing to the ends of the front and rear purlins.

Next, cut and fasten by nailing the three 2 × 3in (50 × 75mm) purlins on the lean-to roofs at the ends of the building. They must be cut to length and angled so that they butt tightly against the hip rafters at the ends, and align at the corner hips with the front and back purlins.

Cut and fit the 3 × 3in (75 × 75mm) veranda support posts in the middle of the end sections to fit between the concrete base and the twin central jack rafters. The base of each post should rest on a small piece of lead, which seals the end grain very effectively. Using connector plates and ½in (12mm) diameter lag bolts, drill and bolt to the floor joists at the base and between the twin jack rafters at the top. Leave overlong for the time being, and later trim flush, angled with the tops of the purlins.

---

1 **Cross-section of the Width Showing the Raised Roof Section**
Note how the furring pieces lift the ridge and raised roof purlins to create the raised roof section. Also look at the eave area and note how the truss ends are trimmed vertically, level with the front top edge of the eave purlin, to give a plumb fastening for the fascia board to which the gutters are affixed.

2 **Trimming the Rafter Ends**
Adjustable bevel marks rafter ends (shown without eave purlin). Use a template to check roof pitch.

Ridge purlin
Plywood gusset
Intermediate purlin
Wall plate purlin
Post
26°
Furring
Raised roof purlin
Eave purlin
Roof pitch template
36°

HIP ROOF ASSEMBLY

Detail 3
Detail 6
Detail 4
Detail 5

The 3 × 3in (75 × 75mm) corner veranda support posts fit between the concrete base and the top sides of the hip boards. Allow 1–1¼in (25–30mm) clearance from the eave purlins. The undersides of the hip rafters are notched to take posts, and the top ends of the posts are cut out with matching notches which allow them to be bolted to the hip rafters (fig. 5). Cut the post tops to the same angles as the roof pitches and to the level of the purlins.

FITTING FASCIA BOARDS

Use an adjustable T-bevel to mark the rafter ends with a vertical line where they will be trimmed. When the fascia boards are affixed onto the rafter ends they will be upright, allowing gutters to be fitted. Trim the rafters in line with the top of the eave purlin. The bottoms of the rafter ends are trimmed level with the bottom of the fascia boards, either before or after the fascias are secured. Also trim the ends of the hip rafters to take the fascia boards.

Cut the fascia boards from 1 × 6in (25 × 150mm) stock.

❸ **Hip Board/Head Plate Join**
Notch hip board to fit over jack rafter top plate. Angle board end to fit against truss. Purlins fit against hip.

❹ **Intermediate Veranda Support Post**
Posts bolt between central jack rafters. Saw tops level with purlins.

❺ **Corner Post/Hip Board Join**
Notch hip boards for corner posts, which are slotted to fit over hips. Bolt and trim tops to roof slope.

❻ **Jack Rafters/Ceiling Joists**
Underside view of the jack rafters nailed to short ceiling joists. Tops of rafters must align.

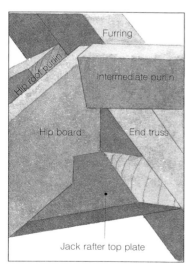

Furring
Hip roof purlin
Intermediate purlin
Hip board
End truss
Jack rafter top plate

Eave purlin
Jack rafter
Twin jack rafters
Intermediate post

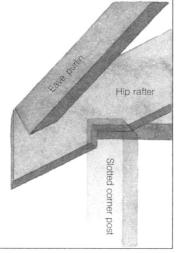

Eave purlin
Hip rafter
Slotted corner post

Purlin
Short ceiling joist
Jack rafter
Jack rafter top plate

Summer Garden House: Detailing

Fitting Corrugated Metal Roof

You can buy corrugated metal sheets cut to any size. Secure the lower sections first by nailing through the peaks of the corrugations into the purlins and screwing through the valleys using special self-sealing screws. Make sure that adjacent sheets overlap by at least two corrugations on each side of the panels.

Install flashing along the lower purlin of the raised roof sections and press the flashing down onto the lower roof sheets using a roller. Apply a similar strip of flashing from the main end trusses onto the end lean-to roof sheets (fig. 1). Nail ½in (12mm) bevel clapboards to the end trusses to form gable ends.

Finally, affix the raised-roof corrugated sheets, screwing and nailing (as above) into the furring pieces. Adjacent sheets must overlap at least two corrugations on both sides of each panel. Fit and fasten metal capping pieces to the ridge and hips of the hip roof sections.

1 **Lower Roof Flashing**
Lay flashing along the lower raised roof purlin; roll the flashing on to the lower roof sheets.

Detailing

With the main walls constructed and the roof in place, the final detailing jobs can be completed.

Between the wall studs on all four walls, fit 2in (50mm) thick fiberglass wall batts for insulation (fig. 4). The material is flexible and will need to be held in place by tapping brads or staples into the studs in much the same way that glass is held in a window frame.

The window and door frames are then cut to length from 1 × 5in (25 × 125mm) S4S (smooth 4 sides) softwood and temporarily screwed in place (figs. 2 and 3). Make up the window sashes from 2 × 2in (50 × 50mm) wood screwed together, and then nail through the outsides of the sashes to affix the glazing bars (these are stocked by lumberyards). Screw the sashes into the frames.

The exterior cladding can now be nailed in place on each wall, starting at the base and working upwards (fig. 4). Cut the clapboarding to fit neatly around the window frames and the door frame (see **Techniques, page 399**).

Cut and nail in place the 1 × 6in (25 × 150mm) fascia boards to the eaves and the 2 × 2in (50 × 50mm) rafter ties.

Corner boards are needed at the four corners of the summer garden house to close off the end grain of the exterior cladding. The boards should be cut to length and set temporarily in place.

Having checked everything over you can now start to decorate. Remove the corner boards while the exterior cladding is treated with exterior-grade preservative, stain, or paint, then paint the boards in a contrasting color before nailing them back in place.

The door and window frames can now be painted, along with the roof and fascia board.

Now secure the gutters, giving them a slight fall toward each corner, where a small hole should be cut. Secure a chain through each outlet and run it down to the ground to channel rain water into a drywell. Alternatively, you could fit a combined stopend and downspout outlet at each corner of the gutter; however, this will mean that you will not be able to run the chains down to the ground at the exact corners of the summer garden house – to the detriment of the overall design.

If the external joists were temporarily removed while the project was being built then re-lay them now on a strip of bituminous felt and secure them to the veranda support posts as described earlier (page 62).

The "duckboard" floor of the veranda is now formed by screwing

1×3in (25×75mm) boards to the joists leaving $\frac{3}{4}$in (19mm) spaces between them. Use 2in (50mm) long No. 8 screws.

The windows can now be glazed using $\frac{1}{8}$in (3mm) glass held in place with glazing bars pinned to the frame. It is important that the glazing bars are set square to each other so that the glass will slot comfortably in place. Check each "window" for square by measuring the diagonals, which should be equal. When ordering the glass, buy it about $\frac{1}{8}$in (2–3mm) smaller than the window opening, both in width and height, to allow for normal expansion.

If you prefer, you can buy a ready-made ledged and braced door; alternatively, you can make one using tongue-and-groove boards with 1×4in (25×100mm) wood for the ledges (cross rails) and braces (diagonals). The door can be full-length or a stable door as here. If you choose the latter, you simply make the two smaller doors with a lower rail for each one. In a full-length door, only one central rail will need to be fitted.

Plywood

Lining

Glass

Frame

Exterior cladding

Glazing bar

Glazing batten

② **Affixing the Door Head**
Screw door lining to the studwork, with $\frac{1}{2} \times 1$in (12×25mm) doorstops nailed to sides and top of frame.

③ **Window Frame Assembly**
Above The top and bottom sections of the frame are fastened to the 1×5in (25×125mm) linings.

④ **Exterior Cladding**
Below Exterior walls are formed from overlapping boards nailed to the studwork; work from bottom up.

Stud

Door Stop

Door lining

SUMMER GARDEN HOUSE: DETAILING

A ledged and braced door is made by simply nailing the boards to the ledges and braces. It is constructed by laying the top and bottom rails on a flat surface and then screwing the tongue-and-groove boards to them (*see* **Techniques, page 399**). The boards should overlap the rails by about 1in (25mm) at either end.

The diagonal brace is then fitted by notching it into the ledges and, again, screwing through the door and into the brace. The purpose of the brace is to transmit the weight to the hinges and so prevent the door from sagging. It is important that the braces are affixed the right way around (*see* Door Assembly, fig. 1).

Use two butt hinges to hang each door. These are affixed to the end grain of the rails. If you make a framed door then also use butt hinges: two 3in (75mm) sizes for each half of a stable door, or three for a full-length door.

Next, fit the $\frac{1}{2}$ × 1in (12 × 25mm) door stops – two vertical pieces and a horizontal top piece – to the door frame(fig 2, page 313)These stops must be positioned accurately: hold the door in place and mark the positions of the stops immediately inside its closed position. This ensures that the stops are fitted accurately. Here, they are positioned about 1in (25mm) back from the front of the door frame.

Complete the interior by cladding the ceiling using tongue-and-groove boards, not forgetting to insert fiberglass insulating batts between the joists (fig. 2), held in place by brads as with the walls. The interior walls can be decorated according to your requirements using exterior paint, varnish stain, or microporous paint.

Finally, at each corner, dig a 12 × 12 × 12in (300 × 300 × 300mm) drywell and fill with gravel or pebbles (fig. 3). Embed the ends of the chains into them so that they are held tautly in place.

Ledge

Brace

Butt hinge

Butt hinge

Hasp and staple lock

Ledge

Tongue-and-groove boards

1 Door Assembly
Above **The ledged and braced door can either be a stable door (as shown) or a single unit.**

2 Insulating the Ceiling
Clad the ceiling with tongue-and-groove boards, and place insulating batts between the joists.

3 Making the Drywells
A chain conducts rainwater from the gutters to a drywell – a hole filled with shingle or pebbles.

DEN . . . GAZEBO . . . HIDEAWAY . . . CHALET . . . SHANTY . . . BOTHY . . . HUNTING BOX . . . CROFT . . . PAD . . . OUTHOUSE . . .

SHACK . . . PLAYHOUSE . . . SNUG . . . CABIN . . . SHED . . . BOLT HOLE . . . STUDIO . . . PAVILION . . . LODGE . . . RETREAT . . .

POTTING SHED . . . HUT . . . SANCTUARY . . . HIDEY-HOLE . . . CUBBYHOLE . . . HAVEN . . . GARDEN ROOM . . . .

SUMMER GARDEN HOUSE

A CHANGE OF SCENERY

In a secluded part of the garden, the summer garden house can be used as a simple retreat. The interior is large enough to function as a tool room and potting shed (right) or as a cozy study (opposite).

PLAYHOUSE

A HOME OF THEIR OWN

Whether as a private den away from their parents or as a "real home" on a miniature scale, a playhouse in the garden will give children hours of fun and laughter.

A playhouse in the garden will attract children like bees to a honeypot. Playhouses are excellent for developing children's learning skills, encouraging them to exercise their imaginations. As they play with other children, they will develop interpersonal skills at the same time as enjoying hours of fun. Depending on the age of your children, you can decorate the interior for them, or encourage them to equip it and paint it themselves. In the latter case, make sure that they only use non-toxic paints, which should also be washable, so that the walls can be painted time and again.

By keeping internal fixtures to a minimum, the children can use the playhouse to represent a variety of structures: from a hospital to a shop, an adult living room to an office, or as a den away from the grown-ups.

When children finally outgrow the playhouse, it can be adapted without too much expenditure or alteration for use as storage space for garden equipment.

The model shown in the photograph is situated in the grounds of Castle Drogo, a Lutyens house near Exeter in the west of England administered by the National Trust. The playhouse was built *circa* 1909 as a birthday present and was transferred to its present home from a house in Sussex *circa* 1928.

Our plans show how a playhouse of a similar style could be constructed. For all the framing use $1\frac{1}{2} \times 1\frac{1}{2}$in (38×38mm) S4S (smooth 4 sides) softwood, as accuracy is important. All the relevant dimensions are shown on the illustrations. Glued and nailed butt joints are used throughout.

PLAYHOUSE ASSEMBLY

FRONT

SIDE

PLAYHOUSE

BASE

A solid, level base is essential; otherwise it will not be possible to build the house. The simplest method is to lay concrete pavers on sand. To prevent damp in the soil creeping up and attacking the floor, lay a polyethylene membrane below the sand as a vapor barrier.

The base should be made slightly smaller than the house so that the wall cladding extends just beyond it all around. This means that rainwater running down the walls will not trickle inside the house, but will instead drip onto the ground.

The overall area of the house is 54 × 48in (1370 × 1220mm) and the base is $\frac{1}{4}$in (5mm) less all round at 53$\frac{1}{2}$ × 47$\frac{1}{2}$in (1360 × 1210mm). The floor itself is constructed as a normal house floor with floorboards nailed at right angles to joists. For the joists, use 1 × 2in (25 × 50mm) rough sawn wood. Five joists running from front to back will be sufficient. The two end joists are just inside the ends of the floorboards, with the other three spaced equally between.

The floorboards can be square edged or tongue-and-groove. The former simply butt up to each other, while tongue-and-groove boards interlock. You can use either 4in (100mm) or 5in (125mm) wide boards for the floor; thicknesses range from $\frac{1}{2}$–1$\frac{1}{4}$in (12–32mm), but buy the thinnest available.

Lay the five joists on the ground, then nail one end board at right angles to each joist. Repeat for the other side. Use 2in (50mm) finishing nails and punch the heads below the surface.

At this point, the floor will be held solidly in position so that you can add more boards, making sure that square edge boards butt up closely and that tongue-and-groove boards are tightly interlocked. You will probably have to remove the last board, affixed earlier, to trim it to size before reinstalling it.

WALLS

Affix $\frac{3}{4}$in (19mm) thick marine plywood over the wall framing. The front of the house is split into two separate frames with the door in the middle. The two frames are identical with allowance made for a window on either side. The windows can be any size provided that they look right proportionately – here, 12in square (300mm square) is about right.

The top horizontal member holds the two frames together, but until the side and back frames are added it will be flimsy. So, as a temporary support, add a strut across the doorway as shown (fig. 1). This can be nailed in place and removed when the frames have been joined and the wall panels added.

Light through the front windows is unlikely to be sufficient: a window up to 20 × 16in (500 × 380mm) can be built into the rear wall.

The side walls are plain. Use a top and bottom horizontal member for rigidity and to strengthen each plywood wall panel.

ASSEMBLING THE WALLS

The front and back wall frames are screwed to the base using 3in (75mm) No. 8 screws. This is especially vital in exposed locations where high wind could easily turn the house over. The horizontal members on each side are now affixed, together with the central supports.

The plywood wall panels can now be cut to size and nailed to the frames using 1$\frac{1}{2}$in (38mm) nails, again punching the heads below the surface. When these are in place, the house will be very solid. Remember to cut the panels to extend just below the base.

ROOF

First fix the roof dormer in position. This is made from two A-shaped frames joined with a glued miter joint and reinforced with two 1$\frac{1}{2}$in (38mm) corrugated fasteners. Plywood offcuts nailed in place strengthen the roof-to-wall joints and reinforce the miter joint at the apex of the A-frame, while a batten the length of the side wall frames runs between them at the apex. These frames are then clad with bevel clapboards, nailed in place with 2in (50mm) finishing nails.

Start at the bottom and work up to the ridge. The boards are nailed

① Constructing the Front Frame

Build all of the frames from 1$\frac{1}{2}$ × 1$\frac{1}{2}$in (38 × 38mm) S4S softwood. Brace the opening for the door at the front and allow for a window on either side. Roof dormer frame rests centrally on top.

② Constructing the Back Frame

The back frame is a very simple construction of glued and nailed butt joints. A central window can be fitted at the back to improve the amount of light inside the playhouse.

with the thinner edge uppermost so that the thicker edge of the board above overlaps it by $\frac{1}{2}$in (12mm) (see **Techniques, page 399**).

At the top, you will probably have to trim the last board to fit. The ridge is sealed by using self-adhesive aluminum flashing tape. Cut the strip to the required length from the roll, peel back a little of the backing paper and position the tape on the roof. Press the tape into place with a cloth, peel back more of the backing paper and continue in this manner until the ridge is covered. Do not peel away all of the backing paper at once – the adhesive is powerful and will start to stick itself to the roof in the wrong place. Add two triangular plywood panels to enclose each end of the dormer. These are inset into the A-frames and glued in place using an epoxy resin.

When the dormer is complete it can be lifted into place and screwed and glued in place to the top of the wall frames.

The main roof is constructed similarly except that the A-frames are screwed in place and then the bevel clapboarding, cutting it to fit around the dormer as necessary.

Use plywood offcuts to strengthen the joints as before, and use triangular plywood panels inset into the A-frames and glued in place at either end.

WINDOWS

You have a choice for the windows: you can either use plain acrylic, or else you can decorate it with self-adhesive strips as imitation leaded lights. A similar effect can be achieved with self-adhesive black tape. An alternative is to use thin battens to form small "windows" within the main frame. For safety reasons, do not use glass.

DOOR

Construct the door from floorboards and affix two 1 × 4in (25 × 100mm) boards horizontally to serve as bracing and to prevent the door warping. Alternatively, you can use shiplap cladding smooth side out, which will give slightly better weather resistance (see **Materials, page 394**).

CHIMNEY

The chimney is optional. Make it from plywood offcuts joined with 1in square (25mm square) plywood strips in each corner, or use plastic joint blocks. A piece of plastic pipe forms the pot.

PAINTING

Before painting, all the wood which the children will be able to touch should be very carefully smoothed by sanding it down with a power sander to remove any splinters.

Use masonry paint for the main walls and treat the door with primer, undercoat, and exterior gloss. Coat the floor with an appropriate wood dye and exterior-grade varnish or a varnish stain; alternatively, it can be painted with masonry paint.

GUTTERS AND PIPES

The gutters and drainpipes are purely decorative. Use offcuts of plastic guttering – the smallest section made for sheds will do. Make the drainpipes from waste pipe held in place with pipe clips.

3 **Constructing the Roof Dormer Frame**
Reinforce the A-shaped frames with plywood offcuts at the apex. Additional plywood offcuts strengthen the roof-to-wall joints at the front and back. A batten the length of the side walls runs between the A-frames.

4 **Making the Door**
Make door from floorboards braced top and bottom. Weather bar at bottom throws rain clear of base.

5 **Making the Chimney**
This is purely decorative. Angle the plywood to sit on the apex of the roof. Add plastic pipe to form pot.

RABBIT RUN

RUN RABBIT, RUN
Pet rabbits can exercise in safety if you build a rabbit run. The dimensions can be adjusted according to the size and number of rabbits. The enclosed end section provides shelter in bad weather.

An enclosed run such as this will provide your rabbits with an area for safe daytime exercise. One section of the run is fully enclosed for occasions when the weather turns nasty. Be sure to anchor the run firmly to the ground to ensure that the rabbits cannot escape.

Treat all the wood with a good quality, non-toxic wood preservative that will not harm your rabbits and allow it to dry thoroughly before you start assembly. For the side cladding panels use $\frac{1}{4}$in (6mm) thick exterior-grade plywood; use the same material for the doors, but use $\frac{3}{8}$in (9mm) thickness for the floor.

Make up four A-shaped frames using 1 × 2in (25 × 50mm) softwood and strengthen them with 1 × 1in (25 × 25mm) cross pieces. The apex of each frame needs to be mitered and this joint can be

secured with a 1in (25mm) wide corrugated fastener. The other joints are secured using 1$\frac{1}{2}$in (38mm) No. 8 galvanized screws. Use waterproof adhesive on all joints.

Position the frames at 24in (600mm) spacings, then link them at either side with 72in (1800mm) lengths of $\frac{1}{4}$ × 1$\frac{1}{2}$in (6 × 38mm) plywood battens, top and bottom, attached using 1in (25mm) No. 8 screws driven into the A-frames.

Add the floor to the section that will be beneath the side cladding panels, pinning it to the two cross rails at the bottom of the A-frames with 1in (25mm) panel pins.

Use $\frac{1}{2}$in (12mm) plastic-coated wire mesh, which should be cut to finish 2in (50mm) inside the position of the plywood side panels. Use $\frac{3}{4}$in (19mm) staples to secure it to the frame of the run and secure it very strongly with staples at 3in (75mm) intervals. Cut out a triangle of mesh for the back frame of the run and secure it in the same way as for the sides. Nail the side panels in place on the frame, enclosing the edges of the mesh. The frame battens will create a small gap between the A-frame and the panels – add a filler piece if you want the panels flush.

The outer door should be cut out to sit snugly inside the end frame. Add small spacer blocks to bring it flush with the frame, then add a turnbutton for each corner to hold it in place. Make a turnbutton from a scrap piece of the $\frac{1}{4}$in (6mm) plywood and a 1in (25mm) No. 8 screw. Drill $\frac{1}{2}$in (12mm) ventilation holes in the door and nail a spare piece of wood to act as a handle.

The internal door is nailed in place inside the rabbit run to give access between the covered and uncovered sections. Drill $\frac{1}{2}$in (12mm) ventilation holes and cut the entrance with a saber saw.

Add a cap of building paper and shingles to seal the apex of the roof. Use bitumen-based adhesive to attach it.

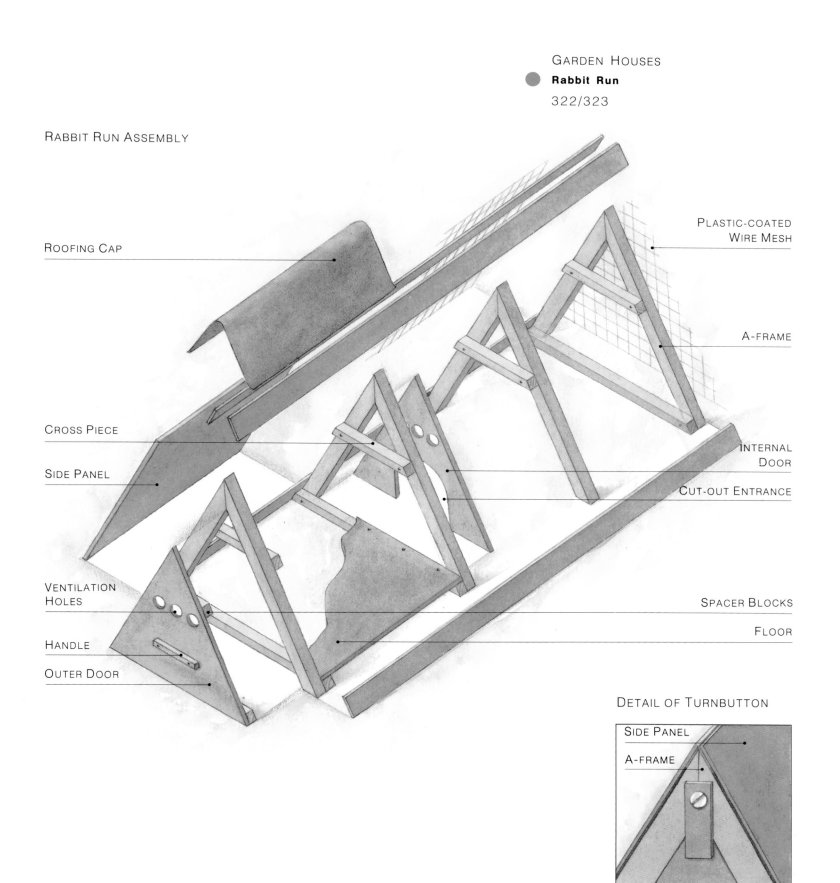

RABBIT RUN ASSEMBLY

ROOFING CAP

PLASTIC-COATED WIRE MESH

A-FRAME

CROSS PIECE

INTERNAL DOOR

SIDE PANEL

CUT-OUT ENTRANCE

VENTILATION HOLES

SPACER BLOCKS

FLOOR

HANDLE

OUTER DOOR

DETAIL OF TURNBUTTON

SIDE PANEL

A-FRAME

BIRDHOUSE

The introduction of a birdhouse into your garden will help to conserve bird life and provide entertainment for the family. Given time, the birds will gain in confidence and come closer to your home.

The sizes given for this particular box (similar to the one in the photograph) are not critical so they can be altered by 1–2in (25–50mm) if preferred. The only thing that must be specific is the diameter of the entrance hole since this will govern the species of bird that will be encouraged to nest. The height that the box is sited above the ground is also important, but is generally not as critical as that of the entrance hole. A table of entrance hole diameters and above-ground heights is given opposite.

Rough-sawn wood is ideal for boxes, and a thickness of $\frac{5}{8}$in (16mm) makes joining easy. All joints are butted, and secured with waterproof wood adhesive and galvanized or alloy nails. Wood is a good insulator against heat and cold, it resists condensation, and blends well with any environment.

First, cut out the two side pieces, each measuring $4\frac{3}{4} \times 8$in (120 × 200mm). Next, cut a groove along the inside front edge of both pieces to serve as a channel for the door to slide in. The channels must be perfectly aligned; laying out, therefore, must be very accurate.

If you have a router then the channels can be cut out quickly and precisely using a straight-sided router bit. If you do not have a router then use a marking knife to scribe the edge of the groove. Next, use a back saw to cut the groove to the required depth along each edge before paring out the waste with a chisel. Work slowly and carefully until the sides and base of the channels are flat.

The back panel is a complete piece, shaped to support the roof panels. In position, it is slightly inset between the side panels.

The front is constructed from two separate pieces. The top triangular section is secured to the roof and has a hole of the required diameter drilled through it. The hole can be drilled using either an auger bit or, if you have one, an expansive bit fitted in a bit brace.

Should you not have a bit suitable for cutting large diameter holes then use a compass saw or a saber saw. First, drill a hole inside the outline of the hole to leave a starting position for the saw blade. Drill the hole with a normal twist drill. Cut out the shape and finish by sanding the edges (see **Techniques, page 397**).

The door is cut to dimensions of $6\frac{1}{2} \times 8$in (160 × 200mm). A rabbet is taken from each side so that the door sits neatly in the side panels.

The rabbet is cut easily with a router and straight-sided bit or with a back saw and chisel (see **Techniques, page 398**).

The roof is comprised of two panels; each panel measures $6 \times 8\frac{1}{2}$in (155 × 215mm). The roof is joined at the top using a miter joint. The joint, as throughout, is glued but this time it is secured with a 1in (25mm) corrugated fastener, tapped home flush with the surface.

When all the pieces have been cut to size, treat the exterior faces and edges only with a water-based wood preservative. It is best to leave internal faces untreated to avoid any toxic risk to the birds.

To assemble the birdhouse, first join the two side panels to the floor and then add the back panel.

Make up the roof, including the triangular front section, and attach this to the lower part.

Finally, with the sliding door in the closed position, drill a hole through either side of the birdhouse and into the door to a depth of 1in (25mm). Insert a 2in (50mm) galvanized steel nail into each hole to hold the door in place. The holes should be of a diameter to give the nails a tight but sliding fit.

BACK YARD BIRD-LIFE
A birdhouse provides a safe haven for small birds and their young. By encouraging birds to nest in your garden, you will derive personal satisfaction and the enjoyment of observing wildlife close at hand.

Siting is not crucial, although a location within view of your house is obviously desirable for the family's enjoyment. Try to avoid anywhere where water is likely to cascade down, and, if your garden is exposed, position the birdhouse on the most sheltered side to avoid strong winds. Most birds prefer a direct flight line to the entrance.

If you are lucky, the birdhouse may lodge conveniently in the fork of a tree, but in most cases some form of attachment will be required. The simplest way is to secure plastic-coated garden wire to the back of the house using fencing staples, and then to wire the house to a tree trunk. With an immature tree, attach the wire fairly loosely to allow for growth of the trunk. It is best not to nail or screw directly into the tree as this may damage it.

Alternatively, you can place the birdhouse on top of a post. Sink a post support into the ground at the chosen site and insert a 4 × 4in (100 × 100mm) post cut to the appropriate height (see **Techniques, page 400**). Remove the sliding door from the birdhouse, drill a pilot hole through the base and into the post, and screw in place.

Remember to clear out the birdhouse annually, after the fledglings and their parents have flown.

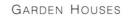
BIRDHOUSE ASSEMBLY

SPECIES	HOLE DIAMETER	HEIGHT ABOVE GROUND
TITMOUSE	1in (25mm)	6–15ft (2–5m)
NUTHATCH	1¼in (32mm)	12–15ft (4–5m)
TREE SPARROW	1¼in (32mm)	12–15ft (4–5m)

5in

FRONT TOP PANEL

7¼in

6¼in

8½in

ROOF PANEL

SIDE PANEL

BACK PANEL

5in

⁵⁄₈in

8in

SLIDING DOOR

8in

8in

INSET FLOOR
3½ × 6in

4¾in

5¾in

⁵⁄₁₆in

6in

6in

PART 7

PATIOS, PATHS, AND PONDS

The contrast between various garden surfaces – hard and soft, paved, turfed, planted, or water-filled – gives a garden its fundamental shape and design. Considerations such as where to build a patio or a flight of steps, which area to link with paths, or how to edge a flowerbed are not details to be decided piecemeal but basic issues which should be resolved at the outset.

All gardens, even informal ones, need some hard surfaces. Modern gardens are generally small and demands on the space available are high. One of our most important requirements today is that the garden should function as an extension of the house, as an outdoor room, which usually means that there must be some sort of paved seating area for relaxation. And there will always be the need for paths to connect one part of the garden to another, as a practical surface for walking and tending beds, and visually to divide flowerbeds from the lawn. Wherever possible, construct hard surfaces from natural materials that weather and age, and allow plants or grass to grow in the crevices of paving and paths, softening the edges so that these areas blend harmoniously with the rest of the garden.

PATIOS, PATHS, AND PONDS

Because hard surfaces are relatively expensive, fairly permanent, and take time and effort to install, it is critically important to work out your ideas on paper first. This is also the stage at which to plan changes of level or to work out how to accommodate an existing slope in the form of steps or terraces. Look at the shapes – the overall pattern – that the paved areas will create. Make sure that paths do not leave useless margins of lawn or awkward-shaped flowerbeds. Plan the connections so that the paths really go somewhere, rather than meander aimlessly. Establish the basic proportion of patio to lawn so that the paving reinforces the overall design of the garden. A formal layout, for example, usually relies on a strong, symmetrical grid which can be expressed in a higher proportion of paths and paved areas. In an urban garden, you may decide to dispense with a lawn altogether and work out a series of connecting paved areas and raised beds.

The range of materials suitable for hard surfacing is so great that there really is no need to rely solely on concrete. All the natural materials are much more sympathetic in the garden and they not only work well with plants but also with each other, so that you can mix materials to create interesting contrasts of texture and pattern. Bricks can be laid to create herringbone or basketweave patterns as well as simple coursing; be sure to choose frost-proof varieties for outdoor use and avoid ugly stock bricks which never weather. Stone – including bluestone, slate, and granite slabs – is traditional and expensive but can sometimes be reclaimed much more cheaply from building sites or builders' yards. Gravel can be rather dull; pebble paths are much more positive. Sea pebbles, in particular, set into concrete look wonderful laid in a mosaic. Treated wood is an excellent

garden material. Railway ties, which have a uniform thickness and are already treated against rot, can be put to a number of uses, from making steps, to forming the sides of raised beds. Slices can be cut from the trunks of fallen trees, treated, and used end grain-on for paths, steps, and patios. Decking, as a terrace or around the perimeter of a pond, is contemporary-looking and absorbs the heat of the sun to make a warm, comfortable surface.

Whatever material you choose will probably depend to a large extent on the amount of money you can spend, but try to form some kind of connection with the overall style of the house and the materials from which it is built. This is an important consideration, particularly for terraces or patios that immediately adjoin the house and create a relatively large surface area which has an impact on how the house is viewed.

If you cannot avoid the use of concrete, there are many ways of improving its rather dull and uniform appearance. Pavers are much better than a poured concrete slab and can be enormously improved if, instead of setting them in cement, they are laid with gaps in between. You can then fill the gaps with pebbles or plants such as creeping thyme or camomile to soften the edges. Choose pavers of a neutral shade and let color come from lichens and mosses: you can encourage lichen to grow by treating concrete with nonpasteurized milk or houseplant food. Even if most of the paving is concrete, an edging of brick or another more harmonious material will lift it out of the ordinary.

A path makes a good edge for a flowerbed or herbaceous border, separating planted areas from lawn and making mowing easier. In the absence of a path, beds need some form of containment. Conventional edging includes brick,

OUTDOOR FLOORING

The surfaces you choose for outdoor flooring can reinforce the overall style and design of the garden. A regular gridded pattern of smooth stone slabs suits the modern formal style of an urban garden (above). Decking is particularly sympathetic surrounding the perimeter of a pool, where it makes a comfortable surface for bare feet (above right). Slate tiles create a sleek paved area in an urban garden (above far right). For a more informal, country setting, a sweep of large cobblestone makes an attractive paved area (below right).

PATIOS, PATHS, AND PONDS

looped wire which also serves to prop up plants, and concrete bricks. Traditional terracotta edging, particularly the Victorian rope design, is also available. Less conventionally, you can make effective edging with whatever comes to hand: slivers of stone, old roofing slates, or thin horizontal slats of treated hardwood nailed to posts.

Water is one of the most delightful of all the elements in garden design, providing another contrast of surface, and retaining its interest even in winter when the garden is bare. A sheet of water, reflecting the sky, has always been a feature of formal designs; surrounded by moisture-loving plants and filled with fish and lily pads, a pond can come close to fulfilling everyone's dream of having a river running through the garden. Moving water – a jet, a fountain, a cascade, or a water sculpture – adds another dimension: sound. The tinkling noise of running water in the garden is extremely pleasant and restful.

There are also good, practical reasons for incorporating water into a garden design. A pond or pool provides a supply of water at air temperature, which presents far less of a shock to young seedlings than water from a hose. Even in a dry

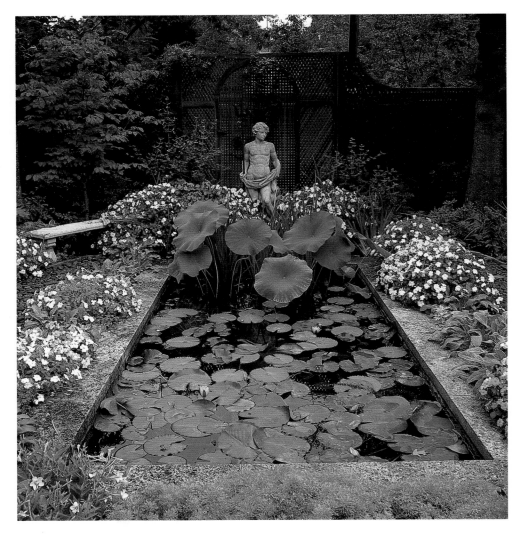

COOL WATER
Formal pools of water can be incorporated into even the smallest garden (right and above right), although pools designed to look like natural lakes need more space around them to be successful.

SURFACE INTEREST
A contrast of different surfaces – terracotta, stone, brick, or concrete – enlivens a garden design (opposite and above opposite.).

area, a pond will create its own microclimate where you can grow species such as arum lilies, irises, and other plants which flourish in damp conditions. And you do not have to stock your pond with fish for it to be attractive to insects, butterflies, and other wildlife.

In whatever form, water is a natural focal point in the garden. If the garden slopes, it is a simple proposition to create channels where water flows down the incline and collects in a pool, to be pumped back by an inexpensive recirculating pump. In hot countries, water in channels or running down stepped terraces has long been a means both of irrigating vegetable crops and, in courtyard gardens, of cooling the air. A still pool of water in a geometric shape is often the centerpiece of a formal garden, and formal cascades, for example, were an important feature of Italian Renaissance gardens. Sunken or raised pools in rectangular, circular, square, or L-shapes are relatively easy to build from concrete block with waterproof facing, the edges softened by clumps of rushes and irises. And in a small urban garden, the suggestion of water can be created very simply by the addition of a water sculpture. Water falling over large urns, slabs of stone, or boulders is much more effective and attractive than a waterfall or fountain which involves a contrived, rather crudely cast garden ornament.

Informal ponds and pools, where the intention is to create as natural an effect as possible, demand a larger garden to be successful. Groups of boulders, wooden decking, dense perimeter planting, and perhaps a flat, low bridge can give an informal pond a Japanese quality. Water on this kind of scale demands more attention and general maintenance than a simple formal pool if it is to be convincing and appealing.

WATER SCULPTURE

The delightful sound of running water in the garden is especially restful and pleasing. A water sculpture can be made very simply and economically, requiring only a minimal outlay for a small pump and the careful installation of a power supply.

This fountain consists of a large ribbed terracotta pot set into a pool which is in turn sunk into the ground and overhung with a brick surround. The dimensions of the pool have been calculated using standard bricks as a module.

A black polyethylene pond liner is fitted inside the pool and bricks and a tile make a central platform on which the pot rests. A waterproof power cable runs from the pump through a special conduit to connect with the main power source. A word of caution: special care must be taken to ensure that there is no leaking where the cable exits from the pool. It is also vital to lay the correct conduit for the cable so that it cannot be accidentally cut when digging above it.

An earthenware pot makes the best choice for the sculpture since terracotta is easier to drill than stoneware. A copper pipe is inserted through a hole drilled in the base of the pot. When the pool is filled with water, the pump sends a jet of water up through the pipe to fill the pot and overflow down the sides.

During the winter months, the power supply should be switched off and the pot emptied to prevent the risk of it being cracked by a hard frost.

WATER SCULPTURE

The sight and sound of moving water are among the most pleasurable experiences to be had in a garden on a hot summer's day. You need not go to the trouble and expense of installing an elaborate pond complete with waterfall, fish, and plants to enjoy this in your own garden – you can build a simple yet very effective water sculpture. The size of the pool is entirely optional, as is the centerpiece. We chose a pot with ridged sides since it gives an interesting surface for the water to splash onto and run down.

A submersible pump pushes the water up and out of the pot. Because the pump is electrically operated from the service at the house, it makes sense to keep the water sculpture as close to the house as possible; this saves having to run the buried cable a long distance. The submersible pump can be hidden beneath the pot or in a corner of the pond, covered by pond weed or water lilies.

With any water feature in the garden, safety must be paramount: a child can drown even in shallow water. If you have children and choose to install a pool then do make sure that it is made child-proof.

BUILDING THE POOL

Choose a level site and mark out the ground using a string line and pegs or a hose. This will give you a good idea of whether the position and size is satisfactory. Our pool is 39in square (1000mm square).

Dig out the hole to a depth of about 12in (300mm). The four sides should be tapered outward slightly and the base should be flat.

Cut out four pieces of exterior-grade plywood to form the pool sides. The top edge of the plywood should align with the level of the surrounding soil once you have cut around the edge of the pool to bed the brick or stone surround which will lie flush and overlap the edge of

TOOLS

SMALL CROSSCUT SAW

SPADE

CARPENTER'S LEVEL

SANDING BLOCK and SANDPAPER

STEEL BENCH RULE

TROWEL (if paving laid on mortar)

MALLET

POWER DRILL

ADJUSTABLE WRENCH

HACKSAW

SCREWDRIVER

MATERIALS

Part	Quantity	Material	Length
POT	1	Terracotta	As required
TUBE	1	½in (12mm) copper tubing	Height of pot
TILE	1	Terracotta	12 × 12in (300 × 300mm)
PAVING SLAB	1	Concrete	24 × 24in (600 × 600mm)
SIDES OF POOL	4	¾in (19mm) shuttering plywood	As required

Also required: 1 submersible pump and outdoor cable; ½in (12mm) compression tank outlet; clip and rubber washers; PVC or butyl pond liner; sand for lining pond; bricks for supporting terracotta tile and for pool surround; sand or soil for setting brick surround

the pool slightly. In our case, the plywood was 8¾in (220mm) deep. Sand the plywood pieces to remove splinters and place in position.

Set a concrete paver in the middle. If you lay it on sand it will be simple to level. Lay a sand screed across the excavation, covering the paver by about ½in (12mm).

The brick or paved surround will be far more appealing if weathered, second-hand material is used. Dig out the area around the pool to the width and depth required for the bricks or pavers being used. In our case, the area was 15in (375mm) wide all round to allow for a double row of 8in (200mm) bricks overlapping the pond edge by 1in (25mm). The depth was approximately 3in (75mm) to allow for the 2¼in (60mm) brick depth plus a ⅝in (15mm) layer of fine soil or sand underneath. If you lay the bricks so that they will be level with the lawn, mowing will be easier.

FITTING THE LINER

The length of liner equals twice the pool depth plus the overall length of the pool (including the brick surround); the width of liner should be twice the depth of the pool plus the overall width.

Lay the pond liner in place following the manufacturer's instructions. Allow the excess edges of the liner to lap up over the sides of the pond, then weight it down temporarily with bricks while the pond is being filled. The weight of the water will gradually force the liner to stretch to the shape of the plywood walls. Check with the instructions as to how long you should allow the liner to stretch until it will be smooth.

Remove the temporary bricks and trim the liner to leave an overlap of about 6in (150mm) to lie below the brick surround.

Next, lay the bricks. Lay the course surrounding the edge of the pool first so that the bricks will overlap the water by 1in (25mm). It is a good idea to lay the corner bricks first and then to rest a straight-edge and carpenter's level across them; bring them level by adjusting the bed of sand or fine soil below and tapping each brick with the shaft of a mallet. It is then easy to fill in the remaining bricks, leveling each one with neighboring bricks, and filling in the gaps with sand or soil so that plants and moss can grow up in the cracks. Although reasonable alignment of the bricks is important, second-hand bricks can tend to be

slightly off center, but that gives the surround a rustic charm. However, it is important that the surface is level so that no one will trip. Note the brick arrangement used to turn the corners (fig. 1).

PREPARING THE POT

The base of the pot sits on a 12in square (300mm square) terracotta tile, itself supported by two leveled bricks, laid on edge and spaced at the required distance (fig. 2). The water level should be slightly above the tile so that the bottom of the pot is just submerged. The pump is placed below the tile.

Drill a ¾in (19mm) diameter hole through the center of the base of the pot to take a ½in (12mm) tank outlet fitting. Use a carbide drill bit at slow speed. A larger hole is needed in the tile to take the pipe from the pump; to make this, drill a series of small holes closely together in a circle. As the small holes are joined up, a larger hole will be formed.

FITTING THE PUMP

Fit the compression tank outlet through the holes in the pot and tile ensuring that rubber washers are used on both sides and that the nuts are not overtightened; otherwise the pot could crack. Using a hacksaw, cut a length of copper tube to extend from inside the compression joint to the rim of the pot (fig. 3).

Attach the rubber tube from the pump to the compression outlet, if necessary using a clip to secure it. If the base of the pot is too thick then there might not be sufficient thread left to attach the tube. If so, screw on an extension piece.

The pump is powered from the house electrical service. It can be operated directly from the main but it is safer to feed it back through a transformer situated in the house which makes the supply low voltage for safety but adequate to power a pump. The cable should be armored for outdoor use and laid in a plastic conduit underground and fed into the pool from below the brick surround. There will be local regulations about this, so check first.

You can then switch on the power supply to the pump and enjoy the results. It is a good idea to remove the pot and store it inside during the winter as it may crack in freezing weather.

WATER SCULPTURE ASSEMBLY

COPPER TUBE

TERRACOTTA POT

CABLE FROM POT

BRICK SUPPORT

POND LINER

PLYWOOD

CONCRETE PAVER

SAND

PUMP

TERRACOTTA TILE

OUTLET

TRANSFORMER

❶ Detail of Brick Surround
At each corner of the surround the bricks are laid in pairs perpendicular to the adjoining pair.

❷ Terracotta Pot Support
Pot rests on tile supported by two bricks. Copper tube is connected to pump through holes in pot and tile.

❸ Connecting Pump to Pot
Pump pipe is connected to copper tube by compression tank outlet which feeds through pot and tile.

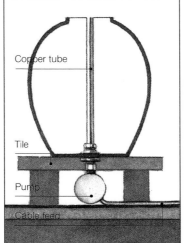

Copper tube

Tile

Pump

Cable feed

Compression joint

Rubber washer

Base of pot

Clip

Tile

Rubber pipe

PLANT STAND

This elegant, rectilinear plant stand, or jardiniere, is inspired by the work of the early twentieth-century designer Josef Hoffmann (1870–1956). He was a Viennese architect, a founding member of the Wiener Werkstätte and a pioneer of functional design. His furniture displays a lack of embellishment and an interest in proportion that was developed further by designers of the Modernist Movement.

Essentially a simple structure, it is made slightly more complicated by the number of right-angled joints. The plant stand incorporates a shallow tray at the top and a shelf at the bottom to hold a collection of plant pots. It is intended for both outdoor and indoor use. The gridded design has been painted a pale "bone" color, but other neutral shades would be equally effective.

The idea of grouping elements together to increase their impact is as important in garden design as it is in the design of interiors. Filled with geraniums, the plant stand would brighten up a corner of a patio or seating area, while, positioned near the kitchen door, either outside or in, the stand would also make a convenient home for a collection of herbs grown in containers.

PLANT STAND

This simple stand for plants and flowers looks equally good in the garden or the conservatory. The plant stand shown here is made from S4S (smooth 4 sides) softwood and then painted. However, if you want to retain the natural wood finish, then be sure to make it from good-quality softwood or even from hardwood, which can afterward be treated with a water-repellent preservative stain.

The design of the frame uses a number of wood joints, and for ease of assembly we suggest that these are doweled together. For a stronger job, the joints could be mortised and tenoned, but unless you have a mortising machine it would be too time-consuming (and complicated) to attempt to construct the frame by this method.

TOOLS

WORKBENCH (fixed or portable)

UTILITY KNIFE

STEEL MEASURING TAPE

STEEL BENCH RULE

TRY SQUARE

SMALL CROSSCUT SAW (or circular power saw)

BACK SAW (or power saber saw)

CHISEL

MARKING GAUGE

POWER DRILL

TWIST DRILL BIT – $\frac{1}{8}$in (3mm)

DOWELING JIG

BRAD-POINT BIT – $\frac{3}{8}$in (10mm)

MALLET

SCREWDRIVER

POWER SANDER (or hand sanding block)

MATERIALS

Part	Quantity	Material	Length
CORNER POSTS	4	2 × 2in (50 × 50mm) S4S softwood	30$\frac{5}{8}$in (779mm)
MIDDLE POSTS	2	As above	28in (711mm)
LONG RAILS	6	As above	33$\frac{3}{8}$in (847mm)
END RAILS	6	As above	9$\frac{5}{16}$in (237mm)
VERTICAL PIECES	10	As above	4$\frac{3}{4}$in (122mm)
SHELVES	2	$\frac{1}{4}$in (6mm) plywood	10$\frac{5}{8}$ × 34$\frac{5}{8}$in (270 × 880mm)
FEET	4	Offcut of hardwood or softwood	3$\frac{1}{2}$ × 3$\frac{1}{2}$ × 1$\frac{1}{8}$in (90 × 90 × 30mm)

Also required: $\frac{3}{8}$in (10mm) diameter doweling; 2in (50mm) No. 8 galvanized screws; brads

FRAME CONSTRUCTION

Cut all the components to length, following the Materials chart.

MAKING THE END FRAMES

Cut a half-lap joint to form the intersection of the middle post with the middle end rail (see **Techniques, page 400**). Mark off on the middle post where the middle end rail will cross it using one of the short vertical pieces as a spacer. The top of the cross half-lap joint will be this distance down from the top of the middle post.

Carefully mark out and cut the half-lap joint on the middle post and the middle end rail (fig. 1). Repeat for the other end frame.

Strike diagonal lines to mark the center points for the dowel holes on the ends of all the end rails, on the ends of the middle posts, and on the ends of all the short vertical pieces. Using a doweling jig and a dowel bit (or a drill fitted with a brad-point bit and held in a vertical drill stand) drill $\frac{3}{8}$in (10mm) diameter holes centrally into the marked positions. The hole depths should be slightly over half the dowel lengths (ie, $\frac{7}{8}$in [22mm] deep holes for 1$\frac{1}{2}$in [40mm] long dowels). This gives a small cavity at the end which will accommodate trapped air and glue (see **Techniques, Dowel joint, page 402**).

1 **Affixing Middle End Rail**
Mark position of middle end rail on middle post and cut half-lap joints to affix the two pieces together.

2 **Top and Bottom End Rails**
Mark dowel hole positions centrally on both ends of middle rail. Dowel to top and bottom end rails to affix.

3 **Adding Corner Posts**
Dowel posts to end rails: top end rail is flush with top of posts, bottom end rail flush with bottom of posts.

PLANT STAND ASSEMBLY

TOP LONG RAIL

TOP END RAIL

MIDDLE LONG RAIL

MIDDLE END RAIL

CORNER POST

MIDDLE POST

DOWELS

BOTTOM END RAIL

END FRAME

SMALL VERTICAL PIECES

LADDER SECTION

TOP SHELF

BOTTOM LONG RAIL

BOTTOM SHELF

PLANT STAND

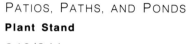

Mark out the position of the top and bottom end rails onto the inside faces of the corner posts and strike diagonals again to mark the positions of the dowel holes. Drill the holes as before. Also mark out on each corner post the dowel hole positions for the middle rail, which is the same distance down as the length of a short vertical piece plus the $1\frac{1}{2}$in (38mm) depth of the top end rail. Square around onto the other internal face of each corner post to mark the dowel hole positions to take the top, middle, and bottom long rails.

Dry assemble the middle post and the middle end rail together to form a cross, and then dowel on the top and bottom end rails, again without glue (fig 2, page 338). Complete the dry assembly of the end frames by adding the corner posts (fig. 3, page 338).

FRONT AND BACK FRAMES

To make up the front and back frames, which look like ladders, mark the positions of the short vertical pieces along one long rail,

and mark dowel hole centers regularly and centrally along the rail (fig. 1). There is an internal spacing of $4\frac{1}{2}$in (110mm) between each short vertical piece, and also between the end-most vertical pieces and each of the corner posts.

Use this rail as a pattern to transfer the marks onto three of the other long rails. Drill all the dowel holes to the required depth and dry assemble the ladder frame sections.

Drill the dowel holes on the inside of the corner posts, using the marks transferred from the front and back ladder frame construction.

Mark the dowel hole positions centrally on the ends of the bottom long rails, then drill the holes in them and in the bottoms of the corner posts as before.

Dowel and dry assemble each ladder frame section, together with the long bottom rails, into the corner posts of the end frames (fig. 2).

Make sure that the assembly is square and fits together perfectly, dismantle in reverse order, then re-assemble, this time gluing the joints using waterproof wood adhesive.

SHELVES

The two shelves are cut so that they finish half-way across the thickness of the frame, rather than fitting flush with the outside edges of the frame rails. Notch out the corners and the central part at the ends to fit around the middle and corner posts.

Cut out the bottom shelf to fit onto the bottom rails, and glue and nail it down to the frame (fig. 3).

The top shelf is glued and nailed to the underside of the middle rails.

FEET

The feet are fitted underneath each corner and protrude at the sides and ends by the same amount as the "step" for the bottom shelf (that is, approximately $\frac{3}{4}$in [19mm]) (fig. 4). Any offcut of softwood or hardwood can be used to make them.

Apply waterproof wood adhesive, then screw the feet to the rails using two screws for each foot.

Fill any gaps using an exterior-grade wood filler. Finally, paint as required or apply a water-repellent wood preservative stain.

❶ Adding Vertical Pieces
Vertical pieces are doweled in place at equal internal spacings between top and middle long rails.

❷ Frame Assembly
Mark dowel positions on corner posts and ends of top, middle, and bottom long rails. Drill and join.

❸ Adding Bottom Shelf
Cut shelf to finish half-way across frame rails. Notch ends to fit around posts. Glue and screw in place.

❹ Adding the Feet
Cut feet from offcuts of wood. Glue and screw them up into rails so that they protrude by about $\frac{3}{4}$in (19mm).

Ponds

An ornamental fish pond will enhance even the smallest garden, providing interest and pleasure with water lilies, reeds, and fish mingling with dragonflies, water beetles, and small frogs. Ponds are easy to install and require little maintenance.

There are various ways to build a pond, but to ensure success, the whole project needs to be carefully planned in advance, taking into account the way in which the pond will be constructed, its size, shape, and location.

First, consider shape and location. The former is purely a matter of taste – a question of whether you want a formal rectangle or would prefer a more natural, curved outline. The main consideration is how you see the whole design blending with your garden, although you should avoid an over-complicated design as this will make the pond more difficult and more expensive to build. The location of the pond is critical, however. Ideally, it should receive sunlight for at least half the day to enable flowering pond plants to thrive. You should try to keep it away from overhanging trees since the shade will not be good for plants and mosquitoes will be encouraged. Deciduous trees pose a particular problem in the fall, when leaves falling into the water can have a harmful effect on pond life if they are left to rot.

A pond at the end of a long garden may sound appealing, but remember that if you want to include a waterfall, underwater lights, or a fountain, you face the problem of running an electricity supply a considerable distance. Also, you may not be able to enjoy the sight of the pond from indoors.

The basic factors governing the size are the proportions of the garden and how much time and money you want to spend on the pond. You must ensure that the pond is not "lost" in the garden, nor must it completely dominate it. Do not make a pond too small since a "puddle" will not provide the right conditions for water, plants, and fish to harmonize. The minimum surface area is really about 38 square feet (3.5 square meters). A smaller pond will not allow the water to be aerated and so it may become cloudy, in which case you would need to install a filtration system.

Water depth should not create major problems. The main hazard is with water that is too shallow, causing the pond to overheat in hot weather (leaving the fish short of oxygen) and to freeze in winter. Anything between 16–30in (400–750mm) will enable an excellent selection of plants to flourish. You should include a 9in- (225mm-) wide planting shelf, about 9in (225mm) below the water surface. The shelf should run around most, if not all, of the perimeter of the pond.

Pond Types

Although a pond can be built using concrete to form the walls and base, few people would attempt this method nowadays since construction can be both tedious and difficult, and the pond may be prone to leaking and cracking. The two most common methods today involve using a preformed pond or a liner.

With a preformed pond, the size and shape of the pond is governed by the models available, whereas a liner allows you to create whatever shape you want. If you decide on a special shape or a very large pond, then you will have to use a liner, but otherwise both types have advantages and disadvantages when it comes to installation.

The choice of material to line a pond is between synthetic rubber and PVC. Although any type of liner can be pierced by sharp objects such as stones or digging implements being thrust into the water, this is less likely to happen with the thicker, better-quality types. Even an economy-grade liner can

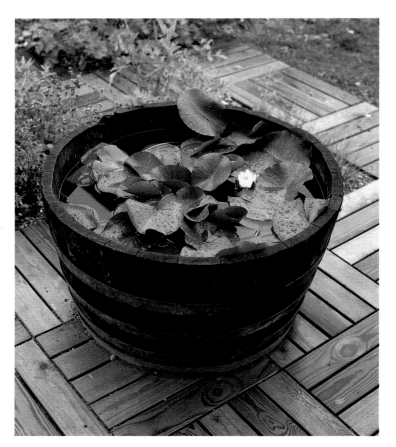

A Pond for a Patio

Not all gardens will have space for a full-size pond. A half-barrel provides a simple solution that is easy to maintain and will have space for two or three small goldfish and for colorful water lilies.

be expected to last ten years if it is properly installed and respected.

Colors readily available are black, stone, blue or gray. Although stone, blue and gray are more natural, many people prefer black since it is much less obtrusive in use. However, color is not vitally important since, after a while, the base of the pond will be covered with a thin layer of mud and its sides will be coated with algae.

A liner can be used in an above ground pond where the walls are constructed from brick or ornamental stonework. It can also be set into the ground in a level excavation made to the required depth and shape. In this case, sharp objects must be removed from the excavation and a 1in (25mm) layer of sand spread across the bottom. The liner is then placed in the excavation, the edges weighted with bricks, and water then added. The pressure of the water stretches the liner to the shape of the excavation.

Finally, paving slabs are used to make a border around the pond and to conceal the edge of the liner.

Preformed ponds are made from plastic or (more expensively) fiberglass and can also be used above or below ground. In both cases, it is vital to support the sides and to ensure that the rim is exactly level.

The lesser-quality plastic ponds are neither as big nor as strong, but should certainly last for at least ten years and enable you to enjoy a wildlife pond in that time. However, if you really want a stock of outstanding fish and plants then you will need one of the better-quality models, which will last for years if it is properly installed and not damaged by sharp objects.

Whether you plan the pond to be below or above ground, it is vital that the excavation of the framework of bricks or ornamental stonework is lined with sand to provide adequate support for every nook and cranny of the pond's outline as the water exerts pressure on it.

PLANTS

Choose a mixture of types for the best effect; most are grown in plastic containers resting on the base of the pond or on the shelf.

Water lilies are a must, really, while shallow water marginals can be either tall and spikey or ground-covering. Deep water aquatics have their roots in containers but their leaves float on the surface, giving interest and shade to the water. Floating plants do not need soil for their roots and some only rise to the surface when flowering. Oxygenating plants, as the name suggests, supply oxygen to the pond and discourage algae. Use four or five for every square yard (meter) of water surface.

Almost inevitably, weeds will build up in the pond. Pull up weeds regularly: if the size and location of the pond allow, simply reach into the water and weed by hand; otherwise, use a rake or a long stick for any parts of the pond that are inaccessible. On no account, however, should you use a chemical algicide. Not only will it kill off the weed, leaving it to decompose in the pond, it may also contaminate your plant and fish stock.

There are many kinds of fish you can use to stock the pond apart from the ubiquitous goldfish, so read a bit about the subject and visit a good local specialist shop or a garden center with a pond department to see what is available.

BARREL POND

Any watertight container can be used for a small water garden and a half-barrel is one of the most popular choices. Half-barrels that previously contained beer, wine, or vinegar are normally available from large garden centers.

It is important to scrub clean the inside of the barrel first using only clean water, never detergent. A clean barrel is important because otherwise the water will quickly become contaminated, posing a threat to your plants and fish. For this reason do not use a barrel that previously contained either wood preservative or oil.

When you are satisfied that the barrel is thoroughly clean, spread 3–4in (75–100mm) of clean soil in the base of the barrel – keep out weeds or vegetation which will rot and pollute the water. Add enough water to enable you to mix the soil into a slurry of mud.

Planting should be carried out in spring or early summer. Use miniature water lilies and some other small, less vigorous plants. Include oxygenating plants to help keep the water clear.

Next, spread a 2in (50mm) layer of fine gravel over the soil to prevent the fish stirring it up and to help prevent the plants from becoming uprooted. Then fill the barrel with water through a hose with its nozzle inside a polyethylene bag (fig. 2); this prevents the jet of water disturbing the soil.

When the barrel is almost full, turn off the water and remove the bag and hose. Allow about a week for the water to settle and the temperature to stabilize before introducing the fish – two or three small goldfish – and a few snails. The fish will discourage mosquitoes in summer, but do transfer them to a larger pond or to a fishtank indoors for the winter as the small amount of water in a barrel is almost certain to freeze over in a cold winter. In early spring, before returning the fish to the barrel, replace most or all of the water and allow it to settle and the temperature to stabilize as before.

① Through-section of Pond with Liner
A hole of the required dimensions is dug and lined with sand before the liner is laid in place. Include a planting shelf around the perimeter. The liner is held in place at the edges by bricks, stones, or paving slabs.

Paving slab

Oxygenating plant

Planting shelf

Liner material

Marginal plant

Layer of sand

② Making a Pond from a Half-barrel
Scrub the barrel clean and place a layer of soil at the bottom for planting. A layer of fine gravel prevents soil mixing with water. Fill pond with water through a hose with its nozzle in a polyethylene bag.

Fine gravel

Hose

Polyethylene bag

Soil

PART 8

SUPPORTS AND DIVIDERS

The opposition of closed and open space is fundamental in garden design. All gardens have boundaries, more or less secure perimeters defined by walls, fences, or hedges. But often there is a need to break up space within the garden, dividing one part from another, screening the view of a utility area or vegetable garden, or making a garden "room," an enclosed area which can create a heightened sense of "hazard and surprise." Simple boundaries can be made from living dividers such as hedges, through semi-transparent picket, wattle, and beanstick fencing to proper garden walls of brick or stone.

Moving from a rose-covered pergola to an expanse of lawn is far more pleasing than walking along an exposed path. Framing a view with a simple arch, dissolving a boundary wall with climbers trained over a trellis, creating an arbor in a corner of the garden are all design devices which add depth and perspective to what might otherwise be flat and monotonous. By growing plants up pergolas, arbors, and other dividers you have the opportunity to add light and shade: the dappled sunlight created by foliage is one of the most appealing sights in the garden.

SUPPORTS AND DIVIDERS

Lattice is indispensable. Off-the-shelf square or diamond wooden mesh is available very cheaply, ready treated, in panels which can be assembled to create a variety of structures or to cover a large surface area. As an extension to a boundary fence, trellis covered with climbing plants filters the wind so that it cannot cut across the garden, and gives a degree of privacy without entirely blocking airflow and light. It is also one of the most economical ways of getting rid of eyesores – ugly sheds, bare blank walls in stock brick, concrete blocks, anything which cannot easily be removed can be covered with trellis and plants encouraged to grow. Climbers such as Russian vine (*Fallopia aubertii*) and flowering plants such as clematis, climbing roses, honeysuckle (*Lonicera* sp) and Virginia creeper (*Parthenocissus quinquefolia*) can materially alter the appearance of any structure. Wisteria will need a greater degree of support, and ivy should be avoided at all costs: its aerial roots dig into mortar and damage brickwork. You can also use trellis to make free-standing structures to block unwelcome views.

Trellis can be put to more positive use, to create a whole range of effects. *Treillages*, intricate flat wooden frameworks, were a feature of French formal gardens, traditionally painted green and used against ecru walls. These were often arched, with tapering lines that gave a subtle sense of perspective – a simple *trompe l'oeil* that enlivened Parisian courtyards. Less elaborate trellis still has this ability to "dissolve" a flat, dull expanse of wall. Depending on how positive you want the trellis to be, you can stain or paint it to add interest in the winter when the leaves have fallen. Trellis helps to blend and merge the garden with the house, taking greenery up onto walls, the sides of buildings and fences.

A pergola is another type of support for plants, but one which involves some kind of canopy, either as a free-standing arch, a covered walkway or a simple framework projecting out from the side of the house. It is commonplace in Mediterranean countries to attach a plain metal framework and wiring to the house over a rear courtyard or front entrance and allow a vine to create a type of living awning. The leaves of the vine keep the sun off and deflect the heat in the summer; in the winter, the frame and the house are revealed: a cheap, effective solution and one which generates interest by changing from month to month. Plain or painted trellis can also be used overhead; the grid takes the strength out of the sun and makes a lively pattern of light and shade.

In design terms, a pergola acts as a kind of picture frame, intensifying a view. It usually demands some type of focal point – a seat or urn at the end of a walkway, for example. But it also produces a contrast of light and shade which is so attractive in a garden, and it makes an ideal support for plants, since they are freely exposed to sunlight, air, and rain.

While there is something especially English about a rose-covered pergola, it is the French who excel at garden ironmongery, including that wonderful green iron which goes to make curved frameworks, such as the one which forms the laburnum avenue in Monet's garden at Giverny. There are different ways of making a pergola, but, generally, if you want the top to curve it must be made of metal, although it is possible to wire beanpoles to achieve a curve. A simple version is to attach small sections of curved metal to wooden uprights. Wires for training plants can be passed through holes in the metal frame or trellis attached to the posts to support climbing roses, honeysuckle, and espaliered and cordoned fruit trees.

TRELLISWORK

Trellis is much more than just a support for plants. Trompe l'oeil *designs add wit and interest to plain expanses of wall (opposite above and opposite center). Trellis can also be attached to free-standing copper pipes or posts and used to support climbing roses and other plants (opposite below). For an urban garden, with little horizontal growing space, trellis provides a vertical extension, acting as a support for potted plants (left).*

ALL FENCED IN

Most people need some means to mark boundaries, either with a neighboring house or between different areas of the garden (overleaf). The style of fencing you choose should reflect and enhance the overall design of your garden: use white painted fencing to contrast with bright flowers, natural wood posts for a country feel, or strongly geometric panels for a look of urban chic.

SUPPORTS AND DIVIDERS

Another type of garden enclosure or room is the arbor. Essentially a seat shaded by a canopy of plants, the arbor always adds a certain mysterious, romantic quality to a garden. As well as its visual impact, there is often the added dimension of the perfume of scented flowers growing overhead. The framework itself can be as simple as you like. Trellis is a good component, but special metal arbor frameworks are also available.

There is great diversity in the materials and methods used to create boundaries in a garden. While there is no need to look for an exact match to the design of your house, some styles of fence and wall will be more appropriate than others. Metal railings, of the kind seen in public parks, are generally better in town situations; stockade fencing and split rail fencing are really for the country. Avoid, if you can,

building walls in cheap stock bricks which never weather; concrete blocks and concrete posts and wire mesh fencing can also be unappetizing. An existing wall which presents this kind of eyesore can be ameliorated either by covering it with trellis or, in the case of a concrete structure, encouraging the growth of lichens and moss.

Semi-transparent boundaries can be made cheaply with trellis, using standard panels secured to posts. Today you can buy spiked steel socket-type supports which make the job of sinking posts much easier. Inspiration for other types of wooden or panel fencing can be taken from the Japanese, who excel at Mondrian-type arrangements of panels and screens using bamboo uprights and woven rush, roughly equivalent to European traditional wattle fencing.

Wall building is an art in itself. There are many intriguing and inspiring examples: stone inset with flints, shells, pebbles, or bottle ends; dry stone walling; brick walls built with spaces to let air and views through; walls made of logs and driftwood. It is a good idea, if you are building a wall from scratch, to leave pockets so that plants can be grown on the vertical face. Alyssum, thrift, aubrieta, campanula, and other rock plants will grow in cornices, wall pockets and on tops of dry stone walling.

Hedges are the living boundaries in a garden, easy on the eye, good at creating windbreaks and relatively simple to maintain. As far as types are concerned, there are many alternatives to the ubiquitous privet. Box (although slow-growing), beech, yew, and hawthorn all make excellent and attractive hedges.

ARBORS

Structures which provide a support for climbing and trailing plants also make ideal locations for garden seats, creating a shady, scented retreat from which to view the garden. Aesthetically, an arbor also provides contrast of light and shade which is so important in giving depth and definition to a layout.

WALK-THROUGH PERGOLA

In a small garden, a pergola, or framework for climbing plants, makes an architectural addition which gives focus to the entire layout, especially when centrally positioned. In a larger garden, a pergola can be extended further to create a proper walkway, a semi-enclosed space to contrast with the open areas of lawn and flowerbed. This particular design can be adapted to vary the length as required, but would not really be effective if made any shorter than three units long.

The structure and the dimensions of the pergola are based around standard trellis panels, which are much cheaper than any you could make for the purpose.

The easiest way to assemble the structure is to construct the top frame first, adding the struts to make the pyramid roof afterwards. Then the position of the posts, or uprights, can be marked out on the ground where you want the pergola to go and metal shoes or spiked steel supports driven in.

The final stage is to cover the outside of the structure with trellis. When viewed from the side, the trellis wall appears to be continuous, but, because the trellis is affixed to alternate bays, you will get glimpses of the garden as you walk through. As a plain, undressed structure with no covering of plants the pergola has its own attractions, especially when painted a strong positive color. To support climbing plants over the roof, simply staple wire around the pyramids.

WALK-THROUGH PERGOLA

The light and airy framework of this pergola can be built over a garden path to form a covered walkway of colorful and sweet-scented climbing plants trained over the easy-to-make, but distinctive, trellis and wire-covered framework. Good plants to use include clematis, especially the small-flowered species such as *C. montana* and *C. armandii*, climbing hydrangea (*H. petiolaris*), sweet-scented plants such as jasmine and honeysuckle, and wisteria. The many varieties of ivy are quickly established, although they can be difficult to contain; instead, you could try ornamental grape vines, the leaves of which turn to spectacular colors in the fall.

The "roof" is a series of simple pyramids on a wooden framework which is affixed on top of fence posts held upright by hammer-in steel fence post supports. Training wires for climbing plants are stapled around the pyramids, and trellis panels are attached at the sides between the post supports.

Trellis panels (lattice) usually come in 72in (1830mm) widths, and in heights of 24in (600mm), 36in (900mm) and 48in (1220mm). For this project, the panels are turned to give a height of 72in (1830mm) and a width of 48in (1220mm).

The size of the trellis panels also determines the dimensions of the pergola – ours is 48in (1220mm) wide, and the posts are spaced 48in (1220mm) apart. It is best to keep these measurements the same so that the "base" to each pyramid is a square, ensuring that the struts are in proportion to the main frame. The height of the posts is 6ft 6in (2m) which means that the trellising is raised off the ground 6in (150mm). We have only fixed trellising to alternate bays, but this is simply for effect. Our pergola is four bays long, but this is variable and you can have more or fewer bays, according to your requirements.

All wood used is sawn and preservative-treated softwood, as used for fencing.

PYRAMID ROOF STRUCTURE

The series of pyramids that form the "roof" of the pergola add visual interest to the design. Training wires are stapled around the struts, enabling plants to grow and thrive and to form a "living ceiling."

MATERIALS

Note: All lumber is sawn and preservative-treated softwood

Part	Quantity	Material	Length
LONG RAILS	2	2 × 3in (50 × 75mm)	17ft 3in (5.25m)
CROSS RAILS	5	As above	48in (1200mm)
PYRAMID STRUTS	16	1 × 3in (25 × 75mm)	53in (1350mm)*
POSTS	10	3 × 3in (75 × 75mm)	6ft 6in (2m)
TRELLIS PANELS (LATTICE)	8		72in (1830mm) high × 48in (1200mm)
HAMMER-IN POST SUPPORTS	10		
TRAINING WIRE	1 large coil		
SCREWS		Galvanized steel	2in (50mm) No. 8
STAPLES		Galvanized fencing type	¾in (19mm)

* Approximate length only – measure and cut on site for accuracy

TOOLS

WORKBENCH (fixed or portable)

STEEL MEASURING TAPE

STEEL BENCH RULE

TRY SQUARE

COMBINATION SQUARE

SMALL CROSSCUT SAW (or circular power saw)

BACK SAW

MARKING GAUGE

POWER DRILL

DRILL BIT – approximately ⅛in (3mm) diameter to drill pilot holes for screws

SLEDGE HAMMER

CLAW HAMMER

CHISEL – about 1in (25mm)

MALLET

WALK-THROUGH PERGOLA ASSEMBLY

TRAINING WIRES

PYRAMID STRUT

CROSS RAIL

LONG RAIL

STEEL POST SUPPORT

POST

TRELLIS PANEL

WALK-THROUGH PERGOLA

TOP FRAME

Start by making the top frame on which the "roof" of pyramids is affixed and which will eventually be supported on the vertical posts. The top long rails are made from 2 × 3in (50 × 75mm) sawn and preservative-treated wood, ideally in one full length (that is, if you are making the pergola to the proportions shown in the photograph, the length of four trellis panels plus the five posts of nominal 3in [75mm] width). If it is impossible to buy wood the length required, two shorter lengths can be joined end to end with a simple cross-lap joint (*see* **Techniques, page 400**).

Cut the cross rails to the width required, in our case 53in (1345mm) (the spacing between two posts plus the thickness of the posts).

Mark out the positions of the posts on the long rails to suit the width of the trellis panels, in our case at *internal* intervals of 48in (1220mm). Cut cross-lap joints at the appropriate places on the long rails and at the ends of the cross rails, so that they form end-lap joints on the cross rails at either end (fig. 1) and half-lap joints on the intermediate rails (*see* **Techniques, page 400**). Form the joints so that the long rails are on top.

Screw the joints together through the cross rails from the underside.

PYRAMID ROOF SECTIONS

To work out the exact length of the pyramid struts, measure the diagonal of the base across the frame. Mark this length on a flat floor and strike equal length lines at 45° to this line at either end to give the point of the apex of the pyramid. This gives the lengths of the timber required for the structure forming the pyramid – the measurement should more or less correspond to the length of the cross rails.

Cut the required number of struts slightly overlength and then miter them all at 45° at both ends in opposite directions and to the correct length required.

To assemble, hold two of the struts in a vise so the mitered faces of one end meet. Screw through each side using 2in (50mm) No. 8 galvanized woodscrews (fig. 2).

Hold this frame upright in a workbench and lay a third strut against the joint and pilot drill through at approximately 45° into the other frame (fig. 3). Repeat for the fourth pyramid strut (fig. 4).

Make up the required number of pyramid structures. These are delicate, so handle them carefully.

Place each pyramid on top of the frame already made and screw down into it with a single screw at each corner (fig. 5). Once secured, this is a very strong structure. Repeat for all of the pyramids.

Staple training wires at 6in (150mm) intervals up the pyramids.

AFFIXING THE POSTS AND FINAL ASSEMBLY

Carry the top structure to its final position and use it to mark on the ground the positions of the fence posts. The posts are spaced at internal intervals of 48in (1220mm) so that they coincide with the cross rail positions.

The easiest way to secure the posts is with steel post supports. These are simply hammered into the ground and the posts slotted into sockets at the tops of the supports.

Stretch a string line along the line of the posts. This string line will help you to line up the supports and will also give some idea of levels. Push the tip of the support into the ground and use a carpenter's level to check that it is upright. To drive the support into the ground, a heavy hammer, such as a sledge hammer, will be required. Insert a short length of 3 × 3in (75 × 75mm) wood post into the socket to protect the support from hammer blows, or use a proprietary metal-capped driving tool which should have a handle allowing you to steady the socket and prevent it from twisting as it is hammered in place.

Drive the support into the ground with firm, slow blows of the hammer. At regular intervals, insert a post into the socket and use a carpenter's

---

❶ Joining Top Frame Rails
Frame rails form end lap joints at ends and half lap joints (not shown) at intermediate points.

❷ Joining First Two Struts
Miter ends of struts at 45° and butt cut faces together. *Inset* Affix with screws at oblique angles.

❸ Adding Remaining Struts
Hold frame in a workbench. Screw through from sides of third strut to face of joint; repeat for fourth strut.

❹ Apex of Finished Pyramid
Finished joints form pyramid apex. *Inset* Angled screws attach third and fourth struts to first two struts.

level on two adjacent faces to check that the spike is going in vertically. Adjustments can be made by pulling or twisting the sockets as necessary.

When the supports have been inserted the posts can be fitted. In some designs of post supports, two bolts have to be tightened to clamp the posts in position, while in others the posts are held with large screws. Double-check that the posts are upright and use a length of straight lumber and a carpenter's level to check that the tops of the posts are level. On flat or slightly sloping ground this will be easy to achieve, but on steeply sloping ground it may be acceptable if the tops of the posts follow the slope of the ground. Use a length of string or a long batten to level the post tops which can be trimmed to an even height, if necessary, using a crosscut saw.

The next stage is to install the trellising between the posts (we installed it only to alternate bays of the pergola). Place bricks or blocks on the ground to support the trellis panels about 6in (150mm) from the ground. We used metal clips to hold the panels of trellis in place and the clips are first nailed to the posts so that they are vertical and inset by the same amount – about 1in (25mm). The panels are then lifted into place and a check is made that the horizontal rails of the trellis panels are level. The panels are then secured to the clips using galvanized screws (*see* **Techniques, page 400**).

If required, the trellis panels can be secured directly to the posts. Position and level them as above, then drill through the side frames of the panels so that 3in (75mm) long galvanized fencing nails can be driven through the panels, without splitting them, and into the posts. Three fixings will be required on each side of a 72in (1830mm) high trellis panel.

You will need some help to lift the pyramid roof onto the posts. Adjust the roof so that the vertical posts coincide with the corner and cross rail joints, then nail the frame to the tops of the posts using two 4in (100mm) nails toe-nailed through the top frame and into each post.

❺ Affixing Pyramids to Frame
Screw the pyramids to the top frame using a screw through each corner and into the frame rails.

TRELLIS WITH FALSE PERSPECTIVE

Trellising has varied garden applications. This project goes a stage further and follows the French tradition of using trellis to give blank walls a sense of depth and perspective. The result, although simple to construct, is a memorable and effective exercise in *trompe-l'oeil*. You can adapt this idea to cheer up any featureless expanse of wall or disguise unsympathetic stock brick or concrete block.

Perhaps the easiest project in the book to accomplish, this false-perspective trellis could be assembled without too much trouble during the course of a single afternoon once you have established your required dimensions and perspective.

The first step is to draw up a full-size plan: you can adapt the design shown here to fit your space. A false perspective is generally more effective if you arrange it so there is a contrast with a real view. Incorporating a doorway, as here, or any other kind of opening heightens the element of "hazard and surprise."

The next stage is to nail together slats of wood to make the required design. Bend the nails over and hammer them flat as they go through the back so they will not pull out. If you want a curved arch, you could make the curve out of exterior-grade plywood cut with a saber saw.

This trellis design was painted a pale gray to blend with the lichened wall. Trellis looks very effective painted, but the colors should not be too harsh and bright or the illusory effect will be lost.

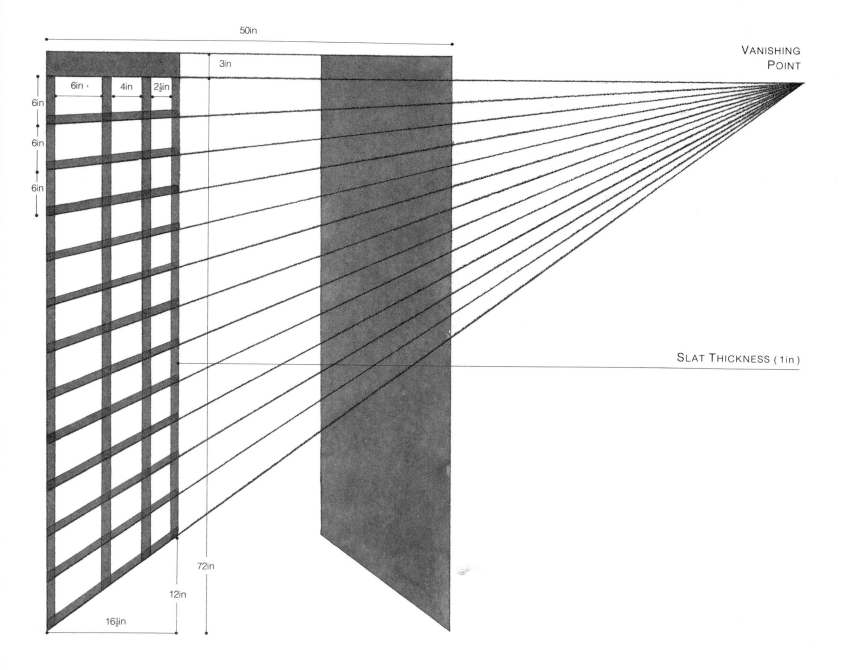

DRAWING UP A PLAN OF THE TRELLIS STRUCTURE

You will need to draw up a full-size plan to calculate the length of the slats and the degree of perspective. The overall height and width shown here are based on the dimensions of the door alongside which we built this project, and can be altered according to the space available.

TRELLIS WITH FALSE PERSPECTIVE

This trellis is constructed so that when it is fixed against a wall, it deceives the eye into believing it is looking at a three-dimensional arch, or a series of three-dimensional arches if several are installed side by side as shown here.

If you fit the trellis around a door or gateway, sizes are dependent on the dimensions of the door. We used three archways alongside a garden door, which has a matching trellis "roof" above it. Our arches are separated by 1 × 3in (25 × 75mm) wooden "posts" beveled at the top. However, the principles of construction are easy to adapt to other sizes and designs according to the size of your garden, the amount of wall space, and personal preference.

A wider batten has also been incorporated at the top to align with the top of the door frame, replacing one of the "normal size" trellis slats, but again this is optional.

The density of the trellis and the amount of perspective incorporated is entirely up to individual taste, but the dimensions here are a good standard to work from.

Obviously, you will need a wall on which to affix the trellis. This need not be a garden boundary wall: it could be a plain wall of the house, or the wall of a garage or outbuilding.

1 **Drawing Up a Plan of the Roof Structure**
Above Draw a line to trellis width. Draw a line perpendicular to center point – top of this line represents apex. Draw in slat thickness, then two sides of triangle. Mark where vertical slats of side panels fall along base and extend lines to center line, parallel with triangle sides. Mark five equally spaced points on each side and join to center of base.

TOOLS

WORKBENCH (fixed or portable)

STEEL MEASURING TAPE

TRY SQUARE

BACK SAW (or saber saw)

CLAW HAMMER

POWER DRILL

DRILL BIT – $\frac{3}{16}$in (4mm)

MASONRY DRILL BIT – $\frac{1}{4}$in (6mm)

SCREWDRIVER

CARPENTER'S LEVEL

MATERIALS

Note: If you experience difficulty buying $\frac{1}{2}$ × 1in (12 × 25mm), you can cut your own slats by ripping down 1 × 8in (25 × 200mm) wood using a circular saw; this will give 16 slats per board if saw blade is not too thick

Part	Quantity	Material	Length
VERTICAL SLATS	8 per trellis arch	$\frac{1}{2}$ × 1in (12 × 25mm) sawn softwood	72in (1800mm)*
CROSS SLATS	As required	As above	As required
ROOF SLATS	As required	As above	As required
TOP BATTEN (optional)	1 per arch	$\frac{1}{2}$ × 3in (12 × 75mm) sawn softwood	50in (1270mm)**
POST	1 between each arch	1 × 3in (25 × 75mm) sawn softwood	As required

* Finished size – cut overlong and then cut to size after nailing (see text for details)

** Length given is width of each trellis arch; top battens can be cut from two shorter lengths of softwood because center section is cut away on assembly

CONSTRUCTION

The easiest way to make this trellis is first to draw up full-size plans on a large, reasonably flat surface such as a garage floor, tables pushed together, or a flat area of concrete, such as a driveway.

You may be able to draw the plan directly onto your flat surface, but it is more likely that you will have to make the drawing on several sheets of paper which can then be taped together to produce a full-size plan. Wherever you construct the trellis, it will be necessary to have enough space for all the pieces to be laid out on this plan and nailed up in place on top of the drawing.

DRAWING UP PLANS

Using our diagrams as a guide, draw up plans for one side of the upright trellis. You need to decide on the height and spaces required. Ours is 72in (1800mm) high, with 12 equal spaces down the outer side, giving 6in (150mm) centers (actually from the base of one slat to the base of the next).

Mark off the width of this one side of trellis; ours is 16¼in (410mm) from the outside edge of the outermost vertical slat to the inside edge of the innermost vertical slat. Two more vertical slats are placed between them to give *internal* spacings of 6in (150mm), 4in (100mm), and 2½in (60mm) respectively.

The innermost vertical slat is only 60in (1500mm) long and is placed 12in (300mm) up from the ground. Join the bottom two points and continue this angled line up until it meets a horizontal line drawn across at the very top. This gives you a vanishing point where the two lines cross. All the other cross lines must converge at this point.

Use a slat to mark off the thickness of all the slats across the width and down the length of the trellis.

Draw up the "roof" section next,

starting with the base line of the triangle. Find the center and draw a vertical line (at exactly 90°) up, 24in (600mm) long, to give the apex of the triangle. Draw in the slat thickness over this center line. Then draw in the outer lines of the triangle.

If you have made this drawing separate from the main trellis, mark off where the vertical slats of the main trellis will fall along the base line. Draw lines from these positions onto the roof section, parallel with the outer lines of the triangle, joining them all at the center line.

Equally space five points along each of the upward-sloping sides of the triangle (giving six equal spaces on each side) and join these points to the center of the base line. Start with the central one, and then space two slats on either side.

Draw in the other slat thicknesses as before, finishing the cross slats at the innermost roof slat (fig. 1).

Use the drawings to measure off for the lengths of slats that will be required (remembering to multiply the number of slats in the vertical structure by two), and then multiply the total by the number of arches required. Add on a little extra to each length to allow for trimming the angles at the ends.

When the slats have been obtained, cut them all to length, again allowing a small surplus to allow for trimming at the ends.

MAKING UP ONE SIDE

Start by laying all the cross slats accurately on the drawing, and then place the vertical slats on top.

Apply a dab of waterproof wood glue at every intersection of the slats, then affix by driving an annular threaded nail through each intersection. If you are nailing up on a workbench, a good way to hold the slats firm while nailing is to drive nails temporarily into the bench at all corners, where the slats cross each other. Make up the required number of trellis frames.

MAKING UP OPPOSITE SIDE

Turn over the first side of trellis panel, then draw around it onto the worksurface to give a mirror image of the plan. Make up the required number of trellis frames to this pattern in the same way as before.

MAKING UP THE ROOF

The roof is made in the same way as the side panels. Position the cross slats on the plan, and then place the long parallel slats on top. Glue and nail the intersections.

FINISHING OFF

Saw the protruding ends of the slats flush with the edges of the frames.

Prepare the "posts" and the top battens. In the latter case, the center section will be cut out on assembly, so you could use two offcuts for these pieces, rather than a batten the full width of the trellis arch.

Ideally, you should use preservative-treated timber. If not, at this stage treat the whole trellis with a water-repellent preservative. The finished trellis is painted with three coats of microporous paint, or one coat of exterior primer and two coats of exterior gloss paint.

AFFIXING THE TRELLIS

If the trellis is going to support climbing plants, spacers must be inserted between it and the wall so that plants can twine behind the trellis. Otherwise, the trellis can be screwed directly to the wall.

Position a post against the wall, and use a carpenter's level to check it is vertical. Drill clearance holes for two screws through the post and allow the drill tip to mark the wall. Remove the post and, using a masonry bit, drill the holes for the anchors. Insert the anchors, then drive galvanized screws through the post and into the plugs. The screws should penetrate the wall by about 1½in (38mm).

Affix the adjacent side panel and, using an offcut of top batten as a spacer, fit the roof section, then the next post, then the next roof trellis, then the next post, and so on right across. After this, add the other side trellises, with lengths of top batten, if required, attached between the top of the side panels and the undersides of the roof panels.

② Nailing the Trellis
Lay cross slats on plan, then position vertical slats above them. Glue and nail through intersections.

HEXAGONAL ARBOR

An arbor makes a distinctive feature in any garden, displaying climbing plants to great advantage and exposing them to optimum conditions of light and air. Arbors are often all-metal structures, but this simple but elegant framework makes use of ordinary copper tubing and plain wooden rustic posts, readily available from most garden centers. The construction process is fairly quick and easy to do.

The three sections of copper tubing (which have been rubbed with plumbers' flux to give them a green color) are cut to precisely the same length and bent into shape using a curved piece of plywood or particleboard as a form. Holes are drilled about 6in (150mm) apart along the tubes. Thin green plastic-covered wires are threaded through the holes to make a support for the plants.

As is the case with all posts that need to go into the ground, it is much easier to use spiked steel supports with sockets. The metal spikes are readily driven into the ground and the end of the post can be dropped into the shoe and held in place.

The uprights and cross rails must be treated with a preservative and the resulting dark brown makes a pleasing contrast with the greenish copper.

HEXAGONAL ARBOR

This arbor is made from six preservative-treated rustic poles set into the ground at equal intervals and joined by cross rails, with a dome above made from copper tubing. If you brush the tubing with plumbers' flux, a green patina will result. Garden wire is fed around the tubing as a support for climbing plants.

WOODEN FRAME

The height of the frame can be varied slightly. However, the poles should not be less than about 6ft 6in (2m) above ground, otherwise some people may hit their heads on the cross rails; and, for stability, the poles should not be much higher above ground than 8ft (2.5m).

PREPARING THE SITE

Choose a flat site and, using pegs and string lines, mark out the hexagonal shape (fig. 1) for the positions. The posts are spaced at 39in (1000mm) centers, with 6ft 6in (2m) between any two opposite posts. It is essential that the post positions are accurately marked.

Dig 24in (600mm) deep holes for the posts. This can be done using a narrow spade or, if available, a posthole digger which is driven into the ground and then removed to deposit excavated earth. Fill the bottom 6in (150mm) of each hole with gravel to ensure good drainage and prevent the bottoms of the posts from rotting.

MAKING THE FRAME

Make up six L-shapes comprising a post and a cross rail as follows.

Position two posts in neighboring holes and wedge them vertically. Measure the internal distance between them and add 2in (50mm) to allow for shaping the ends of the cross rails. Remove the posts.

Use a saber saw to make a curved cut in the ends of the cross rails so that they fit against the post sides. Alternatively, use a hand saw to cut out V-shapes in the cross rails.

At the top of each post, draw 60° angles as a guide to aligning the cross rails (fig. 2, below). Continue the lines to the opposite sides of the post as a guide for the dowel affixing positions. Cut the doweling into 6in (150mm) lengths.

Lay one post on a flat piece of ground. Position a cross rail against the post and drill through the post and into the rail to accept the dowel (fig. 3). At least 2in (50mm) of dowel should enter the rail. Fit the dowel using waterproof wood adhesive. Repeat to make five more L-shapes.

ERECTING THE FRAME

Position two posts in their holes and align the cross rail that falls between them with both posts. Use a straight edge and a carpenter's level to align the posts – if necessary, add or take away a little of the gravel in the base of the hole. Drill through the "free" post into the end of the cross rail to align with the angles marked on the top. Join the "free" post to the cross rail with a length of dowel as you did before (fig. 3).

Continue to join up the L-shaped sections in the same way, checking that the tops of the posts are all at the same height, and then saw off any protruding dowel ends flush with the posts.

MATERIALS

Part	Quantity	Material	Length
POSTS	6	3–4in (75–100mm) diameter treated rustic poles	7ft 8in (2.4m)
CROSS RAILS	6	2–3in (50–75mm) diameter treated rustic poles	As required
DOME BARS	3	$\frac{7}{8}$in (22mm) diameter copper tubing	As required

Also required: Approximately 6ft 6in (2m) of $\frac{1}{2}$in (12mm) diameter hardwood doweling

TOOLS

WORKBENCH (fixed or portable)

SPADE or POST-HOLE DIGGER

PANEL SAW

CARPENTER'S LEVEL

STEEL BENCH RULE

SABER SAW

POWER DRILL

HAMMER

SCREWDRIVER

PLIERS

HACKSAW

CLAMPS

SHOVEL

1 Drawing up a Ground Plan
Posts are spaced 39in (1000mm) apart: mark center and strike off 39in (1000mm) lines at 60° angles.

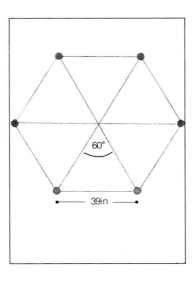

2 Shaping the Cross Rails
Angle ends of rails to fit around posts. Use saber saw for curve or make V-cuts with crosscut saw.

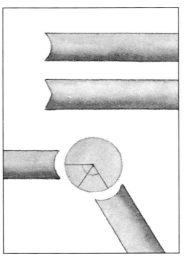

3 Affixing the Cross Rails
Drill holes through posts into cross rails. Insert dowels to affix in place. Angled screw holds dowel in place.

To secure the joints, use a 3in (75mm) screw inserted diagonally through each cross rail (fig. 3).

Finally, tie a length of garden wire around the top of the posts, holding it in place on each post using 1½in (38mm) staples. To make the wire taut, twist the two ends together using pliers.

THE DOME

Draw a semi-circle on a large sheet of plywood or particleboard (fig. 4) using a pencil and a piece of string to act as a compass. This will mark out the section of the dome. When this is done, mark off at 6in (150mm) centers for the positions of holes through which training wires will later be threaded.

Use a piece of ¾in (19mm) particleboard or plywood to make a form for bending the tube into shape. Trace the curve onto the form and cut it out using a saber saw.

BENDING THE TUBE

Cut the copper tubing to length using a hacksaw. Our tubes were 10ft 4in (3.14m) long. Since the copper will need to be bent a little tighter than the arc, bring it down about 1½in (38mm) at each end.

Clamp the form to a workbench or table and start to bend the piece of tube around it. You will need someone to help you with this: each person should exert a little pressure until the tubing is bent to follow the shape of the form. If you find that the ends lose their shape then you can use a ⅞in (22mm) internal pipe bending spring.

Lay the bent tube on the original dome profile and mark off the 6in (150mm) spacings onto the tube. Drill ⅛in (3mm) diameter holes through the tubing at these marks.

Bend the other two tubes to the shape of the form and then drill the holes as before. Always mark off the spacings on the tubing against the original dome profile.

ASSEMBLING THE DOME

Mark the middle point of each tube, then hammer it flat so that you can drill a ¼in (6mm) diameter hole through each piece (fig. 5). Bolt the three pieces together.

Next, drill a 1in (25mm) diameter hole, 2in (50mm) deep in the center of the top of each post.

The dome can now be lifted onto the top of the posts and the tube ends located in the holes (fig. 6). There is sufficient movement in the structure to enable the dome to be positioned.

Thread garden wire through each row of holes, tying each length securely in place.

To affix the dome to the rustic poles, drill straight through the tube horizontally above each post and slip a 2in (50mm) nail through.

Finally make up a dryish concrete mix of five parts sand to one part cement and pour it into each hole along with some small pieces of stone. Tamp it down, then shape it into a concave collar so that rain water will drain away.

4 **Dome Section and Form**
Mark off 6in (150mm) spacings on semi-circle. Transfer section of curve to plywood to make form.

5 **Affixing the Dome**
Flatten out tops of the pieces of tubing, drill a ¼in (6mm) diameter hole through them and bolt together.

6 **Affixing Dome to Posts**
Drill a hole centrally in the top of each post. Slot dome into post and drive nail through tubing.

HEXAGONAL ARBOR ASSEMBLY

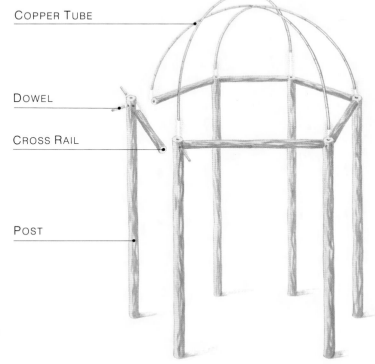

COPPER TUBE

DOWEL

CROSS RAIL

POST

BEANSTICK FENCE

New fencing can look rather harsh and brash and hedges, even when composed of the most quick-growing species, are unfortunately not instant solutions to the problem of garden enclosure. This bean-stick fence was designed to provide a more natural-looking boundary than the standard commercial wood fencing; almost, in fact, a "man-made hedge." The look is reminiscent of the traditional wattle fence; another source of inspiration was the type of wonderful screens and panels seen in Japanese gardens and walk-ways. Here the effect is created by combining a strong rectilinear framework with the natural, random texture supplied by the beansticks.

The fence is very easy to make. The beansticks are trapped in the sawn frame, held in place in two grooves made top and bottom between the top rails and a couple of battens between the bottom rails. The sticks are cut to the same length, slotted into the groove and pushed up together.

The sticks themselves do not need to be treated, although the ends could be dipped in preservative to prolong their life. If sticks do become broken or damaged, it is easy to replace them.

This fence, formal enough for a front yard, would also be a good choice for a new house where the planting had not yet had a chance to become established. The beansticks are sufficiently firm and resilient to be animal-proof but chinks of light lend it a lively and varied effect.

BEANSTICK FENCE

This rustic-looking fence is an ideal project if you want your boundary to look just a bit different from those of your neighbors. It is made from beansticks secured between a frame of sawn and preservative-treated wood. This can be left in its natural state, it can be stained a darker wood color, or it can be painted as shown in our example – microporous paint is ideal for covering the wood, being easy to apply without a primer, and easy to re-paint in future as the need arises.

It is unlikely that you will be able to buy the beansticks from a lumber-yard. More likely sources are either from fencing suppliers or from garden centers.

Cutting of the beansticks is done in winter and early spring, and this is the best time to obtain the sticks. You will need large numbers for this project, and it is a good idea to buy one or two bundles of sticks to start with to see what proportion of the fence they cover. Then you will be able to put in an order for a quantity to cover the full length of the fence you will be making.

The spacing of the posts depends on the length of the rails you will be using. Rails must be joined at post positions, so if you have 10ft (3m) rails, posts must be spaced 60in (1500mm) apart. For 8ft (2.4m) rails, the post spacing will be 48in (1200mm). Once this is decided, you will be able to work out how many posts are required.

You also need to decide on the height of the posts. Our fence is about 40in (1000mm) high, and in this case the posts are 60in (1500mm) long which allows 20in (500mm) of post to be in the ground. A good rule is to allow a minimum of 20in (500mm) of post in the ground, or one third of the fence height, whichever is greater.

Alternatively, you can fit the posts into metal spike post supports which are simply hammered into the ground. The posts fit into sockets in the tops of the spike supports. In this case, 24in (600mm) long spikes are suitable for fences up to 48in (1200mm); for fences up to 72in (1800mm) high use 30in (760mm) long post supports.

The metal post supports are driven into the ground with a scrap of loose-fitting fence post in the socket to protect the socket from sledge hammer blows, keeping a check with a carpenter's level on all sides of the socket that the spike is going straight into the ground. You will also be able to push on the spike to correct any tendency for it to go into the ground out of plumb (vertical) Stretch a horizontal string line along the line of the proposed fence to ensure the metal spikes are driven into the ground in line and to the same height.

If you do not use metal post spikes, it is possible on soft ground to sharpen the ends of the posts into spikes and simply hammer them into the ground. However, using this method usually makes it difficult to get the posts absolutely in line and vertical, and it is better to dig a hole for each post using a metal post-hole digger, which can be rented. This hand-operated tool removes a plug of soil to leave a neat circular hole about 9in (225m) in diameter, and up to 24in (600mm) deep.

Posts can then be stood in the holes, lined up against a string line, and their heights adjusted to bring them all level by packing the holes as necessary. The posts are held upright by ramming gravel around them, and finally topping off with a collar of concrete around the post at ground level to throw rain-water clear of the post.

PREPARING AND AFFIXING POSTS

If you decide to point the posts to drive them into the ground (see above), the joints can then be cut with the posts in position. In all other cases it is better and easier to cut the joints with the post on a bench.

Hold a side rail flush with the top of the post and mark its depth on the post. Repeat for the other side of the post, and notch out 1in (25mm) wide recesses to the depth of the rails at the top of each post (fig. 1).

Position the posts by either dropping them into metal post support sockets or setting them into the ground, adjusting them to the same height. Place a long, straight batten across the post tops or post support sockets and use a carpenter's level to check that they are level.

If using metal post supports, screw or clamp the post bottoms into the supports. If placing posts in holes in the ground, pack around them with gravel and a concrete collar. Double check that all posts are in line, that they are vertical, and that the tops are level.

AFFIXING TOP RAILS

Anchor the top rails to the posts using two lag screws each side.

If it is necessary to join two rails, cut the rails to coincide with a post position and make a spliced joint (fig. 2). To maintain the strength of the fence, you should have only one spliced joint per post, staggering them from side to side.

At the fence ends, cut the rails flush with the edge of the post.

TOOLS

WORKBENCH (fixed or portable)

STEEL MEASURING TAPE

TRY SQUARE

SMALL CROSSCUT SAW (or circular saw)

TREE-PRUNING SAW

HAMMER

DRILL (hand or power)

DRILL BIT – $\frac{1}{4}$in (6mm)

WRENCH

CARPENTER'S LEVEL

CHISEL

MALLET

BILLHOOK (or ax or sharp knife)

MATERIALS

Part	Quantity	Material	Length
POSTS	As required	3 × 3in (75 × 75mm) sawn and treated softwood	As required*
RAILS	As required	1 × 3in (25 × 75mm) sawn and treated softwood	As required
BATTENS	As required	1 × 1¼in (25 × 32mm) sawn and treated softwood	As required
CAPPING BOARD	As required	1½ × 3in (38 × 75mm) sawn and treated softwood	As required
BEANSTICKS	As required	Hazel, birch, or chestnut	As required

* Post length will depend on the height of the fence and whether you are inserting posts into the ground or into metal spike post supports

AFFIXING BOTTOM RAILS

The bottom rails are screwed to the outsides of the posts about 6in (150mm) up from ground level. Install a lag screw at one end of the rail, and use a carpenter's level to get the rail level before drilling and screwing the other end into another post. Use two lag screws per post, and make spliced joints if necessary to coincide with post positions.

Measure the distance between the posts and cut pieces of $1 \times 1\frac{1}{4}$in (25×32mm) roofing batten to fit snuggly between them (fig. 3). Fit the battens inside the bottom rails, flush with the top edge, with the narrower edge toward the rails. Drive four galvanized screws through the bottom rails and into each batten. The battens create a gap about $\frac{1}{2}$in (12mm) wide between the bottom rails.

Repeat all along the fence.

If you plan to paint or stain the frame of the fence, do this now.

INSTALLING BEANSTICKS

Measure the distance from the top of the top rail to the bottom of the bottom rail, and cut all the beansticks to this length. They will tend to clog the saw teeth, so use a tree-pruning saw for this job.

Use a billhook, ax, or sharp knife to sharpen one end of each of the beansticks so that they wedge into the gap between the battens.

Starting at one end, feed the sticks in through the gap at the top of the frame and wedge them into the gap at the bottom, bunching them tightly until the frame is filled.

Trim all the beansticks flush with the top of the top rails. Press each stick down firmly as you cut it.

Finally, nail the capping board along the top of the fence, making sure it covers the edges of the top rails. If you cannot buy a capping board, you can cut one from a length of sawn wood. Paint or stain it to match the fence frame.

BEANSTICK FENCE ASSEMBLY

CAPPING BOARD

LAG SCREWS

BATTENS

BOTTOM SIDE RAIL

POST

TOP SIDE RAIL

BEANSTICKS

SECTION VIEW

❶ Affixing Top Rails
Notch out 1in (25mm) recesses to depth of side rail on sides of post at top. Screw rails to post.

❷ Joining Lengths of Rail
Join rails at post positions, if necessary, cutting rails at an angle to form spliced joint.

❸ Affixing Beansticks
Sharpen one end of stick to a point and feed through top to wedge between bottom rail battens.

PART 9

CONTAINERS

Every year at Versailles, it takes the army to bring in the lemon and orange trees for the winter, hundreds of planted tubs comprising what must be the ultimate container garden. Container gardening is not usually on such a grand scale, but in every garden there is a place for at least some plants in pots, whether a pair of bay trees in formal tubs flanking an entrance, a collection of simple terracotta bowls tumbling with flowers, or cheerful hanging baskets providing a splash of summer color.

The versatility of container gardening is one of its main advantages: you can match plants exactly to their soil requirements, and place them where they will look most effective. If the container is not too large, you can move it to a position of prominence when the plant is in bloom. Planters and window boxes are excellent woodworking projects, allowing you to tailor-make your containers to suit their location exactly. If you use the same type of containers inside and out, group pots around entrances, on either side of French doors and on window sills you will create views which will help to dissolve the boundary between your house and the garden.

CONTAINERS

There are many advantages to gardening in containers. Usually, little or no weeding is required, which saves considerable maintenance time for people with only a few hours to spare. Compost and soil can be tailored to the precise needs of the plant, enabling a far greater range of species to be grown in the same location. Plants can also be arranged to suit the demands of the garden design, or to give shape to a flat landscape. You can also furnish an area with plants which might otherwise be barren, such as in the dry shade under a tree or on a roof.

Some plants positively flourish in containers. Figs, for example, like to be contained; a considerable number of other species can live undisturbed for many years in pots. Growing untidy and invasive herbs, such as mint, in containers also benefits the rest of the garden.

If containers provide a quick and easy way of creating a garden, they are also flexible enough to accommodate and express a whole range of garden styles. Containers are often associated with formal garden designs. Symmetrical arrangements of tubs, clipped box in painted wooden planters, and stone urns at the end of walkways or in the center of radiating beds are all ways of using containers to emphasize the geometry or architectural quality of a garden design.

However, containers can also be delightfully informal. Mediterranean gardens and terraces often feature large terracotta pots carefully positioned to make punctuation points in the overall design. In many Italian and Greek villages, painted and planted oil cans crowd windowsills and balconies, adding a jolt of color to the elevations of houses. Window boxes or hanging baskets spilling over with vivid geraniums and lobelia also work well in country locations or cottage-style gardens.

POTS OF PLANTS

Container gardening is flexible and provides an instant garden for a small space. Tubs or pots flanking an entrance are a common feature of formal garden designs, but can work well combined with less structured planting (above left). A variety of species can be grown in containers; you can train climbers to grow up purpose-built trellis from a tub (above) and even grow small trees (right).

CONTAINERS

Whatever the overall style of the garden, containers should be used in a positive way. Place them to create a focal point, in the center of planting, or arrange a series of pots asymmetrically to lead the eye on through the garden. Containers can also introduce changes of height if they are placed on top of a wall or hung from the side of a house, an important consideration if the rest of the garden is fairly flat. You can also delineate an enclosed area or patio with a row of pots or planters, or make a special feature of an entrance by flanking it with a pair of tubs.

Wherever possible, mass containers in groups for increased effect, rather than dot them about the garden where their impact will be lost. You can group pots on metal garden staging which looks very attractive positioned at either side of a door, or adopt one solution seen on a French roadside, where the entire length of a garden wall was lined in shelves, set about 18in (45cm) apart, on which were arranged dozens of planted pots.

Plants should be massed in much the same way, although filling a container with a single variety is often more effective than a careful composition of a small amount of different species. Wooden boxes simply planted with box and ivy provide a graphic line of green at the window and require little maintenance to remain attractive and flourishing.

As far as the container itself is concerned, material, size, and style vary tremendously. Wherever possible, keep to natural materials – stone, wood, and terracotta all look marvelous and age in a sympathetic way. Metal containers, especially when made of lead, zinc, or copper, can be attractive and even rubber – in the form of old tractor tires – can be effective, contributing textural interest. Avoid plastic: it always looks glaringly out of place in a garden; its harshness

seems to stem from the fact that, unlike everything else, it does not weather or change, and usually has no texture.

In terms of size, choose containers which are on the generous side. Small pots will be overlooked and tend to have a prissy appearance which is at odds with the robust and striking effects you should be trying to create.

Ready-made containers include a range of plain terracotta shapes from urns to shallow bowls, from traditional flowerpots to troughs. Simple reconstituted stone containers can also look good, particularly if you encourage a little weathering. Wooden planters and tubs available commercially can be customized by staining or painting them to blend in with your house or to make a vivid color accent. Wooden containers are also, of course, a natural choice and suit a variety of different applications. A wooden tub is an excellent container home for small trees and shrubs, and half a wooden barrel is a classic. Wooden troughs or planters also make excellent raised beds, a practical and enjoyable way of gardening for older people or those with limited physical strength. Planting does not necessarily have to be at a low level in a container: a pyramid of bamboo sticks tied together and placed in a pot and planted with scarlet-flowering runner beans is a colorful and lovely sight!

One of the most appealing features of container gardening is the scope for improvization and humor in the choice of container. In this area, more than any other, there is great opportunity for creative salvage. Everything from half-barrels to old watering cans can be used as a plant container. Old sinks, wash tubs, chimney pots, and stone troughs can all be recycled to great effect, and architectural salvage yards can be a tremendous source of objects in this respect.

POTTED PLANTS

One of the most important advantages of container gardening is its ability to establish a visual connection between the house and garden. The current popularity of the conservatory bears out the common desire of people to include a sense of the outdoors in their homes. An array of the same type of containers can be used indoors and outside to create views that dissolve the boundary between house and garden.

COMPOST BIN AND PLANTER

The compost bin and planter are very similar in construction, made from rough-sawn boards affixed to posts. The simple nature of the design and lack of precision required in the finishing mean that these two structures offer a good means of practicing your woodworking skills and gaining the confidence to move on to more elaborate projects.

A compost bin is an invaluable asset for the gardener, providing a supply of rich organic matter which makes all the differ-ence to the way plants grow. At the same time, recycling your garden and kitchen waste is environmentally beneficial and economically sound.

The front posts of the bin are doubled up, making a slot where boards can be dropped into place as the pile builds up, or easily removed as the compost is taken out. It is worth buying "pressure treated" wood – compost is both hot and wet, so the wood needs the maximum degree of protection.

The planter provides a support for young trees, many of which either blow over or suffer from "windrock," instabi-lity of the root structure where growth stops and starts rather than proceeding at an even pace. The cross supports enable the trunk to be secured firmly in place while the tree becomes established.

The planter is painted with a coat of black tar to preserve the wood. Lag screws are used to bolt the boards to the uprights, giving a smart finishing touch.

COMPOST BIN

The principle of construction for the compost bin is the same as for the planter (pages 383–385). It is made from fencing-quality sawn and preservative-treated lumber.

The size of the bin can be varied to suit the site, but it should not be too large, since air will not be able to get to the center of the heap, hindering the production of good garden compost.

Our bin is about 36in (915mm) square. The height can also be altered according to your own requirements, but you should work in multiples of $5\frac{1}{2}$in (137mm) – the depth of the 6in (150mm) boards after they have been planed – plus an allowance for ventilation gaps between the boards. Our bin is about 39in (990mm) high. Bear in mind that you want a height at which it will be comfortable to tip garden waste into the bin. Also, the heap does not want to be too high or you will not be able to climb onto the heap to tread down the waste material. Opinion varies on the optimum size for ventilation gaps; we suggest $\frac{1}{2}$–$\frac{3}{4}$in (12–19mm).

CONSTRUCTION

Cut all of the components to the lengths specified in the Materials chart below. The posts are left long and are cut down to size after the boards have been affixed to allow for the ventilation gaps between the boards. The bin is held together with lag screws, and C-clamps are useful for holding the boards squarely in place while they are being attached. The lag screw heads are a decorative feature of this compost bin, and it is important that they line up with each other and are the same distance in from the corners.

At the front of the bin, the only fixed board is at the bottom. The other retainer boards slot into the groove between the posts and are built up to the height required. They are therefore easily removed to gain access to the bin contents when the time comes to fork out the rotted compost.

MATERIALS

Note: All lumber is sawn and preservative-treated softwood

Part	Quantity	Material	Length
"LONG" BOARDS	9	1 × 6in (25 × 150mm)	36in (915mm)
"MIDDLE" BOARDS	6	As above	35in (890mm)
"SHORT" BOARDS	4	As above	34in (856mm)
RETAINER BOARDS	6*	As above	As above
POSTS	6	2 × 2in (50 × 50mm)	48in (1220mm)
LAG SCREWS	100	Galvanized steel	$\frac{5}{16}$ × 2in (8 × 50mm)

* Cut 7 retainer boards if you want the boards at the front to be level with the boards at the side and back

TOOLS

WORKBENCH (fixed or portable)
STEEL MEASURING TAPE
STEEL BENCH RULE
TRY SQUARE
SMALL CROSSCUT SAW (or circular power saw)
MARKING GAUGE
POWER DRILL
DRILL BIT – approximately 6mm ($\frac{1}{4}$in) diameter to drill pilot holes for lag screws
WRENCH
ONE PAIR OF C-CLAMPS

1 Securing the First Board to the Posts
A "short" length of board is secured to the two posts flush and square with the ends to form the bottom row of the back of the bin. Two lag screws at each end hold it in place.

2 Adding the Side Posts and First Retainer Board
A "long" board at both sides is screwed in place, flush with the ends of the posts. The first retainer board rests against the back of the front posts and is later screwed to the posts from behind.

COMPOST BIN ASSEMBLY

POST

MIDDLE LENGTH BOARD

LONG LENGTH BOARD

FIRST RETAINER BOARD

LONG LENGTH BOARD

SHORT LENGTH BOARD

MIDDLE LENGTH BOARD

LONG LENGTH BOARD

LAG SCREWS

VENTILATION GAP

LAG SCREW

POST

POST

LONG

MIDDLE

SHORT

PLAN VIEW

COMPOST BIN

SQUARING THE FIRST ROW

Start to form the back of the bin by laying two of the posts on a flat surface. Then lay a "short" length of board across them flush with the bottom ends of the posts, so the outer edges of the posts are 34in (865mm) apart (fig. 1, page 380).

Check that the board is square to one of the posts, then clamp it to the post. Drill pilot holes for two lag screws and insert the screws to affix the board to the post.

Use a second board at the other end of the posts to ensure that they are square to the "short" length of board, then double-check that the post is square to the first board using a try square. Drill pilot holes for the two lag screws to be inserted into the other end of the first board, the same distance in as the lag screws at the other end.

Stand the frame upright and place a "long" board along the side, flush with the post, and secure it to the post with a C-clamp. Pilot drill and screw it to the post using two lag screws centered on the post.

Repeat for the other side with another "long" length of board.

Place another post inside this board flush with the end, check that it is square at the top using another "long" board, and screw into the post through the side board using two lag screws as before.

Take a retainer board and place it on the inside of the front posts (fig. 2, page 380).

BUILDING UP THE ROWS OF BOARDS

Place spacing blocks or a spacing batten about $\frac{1}{2}$–$\frac{3}{4}$in (12–19mm) thick on top of the back board, then lay a "long" length of board across the top (fig. 1). Check that it protrudes an equal distance beyond the outside edges of both the posts, then affix it in place with two lag screws at each end as before. For neatness, make sure that the lag screws line up with those on the board in the row below.

Repeat the process with one "middle" length board on each side; these should both fit flush with the ends of the back board.

Continue working in this way, one row at a time so that the back boards run alternately with "short"/"long" lengths, and the sides with "long"/"middle" lengths to the height required. Ours is six boards high plus spaces.

As you work it is important to check that the structure is square by holding a spare board at the top flush with the posts each time a new board is added.

THE FRONT

With the bottom board at the front, screw through into the back of the front posts using two lag screws at each end.

Place the final two posts in position behind the lag screw heads, leaving at least a $\frac{1}{2}$–$\frac{3}{4}$in (12–19mm) gap from the front board to create a slot in which the retainers will be a very loose fit. Hold a post in position on the side boards using a C-clamp, then mark a vertical line on the outside of the boards for the lag screw positions (fig. 3).

Screw through each board into the post from the outside using two lag screws per board. Repeat for the post on the other side.

Drop the retainer boards into the slots created by the two posts on each side, building the retainers up to the height required. If you want the retainers to finish level with the boards at the sides and back, rip cut the top one to size.

Finally, cut off the tops of the posts so that they are flush with the top edges of the boards.

Place the bin in an appropriate site away from general view. Almost all types of organic matter can be used for producing compost, although anything too bulky should be avoided because it will slow down the rate at which composting takes place. Similarly, large quantities of leaves also tend to slow the process, and are best kept to decompose separately. Farmyard manure, on the other hand, will accelerate production, and it is a good idea to add a layer of manure or proprietary compost accelerator to your bin every 5–8in (125–200mm). Climate will affect when your compost will be ready.

---

1 Building Up the Rows of Boards
Use spacing blocks or a spacing batten to allow for ventilation gaps when affixing subsequent boards to the back and sides. Alternate "short" and "long" boards at the back, "long" and "middle" boards at the sides.

2 Back Corner Detail
Saw the posts so they are flush with top boards. Note that lag screws line up for a neat appearance.

3 Forming the Front Slot
A second post each side is screwed 1½in (38mm) behind front posts and retainer boards drop in place.

Planter

This planter allows you to grow trees, roses, shrubs, and other flowers where normally you would not be able to, such as on a paved patio or on a concrete path or driveway. The planter is made from fencing-quality sawn and preservative-treated wood. Since the finished planter would be too heavy to lift, there is no need for a floor panel – the planter is placed where required, the planting compost is added and the tree or shrub is planted. There is normally room for other plants around the edge, which will enhance your display.

The size of these planters can be varied according to your specific needs – ours is 30in (760mm) square and 30in (760mm) high, which is good for medium-size trees. For smaller shrubs and flowers you can make smaller planters, and if these are of a size that will still be light enough to move when planted, then it is worth putting a floor panel in the planter so that you can reposition it at will (*see* **Making a Floor Panel, page 385**).

The corner posts are extended upward and are joined at the top by two cross pieces which form a useful tree support. Omit the cross pieces and cut shorter posts if making a smaller model just for plants. The planter is held together with lag screws, and it is important that these neatly align with each other.

POSTS – CUTTING THE TOP JOINTS

Cut the corner posts to length, and then use the clean sawn end of the post to mark out the top joint for housing the cross supports. Place the edge of a length of 1 × 3in (25 × 75mm) lumber (cut from 1 × 6in [25 × 150mm]) centrally on the post end at a 45° angle and mark its position (fig. 1).

Place the cross support $\frac{1}{8}$in (3mm) down from the top of the post, ensure it is at right angles, and mark off the bottom edge. Square around on all four faces, then mark lines down the sides of the post from those drawn at the top.

Cut down the marked lines on each side of the post with a back saw and use a coping saw to remove the center section.

Repeat for other three posts.

TOOLS

WORKBENCH (fixed or portable)

STEEL MEASURING TAPE

STEEL BENCH RULE

TRY SQUARE

COMBINATION SQUARE – for marking 45° angles

SMALL CROSSCUT SAW (or circular power saw)

BACK SAW (or power saber saw)

COPING SAW

MARKING GAUGE

POWER DRILL

DRILL BIT – approximately 6mm ($\frac{1}{4}$in) diameter to drill pilot holes for lag screws

WRENCH

ONE PAIR OF C-CLAMPS

HAMMER – if fitting floor panel

MATERIALS

Note: All lumber is sawn and preservative-treated softwood

Part	Quantity	Material	Length
"LONG" BOARDS	10	1 × 6in (25 × 150mm)	30in (760mm)
"SHORT" BOARDS	10	As above	28in (710mm)
CORNER POSTS	4	2 × 2in (50 × 50mm)	53in (1350mm)
CROSS SUPPORTS	2	1 × 6in (25 × 150mm) cut to 1 × 3in (25 × 75mm)	48in (1220mm) cut to length as required
LAG SCREWS	80	Galvanized steel	$\frac{5}{16}$ × 2in (8 × 50mm)

1 **Marking Top Joint on Posts**
Mark cross support centrally on post end at 45°. Gauge lines down post to marked position and remove center.

2 **Securing the Second Frame to Form Main Construction**
Affix "short" boards flush with the ends of two lots of two posts. Screw "long" boards to the sides of one frame, then place the second frame inside the "long" boards so that the ends are square and flush.

PLANTER

MAIN CONSTRUCTION

Lay two of the corner posts on a flat surface and place a "short" length of board across them flush with the ends so that the outer edges are 28in (710mm) apart.

Secure the board to the posts by drilling two pilot holes at one end, about 1in (25mm) from the end, and screw in two of the galvanized lag screws. For a neat finish try to ensure that each lag screw is the same distance from the edge.

Hold a spare board at the other end to make sure that the post is square, double check using a try square and secure the opposite end of the first board in the same way, drilling the holes the same distance in from the outside edge.

Repeat the process with the other two posts, affixing a "short" board betweeen them at the base.

Stand one of the frames upright, and place a "long" length of board along the side flush with the post and secure it in place using a C-clamp. Pilot hole and screw to the corner post with two lag screws centrally on the post. Repeat for the other side of the frame, using a "long" length of board as before.

Place the other frame inside these "long" boards, with the corner posts on the inside (fig. 2, page 135). Affix the sides to the corner posts with two lag screws each side.

BUILDING UP THE ROWS OF BOARDS

Take another "short" length of board and place it on top of the attached "long" board so its ends are flush with the posts. Clamp the board to the posts using a pair of C-clamps and affix it with two lag screws at each end, aligning them with the screws on the board below.

Take a "long" length of board and place it on the adjacent side so it overlaps the end of the "short" board (fig. 1). Make sure the end is flush; screw it into the corner post.

Continue in this way, one row at a time, so that the "short"/"long" boards run alternately, and ends are visible on each side on alternate rows. Build to five boards high (or whatever height you have decided on). It is most important to check that the structure is square as you work: do this by holding a board at the top flush with the posts each time a board is added.

AFFIXING THE CROSS SUPPORTS

Measure diagonally across the corner posts at the top of the planter and add 2in (50mm) so that there will be an overhang at each end. Cut two lengths to this measurement from 1 x 3in (25 x 75mm) stock.

At the middle of these two cross supports, cut two cross lap joints (see **Techniques, page 400**) and slot together. Fit the cross supports into the slots in the corner posts and glue them in place (fig. 3).

Unless you wish to color the wood there is no need to apply a special finish, as preservative-treated lumber is used for this project. If you

1 **Building Up the Sides of the Planter**
Build up the rows one at a time, affixing "short" boards above "long" boards and vice versa. Always check boards are square with the frame and ends are flush before screwing in place. Align screws with those on the boards below.

2 **Joining the Cross Supports**
Cut cross lap joints in the middle of the two cross supports so that they slot together.

do want to change the color of the wood, at this stage apply a water-repellent preservative wood stain of the desired shade. To avoid getting stain onto the lag screw heads, push lengths of plastic or rubber tubing over the heads before staining the planter.

MAKING A FLOOR PANEL

If a floor panel is required, screw 2 × 2in (50 × 50mm) battens to the inside of the planter at the base. Lay 1 × 6in (25 × 150mm) boards across the planter, resting on the battens. Space the boards so that there are narrow gaps about ⅛in (3mm) wide between them to allow drainage of excess water. To assist the base in supporting a heavy weight of soil, you can reinforce it with additional 2 × 2in (50 × 50mm) battens spaced about 9in (225mm) apart under the floor panel and running at right angles to it.

Move the planter to the chosen site before adding the soil and planting the tree or shrub. A layer of small stones at the bottom of the planter will assist drainage.

③ Affixing Supports to Posts
The cross supports fit into the slots cut in top of each post and protrude an equal distance. Glue in place.

PLANTER ASSEMBLY

CROSS SUPPORT

POST

LONG BOARD

SHORT BOARD

LAG SCREW

SHORT BOARD

LONG BOARD

COLD FRAME

If you can't afford a greenhouse, a cold frame is the next best thing. Most important for raising seedlings or growing early vegetables, it can also be used to provide salad ingredients such as lettuce all through the winter: a year-round usage which makes it an invaluable addition to any garden. If you do have a greenhouse, a cold frame can still be used to harden off bedding plants that have been raised in the greenhouse and as a place for overwintering delicate biennials.

The design of this cold frame varies little from the traditional version which is such a common garden sight. Extremely versatile and very simple to make, the wooden base is treated with exterior-grade preservative, contrasting with the crisp, white painted "light" or glazed lid. An important feature of the design is the ability to remove the entire light so that there is free access to the area of ground covered by the cold frame, enabling it to be dug over and planted easily.

Cold frames are best sited in south-facing positions where they will receive maximum sunlight, but, because they are usually portable, the position can be varied from year to year. If there is a danger of scorching at the height of summer, the glass may need to be coated with white "obscuring paint."

Unlike traditional cloches or glass bell-jars, a cold frame can be made simply and economically to provide a versatile extension of the growing season.

Cold Frame

WORKBENCH (fixed or portable)

STEEL MEASURING TAPE

STEEL BENCH RULE

TRY SQUARE (or combination square)

SMALL CROSSCUT SAW (or circular power saw)

BACK SAW

MARKING GAUGE

POWER DRILL

DRILL BIT – approximately $\frac{1}{8}$in (3mm) diameter

COUNTERSINK BIT

SCREWDRIVER

CLAW HAMMER

NAILSET

PLIERS

CHISEL – about 1in (25mm)

MALLET

BAR CLAMPS (or folding wedges)

Materials

Quantities are for the three-bay frame illustrated

Part	Quantity	Material	Length
Frame Structure			
BOTTOM RAILS	4	2 × 2in (50 × 50mm) sawn and treated softwood	48in (1220mm)*
FRONT POSTS	4	As above	10$\frac{1}{2}$in (270mm)*
BACK POSTS	4	As above	16in (400mm)*
TOP RAILS	4	As above	48$\frac{1}{2}$in (1230mm)*
TOP SUPPORT BATTENS	6	1 × 1in (25 × 25mm) S4S softwood	48$\frac{1}{2}$in (1230mm)
FRONT JOINING BATTENS	6	As above	13in (330mm)*
BACK JOINING BATTENS	6	As above	18in (460mm)*
FRONT & BACK CLADDING	As required	$\frac{1}{4}$ × $\frac{3}{4}$ × 6in (6 × 19 × 150mm) bevel clapboarding	Width of glazing frame plus clearance
END CLADDING	As required	As above	44in (1120mm)
Glazed Lights			
SIDE RAILS	6	1$\frac{1}{2}$ × 2in (38 × 50mm) S4S softwood	50in (1270mm)
TOP RAILS	3	As above	31$\frac{1}{2}$in (800mm)
BOTTOM RAILS	3	1 × 3in (25 × 75mm) S4S softwood	31$\frac{1}{2}$in (800mm)
CENTRAL GLAZING BARS	3	1 × 1$\frac{1}{2}$in (25 × 38mm) S4S softwood	50in (1270mm)
GLASS SUPPORT BATTENS – LONG	12	$\frac{1}{2}$ × 1in (12 × 25mm) S4S softwood	46in (1150mm)*
GLASS SUPPORT BATTENS – SHORT	6	As above	16in (400mm)*
GLASS SHEETS	18	Approx. 17 × 16in (425 × 400mm) clear glass	

Also required: 3 D-handles; metal glass clips; mastic for bedding glass; glazier's points for holding glass in place; glazed light supports

* Leave overlong and then cut to size after affixing – see text

A cold frame will be appreciated by all keen gardeners, whether their speciality is flowers, fruit, or vegetables. The frame will be useful for seedlings, propagation, and for growing delicate or early plants.

Our frame has been developed from the tried and tested standard cold frame that has evolved over the years. The main frame is made from sawn and preservative-treated softwood, put together in a series of inset "bays" clad with bevel clapboarding affixed between the main frames. This gives the frame a distinctive style and avoids the bland appearance of a conventional cold frame. However, you may prefer to run the clapboards along the whole length of the frame, which is quicker and easier.

The size of the frame from front to back and end to end is optional and can be varied as you wish according to what you want to grow. Our frame is a good average size, being 14$\frac{1}{2}$in (370mm) high at the front, 20in (500mm) high at the back, and 48in (1220mm) from front to back. The beauty of this design is that you can have a single section, or make a block of two, three, or more. We have built a three-section frame, and quantities in the Materials chart are for a frame of this size.

The glazed lights in our design are loose, giving flexibility in use. You have the option of sliding them back a little way for ventilation, farther back to tend for plants within the frame, or they can be lifted at the front and propped open a little way for ventilation. Alternatively, they are easy to slide off, either from the front or the back, allowing them to be removed completely. However, you could glaze the lights with sheets of clear plastic, which is also a safer option if young children play in the garden. In this case, you would affix the lights at the back with hinges; you will need a 2 × 3in (50 × 75mm) wood rail along the back, level with the support battens.

COLD FRAME ASSEMBLY

SIDE RAIL

GLASS SUPPORT BATTEN

END JOINING BATTEN

BOTTOM RAIL

CLAPBOARDS

FRONT POST

FRONT JOINING BATTEN

TOP RAIL

CENTRAL GLAZING BAR

GLASS SHEET

TOP RAIL

BACK JOINING BATTEN

BACK POST

20in

TOP SUPPORT BATTEN

48in

36in   14½in

FRAME STRUCTURE

MAKING THE DIVIDERS

The ground frame structure is built around four dividers (if you are making a three-bay cold frame), and construction starts with these. Start by cutting out the four components of the dividers – the top and bottom rails, and the front and back posts – from 2 × 2in (50 × 50mm) sawn softwood all at least 2in (50mm) overlong.

Lay the bottom rail down and mark off its final length centrally on one side. Place the front and back posts in position alongside.

Mark off the final heights of the front and back posts, and then lay the top rail alongside these top marks (with the correct post heights on the outer edges of each) so that the correct angles to cut the tops of the posts can be marked. Cut the posts to length.

Nail up the frame by toe-nailing through the bottom and top rails into the front and back posts.

Once the frame has been finished, check it for square, then cut off the "horns" (protruding ends) of the top and bottom rails so they are flush with the posts. Make up the required number of frame dividers – four in our example.

SUPPORT AND JOINING BATTENS

Place an offcut of the 1½ × 2in (38 × 50mm) glazing frame side rail, 1/16in (2mm) down from the upper edge of the top rail to position the top support battens. You will need one on each side of the central dividing frames and on the inner sides of the end frames. Nail them in place, then saw the ends flush with the front and back posts.

Unless you are nailing the cladding in continuous lengths to the front and back of the dividing frames, you will need to nail joining battens to the front and back posts.

Hold the battens in place so that the tops can be marked at the angle of the top support batten. Cut the battens to this angle, then screw them in place so that they are flush with the inside edges of the front and back posts (fig. 1, page 142). Saw the ends of the battens flush with the bottom edge of the bottom rail. Affix side battens on both sides of the dividing frames, and on the inner sides of the end frames.

To support the cladding at the ends, measure internal heights of the front and back posts on the end frame. Cut battens to these lengths and affix to the inside edges of the end frames (fig. 2, page 390).

COLD FRAME

GLAZED LIGHTS

Cut out all the components. Each glazed light frame will require two sides, one top rail, one bottom rail, and one central glazing bar (fig. 3).

Mark out all the joints as shown (fig. 3). The sides are joined to the top rail using corner half-lap joints (*see* **Techniques, Half-lap joint, page 400**). The bottom rail is lapped onto the sides so that the bottom rail is on the underside.

The glazing bar is joined to the top rail with a T-half-lap joint and to the bottom rail with a lap joint on the *opposite* side (the underside) so that it laps onto the bottom rail as shown (fig. 3).

Letter all the joints clearly to identify them for assembly, and then cut them all out.

MAKING UP THE GLAZED LIGHT FRAMES

Glue all the joints to the top and bottom rails, starting with the central glazing bar. Use a waterproof woodworking adhesive such as epoxy resin. Turn the frame over so that it can be screwed together from the underside. Use a try square to make sure that the frame is square, and hold it with clamps to keep the joints tight while drilling two pilot holes and a countersink for each of the three top joints. Screw the top joints together.

Drill and screw the bottom corner joints with three screws each. Measure to check that the central glazing bar is central on the bottom rail, then drill two holes and screw the bar to the bottom rail.

Lay the frame on a flat surface and check it is square by measuring the diagonals. Then nail on a bracing batten to keep the frame square while the glue is drying. Clean off any excess glue with a damp cloth and leave the joints to dry.

Repeat the process for the required number of frames – in this case three.

GLASS SUPPORT BATTENS

Cut four lengths of $\frac{1}{2} \times 1$in (12×25mm) batten to the internal length of the glazing frame and nail them so that they are flush with the underside of the frame.

Then cut two lengths to the internal widths between the side battens at the top. Nail the battens at the top between the two pairs of side battens, with the lower edge flush with the underside of the frame.

Repeat for the other frames.

CLADDING

Although we used bevel clapboarding for cladding the frame, other cladding boards could equally well be used – for example, shiplap, tongue-and-groove, or V-jointed.

For the sides, cut the cladding to the internal dimensions of the end frames. Affix the cladding, working up from the bottom board, nailing into the joining battens. When using bevel clapboards, the cladding boards should overlap by about $\frac{1}{2}$in (12mm), and the nails holding the lower edge of each board should pass through the top edge of the board beneath to hold it securely. Use galvanized round head nails.

When affixing the end cladding, the top boards must be shaped to the slope of the top rail.

The front and back clapboards are cut to fit between the dividing frames so that the glazed frames, when fitted, will be a loose fit. You will need to leave enough clearance to allow for the wood to swell when it gets wet. Check that the main dividers are spaced so that there is about $\frac{1}{16}$in (2mm) of clearance between the dividers and the sides of the glazing frames so that they will slide in place easily.

Nail the bevel clapboards to the front and back joining battens, working up from the bottom boards as before. The upper corners at each end of the top boards will have to be notched out so that the clapboards will fit tightly around the top support battens.

If you are affixing the front and back cladding in a continuous strip, dispense with the front and back joining battens, and nail the clapboards directly to the front and back posts of the dividing frames. If the boards are of insufficient length to

1 **Fitting the Top Support Batten and Side Joining Battens**
Left Detail shows spacing block held $\frac{1}{16}$in (2mm) down from top rail to position top support batten. *Below* Top support batten runs length of top rail; side joining battens fit flush with inside edges of front and back posts and are angled at top to fit beneath top support battens.

2 **Affixing End Battens**
Cut end panel joining battens to internal heights of posts, and fit flush to inside edges of frame.

③ Making the Frames for the Glazed Lights
Top Corner half-lap joints fit side rails to top rail; T-half-lap joint fits glazing
bar to top rail; lap bottom rail to underside of side rails and glazing bar.
Below Glue and screw from underside; bracing batten holds frame square.

clad the frame in continuous strips, shorter lengths of clapboards can be used: simply butt joint them together so that the joint coincides with the midpoint of a front or back post. Stagger these joints so they do not line up with joints in boards directly above or below.

PRESERVING AND FINISHING OFF

It is most important to treat the whole of the frame assembly with at least two coats of clear or colored wood preservative. When dry, this can then be painted with a microporous or exterior gloss paint, or it can be treated with a water-repellent preservative stain if a natural wood color is required. You must not use creosote or any wood preserver that is harmful to plants.

FITTING THE GLASS, HANDLES, AND HINGES

Have the glass cut to fit the glazed frames. We had ours cut in three sheets on each side, with the bottom sheet feeding first and subsequent sheets overlapping the previously affixed sheet. The bottom sheet is held by small aluminum clips, nailed to the bottom glazing frame rail and bent back over the edge of the glass to prevent it from slipping out. All the sheets are bedded into mastic on the glazing support battens. The glass sheets are held with small nails, called glazier's points, nailed into the side rails so that they are horizontal and hold the glass down. The bottom edges of the overlapping sheets of glass rest against two glazier's points which prevent the sheets from sliding down.

As an alternative to glass, the lights can be glazed with clear plastic sheeting, which is cheaper and much safer. Make sure that you buy purpose-made horticultural plastic which will encourage the plants to thrive and will also prevent premature yellowing and cracking of the plastic. Do *not* buy plastic containing an ultra-violet (UV) inhibitor as nothing will be able to grow in the cold frame.

To make it easier to lift the glazed lights for ventilation and access to the plants, screw a D-handle into the bottom end of the glazing bar.

If the glazed lights are left loose, they can be lifted at the front edge and wedged open with a wooden block for ventilation; the lights can also be slid backward or forward to gain access to inside the frame.

Alternatively, the glazed lights can be hinged at the back, and this is a particularly good option when the lights are glazed with plastic and are therefore lighter. In this case, cut a 2 × 3in (50 × 75mm) batten to the total length of the frame and bevel the top edge to allow the glazed light to fold back beyond 90° (so that it will rest open against a wall or fence behind the frame). With the batten level with the top support battens, screw it to the back posts. Then screw hinges into the back edges of the glazing frames, and into the top edge of the beveled batten (*see* **Techniques, page 400**).

A simple ventilation prop can be made simply from a 2 × 4 × 6in (50 × 100 × 150mm) wood block with 1in (25mm) steps cut along one edge to allow variable ventilation up to 6in (150mm). Another method is to install a swing-down prop to hold the glazed light partially open. The prop can be affixed to the underside of the central glazing bar and held out of the way in a tool clip when not in use.

If the frame is glazed with plastic lights and hinged at the back, affix hooks and eyes to the front edge of the frame to hold the lights firmly closed in windy conditions.

The frame should be positioned in a sunny place, and can simply be rested on the soil. Alternatively, you could place it on a partially buried row of bricks which will help to keep the wood dry. If the frame is to be permanently sited, it should be placed on a strip of damp-proofing placed on two rows of bricks over a concrete foundation (to act as a vapor barrier). Affix the frame using expansion bolts inserted into the brick foundation through the bottom rails, or use metal strips screwed to the foundation and to the inside of the frame structure.

④ Glass Support Battens
Cut side battens to internal lengths of frame and top battens to internal length between side battens.

TOOLS, MATERIALS, AND TECHNIQUES: TOOLS

TOOLS FOR PREPARATION

Adjustable T- bevel   This is a type of square used to mark out timber at any required angle.

Bench stop and vise   A vise is fitted to the underside of a bench, the jaws level with the bench top. The jaws are lined and topped with hardwood to protect the work and any tools being used. Some vises incorporate a small steel peg (a "dog") that can be raised above the main jaw level. This allows awkward pieces of wood to be clamped in position when used with a bench stop fixed at the opposite end of the bench.

Drill stand   Enables a power drill to be used with extreme accuracy when, for example, dowel jointing. The hole will be perpendicular to the surface and its depth can be carefully controlled. The drill is lowered onto the work with a spring-loaded lever which gives good control.

Marking gauge   This is used to mark both widths and thicknesses with only a light scratch. The gauge comprises a handle, on which slides a stock bearing a steel marking pin which can be fixed at a precise point.

Mortise gauge   Similar to a marking gauge, it has two pins, one fixed, one adjustable, to mark out both sides of a mortise at the same time.

Utility knife   Used to score a thin line for a saw or chisel to follow, ensuring a precise cut.

Miter box   A simple open-topped wooden box which is used to guide saws into materials at a fixed 45° or 90° angle, to ensure an accurate cut.

Plumb bob and chalk   Used to check or mark accurate vertical lines on walls. A plumb bob is simply a pointed weight attached to a long length of string. The string can be rubbed with a stick of colored chalk to leave a line on the wall.

Portable workbench   A collapsible, portable workbench is vital for woodworking. It is lightweight and can be carried to the job, where it provides sturdy support. A portable bench is like a giant vise – the worksurface comprises two sections which can be opened wide or closed tightly according to the dimensions of the work and the nature of the task.

Carpenter's level   Used for checking that surfaces are horizontal or vertical. A 24in (610mm) long level is the most useful size. An aluminum or steel level will withstand knocks and it can be either I-girder or box-shaped in section. A 9in (225mm) "torpedo" carpenter's level is useful for confined spaces and can be used with a straight-edge over longer surfaces.

Steel measuring tape   A 12ft (3.6m) or 18ft (5.5m) long, lockable tape (metal or plastic) is best, and one with a top window in the casing makes it easier to read measurements.

Steel bench rule   Since the rule is made of steel, the graduations are indelible and very precise. A rule graduated on both sides in imperial and metric is the most useful. The rule also serves as a precise straight-edge.

Straight-edge   Can be made from a length of 1 × 2in (25 × 50mm) scrap wood. It is used in combination with a carpenter's level to tell whether a surface is flat and also for checking whether two points are aligned with each other.

Try square   An L-shaped precision tool comprising a steel blade and stock (or handle) set at a perfect right angle to each other on both the inside and outside edges. Used for marking right angles and for checking a square.

Combination square   A versatile measuring and marking tool comprising a steel ruler, try square, miter square, and carpenter's level.

TOOLS FOR SHARPENING AND CUTTING

Chisels   Used to cut slots in wood or to pare off thin slivers. Some chisels may be used with a mallet when cutting slots. When new, a chisel's cutting edge is ground and must be honed with an oilstone to sharpen it before use.
Mortise chisel   Used for cutting deep slots.
Firmer chisel   For general-purpose use.
Bevel-edge chisel   Used for undercutting in confined spaces.
Paring chisel   Has a long blade for cutting deep joints or long grooves.

Doweling jig   Clamps onto a piece of work, ensuring that the drill is aligned over the center of the dowel hole to be drilled.

DRILLS

Hand drill   For drilling holes for screws or for making large holes, particularly in wood. It will make holes in metal and is useful where there is no power source. A handle attached to a toothed wheel is used to turn the drill in its chuck.
Power drill   These range from a simple, single-speed model (which will drill holes only in soft materials) to a multi-speed drill with electric control. Most jobs call for something in between, such as a two-speed drill with hammer action.

DRILL BITS

You will need a selection of drill bits in various sizes and of different types for use with a drill.

Auger bit   Has a tapered, square shank that fits into a carpenter's brace. It is used to make deep holes in wood, the usual lengths being up to 10in (250mm). Diameters range from $\frac{1}{4}$in (6mm) to $1\frac{1}{2}$in (38mm). The tip has a screw thread to draw the bit into the wood.
Countersink bit   After a hole is drilled in wood, a countersink bit is used to cut a recess for the screwhead to sit in, so ensuring that it lies below the surface. Different types are available for use with a carpenter's brace or a power drill.
Brad-point bit   Used to make dowel holes. The top has two cutting spurs on the side and a center point to prevent the bit from wandering off center.
Forstner bit   Primarily used for boring flat-bottomed holes to accept the hinge bosses on concealed hinges. Forstner bits are used in electric drills, ideally fitted in drill stands, and should be set to drill no deeper than $\frac{1}{2}$in (12mm).
Spade bit   Is used with a power drill. For maximum efficiency the bit must be turned at high speed from about 1000 to 2000 r.p.m. It drills into cross grain, end grain, and man-made boards.
Masonry bit   Has a specially hardened tungsten-carbide tip for drilling into masonry to the exact size required for an anchor. Special percussion drill bits are available for use with a hammer drill when boring into concrete.
Twist drill bit   Used with a power drill for drilling small holes in wood and metal.

Power router   This portable electric tool is used to cut grooves, recesses, and many types of joints in lumber, and to shape the edge of long lumber battens. A range of cutting bits in different shapes and sizes is available and when fitted into the router the bits revolve at very high speed.

SAWS

Back saw For cutting the tenon part of a mortise and tenon joint, and for other delicate work. It has a stiffened back and the blade is about 10–12in (250–300mm) long.

Circular saw For cutting large pieces of wood or sheets of board, as well as grooves and angles. The most popular size has a diameter of 7¼in (184mm). Circular saws can be extremely dangerous and must be used carefully. The piece of work must be held securely, supported on scrap battens, and the blade depth set so that it will not cut into anything below the work. The tool should be fitted with an upper and a lower blade guard.

Compass saw Has a narrow, tapered blade to cut holes and shapes in wood. A hole is drilled and the saw blade is inserted to make the cut.

Coping saw Used to make curved or circular cuts. It has a narrow blade, which can be swiveled. When cutting, the blade can be angled so that the frame clears the edge of the work.

Hacksaw For cutting metal. A traditional hacksaw has a wooden handle and a solid metal frame. The blade is tensioned by a wing-nut. Modern hacksaws have a tubular frame which is adjustable for different lengths of blade.

Hand saw A saw used for rough cutting rather than fine carpentry. It has a flexible blade of 20–26in (510–660mm).

Saber saw More versatile than a circular saw, although not as quick or powerful. It cuts curves, intricate shapes, angles, and holes in a variety of materials. Good models offer variable speeds.

Rasp A coarse file, available with flat or half-round surfaces, used to shape wood.

Surforms Available in a range of lengths from approximately 6–10in (150–250mm), these rasps are useful for the initial shaping of wood. The steel blade has a pattern of alternating small teeth and holes through which waste wood passes, so that the teeth do not get clogged up.

HAND TOOLS

Abrasive paper *see* **Sanding block**

CLAMPS

For securing glued pieces of work while they are setting. There are many types of clamp, but the C-clamp is the most commonly used and is available in a wide range of jaw sizes.

C-clamp Also called a frame clamp or fast-action clamp, it is important for our projects that the jaws of the clamp open at least 8in (200mm). The wood to be held in the clamp is placed between the jaws which are then tightened by turning a thumb-screw, tommy bar, or other type of handle. With a fast-action clamp, one jaw is free to slide on a bar, and after sliding this jaw up to the workpiece, final tightening is made by turning the handle. To protect the work, scraps of wood are placed between the jaws of the clamp.

Bar clamps These employ a long metal bar, and are indispensable for holding together large frameworks, although you can improvise in some cases by making a rope tourniquet. This consists of a piece of rope which is tied around the object, and a length of stick to twist the rope and so clamp the frame tightly.

Band clamp The webbing, like narrow seat-belt type material, is looped around the frame, pulled as tight as possible by hand, and then finally tightened by means of a screw mechanism or ratchet winder.

HAMMERS

Claw hammer The claw side of the head of the hammer is used to extract nails from a piece of work, quickly and cleanly.

Cross-peen hammer The peen is the tapered section opposite the flat hammer head, and it is used for starting off small brads and tacks.

Tack hammer A smaller version of the cross-peen; this is useful for light work.

Hand staple gun A trigger-operated tool which fires a staple straight into a surface, usually fabric, fiberboard, or thin wood over a wooden batten. Its advantage over conventional nailing with a hammer is that it is used one-handed.

Mallet Most commonly used to strike mortise chisels, although if a chisel has an impact-resistant handle then a hammer may also be used. The tapered wooden head ensures square contact with the object being struck.

Nailset Used with a hammer to drive nails and brads below the surface so that they are hidden and the holes can then be filled.

Orbital sander This gives a fine, smooth surface finish to wood. A gritted sanding sheet is fitted to the sander's base plate. Sheets are graded from coarse to fine, and the grade used depends on the roughness of the surface to be sanded. Orbital sanders produce a great deal of dust, so always wear a mask when using one.

Paintbrushes A set of paintbrushes for painting and varnishing should ideally comprise three sizes – 1in (25mm), 2in (50mm), and 3in (75mm). A better finish is always achieved by matching the size of the brush to the surface – a small brush for narrow surfaces, a large brush for wide areas.

PLANES

Block plane Held in the palm of the hand, it is easy to use for small work and chamfering edges. Also useful for planing end grain.

Jack plane A good all-purpose tool with a long blade used for straightening long edges.

Power plane Finishes lumber to precise dimensions. A one-hand model is lightweight and can be used anywhere, whereas the heavier two-hander is intended for workbench use. A power plane will also cut bevels and rabbets.

Smoothing plane A general-purpose, hand-held plane for smoothing and straightening surfaces and edges. The plane is about 10in (250mm) long and its blade 2–2¼in (50–60mm) wide. The wider the blade the better the finish on wide lumber. There is a fine adjustment for depth of cut and a lever for lateral adjustment.

Sanding block and sandpaper A sanding block is used with sandpaper to finish and smooth flat surfaces. The block is made of cork, rubber or softwood and the sandpaper is wrapped around it. Make sure that the paper is not wrinkled. Coarse paper is used for a rough surface and fine paper for finishing.

Screwdrivers Come in many shapes and sizes, the main differences being the type of tip (for slotted or Phillips screws), the length, and the shape of the handle, which varies from straight or fluted to bulb-shaped.

Ideally, you should have a range of screwdrivers for dealing with all sizes of screws. Ratchet models, which return the handle to its starting point, are easy to operate since your hand grip does not need to change.

Wrench A wrench is required for tightening carriage bolts, and any type that fits the head of the bolt is suitable. If the correct-size open-ended or ring wrench is not available, any type of adjustable wrench may be used.

MATERIALS

LUMBER AND SHEET BOARDS

Lumber This is classified into two groups – softwoods and hardwoods. Softwoods come from evergreen trees and hardwoods from deciduous trees. Check your lumber for defects before buying it. Avoid wood which is badly cracked or split, although you need not be concerned about fine, surface cracks since these can be planed, sanded, or filled. Do not buy warped wood, as it will be impossible to work with. Check for warping by looking along the length of a board to see if there is any bowing or twisting.

Wood for outdoor projects must be protected from rot and insect attack. It can be bought pre-treated with preservative, but this is expensive and not always readily available. Alternatively, you can buy untreated wood and treat it, as soon as possible, with one of the finishes described here. Pay special attention to end grain and to posts which will be buried below ground – a double coating is a good idea here.

Softwood Softwood is much less expensive than hardwood and is used in general building work. Softwood is sold either by the *lineal* foot or the *board* foot. The former is based on the length of a piece of wood – for example, 8ft of 1 by 2 (1 × 2in [25 × 50mm]). The board foot is calculated by the thickness in inches × width in feet × length in feet – for example, 10ft of 1 by 6 would be 5 board feet: $1in × \frac{1}{2}ft$ (6in) × 10ft.

It is important to remember that standard softwood sizes refer to sawn sizes – that is, how it is sawn at a mill. Sawn timber is suitable for most of the projects in this book. However, where a smooth finish is specified, where appearance and accuracy are important, it will need to be planed. Such wood is referred to as S4S (smooth 4 sides), and, since planing takes a little off each face, it is $\frac{1}{4}–\frac{3}{4}in$ (6–19mm) smaller in width and thickness than stated.

Hardwood Expensive and not as easy to obtain as softwoods, hardwoods often have to be ordered or bought from a specialist lumberyard. Many lumberyards will machine hardwood to your exact specification.

Sheet boards Mechanically made from wood and other fibers, they are versatile, relatively inexpensive, made to uniform quality and available in large sheets. You need to know the advantages of each type before making your choice.

Plywood Made by gluing thin wood veneers together in plies (layers) with the grain in each ply running at right angles to that of its neighbors. This gives it strength and helps prevent warping. The most common boards have three, five, or seven plies. Plywood is graded for quality: N is perfect, followed by A, B, C, and D in decreasing order of quality. Usual thicknesses of plywood are $\frac{1}{8}in$, $\frac{1}{4}in$, $\frac{1}{2}in$, and $\frac{3}{4}in$ (3mm, 6mm, 12mm, and 19mm). WBP (weather and boil proof) grade board must be used for exterior work.

Lumber core Made by sandwiching natural lumber strips between wood veneers, the latter usually of Far Eastern redwood or plain birch. Although plain birch is a little more expensive than redwood it is of a much better quality. Lumber core is very strong, but can leave an ugly edge when sawn, making edge fixings difficult. Lumber core is graded in the same way as plywood and common thicknesses are $\frac{1}{2}in$, $\frac{3}{4}in$, and 1in (12mm, 19mm, and 25mm).

Tongue-and-groove boarding Also called match boarding, or matching, this is widely used for cladding frameworks. The boarding has a tongue on one side and a slot on the other side. The tongue fits into the slot of the adjacent board; this joint expands and contracts according to temperature and humidity without cracks opening up between boards. Make sure you use exterior grade boarding for outdoor projects.

Bevel clapboards These taper from a thick edge across to a thin edge. When fixed in place, the thick edge of one board overlaps the thin edge of the next board.

ADHESIVES AND FILLERS

Adhesives Modern adhesives are strong and efficient. If they fail, it is because the wrong adhesive is being used or the manufacturer's instructions are not being followed carefully. For outdoor woodworking, you must always use either a synthetic resin adhesive that is mixed with water (this has gap-filling properties, so is useful where joints are not cut perfectly) or a two-part epoxy resin adhesive where the parts are applied separately to the surfaces being joined.

Fillers For outside work, always use an exterior grade filler which has been specially formulated to withstand the natural movement of cracks and holes caused by weather changes.

If the wood is to be painted over, use an exterior painter's caulk. This dries white and will be evident if used under any other kind of finish. When a clear finish is needed, fill cracks and holes with a proprietary wood filler. These are thick pastes and come in a range of wood colors. You can mix them together or add a wood stain if the color you want is not available. Choose a color slightly paler than the surrounding wood, since fillers tend to darken when the finish is applied. Some experimentation may be needed on a waste piece of matching wood.

FINISHES

The choice of finish is determined by whether the wood or board is to be hidden, painted, or enhanced by a protective clear finish.

Paint A liquid gloss (oil-based) paint is suitable for wood, and is applied after undercoat. Generally, two thin coats of gloss are better than one thick coat. Non-drip gloss is an alternative. It has a jelly-like consistency and does not require an undercoat, although a second coat may be needed for a quality finish. If you intend to spray the paint, you must use a liquid gloss.

Microporous paint This is applied directly to the wood – neither primer nor undercoat is needed. The coating will not flake or blister as the special formulation allows trapped moisture to evaporate. If applied over old gloss paint, it will lose the quality that prevents flaking or blistering.

Preservative Unless wood has been pre-treated with preservative and it is not to receive an alternative decorative finish, you must use a coat of preservative. Modern water-based preservatives are harmless to plant life. They are available in clear, green, and a number of natural wood colors. The preservative sinks well into the wood, preventing rot and insect attack.

Varnish For outdoor use, you must always use an exterior grade varnish – stated on the container – or a yacht varnish. It is available as a gloss, satin, or matt finish, all clear. Varnish also comes in a range of colors, so that you can change the color of the wood and protect it simultaneously. The color does not sink into the wood, so if the surface becomes scratched or marked then its original color will show through. A wood stain or dye can be used to change the color of wood. It sinks into the wood, but offers no protection, so varnish is also needed.

CONCRETE

Concrete Made by mixing Portland cement and ballast (a mixture of sand and aggregates) with water. The usual mix for paths, bases and foundations is one part cement to four parts ballast. Although concrete mix is available dry-mixed in bags, it is only economically viable for small jobs. Concrete can be mixed by hand, but it is an arduous task, and it is advisable to hire a small electric mixer.

Precast concrete paving slabs These come in a range of shapes and sizes with 450mm square (18in square) being the most popular, since anything larger is difficult to handle. There is a limited range of colours, and surface finishes are smooth, patterned or textured. Thicknesses are usually 35–40mm (about $1\frac{1}{2}$in).

Bricks and **Mortar** *see* **Techniques: Bricklaying, pages 156–7**

DIVIDERS

Fences Required principally to mark boundaries and to create privacy and security. Among the most popular types are:

Vertical closeboard A solid, secure fence which can be of any height. Feather-edge boards are nailed to horizontal arris rails which, in turn, are fixed to timber or solid concrete posts.

Waney-edged panels Pre-fabricated panels made from larch or pine planks which overlap horizontally. The panels are normally 1800mm (72in) wide and 600–1800mm (24–72in) high, and are fixed to timber or concrete support posts.

Palisade Vertical timber pales (stakes) nailed to arris rails at 50mm (2in) intervals and in turn fixed to timber posts. Pales can have ornate or square tops. Heights vary, but 900mm (36in) is the most popular. Usually used for front gardens.

Ranch-style Horizontal timber rails nailed at intervals to timber posts. A two-rail fence is usually about 1000mm (39in) high; a four-rail fence is about 1300mm (51in) high.

Chain link A secure fence, 900–3600mm (36–144in) high. The metal mesh can be galvanized or plastic-coated. Posts are iron or concrete.

Plastic wire Ornamental fencing commonly used to mark a boundary or surround a fish pond or herbaceous border. The fencing can be fixed directly into the ground, but it should be fixed to posts if it is over 600mm (24in) high. It is sold in rolls and cut to the required length.

Rustic poles Hazel, birch or chestnut poles are available from garden centres. Diameters generally range from 50–125mm (2–5in). You will need the larger sizes for main uprights and bearers and the thinner ones for cross beams. The poles have bark attached; this will peel off in own time.

Trellising Square trellis is available in panel heights from 600–1220mm (24–48in) and in 1800mm (72in) long sections. The squares are each about 150mm (6in) and the trellis is made from hardwood battens. Diamond trellis comes in heights from 300–1220mm (12–48in) and lengths of 1800mm (72in).

FIXINGS

The choice of fixing depends on the size and weight of the materials being fixed.

Nails For general-purpose frame construction.
Round wire nails With large, flat, circular heads, these are used for strong joins where frames will be covered, so that the ugly appearance of the nails does not matter.
Annular ring-shank nails Used where really strong fixings are required.
Round lost-head nails or **oval brads** (*oval wire nails*) Used when the finished appearance is important.
Panel pins For fixing thin panels, these have unobtrusive heads that can be driven in flush with the wood's surface or punched below it.
Masonry nails For fixing timber battens to walls as an alternative to screws and wallplugs.

Screws All types of screws are available with conventional slotted heads or cross-point heads. The latter are the best type to use if you are inserting screws with an electric screwdriver.

For most purposes, screws with countersunk heads are ideal as the head lies flush with the surface after insertion. Round-head screws are for fixing metal fittings such as door bolts, which have punched-out rather than countersunk screw holes. Raised-countersunk head screws are used where a neat appearance is important.
Wood screws These have a length of smooth shank just below the head. This produces a strong cramping effect, but there is a possibility of the unthreaded shank splitting the wood.
Twin-thread screws Less likely to split wood than wood screws. Except for larger sizes, they are threaded along their entire length, giving an excellent grip in timber and boards.

Coach screws For heavy-duty fixings when making frameworks requiring a strong construction. The screws have square or hexagonal heads and are turned with a spanner. A washer is used to prevent the head cutting into the timber.

Wallplugs Use a masonry drill bit to drill a hole which matches the size of screw being used (a No 10 bit with a No 10 screw, for example). Insert the plug in the hole, then insert the screw through the object being fixed and into the plug.

Wall anchor bolt Similar to a wallplug, but with its own heavy-duty machine screw. You need to make a much larger hole in the wall, typically 10mm ($\frac{3}{8}$in) in diameter. The anchor sleeve expands in the hole as the bolt is tightened.

Expanding wall bolt This comprises a segmented body which expands as the bolt inside it is tightened. The body grips concrete, brick or stone securely. There are various lengths and diameters and there are also versions containing a hook or an eye. Most bolts are zinc-plated, but aluminium bronze versions are available where greater resistance to corrosion is required.

Corrugated fasteners For strengthening glued joints in frameworks. Sizes are 6–22mm ($\frac{1}{4}$–$\frac{7}{8}$in) deep and 22–30mm ($\frac{7}{8}$–$1\frac{1}{4}$in) long.

Staples A useful means for quickly anchoring plastic mesh fencing to timber posts.

Battens A general term used to describe a narrow strip of wood. The usual sizes are 25 × 25mm (1 × 1in) or 50 × 25mm (2 × 1in).

Battens can be screwed to a wall to serve as bearers for shelves or they can be fixed in a framework on a wall, with sheet material or boards mounted over them to form a new 'wall'.

Dowels Used to make framework joints or to join boards edge-to-edge or edge-to-face.

Hardwood dowels are sold in diameters ranging from 6–10mm ($\frac{1}{4}$–$\frac{3}{8}$in). Generally speaking, dowel lengths should be about one-and-a-half times the thickness of the boards being joined.

Dowels are used with adhesive and, when the joint is complete, it is important to let excess adhesive escape from the joint. Dowels with fluted (finely grooved) sides and chamfered ends will help this process. If you have plain dowels, make fine sawcuts along the length yourself.

Techniques: Sawing and Cutting

Measuring and Marking Square

Mark the cutting lines lightly with a hard pencil first, and then use a utility knife, straight-edge, or try square along a steel rule to create a sharp, splinter-free line.

To mark wood square, use a try square with the stock (handle) pressed against a flat side of the wood, called the face side or face edge. Mark a line along the square, using a knife in preference to a pencil, then use the square to mark lines down the edges from the face mark. Finally square the other face side, checking that the lines join up right around the wood.

If you are measuring and marking a number of pieces of the same length, then clamp them together and mark across several of them at the same time.

Spacing Batten

This is simply an offcut of wood, about ¾in or 1in square (19mm or 25mm square), which is used to ensure that any slats to be affixed across a frame are spaced an equal distance apart. To ascertain the length to cut the spacing batten, simply bunch all the slats at one end of the frame. Measure to the other end of the frame and divide by the number of spaces (which you can count while you have the slats laid side by side). The resulting measure is the length to cut the spacing batten, which is used to position each slat exactly.

Bracing

When making a frame, it is vital that it should be square, with corners at perfect right angles. You can ensure this using one of two methods.

3-4-5-method Measure three units along one rail, four units down the adjacent rail, then nail a bracing batten accurately to one of the unit marks. Pull into square so that the bracing batten measures five units at the other unit mark, forming the hypotenuse of the triangle. Saw off the batten ends flush with the frame, but do not remove the batten until the frame is fitted in place.

Try square method Nail a batten into one rail, pull into square by using a try square, and then nail the batten into the adjacent rail.

Making Folding Wedges

Folding wedges are very useful for clamping large frames on a bench top during assembly. The wedges are always used in pairs, but more than one pair may be used to hold a large framework.

Make each pair of wedges from a piece of lumber (hardwood is an ideal material for this) measuring $1\frac{1}{2} \times 1\frac{1}{2} \times 13$in ($38 \times 38 \times 330$mm). Make the wedges by sawing the lumber diagonally into two pieces.

To use the wedges, a wooden batten is first nailed to the bench and the item to be clamped is placed against the batten. Another batten is nailed to the bench, parallel with the first, and about $1\frac{3}{4}$in (45mm) away from the item. The wedges are now placed between the item and the second batten. Next, the ends of the wedges are knocked inwards with two hammers, thereby clamping the frame.

Sawing and Cutting

Cross-cutting to length by hand Hold the lumber firmly with the cutting line (see **Measuring and Marking Square,** above) overhanging the right-hand side of the bench (if you are right-handed). With the saw blade vertical and the teeth on the waste side of the line, draw the handle back to start the cut. To prevent the saw jumping out of place, as you start hold the thumb joint of the other hand against the side of the saw blade.

Rip-cutting by hand With the lumber or board supported at about knee height, start the cut as described above, then saw down the waste side of the line, exerting pressure on the down cut only. If the saw blade wanders from the line, clamp the edge of a wood batten exactly above the cutting line on the side to be retained, and saw along it.

Using a portable power saw If the cutting line is only a short distance from a straight edge, adjust

---

① Marking Lumber to Length and Square All Around
Mark across the face of the lumber with a utility knife held against a try square blade. Move knife around corners and mark sides, and finally mark other side to join up the lines.

② Using Spacing Battens
Measure distance from bunched slats to frame end. Divide by number of spaces to calculate batten size.

③ Making Folding Wedges
Saw wood diagonally. Nail batten to bench; wedges fit between batten and item being clamped.

the saw's fence so that when it is run along the edge of the lumber, the blade will cut on the waste side of the cutting line. If the lumber is wide, or the edge is not straight, clamp a batten to the surface so that the saw blade will cut on the waste side of the line when run along the batten.

Ensuring a straight cut When cutting panels or boards using a power circular saw or Saber saw, the best way to ensure a straight cut is to clamp a guide batten to the surface of the work, parallel with the cutting line, so the edge of the saw sole plate can be run along the batten. The batten position is carefully adjusted so that the saw blade cuts on the waste side of the cutting line. Depending on which side of the cutting line the batten is clamped, when using a circular saw, it is possible the motor housing will foul the batten or C-clamps used to hold it in place. In this case, replace the batten with a wide strip of straight-edged plywood clamped to the work far enough back for the motor to clear the clamps.

⑤ Straight Power-saw Cutting
Top Use the rip fence of the saw if cutting near the edge. *Above* Cutting alongside the batten as a guide for obtaining a straight cut.

CUTTING A CIRCLE

With a coping saw Mark out the circle, score the cutting line, and drill a hole about ⅜in (10mm) in diameter just on the inside of the circle. Disconnect the blade from one end of the frame, pass the blade through the hole, and re-connect it to the frame. It will be best to clamp the piece of work vertically when cutting the circle. The blade can be turned in the frame to help the frame clear the piece of work, but even so, with a coping saw you will be restricted in exactly how far you are able to reach away from the piece of work. If the circle is some way from the edge, use a compass saw to cut it.

With a compass saw A compass saw, similar to a keyhole saw, has a stiff, triangular pointed saw blade attached to a simple handle. A very useful saw blade is available for fitting in a regular knife handle.

Because this saw has no frame, it is ideal for cutting circles and other apertures, like keyholes, anywhere in a panel.

Preparation of the circle for cutting is the same as for a coping saw. When cutting with a compass saw, keep the blade vertical and make a series of rapid, short strokes without exerting too much pressure.

CUTTING GROOVES

By hand Start by marking out the groove with a utility knife. Hold the piece of work on a bench and, with a back saw, make vertical cuts just inside the marked lines to the depth of the groove. If the groove is wide, make a series of other vertical cuts in the waste wood. Now chisel out the waste, working from each side to the middle. Finally, with the flat side of the chisel downwards, pare the bottom of the groove so that it is perfectly flat.

With a router Use a straight-sided router bit set to the depth required for the groove. Ideally, the bit should be the exact width of the groove. Make the cut along the waste side of the line with a batten clamped in place to guide the base of the router.

④ Cross-cutting to Length
Hold the lumber firmly. Steady the saw blade with the thumb joint as you start to saw.

⑥ Cutting with a Back Saw
Start the cut as for a hand saw. As the cut progresses keep the blade horizontal.

⑦ Straight Rip-cutting
Clamp a straight batten alongside the cutting line and saw beside the batten. A wedge holds the cut open.

⑧ Cutting Circles by Hand
1 Drill a small hole and cut circle using a compass saw. *2* Making the cut with a coping saw.

TECHNIQUES: DRILLING AND FASTENINGS

CUTTING RABBETS

A rabbet is an L-shaped step in the edge of a piece of wood.

By hand Use a marking gauge to mark the rabbet width across the top face of the piece of work and down both sides. Mark the depth of the rabbet across the end and sides.

Hold the wood flat and saw down on the waste side of the marked line to the depth of the rabbet. Chisel out the waste one bit at a time along the end grain.

With a router It is not necessary to mark out the rabbet unless you want a guide to work to. However, do practice on scrap wood to be sure of setting the router correctly.

If using a straight cutter, adjust the guide fence on the router so that the correct width is cut, then plunge and adjust the cutting depth so that the router will cut to the correct depth. When the router is correctly set up, simply hold it flat on the piece of work and move it against the direction of the cutter's rotation.

If you are using a cutter with a guide pin, simply adjust the depth of cut and then run the cutter along the edge of the wood to form the rabbet. The cutter will follow irregularities in the wood, so make sure your wood is perfectly straight.

PLANING

By hand Make sure that the plane blade is sharp and properly adjusted. Stand to one side of the work with feet slightly apart so you are facing the work. Plane from one end of the work to the other, starting the cut with firm pressure on the leading hand, transferring it to both hands, and finally to the rear hand as the cut is almost complete. Holding the plane at a slight angle to the direction of the grain can sometimes improve the cutting action.

With a power plane Remove loose clothing, and wear goggles and a dust mask. Clamp the work in place. Start the plane and turn the adjuster knob to set the depth. Start with a shallow cut and increase the depth if necessary.

Stand comfortably to one side of the work and, holding the plane with two hands, set it into the work at one end and pass it over the surface to the other end. When you have finished, switch off and make sure the blades stop spinning before resting the plane down with the cutting depth at zero.

DRILLING

To minimize the risk of splitting wood, drill pilot and clearance holes for screws.

The **clearance hole** in the wood should be fractionally smaller in diameter than the screw shank.

The **pilot hole** to receive the screw should be about half the diameter of the clearance hole. The hole depth should be slightly less than the length of the screw.

To ensure that screwheads lie level with the surface of plywood, particleboard and hardwood use a **countersink drill bit**.

Drilling vertical holes To ensure vertical holes, mount the drill in a stand. If this is not possible,

stand a try square on edge so that its stock is resting on the work alongside the drilling position, and the blade is pointing up in the air. Use this as a siting guide and line up the drill as close as possible with the square to ensure the drill is vertical. It is also helpful if an assistant can stand back and sight along the drill and square from two sides to ensure the drill is straight.

SCREWING

When screwing one piece of wood to another ensure that half of the screw penetrates through the bottom piece of wood. Its thickness should not exceed one-tenth of the width of the wood into which it has to be inserted. Keep screws at a distance of five times their shank diameter from the side edge of the wood, and ten times the shank diameter from its end.

NAILING

The correct length of nail to use is two-and-a-half to three times the thickness of the lumber being nailed. However, check that the nail

1 Chiseling a Groove
After making saw cuts at side, chisel out waste from each side. Finally pare base flat.

2 Drilling Vertical Holes
With a drill stand, not only will the drill bit be held vertical, but depth is also controlled.

3 Freehand Drilling Guide
When drilling it can be helpful to stand a try square alongside the drill to ensure accuracy.

4 Drilling Depth Guide
There are various guides to control drilling depths, such as rings for drills and masking tape.

will not pierce right through two pieces being nailed. Wherever possible nail through the thinner piece of wood into the thicker piece.

Nails grip best if driven in at an angle ("toe-nailing"). A row of nails should be driven in at opposing angles to each other. Framework joints are usually held in by toe-nailing. Clamp or nail a block of wood temporarily against one side of the vertical piece to stop it sliding as the first nail is started.

To prevent wood from splitting, particularly if nailing near an edge, blunt the points of the nails by hitting them with a hammer before driving them home. Blunt nails will cut through lumber fibers neatly, while pointed nails are more likely to push the fibers apart like a wedge.

FASTENINGS

Solid wall The normal attachment for a solid wall is a wood screw and plastic or fiber anchor. Before drilling the hole, check with a metal detector that there are no pipes or cables hidden below the surface. Drill the holes for the anchor with a

6 Toe-nailing for Strength
Hold the frames together in a clamp and join them by toe-nailing (driving nails at an angle). The joint will not then pull apart.

masonry drill bit in an electric drill. The anchor package will indicate the drill size to use. Switch to hammer action if the wall is hard. The screw should be long enough to go through the fixture and into the wall by about 1in (25mm) if the masonry is exposed, and by about $1\frac{3}{8}$in (35mm) if fastening into a plastered wall.

If the wall crumbles when you drill into it, mix up a cement-based plugging compound (available from home improvement stores). Turn back the screw half a turn before the compound sets (in about five minutes). When hard (in about one hour) the screw is removed and a heavy attachment made.

If your drill sinks easily into the wall once it has penetrated the plaster layer, and a light gray dust is produced from the hole, you are affixing into lightweight concrete blocks. In this case, special winged anchors should be used.

To make a quick, light-to-medium weight attachment in a solid wall, a masonry nail can be used. Choose a length that will penetrate the

material to be attached, and pierce an exposed masonry wall by $\frac{5}{8}$in (15mm) or a plastered wall by about 1in (25mm). Wear goggles in case the nail snaps; hammer it gently through the material to be attached and into the wall.

Expansion bolts In rugged construction work, wall attachments are made with expansion bolts. The hole drilled in the wall must be deep enough to accept the segmented body of the bolt. Check the manufacturer's instructions for the exact diameter of the hole. The body of the bolt is placed in the hole, the bolt passed through the fixture to locate in the body, and then the nut of the bolt turned with a wrench, expanding the segmented body and causing it to grip tightly.

Installing cladding Always install boards from the bottom upwards. Use a carpenter's level to check that the first board is exactly horizontal – if it is not, the boards above will start to run out of true, making it impossible to secure them.

5 Drilling Holes for Screws in Lumber
Drill a clearance hole in the thinner piece. Countersink this hole, then drill a pilot hole to slightly less than screw length. *Inset* To counterbore, drill to the diameter of the screw head to required depth, then as above.

7 Techniques for Joining Wood by Nailing
Nails should be two-and-a-half to three times the thickness of the wood being joined. Assemble frames on bench by nailing against batten. *Inset* Blunt nail points to avoid splitting wood.

TECHNIQUES: WOOD JOINTS

Nail through the center of the first board into each of the vertical support battens behind, using 1in (25mm) galvanized common nails. If boards have to be joined to span the full width of the structure, then butt the edges closely and ensure that joints are always made against a vertical support batten.

If you are installing bevel clapboards, it is important that they overlap uniformly and you will need to use a spacing block cut from a spare piece of wood. If the boards are 6in (150mm) wide and the spacer is 4½in (112mm) wide then, by aligning the spacer with the bottom edge of the previously fixed board and resting the overlapping board on top, you will get a consistent overlap of 1½in (38mm). Nail through the lower edge into the top edge of the board it overlaps and through into the batten.

Tongue-and-groove boards are installed by driving the nail at an angle through the tongue and tapping the head below the surface. The groove of the next board slides over the tongue to conceal the nail.

Shiplap cladding is installed in the same way except that the boards do not interlock, but simply overlap.

Installing trellis Trellis should be affixed about 6in (150mm) clear of the ground so that it will not rot at the base. Stand the trellis on blocks of the correct height while it is being secured to wood uprights or a wall. Use a carpenter's level to check that the horizontal rails are true, then drill holes into the side uprights of the trellis through which galvanized nails are inserted and then driven into the posts behind. If you nail directly into the trellis there is a chance the wood will split. Three nails either side of an 72in (1800mm) high trellis panel will suffice. Alternatively, use purpose-made clips screwed to support posts. The trellis slots into clips.

When securing to a wall, use 1in (25mm) thick wood blocks behind each attachment point to keep the trellis clear. Pre-drill the holes and use about 3in (75mm) long No. 8 or 10 galvanized screws and anchors to secure the trellis.

Installing posts and poles On concrete paths and pavers laid on mortar you can use a steel base as an attachment point for posts. The base is a square plate with a projecting cup into which the post is located. The base is bolted in place.

Metal post spikes are driven into the earth. Again, the post fits into a square cup and is clamped in place. As the post is above ground it is far less susceptible to rotting at the base.

Posts and poles can be inserted directly into soil. In firm soil and where shorter posts are used, then well-compacted gravel is usually adequate support. In loose soil and for longer posts and poles, a combination of stones and concrete should be used. For a post 72in (1800mm) high, at least 24in (600mm) should be buried below the ground.

FITTING HINGES

Butt hinges These are conventional flapped hinges and are available in steel (commonly) or in brass, which is better for high-quality work.

They are relatively simple to install, except that the hinge flaps have to be recessed into the wood using a chisel or router.

Mark out the hinge positions on the frame of the item to be hung, making sure that the hinges are not positioned so that the screws will go into the end grain of cross members and be likely to pull out.

The length of the hinges is marked out first, using a utility knife, then the width of the hinge and the thickness of the flap are marked using a marking gauge. With a chisel held vertical, and a mallet, cut down around the waste side of the recess, then make a series of vertical cuts across the full width of the recess. Remove the waste by careful chiseling, then finally pare the bottom of the recess flat using the chisel held flat side downwards (fig. 4).

If you are careful, you can remove the bulk of the waste from a hinge recess using a straight bit fitted in a router. The bit is set to cut to the depth of the recess required, and afterwards the corners can be finished off using a chisel.

WOOD JOINTS

Butt joint This is the simplest frame joint of all. The ends of the wood to be joined must be cut square so that they butt together neatly. Corner and "T" joints can be formed, which are glued and nailed for strength. Corrugated fasteners can also be used to hold these joints, especially where the sides of the frames will be covered to hide the fasteners. When "T" joints are being formed from inside a frame, they can be toe-nailed.

Half-lap joint Also known as a halving joint, these may be used to join wood of similar thickness at corners or to "T" or "X" joints. The joint is formed by cutting each piece to half its thickness. Use a try square to mark the width of the cut-outs and a marking gauge set to half the

① Installing Cladding
Above Nail tongue, then slot groove of next board over. *Below* Use spacing block for bevel clapboards.

② Installing Posts
Left and top right Post spikes affix posts in place. *Below right* Post-hole digger makes hole for post.

③ Installing Trellis Panels
Panel clips are screwed to vertical support posts. Trellis panels slot into clips and are screwed in place.

thickness of the wood to mark their depth. Be sure to cross-hatch the waste wood with a pencil so that the correct side is removed. To form an end-lap joint, saw down as for making a tenon joint (see **page 402**). To form a "T" or "X" half-lap, saw down each side of the "T" cut-out to the depth of the central gauge line, then chisel out the waste.

Dado joint Used mainly for shelving, this is basically a slot into which a shelf fits. The "through" dado joint goes to the full width of the shelf, while a "stopped" dado joint is taken only part of the way across the board. Chisel the waste away from each side. In the case of a stopped dado, chisel the waste from the stopped end first. If you have a router, it is easier to cut a dado joint by running the router across the board against a batten which is clamped firmly at right angles to the board.

A rabbet joint is similar to a dado joint, but positioned at the top of a piece of board; it can be cut in a similar way.

④ The Stages in Fitting a Butt Hinge

Using a try square and a utility knife, mark out the length of hinge. With a marking gauge mark width and thickness of hinge flap. With chisel vertical, cut around outline of hinge. Make series of cuts across width of recess. Pare out the waste then check that flap lies flush. Screw the butt hinge in place.

⑤ Simple Butt Joints

Top Corner and *Below* "T" joints can be formed by toe-nailing or by using corrugated fasteners.

⑥ Types of Half-lap Joints

Top An end-lap joint. *Bottom left* A "T" half-lap joint. *Bottom right* A "X" half-lap joint.

⑧ Types of Dado Joints

Top A through dado joint; *Middle* Through dado joints on the side of a central support; *Bottom* A corner dado joint.

⑦ Forming a Half-lap Joint in Wood Battens

Mark width of the cut-out. Mark half the thickness of the wood with a marking gauge. Cross hatch area to be removed. Saw down sides with a back saw, then chisel out the waste.

TECHNIQUES: WOOD JOINTS

Dowel joint   Dowels are a strong, simple, and hidden means of joining wood together.

Use pre-cut grooved dowels with beveled ends (*see* **Materials, page 395**). These range from ¼in (6mm) diameter by 1in (25mm) long to ⅜in (10mm) by 2in (50mm). The dowel length should be about one-and-a-half times the thickness of the wood being jointed. When making your own dowels, their length can be twice the thickness of the wood. Cut grooves down the length of dowel to allow glue and air to escape, and bevel the ends.

On both pieces of wood, use a marking gauge to find the center line, and mark with a pencil. Drill the dowel holes to half the dowel length with the drill held in a drill stand, or aligned with a try square stood on end. Drill the dowel holes in one of the pieces to be joined, insert center points in the holes, then bring the

① **Dowels to Join Panels**
Right Mark dowel positions. Drill holes, insert center points. Mark second piece.

② **Types of Dowel Joint**
Dowels can join panels edge to edge and join frames at corners. They can be hidden or have ends exposed.

③ **Making a Doweled Frame**
If edge of frame will not be seen, drill holes for dowels after making frame. Hammer dowels home; cut ends flush after glue dries.

④ **Using a Doweling Jig**
If dowels are to be hidden, a doweling jig makes it easy to drill holes that align in both pieces.

two pieces of the joint together so they are carefully aligned. The center points will make marks in the second piece of wood where the dowel holes should be drilled. Drill the holes to half of the length of the dowels, plus a little extra for glue. Where dowels are used for location rather than strength, set the dowels three-quarters into one edge and a quarter into the other.

Put adhesive in the hole and tap dowels into the holes in the first piece with a mallet. Apply adhesive to both parts of the joint; bring the pieces together and clamp them in position until the adhesive has set.

Using a doweling jig   A doweling jig enables accurate dowel holes to be drilled. It is clamped over the workpiece above the pre-marked hole centers. A bush of the same diameter as the drill bit is selected and fitted on the jig. The bush holds the drill vertically as the hole is made. A depth gauge ensures that the hole is the required depth. The jig is then set up on the mating piece of wood and the process repeated.

Miter joint   A simple miter joint is glued and nailed; a stronger one is made using dowels, or by sawing oblique cuts into which wood veneers are glued. Cut the joints at 45° using a miter box as a guide.

Mortise and tenon joint   A mortise and tenon joint can be marked out with a mortise gauge. Mark out the tenon (the tongue) so that it is one-third of the thickness of the piece of wood. The mortise (the slot) is marked at the same width in the other piece. The length of the mortise should match the width of the tenon being fitted. Drill out most of the waste with a series of holes using a bit slightly smaller than the mortise width. Working from the center, chop out the mortise with a chisel to the depth required. If making a through joint (in which the end of the tenon is visible), turn the wood over and finish chiseling out the mortise from the other side.

Hold the tenon piece upright, but sloping away from yourself, secure in a vise, and use a back saw carefully to cut down to the shoulder. Then swivel the wood around to point the other way, and saw down to the other side of the shoulder. Next, position the wood vertically and cut down to the shoulder. Finally, place the wood flat and saw across the shoulder to remove the waste. Repeat for the waste on the other side of the tongue. Check that the two pieces fit well before gluing and assembling the joint. For added strength, cut small additional shoulders at each end of the tenon.

Bare-faced mortise and tenon joint If the tongue of a tenon joint is offset to one side, this produces a bare-faced tenon as shown (fig. 8). This produces a strong joint where narrow rails meet thicker frame rails.

A bare-faced tenon is cut in the same way as a half-lap joint.

6 **Marking and Cutting a Mortise and Tenon Joint**
Mark the length of the mortise slot to match the size of the rail being joined. Set the mortise gauge to the width of the chisel being used to cut out the mortise slot. (Chisel should be about one-third the width of wood being joined.) Use the mortise gauge to mark the mortise, and also the tenon, on the rail. Drill out the mortise and complete the cut with a chisel. Use a back saw to cut out the tenon.

5 **Cutting Miter Joints**
Miters make right-angled joints. Use a miter box to ensure a 45° angle and cut joint with a back saw.

7 **Mortise and Tenon Joints**
Top A common or stopped mortise and tenon joint. *Below* Through mortise and tenon joint.

8 **Making a Bare-Faced Mortise and Tenon Joint**
Tenon is offset to one side. Mark and cut as shown here.

9 **Shouldered Tenon Joint**
For enhanced strength, saw down small additional shoulders at each end of the tenon.

TECHNIQUES: BRICKLAYING

TOOLS

Bricklayer's chisel and hammer For cutting bricks.

Brick trowel Used to spread mortar on bricks.

Buckets You will need two of the same size, one for measuring mortar ingredients, the other for cement.

Builder's square Three battens in the proportions 3:4:5 nailed to form a right-angled triangle. Used to check that each course is vertical.

Hawk board For holding small amounts of mortar.

Mason's level For checking brickwork horizontally and vertically.

Pointing trowel Small trowel for shaping mortar joints.

Profile board Made from a piece of scrap wood about 20in (500mm) long, nailed across two battens which are driven into the ground. You will need two – one for either end of the wall. The top of each board is notched at appropriate intervals to represent the edges of the foundation and the wall. The notches then hold the string line taut for accurate bricklaying.

Shovels You will need two of these, one for mixing and one for lifting cement from its bag.

Story pole This is a 1 × 1in (25 × 25mm) batten marked off in 2¾in (70mm) increments. It is used to check that courses of bricks are vertical. It should be slightly longer than the intended wall height.

String line Needed as a guide to laying the brick courses horizontally.

Watering can For adding water to the mortar mix.

MATERIALS

Bricks Modular bricks are made to an actual size of 7⅝ × 3⅜ × 2¼in (190 × 96.5 × 60mm). Since allowance has to be made for ⅜in (10mm) thick horizontal and vertical mortar joints, they are regarded as being 8 × 4 × 2⅝in (200 × 100 × 65mm).

Bricks come in many colors, sizes, and textures, and it is important to choose a type that will harmonize with your garden and house. Second-hand bricks are popular for garden projects since they blend well with any environment. Lumberyards stock a selection of bricks; local demolition sites or architectural salvage yards are good hunting grounds for second-hand bricks.

Mortar This is needed to bond the bricks together. It is made by mixing cement, soft builders' sand, and lime or plasticizer in the proportions of 1:5:1 with water. Bags of ready-mixed mortar are available, but they are economical only for very small jobs such as repair work.

Ordinary Portland cement (sold in large bags) is usually used although white Portland cement is available if you want pale joints to match pale bricks.

Builders' sand is sold by the cubic yard (meter). Most lumberyards will sell smaller quantities in bags – larger quantities are tipped from a truck into a loose pile.

Lime is sold in bags, liquid plasticizer in containers.

When calculating how much to buy, a good rule of thumb is to allow one bag of cement and 0.2 cubic yards (meters) of damp sand for every 400 bricks.

Should you need to store cement before use, keep it under cover and raised off the ground. A pile of sand will attract children and animals, so cover this, too.

Mix mortar on a clean surface. In hot weather, mix only as much as you can use in an hour, since the mortar will start to stiffen. Never try to reactivate mortar by adding more water: it will crack up. On a hot day, it is worth dipping each brick in water before laying it.

First, mix the dry ingredients until the pile is a uniform gray colour. Make a crater in the top and pour in some water, then turn the pile over continuously, adding a little more water from time to time until the mix is buttery. A good test for the right consistency is to chop the mixing shovel through the pile until the ridges remain intact.

TECHNIQUES

Laying foundations Unless the brickwork is built on a firm base it will soon start to settle unevenly. Judging foundations is a matter of common sense, although you must check codes and regulations.

Whereas a low brick planter or barbecue can be built on a sound existing patio or drive, more ambitious projects require tailor-made solid concrete foundations. For a garden wall up to 39in (1000mm) high (two brick thickness), dig a trench 20in (500mm) wide and deep, and lay a leveled bed of concrete in the trench to a depth of 9in (230mm). For a single brick thickness wall, you will need to dig a

① Single Brick Foundation
Dig trench and lay concrete bed as indicated. Lay bricks and backfill with soil once mortar has hardened.

② Laying First Two Bricks
Lay first brick using profile board as guide. Lay second brick 60in (1500mm) away; check it is level.

③ Laying the Second Course
Begin with a half brick to stagger courses, then continue along. Always check bricks are vertical and level.

trench 12in (300mm) wide and 14–16in (350–400mm) deep, and lay a 6in (150mm) deep bed of concrete in the trench.

The concrete mix should be one part cement to four parts of ballast. Allow it to harden for four days and keep it covered with polyethylene in wet weather. In hot weather, cover the concrete with damp sacking, spraying it occasionally with water.

Cutting bricks To cut a brick, score a continuous line around all four faces using a bricklayer's chisel and hammer. Place the brick on a pile of sand, put the blade of the chisel in the groove, and tap sharply with the hammer for a clean cut.

Brickwork bonds For stability, a wall must be built in a definite bond formation such as one of the examples illustrated (fig. 7). Running and open bond formations are suitable for single brick thickness walls up to a height of 39in (1000mm). Piers (support columns), as indicated (fig. 5), are essential at both ends and at 72in (1800mm) centers.

A double brick thickness wall requires bricks to be cut near the corners to ensure that the vertical joints are staggered.

Laying bricks Set up string lines at either side of the foundation trench as a guide to laying the first course of bricks. Make profile boards from pieces of scrap wood notched as appropriate for a single or double brick wall – the notches trap the string, pulling it taut.

Spread a layer of mortar about 60in (1500mm) long and lay the first brick in place with the indentation facing upwards. Lay a second brick 60in (1500mm) or so away. Place a mason's level on a straight-edge piece of wood spanning the two bricks and tap the higher brick down until both are level.

Mortar should always be a little thicker than ⅜in (10mm) since the bricks will compress it slightly.

As each brick is laid, spread ⅜in (10mm) of mortar on the end to form a vertical joint with the preceding brick. Use the level and trowel to level bricks. Complete first course.

Cut a brick in half to start the second course. Build up the ends of the wall as shown (fig. 4), so that you are always working three or four courses above the course being filled. The course being completed must be laid to match against a taut string line which you will need to anchor into the course above using bradpoint nails.

Check continually with the story pole that the courses are accurate. Also check the face of the brickwork to ensure it is plumb.

The top course of bricks (the coping course) protects the wall from the weather. On a single brick wall, stand half bricks on edge. Whole bricks on edge complete a double thickness wall.

Joint finishes It is best to finish the joints as each course of bricks is completed. The simplest joints to make are flush joints, made by scraping away excess mortar using the edge of a trowel.

Beaded joints are more decorative and are made by drawing a steel rod through the mortar.

Running bond

Open bond

English bond

Flemish bond

7 Brickwork Bonds
Lay bricks to stagger with the course above and below. Four popular bond formations are shown here.

4 Laying Additional Courses
Build up the ends of the wall first, then fill in the intervening bricks, completing one course at a time.

5 Forming Piers
For long walls, stagger the brick formations as shown to form piers at centers 72in (1800mm) apart.

6 Forming the Ends
Use a combination of half bricks and whole bricks to form the bonding necessary at either end of the wall.

8 Cutting a Brick
Score line around faces of brick. Lay it on bed of sand, insert chisel in groove, tap sharply with hammer.

½ brick

¾ brick

¾ brick

Whole brick

Whole brick

½ brick

INDEX

INDEX

ACKNOWLEDGMENTS

The publisher thanks the following photographers and organizations for their kind permission to reproduce the photographs in this book:

10 left Camera Press; 10 right Michael Freeman; 11 (c) Jon Jensen; 48 left Camera Press; 48 centre Richard Bryant/Arcaid; 48 right Ken Kirkwood; 49 Simon Brown/Conran Octopus; 50 Karen Bussolini (House Beautiful Specials); 51 Aldo Ballo; 52 left Jean-Pierre Godeaut; 52 right Fritz von der Schulenburg; 53 left La Maison de Marie Claire (Sarramon/Forgeur); 53 right Pascal Chevalier/ Agence Top; 54 above Neil Lorimer/Elizabeth Whiting & Associates; 54 below left Rodney Hyett/Elizabeth Whiting & Associates; 54 below right Tim Street-Porter/ Elizabeth Whiting & Associates; 55 above Tim Street-Porter/Elizabeth Whiting & Associates; 55 below left Elizabeth Whiting & Associates; 55 below centre Lars Hallen; 55 below right Jean-Pierre Godeaut; 56–57 Jean-Paul Bonhommet; 58 above Richard Bryant/Arcaid; 58 below Tim Street-Porter/Elizabeth Whiting & Associates; 59 left Tim Street-Porter/Elizabeth Whiting & Associates; 59 right Jean-Pierre Godeaut (designer Lydia Kumel); 60 left Simon Brown/Conran Octopus; 60 right Rodney Hyett/Elizabeth Whiting & Associates; 61 Rodney Hyett/Elizabeth Whiting & Associates; 62 above designer Rudiger Mahlau (photographer Michael Scheffler); 62 below Jean-Pierre Godeaut (designer Geneviève Lethy); 63 Lars Hallen; 64 Rodney Hyett/Elizabeth Whiting & Associates; 65 Tim Street-Porter/Elizabeth Whiting & Associates; 66 above Neil Lorimer/Elizabeth Whiting & Associates; 66 below La Maison de Marie Claire (Sarramon/Forgeur); 67 Dennis Krukowski (designers Spottswood/Byron); 68 above Rodney Hyett/Elizabeth Whiting & Associates; 68 below left Andreas von Einsiedel/Elizabeth Whiting & Associates; 68 below right Simon Brown/Conran Octopus; 69 Tom Leighton/The World of Interiors; 70 left Garry Chowanetz/ Elizabeth Whiting & Associates; 70 right Jean-Paul Bonhommet; 71 left Vogue Living (Rodney Weidland); 71 right Rodney Hyett/Elizabeth Whiting & Associates; 72 Rodney Hyett/Elizabeth Whiting & Associates; 73 Lars Hallen; 74 left Tim Street-Porter/Elizabeth Whiting & Associates; 74 right Christian Sarramon; 75 above Richard Bryant/Arcaid; 75 below left James Merrell/Homes & Gardens/ Syndication International; 75 below centre Elizabeth Whiting & Associates; 75 below right Belle (Geoff Lung); 114 Rodney Hyett/Elizabeth Whiting & Associates; 115 Camera Press; 116 Pascal Chevalier/Agence Top; 117 Belle (Neil Lorimer); 118 left Derry Moore; 118 centre Camera Press; 118 right Maison Française (Jean-Pierre Godeaut); 119 Juliana Balint (photographer Paul Ryan); 120 above Rodney Hyett/Elizabeth Whiting & Associates; 120 below left Rodney Hyett/Elizabeth Whiting & Associates; 120 below right Jean-Paul Bonhommet; 121 above Trevor Richards/Homes & Gardens/Syndication International; 121 below left Rodney Hyett/Elizabeth Whiting & Associates; 121 below right Jean-Paul Bonhommet; 122 Derry Moore; 123 Michael Freeman; 124 above Tim Street-Porter/Elizabeth Whiting & Associates; 124 centre Ken Kirkwood; 124 below Richard Bryant/Arcaid; 125 Friedhelm Thomas/Elizabeth Whiting & Associates; 126 above Simon Brown/Conran Octopus; 126 below left Roland Beaufre/Agence Top (designer Anne Gayet); 126 below right Jean-Paul Bonhommet; 127 left Jean-Paul Bonhommet; 127 centre Jean-Paul Bonhommet; 127 right Karen Bussolini (designer Russota/Cama Design Associates); 128 above left Jean-Paul Bonhommet; 128 above right Richard Bryant/Arcaid; 128 below left David Montgomery/Conran Octopus (designer Tricia Guild); 128 below centre Jean-Paul Bonhommet; 128 below right Ken Kirkwood; 129 Pascal Hinous/Agence Top (designer Manual Canovas); 130 above Neil Lorimer/Elizabeth Whiting & Associates; 130 centre La Maison de Marie Claire (Chabaneix/Puech Postic); 130 below Jean-Paul Bonhommet; 131 above Rodney Hyett/Elizabeth Whiting & Associates; 131 centre Jean-Paul Bonhommet; 131 below Clive Frost/The World of Interiors; 132 left Belle (Geoff Lung); 132 centre Elizabeth Whiting & Associates; 132 right Michael Dunne/ Elizabeth Whiting & Associates; 133 left La Maison de Marie Claire (Hussenot); 133 centre Lars Hallen; 133 right Jon Bouchier/Elizabeth Whiting & Associates; 134 Juliana Balint (photographer Hannu Mannynoksa); 135 Simon Brown/ Conran Octopus; 136 left Jean-Pierre Godeaut; 136 centre Karen Bussolini (architect William Herman); 136 right Dennis Krukowski (designers Spottswood/Byron); 137 above Richard Bryant/Arcaid; 137 below left Vogue Living (Rodney Weidland); 137 below centre Maison Française (Luc de Champris); 137 below right Simon Brown/Conran Octopus (Elyane de la Rochette); 138 Elizabeth Whiting & Associates; 139 Jean-Paul Bonhommet; 140 left Woman Syndication International; 140 right Lars Dalsgaard; 141 left Fritz von der Schulenburg; 141 right Jerry Tubby/Elizabeth Whiting & Associates; 171 above Fritz von der Schulenburg (designer Mimmi O'Connell, paint finish by Peter Farlow); 171 below left Elizabeth Whiting & Associates; 171 below centre Dennis Krukowski (James Franklin Mitchell); 171 below right Chris Sanders; 172 Richard Bryant/Arcaid; 173 Clive Frost/Homes & Gardens/Syndication International; 174 Rodney Hyett/Elizabeth Whiting & Associates; 175 Simon Brown/Conran Octopus; 176 left Rodney Hyett/Elizabeth Whiting & Associates; 176 centre Fritz von der Schulenburg; 176 right Fritz von der Schulenburg; 177 Friedhelm Thomas/Elizabeth Whiting & Associates; 178 Jean-Pierre Godeaut; 179 Simon Brown/Conran Octopus; 181 above Simon Brown/Conran Octopus; 181 below left Alfredo Anghinelli/Elizabeth Whiting & Associates; 181 below centre Jean-Pierre Godeaut; 181 below right Maison Française (Jean-Pierre Godeaut); 182 above Tim Street-Porter/Elizabeth Whiting & Associates; 182 centre Ken Kirkwood (designer David Pocknell); 182 below Vogue Living (Geoff Lung); 183 left Jean-Pierre Godeaut; 183 above right Andreas von Einsiedel/ Elizabeth Whiting & Associates; 183 centre right Tim Street-Porter/Elizabeth Whiting & Associates; 183 below right Rodney Hyett/Elizabeth Whiting & Associates; 184 Karen Bussolini (designer Nelson Denny); 185 Andreas von Einsiedel/Elizabeth Whiting & Associates; 186 above Richard Bryant/Arcaid; 186 below left Neil Lorimer/Elizabeth Whiting & Associates; 186 below right Rodney Hyett/Elizabeth Whiting & Associates; 187 above Rodney Hyett/Elizabeth Whiting & Associates; 187 below left Camera Press; 187 below right Rodney Hyett/Elizabeth Whiting & Associates; 188 above Lars Hallen; 188 below Michael Crockett/Elizabeth Whiting & Associates; 189 left Camera Press; 189 above right Jean-Paul Bonhommet; 189 below right Rodney Hyett/Elizabeth Whiting & Associates; 190 left Vogue Living (George Seper); 190 centre Richard Bryant/ Arcaid; 190 right Jean-Paul Bonhommet; 191 above Richard Bryant/Arcaid; 191 below left Maison Française (Jean-Pierre Godeaut); 191 below centre Tim Street-Porter/Elizabeth Whiting & Associates; 191 below right Rodney Hyett/ Elizabeth Whiting & Associates; 192 above Simon Brown/Conran Octopus; 192 centre Vogue Living (Rodney Weidland); 192 below Wulf Brackrock/designers Titterio-Dwan for Architektur & Wohnen; 193 Gabriele Basilico/Abitare; 252–253 Fritz von der Schulenburg.

Special photography by Hugh Johnson and Simon Lee for Conran Octopus.

Hugh Johnson 1, 2, 6 right, 7 left, 8–9, 39, 46, 76–83, 106–107, 142 left, 144–145, 150, 151 above, 152–163, 167, 194–197, 209, 214–215, 223–227, 232–233, 239, 242–243.

Simon Lee 6 left, 7 right, 44, 92–101, 102–104, 112–113, 142 right, 149, 151 below, 164, 203, 212, 219–221, 228–230, 240, 247, 249.

PUBLISHER'S ACKNOWLEDGMENTS
The publishers would like to thank the following for their invaluable assistance in producing this book:

Jonathan Chidsey, Lady Caroline Conran, The Conran Studios, Julie Drake, Mike Goulding, Vana Hagarty, Gordon Hurden, Gareth Jones, Sian Jones, Wendy Jones, Harold Lee, Malcolm and Steve and all at Benchmark Woodworking Limited, Alan Rayner and the staff at Servis Filmsetting Ltd, Hickson Timber Products Ltd, Bridget Bodoano and the Conran Shop, the Administrator of Castle Drogo, Tabby Riley and Alex Willcock.

The projects in this book were specially built by SEAN SUTCLIFFE of Benchmark Woodworking Limited.

Special thanks to SIR TERENCE CONRAN for original project sketches and to PAUL BRYANT for his superb original illustrations.

The designs for the projects on pages 270-277,278-285,286-289,300-317,332-335,336-341,352-357,358-363,364-367,368-371,378-385, and 386-389 are copyright © Sir Terence Conran and may be built for personal use only.

The publisher would like to thank the following companies for supplying material for photography:

78 Franke (UK) Ltd. The Conran Shop, David Mellor Design Ltd, Divertimenti, Philips Major Appliances Ltd, The Kitchen Range, Neff (UK) Ltd, Stephen Long Antiques, W H Newson & Sons Ltd; **80** Aston-Matthews Ltd, W H Newson & Sons Ltd, David Mellor Ltd, Heal & Sons Ltd; **83** The Conran Shop, Neff (UK) Ltd; **106** The Conran Shop; **144** The Conran Shop; **159** Authentics, INC Office Equipment, The Conran Shop; **167** General Plumbing Supplies; **196** The Conran Shop, Ideal Standard Ltd, C P Hart Ltd; **209** London Architectural Salvage Company, The Conran Shop, Ideal Standard Ltd; **214** Paul Jones, Eximious Ltd, Sam Walker; **242** Gallery of Antique Costume and Textiles.